Practical Bot Development

Designing and Building Bots with Node.js and Microsoft Bot Framework

Szymon Rozga

Apress®

Practical Bot Development: Designing and Building Bots with Node.js and Microsoft Bot Framework

Szymon Rozga
Port Washington, New York, USA

ISBN-13 (pbk): 978-1-4842-3539-3   ISBN-13 (electronic): 978-1-4842-3540-9
https://doi.org/10.1007/978-1-4842-3540-9

Library of Congress Control Number: 2018949897

Managing Director, Apress Media LLC: Welmoed Spahr
Acquisitions Editor: Natalie Pao
Development Editor: James Markham
Coordinating Editor: Jessica Vakili

Cover designed by eStudioCalamar

Cover image designed by Freepik (www.freepik.com)

Distributed to the book trade worldwide by Springer Science+Business Media New York, 233 Spring Street, 6th Floor, New York, NY 10013. Phone 1-800-SPRINGER, fax (201) 348-4505, e-mail orders-ny@springer-sbm.com, or visit www.springeronline.com. Apress Media, LLC is a California LLC and the sole member (owner) is Springer Science + Business Media Finance Inc (SSBM Finance Inc). SSBM Finance Inc is a **Delaware** corporation.

For information on translations, please e-mail rights@apress.com, or visit www.apress.com/rights-permissions.

Apress titles may be purchased in bulk for academic, corporate, or promotional use. eBook versions and licenses are also available for most titles. For more information, reference our Print and eBook Bulk Sales web page at www.apress.com/bulk-sales.

Any source code or other supplementary material referenced by the author in this book is available to readers on GitHub via the book's product page, located at www.apress.com/978-1-4842-3539-3. For more detailed information, please visit www.apress.com/source-code.

Printed on acid-free paper

Table of Contents

About the Author

Szymon Rozga has 15 years of hands on experience in the software development industry. He found a passion working on front end applications on Wall Street. The interest in attention to user interface details would take him on a tour of the different user interface technologies on the Windows, Web and iOS/Android platforms. He has managed teams of engineers on a variety of projects and since 2016, he has dedicated his time to building chat bots for clients across text and voice channels. He has built a practice around the technologies at BlueMetal, An Insight Company, and is involved in a handful of chat bot projects at any time. As Chief Architect of Emerging Technologies, he keeps cognitively flexible by reading and watching presentations about new technologies, educating clients, leading discovery sessions, scoping and guiding engagements, mentoring engineers and helping clients apply technologies such as Chat Bots, Blockchain and Augmented Reality to business problems.

In his spare time, he enjoys taking walks, reading fiction, going to the beach, playing guitar, and spending time with his wife Kim, his son Teddy, and his Golden Retriever, Chelsea.

About the Technical Reviewers

Alp Tunc is a software engineer with a master of science degree from Ege University in Izmir, Turkey. He has 20 years of experience in the industry as a developer/architect/project manager on projects of various sizes. He has hands-on experience in a broad range of technologies. Besides technology, he loves freezing moments in spectacular photographs, trekking into the unknown, running, reading, and listening to jazz. He loves cats and dogs.

Jim O'Neil is a Microsoft Azure MVP and senior architect at BlueMetal (an Insight Company), a modern application consulting firm headquartered in Watertown, Massachusetts, where he is primarily focused on designing and implementing IoT solutions for a variety of industries. A former Microsoft Developer Evangelist for the Northeast United States, he remains active in the New England software community as a speaker and organizer of technical and nonprofit events, namely, New England GiveCamp. In his spare time, he noodles around in genealogy and DNA testing through which he's found both of his birth parents' families.

Preface

In mid-2016, I started work on a fascinating project. A client wanted to have users with type 2 diabetes be able to get advice from an automated coach, in other words, a chat bot. It was a fascinating idea. I had many questions. Why would anyone want to have a natural language conversation with a machine? Is it possible to make this thing smart enough to accomplish its goals? How do you even begin creating a chat bot? Through which means are users supposed to interact with it? When the project ended, we quickly realized that the technologies we just utilized, natural language understanding, Microsoft's Bot Framework, and custom machine learning models, could serve as the technical base for a wide array of natural language applications between users and computing systems. Natural language interfaces, after all, were all the rage. The Alexa-powered Echo Dot had just been released, and the general population was quickly becoming fascinated with the idea of communicating with digital assistants by talking to them. My friend and I jumped on the opportunity to become experts in this space.

We tried many of the different platforms such as Api.ai (now DialogFlow), Wit.ai, and Watson Conversation but decided to focus on Microsoft's Bot Framework as we felt it best complemented the enterprise space. Chat bot startups sprung up across the landscape promising the best bot or bot platform. The field became saturated, and our customers started paying attention. Suddenly, I found myself talking to multiple clients a day. Initially, these were high-level mentorship sessions. What is a chat bot? How does it work? What channels does it work with? Does it learn by itself? Can it integrate with live chat?

Starting around mid-2017, these conversations slowly shifted from educating clients to scoping the development effort for all types of use cases. Clients were starting to apply the technology to solve their business problems. In the second half of 2017, while working on delivering multiple chat bot implementations, a colleague of mine connected me to the editors who would make this book happen. Taking on this project was an easy decision to make; it was a fascinating topic, it was a new space, and it had lots of possibilities. Being slightly on the naïvely optimistic side about a three-month old's sleep patterns, I jumped on the opportunity.

I decided to write the book in the same way I would mentor engineers on the topics. It is divided roughly into three sections. First, I introduce the topics of chat bots and machine learning (ML) in Chapters 1 and 2. Although chat bots can, and often do, exist independently of any ML algorithms, the truth is that users expect chat bots to exhibit some forms of intelligence, minimally a bit of natural language understanding. As such, I want to set the state on ML and how it may be applied in natural language conversations. Chapter 3 is a deep dive into Microsoft's Language Understanding Intelligence Service (LUIS), which we will utilize to create natural language understanding models for our chat bot.

The second section is all about hands-on Bot Framework development. Chapter 4 introduces the concept of conversation design, which is the practice of modeling a chat bot conversation. Chapter 5 guides us through the creation of a Bot Framework chat bot connected to a LUIS model and its deployment into an Azure app service. In Chapter 6, we take a step back to examine the features and capabilities of the Bot Builder SDK, and in Chapter 7 we integrate our chat bot with an OAuth implementation and external APIs. Chapter 8 is a deeper exploration into Slack bots, and, finally, Chapter 9 explores the ability to connect any channel to our chat bot via the Direct Line API. We marry Twilio Voice into the picture to create a chat bot we can talk to via a phone.

The third section addresses a few additional topics that are essential to chat bot development. Chapter 10 adds extra intelligence abilities to our chat bots by focusing on a select set of Microsoft's Cognitive Services. Chapter 11 explores two manners of creating custom cards for our chat bots: adaptive cards and custom graphic renderings. We explore human handover in Chapter 12, we learn about chat bot analytics in Chapter 13, and, finally, in Chapter 14 we put all our newly gained knowledge to work by creating a simple Alexa skill using Amazon's Alexa Skills Kit and then replicate the same experience using a Bot Framework bot.

The chat bot space is dynamic. During the development of this book, Facebook acquired Wit.ai and shifted its focus to natural language understanding, Google acquired Api.ai, LUIS changed user interfaces not once but twice, the Bot Framework was officially released and moved to Azure, QnA Maker was officially released, Alexa's user interface changed after I had written all the content, and Microsoft announced tons of new features at Build 2018 (which luckily did not drastically change the topics treated in this book). We have reached a point where the subjects of this book are relatively stable. It is my hope that the content is essential to any developer looking to begin chat bot development using Microsoft's Bot Framework.

This project has been a humbling experience and would not have been possible without a small group of people for whose support I am forever grateful. I would like to thank my wife Kim, without whose patience, kindness, support, and late-night help with editing I would have never completed the process. I would also like to thank Jeff Dodge for the collaboration on building our chat bot practice, Bob Familiar for introducing me to the Apress team, and BlueMetal for allowing me the room to work on this project. Big thanks to Matt, Jimmy, and Andrew, and my parents, Hanna and Krzysztof Rozga, for providing much needed moral support and words of encouragement during times when I felt I was white knuckling it. I would also like to acknowledge the Apress editors Natalie and Jessica for their support during the book writing process.

This book is dedicated to Teddy.

—*Szymon Rozga*
June 1, 2018
Port Washington, New York

CHAPTER 1

Introduction to Chat Bots

In recent years, chat bots and artificial intelligence (AI) have become a hot topic in the tech sector and the public imagination. Chat bots, computer programs that can communicate using natural language, are doing everything from ordering pizza to buying clothes to saving money on parking tickets[1] to negotiating among themselves.[2] Initially, developing a chat bot was tantamount to developing an integration with a messaging platform. There was no easy way to represent a conversation flow in code. When Microsoft created the Bot Framework and the Bot Builder SDK, this changed. Microsoft created a rich environment in which the developer was liberated from the concerns of integrating with individual channels and could focus on writing code that performed the conversational tasks a chat bot needs to accomplish. The Bot Builder SDK provided a generic approach to the development of conversational experiences. Microsoft's Bot Connectors implemented the logic to translate from the generic format to channel-specific messages.

---

[1]Robot Lawyers Makes Case Against Parking Tickets:
http://www.npr.org/2017/01/16/510096767/
robot-lawyer-makes-the-case-against-parking-tickets

[2]Deal or no deal? Training AI bots to negotiate: https://code.facebook.com/
posts/1686672014972296/deal-or-no-deal-training-ai-bots-to-negotiate/

© Szymon Rozga 2018
S. Rozga, *Practical Bot Development*, https://doi.org/10.1007/978-1-4842-3540-9_1

The result is that chat bot development has become significantly more accessible to millions of developers. Engineers no longer have to learn the ins and outs of integrating with something like Facebook's Messenger APIs or Slack's Web API. Instead, developers focus on core bot logic and the conversational experience. Microsoft worries about the rest.

The Bot Builder SDK is available for .NET and Node.js and is run as an open source MIT-licensed project on GitHub.[3] The team is active in both development and responding to the various issues that development teams run into. And the team is friendly to boot!

In December 2017, Microsoft made both the Bot Framework and the Language Understanding Intelligence Service (LUIS) generally available. LUIS is Microsoft's natural language service that will aid us in adding conversational intelligence to our bots. The Bot Framework is now also called the Azure Bot Service; the two refer to the same thing. As implied by the name, the Azure Bot Service is now a full-fledged part of Microsoft's Azure cloud offering. Microsoft has also provided free tiers of the service so we can play with the framework to our heart's content. All of the samples and techniques in the book can be experimented with at no cost!

Over the last years, all the big tech companies like Microsoft, Facebook, and Google, as well as many smaller ones, have been taking a stab at creating the best and easiest-to-use chat bot development frameworks. The field is very dynamic. Frameworks come and go. Things seem to change daily. Despite the space's dynamic nature, Microsoft's Bot Framework remains the best platform for developing powerful, fast, and flexible chat bots. I am thrilled to take you on a journey through chat bot development using this tool.

---

[3]Microsoft Bot Builder SDK on GitHub: https://github.com/Microsoft/ BotBuilder

The Expectations Game

For more than two years now, a substantial chunk of my conversations with customers has been spent on discussing chat bot capabilities, what they are, and, more importantly, what they are not. Our culture largely confounds chat bot abilities with artificial intelligence, and it is easy to see why. Some chat bots employ rich natural language capabilities, leading us to imagine there is more to them. Likewise, voice-based digital assistants such as Cortana, Alexa, and Google Assistant live in our homes and may be spoken to like real humans. Why wouldn't chat bots display more intelligence?

The culture is additionally permeated with references to the likes of IBM's Watson on Jeopardy,[4] the New York Times' feature on the Google Brain team[5] and their feats in language translation using deep learning, self-driving cars, and AlphaZero destroying the world's highest-rated chess-playing engine after only four hours of learning how to play chess.[6]

These and many other stories highlight the investment and interest in these techniques, foreshadowing the kind of AI-driven interactions with our devices that we are heading toward. Developments in the field of AI have changed the way we interact with, as well as what we expect from, our technology. Assigning human attributes and abilities to our devices is becoming more prevalent. Thinkers in the cognition and science-fiction spaces have long grappled with this possibility as popularized by Asimov's Three Laws of Robotics, a set of rules that robots obey to ensure the robots don't go after humans. And now that there are some clear and concrete AI examples in the real world, that kind of reality seems so much closer.

---

[4]IBM Watson: The inside story of how the Jeopardy-winning supercomputer was born, and what it wants to do next: `http://www.techrepublic.com/article/ibm-watson-the-inside-story-of-how-the-jeopardy-winning-supercomputer-was-born-and-what-it-wants-to-do-next/`

[5]The Great A.I. Awakening: `https://www.nytimes.com/2016/12/14/magazine/the-great-ai-awakening.html`

[6]Google's AlphaZero Destroys Stockfish In 100-Game Match: `https://www.chess.com/news/view/google-s-alphazero-destroys-stockfish-in-100-game-match`

Yet, reality does not match the expectations set forth by AI's successes in some very specific problem areas. Although we have made tremendous leaps and bounds in terms of natural language processing, computer vision, emotion detection, and so forth, composing all of these pieces into a human-like intelligence, usually referred to as Artificial General Intelligence AGI, is not yet within our grasp and is not a realistic target for chat bots. For every article that celebrates the tremendous achievements in the AI space, there's a matching article downplaying the hype around the same technology and showing examples of why this type of AI is still far from perfect (think of the articles showing all the images that computer vision algorithms still can't correctly classify). As with any technology that has been hyped up in the media, we must be reasonable with the expectations we set on it.

Are our bots going to be agents with human-level intelligence having conversations with our users? No. Given the technology and the tasks we want our bots to accomplish, can we make our bots perform those tasks very well? Absolutely. This book aims to equip the reader with the necessary skill to build compelling, engaging, and useful chat bots. It is up to the engineer how much of the latest AI techniques you want to incorporate during this journey. Certainly, these techniques are not required for a great chat bot.

What Is a Chat Bot?

At the most basic level, a *chat bot*, also referred to simply as a *bot* throughout this book, is a computer program that can take user input in natural language and return text or rich media to the user. The user communicates with the chat bot via a messaging app, such as Facebook Messenger, Skype, Slack, and others, or via a voice-activated device such as the Amazon Echo, Google Home, or Harmon Kardon's Invoke powered by Microsoft's Cortana.

Figure 1-1 illustrates our first bot built using Microsoft Bot Framework. This bot simply returns the same message to the user prefixed by the string "echo: ". The logic that runs this experience on the Bot Framework is brain-dead simple.

```
var bot = new builder.UniversalBot(connector, [
    function (session) {
        // for every message, send back the text prepended by
            echo:
        session.send('echo: ' + session.message.text);
    }
]);
```

Figure 1-1. A simple echo bot

This is a chat bot. Basic and not terribly useful, right? We can just as easily create a YouTube bot that, given user text input, searches for videos on that topic and sends the user links to those videos (Figures 1-2 and 1-3).

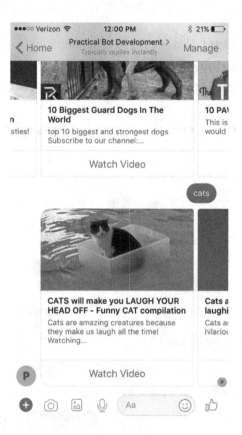

Figure 1-2. *Cats are OK*

This is another basic bot that does just one thing, and it kind of does it well. It integrates with the YouTube API, uses your input as a search parameter, and returns what are referred to in the Bot Framework as *cards*, something we will explore later in the book. The images make for a richer and more engaging experience—a bit more interesting but still rather basic.

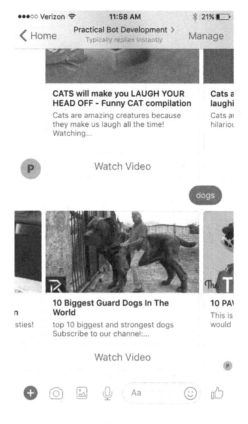

Figure 1-3. *Dogs are way better!*

The code for this one is shown next. We make a request to YouTube and translate the response from YouTube format to Bot Framework cards.

```
const bot = new builder.UniversalBot(connector, [
    session => {
        const url = vsprintf(urlTemplate, [session.message.text]);

        request.get(url, (err, response, body) => {
            if (err) {
                console.log('error while fetching video:\n' + err);
                session.endConversation('error while fetching
                video. please try again later.');
```

```
            return;
        }

        const result = JSON.parse(body);
        // we have at most 5 results
        let cards = [];

        result.items.forEach(item => {
            const card = new builder.HeroCard(session)
                .title(item.snippet.title)
                .text(item.snippet.description)
                .images([
                    builder.CardImage.create(session, item.
                    snippet.thumbnails.medium.url)
                ])
                .buttons([
                    builder.CardAction.openUrl(session,
                    'https://www.youtube.com/watch?v=' +
                    item.id.videoId, 'Watch Video')
                ]);
            cards.push(card);
        });

        const reply = new builder.Message(session)
            .text('Here are some results for you')
            .attachmentLayout(builder.AttachmentLayout.
            carousel)
            .attachments(cards);

        session.send(reply);
    });
    }
]);
```

OK, how about this? We can have a bot that, given a statement, can tell whether it's a neutral, positive, or negative statement and return an appropriate response (Figure 1-4). We don't show it, but the code for this one is as straightforward as the earlier examples: we fetch a sentiment score from a simple sentiment REST API and use it to render an answer.

Figure 1-4. *A simple example of utilizing AI to drive a conversation*

This is a simple example showing how easy our code can integrate with AI, if we were to go that route. Bots don't always have to follow a question-response pattern. Bots can reach out to users proactively. For example, we could have a fraud alert bot (Figure 1-5).

Figure 1-5. *Proactive user messaging*

A bot can be more task driven. Imagine, for example, a calendar bot that can create appointments, check availability, edit or delete appointments, and give you a summary of your calendar (Figure 1-6).

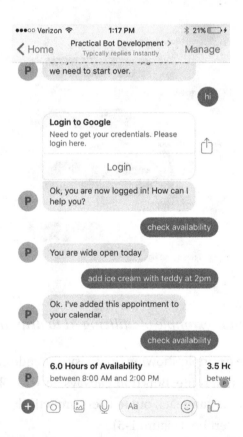

Figure 1-6. *A simple calendar bot integrated with Google Calendar*

Now things are starting to get a bit more interesting. We are starting to take natural language and to act on it.

Why Now?

Why are bots becoming such a big deal? Certainly, they have existed in all kinds of incarnations in old-school apps like IRC[7] and AOL Instant Messenger.[8] And these were not little experiments. IRC bots have been around for a long time. I remember interacting with quite a few bots over IRC. Being young and naïve when it came to technology, I initially thought there was an actual human responding to my messages. I quickly grasped the idea that there was a machine sitting somewhere responding to what I was writing. The more I interacted with IRC bots, the more I treated them like a command line. This, however, was all pretty niche technology at the time. The public wasn't interacting with bots on a daily basis so there was no need to cater to natural language interactions.

Today, the way we interact with the technology around us is completely different, and it is driven by three forces: advancements in AI, the idea of messaging apps as a conversational intelligence platform, and voice-activated conversational interfaces.

Advancements in Artificial Intelligence

Throughout the 20th century, computer scientists, biologists, linguists, and economists have made tremendous strides in the fields of cognition, artificial intelligence, artificial life, machine learning, and deep learning. The very concept of a computer program executing instructions, the

---

[7]IRC Bots: https://en.wikipedia.org/wiki/IRC_bot
[8]SmarterChild: https://en.wikipedia.org/wiki/SmarterChild

Universal Turing Machine[9] and the idea of a computer architecture that can digitally store code and execute the code taking inputs and producing outputs, and the Von Neumann architecture,[10] are recent in human history standards but are the underlying concepts that our work on computers is based on. The beginnings of the ideas around neural networks were first published in 1943 by McCulloch and Pitts in their paper "A logical calculus of the ideas immanent in nervous activity."[11] In 1950, Asimov included the Three Laws of Robotics in his book *I, Robot*.[12] That same year, the first paper describing how a computer can play chess, "Programming a Computer for Playing Chess" by Claude Shannon, was published. He went on to essentially inventing the field of information theory.[13] From the 1960s and onward, the amount of research and growth in the space has been mind-blowing; we see proof of this every day in media coverage of the latest AI applications.

Suffice it to say, since the 1960s, machine learning and the process of building our own models using a variety of algorithms have become better performing and more accessible. Libraries such as scikit-learn for Python and Google's Tensor Flow, among many others, are well documented with strong community support. The big technology firms have also invested enough in their computational capacity and power to be able to work on

---

[9]Universal Turing Machine: `https://en.wikipedia.org/wiki/Universal_Turing_machine`

[10]Von Neumann Architecture: `https://en.wikipedia.org/wiki/Von_Neumann_architecture`

[11]A Logical Calculus of Ideas Immanent in Nervous Activity: `http://www.cs.cmu.edu/~epxing/Class/10715/reading/McCulloch.and.Pitts.pdf`

[12]The Three Laws of Robotics: `https://en.wikipedia.org/wiki/Three_Laws_of_Robotics`

[13]Programming a Computer for Playing Chess: `http://archive.computerhistory.org/projects/chess/related_materials/text/2-0%20and%202-1.Programming_a_computer_for_playing_chess.shannon/2-0%20and%202-1.Programming_a_computer_for_playing_chess.shannon.062303002.pdf`

some of the most computationally intensive tasks in a reasonable time frame. Microsoft, Amazon, Google, IBM, and others are now involved in cloud platforms in one way or another. The next step has been to offer some of these machine learning algorithms on demand. If we simply examine Microsoft's Cognitive Services as an example, we find 30 APIs at the time of this writing. These include computer vision tools like Face and Emotion Detection, Content Moderation, and OCR capabilities. It also includes language tools such as Natural Language Processing, Linguistic and Text Analytics, and Natural Language Understanding. It even includes search and knowledge tools such as Recommendations engines and Sematic Search. The availability of services that any developer can plug into at any time to access these powerful features at a reasonable cost is a significant reason why intelligent systems are becoming so much more prevalent in our lives and is one of the great pieces of infrastructure that our bots can take advantage of. We will look at Microsoft's Cognitive Services in Chapter 10.

Messaging Apps as a Conversational Intelligence Platform

Mobile messaging apps have become all the rage in recent years. Snapchat, Slack, Telegram, iMessage, FB Messenger, WhatsApp, and WeChat are some of the most used apps on a mobile user's phone. In fact, their usage has surpassed that of social networks such as Facebook. According to Business Insider, messaging apps began being more used than social networks sometime around the first quarter of 2015, and the trend has continued since then. Although this book will not get into details around all the relevant players in the U.S. and global markets, the key point is that Asia-based messaging apps such as WeChat and LINE have figured out the best way to grow usage via chat apps and how to monetize that usage. The monetization trend has not yet fully caught up to the U.S. market, but firms like Apple, Twitter, and Facebook have been leading the way by allowing developers to create easy chat bot and even payment integrations I do not mean to limit the discussion to said players; the trend of opening access to messaging platforms is prevalent across the board.

The ability to host these bots within an existing messaging platform opens brands up to significantly more customers. The user experience stays within the messaging application. The bot developer does not need to concern herself with things like animations and memory management as a mobile app developer might; the main concern is the conversation with the user. One of the interesting concepts that we will encounter throughout the book is that bots are not just text. They can include images, videos, and audio as well as buttons to invoke other commands. The creation of a conversational experience within the confines of an existing messaging application is an exercise of writing an app within an app; our bot is constrained by the native features supported by the messaging platform. The Bot Framework has the necessary facilities to maximally take advantage of all these features.

Voice-Activated Intelligent Assistants

Another factor significantly accelerating the development of conversational intelligence technologies is the development of voice-enabled hardware devices. One of the more significant modern virtual assistants, Siri, was introduced by Apple in 2011. Siri, now a household name, is powered underneath the hood by some of the technology behind one of the most well-known desktop voice recognition systems, Nuance's speech-to-text product, Dragon NaturallySpeaking.

Siri was the first to market, seemingly encouraging many other companies to jump into the voice assistant game. Microsoft released its Cortana Assistant in 2014, the same year that the first Amazon Echo device was released. Cortana was initially limited to Windows Phone and Windows desktop operating system but was later made available on mobile operating systems and even Xbox. Amazon's Echo featuring the Alexa voice assistant was the first commercially successful stand-alone hardware device and has allowed Amazon to dominate the voice assistant market early on. In subsequent years, Facebook and Google have introduced M (shut down as of early 2018) and Google Assistant, respectively. Google is jumping into the voice device game with Google Home. Harman Kardon is bringing a product called Invoke into the market, a Microsoft Cortana–powered speaker. Many other players are expanding into the market, further encouraging innovation in the space.

This increased activity and competition have been accelerated by improvements in AI and speech recognition, natural language processing, and natural language understanding technologies. The significant build-up of these technologies has increased the activity in terms of standards, frameworks, and tools to create custom capabilities for these platforms. As we will soon see, these custom capabilities, or skills, can be backed by a chat bot.

Why Should We Create Bots?

Why would we want to write bots and use messaging apps as a platform? We could just as easily write mobile apps, publish to the app store, and be done with it, no? Not exactly. There are a variety of trends in user behavior that are making this approach less feasible.

When it comes to some of the bigger brand names, downloading their app is a simple task. I want to use Facebook? Fine, I'll get the app. I want to check my e-mail; I'll use the app. But, I want to talk to my local flower shop? I don't need an app for that. I don't *want* an app for that. Why should I download an app for every single business I have contact with? Ideally, I would just be able to call them or, really, just text them, right?

The moves that firms are making in the market are allowing users to talk to a business directly. Let's take Facebook as an example. A local flower shop can have a Facebook page and enable messaging on the page. Business employees can respond to customer queries in one place. Twitter has a similar feature with its new Direct Message API. That offers a lot of value for businesses. The removal of the app download friction makes it so much easier for users to begin conversing with businesses. The next step, of course, is to automate some of that communication. This is where bots come in. The messaging platform takes care of numerous concerns such as user identity, authentication, overall app stability, and so forth.

This translates to other use cases as well. Let's take the use case of a productivity tool such as Slack. Slack is a great work collaboration platform that enables people to chat and collaborate with each other across multiple topics. A chat bot on the Slack platform would typically be more productivity oriented. For example, you would probably have a hard time getting people to use a dating bot on Slack as opposed to on a social network like Facebook. Figure 1-7 shows a listing of the top Slack bots. These types of bots are more associated to work tasks such as to-do lists, stand-ups, task assignment, and so on. Clearly, if a team is fully committed and immersed in Slack, creating a bot to carry out common tasks may be more effective than creating an entirely separate web site.

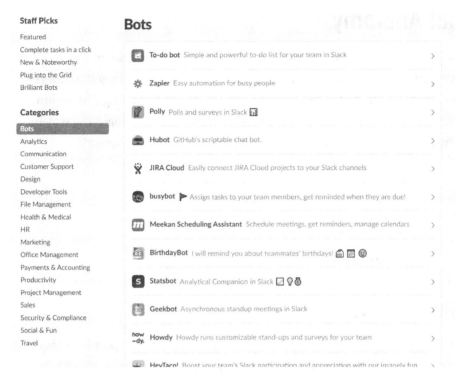

Figure 1-7. Slack bot listing

Although Slack's listing contains a specific category called Bots, the fact is all of these apps are all bots. Some of them might be more conversational, and others could have a more command-line feel to them; as far as we are concerned, a bot is simply listening to messages and acting upon them. For the heavy conversational kinds of chat bots, the topic of natural language understanding, the discipline concerned with understanding human language, is essential for a good user experience. As such, we dedicate the Chapters 2 and 3 to the topic.

Bot Anatomy

As we dive into the Bot Framework, it is worth breaking down the development of chat bots into individual components. In general, there are several approaches to each component. In the following discussion, I attempt to describe the general concepts and then highlight the way in which Microsoft approaches the problem in the Bot Framework.

- Bot runtime

- Natural language understanding engine

- Conversation engine

- Channel integrations

Bot Runtime

At the most basic level, a chat bot is a web service that responds to requests from users. Depending on the messaging platform we integrate with, the details differ, but the idea is the same: a messaging platform calls a bot via an HTTP endpoint with a message that contains the user input. Our chat bot's role is to process the message and respond with a message to the platform that includes the bot's response plus any attachments or platform-specific data. Figure 1-8 illustrates a generic approach. Depending on the platform, we may be able to return exceptional cases with HTTP status codes or some other format. When our bot processes the message, it responds by calling the channel's HTTP endpoint. The channel then delivers the message to the user.

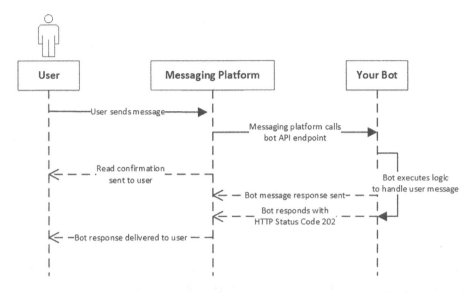

Figure 1-8. *Message exchange between user, messaging platform, and a generic bot*

There are a few problems with this approach, mainly that we are tying the bot to a specific messaging channel, whereas our bots should be channel agnostic so we can reutilize as much logic as possible. The Bot Framework solves this by providing a connector service that sits between the messaging platform and the bot. In reality, the interaction looks more like Figure 1-9. Note that the channel connector owns the connection and communication with the messaging platform and translates messages into a generic format our bot can recognize. We will cover channels in more detail in the "Channel Integrations" section later in this chapter.

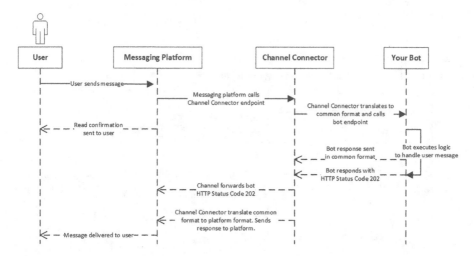

Figure 1-9. *Message exchange between the user, messaging platform, connector service, and bot using the Bot Framework*

Since the bot runtime is simply a computer program listening to an HTTP endpoint, we can develop the bot using any technology that allows us to receive to HTTP messages. We can use .NET, Node.js, Python, and PHP. In fact, we could simply use the Bot Framework to gain advantage of the connectors and implement the HTTP endpoint using any approach we would like. If we did, however, we would lose out on the Bot Builder SDK. We will cover its benefits and reasons to use it in the "Conversation Engine" section later in this chapter.

Natural Language Understanding Engine

Writing a chat bot that reads and understands users' utterances is challenging. Human language is unstructured input with flexible and inconsistent rules. And yet, our bots need to be able to take those inputs and figure out what the user is talking about. At a high level, natural language understanding engines solve two problems for the bot developer: intent classification and entity extraction.

We will show what intents and entities are by way of example. Say we are developing a thermostat-controlling bot. Initially, we would like to support four actions: turn on, turn off, set mode to cool or heat, and set temperature. The categories of actions a user can express in natural language (meaning the turning on/off, setting mode, or setting temperature) are called *intents*. The mode itself (cool or heat) and the temperature value are *entities*. NLU engines allow the bot developer to define a custom set of intents and entities relevant to the application. Table 1-1 lists some sample mappings.

Table 1-1. *A Sample Mapping of User Input to Intent, As Resolved by an NLU System*

Utterance	Intent	Entity
"Turn on"	TurnOn	none
"Power off"	TurnOff	none
"Set to 68 degrees"	SetTemperature	"68 degrees" Type: Temperature
"Set mode to cool"	SetMode	"cool" Type: Mode

Clearly, it is easier for our code to perform logic based on the intent and entity values, as opposed to a raw user utterance.

There are several services a bot developer can utilize to gain this NLU functionality. In the current technology environment, there are plenty of cloud-based APIs available, such as LUIS, Wit.ai, and Dialog flow, among others. LUIS is the richer and best-performing from this group and is the subject of an NLU deep dive in Chapter 3.

Conversation Engine

When building bots, we typically develop a workflow that implements tasks that our bot would like to accomplish. Following the basic thermostat example, we could envision the bot architecture as shown in Figure 1-10.

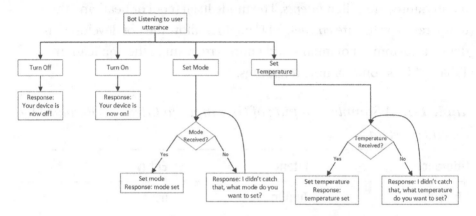

Figure 1-10. *A sample bot conversation design diagram*

The workflow always starts with the bot listening for user utterances. An utterance spoken by the user will be resolved to the intents in Table 1-1. If the intent is TurnOn or TurnOff, the bot can execute the right logic and respond with a confirmation message. If we receive a SetTemperature intent, our bot can verify that the Temperature entity exists. If not, we ask the user for it. Once we receive it, we can execute the right logic and send a confirmation response. SetMode would work similarly to SetTemperature in that we would confirm the existence of the entity and elicit it if it does not exist.

This description of what a bot does based on user inputs is a conversation. The activity of designing the types of inputs, the output, and the transitions is called *conversational experience design*. We cover this topic in depth in Chapter 4.

A conversation engine is the engine that tracks incoming messages, processes them, and executes the state transitions between the conversation diagram nodes (also referred to as dialogs). It does so separately for each user. The state of the conversation is stored so that when the next user message comes into the bot, the bot knows what the user's current state is. The Bot Framework does a great job of providing the conversation engine via the Bot Builder SDK.

Aside: Intents, Entities, Actions, Slots, Oh My!

There are multiple approaches to developing bots, but they can be summarized into two approaches: bot engine and what I call bot conversation as a service. The bot engine was described earlier: we run our bot as a web service, call into NLU platforms as necessary, and use a conversation engine to route messages to dialogs. The bot conversation as a service approach was popularized by the likes of Dialogflow. The approach implies that the NLU resolution, conversation mapping, state, and transitions occur in the cloud on Dialogflow's infrastructure. Your bot is then called by Dialogflow to modify responses or integrate with other systems.

When a user's utterance maps to an intent and a defined set of entities, it is called an *action*. An action has an intent and a set of parameters. Based on our thermostat bot, we could define an action named SetTemperatureAction. This action is the SetTemperature intent with a Temperature parameter. The type of the Temperature parameter is the Temperature entity. When Dialogflow resolves an action, it can call into your bot to fulfill the action. In this model, the bot logic is focused on the execution of logic based on the NLU service's resolution logic; the conversation engine is outsourced to the NLU service.

An advanced topic in this type of approach to bot development is slot filling. This is the process through which a service notices that an action was only partially populated by a user input and automatically asks the user to fill in the remaining slot, or what we called *action parameters*. Tables 1-2 and 1-3 illustrate two sample actions.

Table 1-2. *Action Definition for Setting a Temperature in Our Thermostat Bot*

Action	Name	Type	Required?	Prompt
SetTemperature	Temperature	Temperature	Yes	What temperature would you like to set?

Table 1-3. *A More Complex Action Based on a Flight-Booking Bot*

Action	Name	Type	Required?	Prompt
Book Flight	From	City	Yes	Departure city
	To	City	Yes	Destination city
	Date	Datetime	Yes	When are you traveling?

Figure 1-11 illustrates the entire end-to-end flow between the user, messaging platform, connector, NLU service, and the bot in in this conversation as a service model.

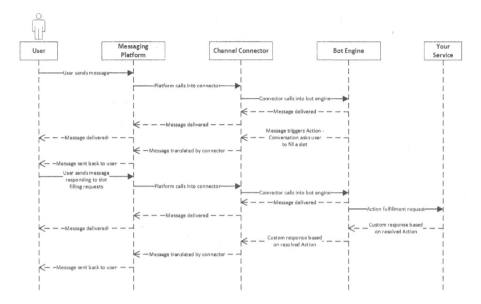

Figure 1-11. *Typical bot conversation as a service flow*

The conversation as a service approach can be good at getting something up and running in short order. Unfortunately, this comes at a loss of some control and flexibility. Using the Bot Framework gets around these issues by allowing us full control over the bot engine.

Channel Integration

Building bots means addressing multiple messaging platforms. Your boss asks you to write a Facebook Messenger bot. You release it, and your boss congratulates you for your great work. He then asks you, "Can we add this as a web chat to our FAQ page?" Your bot code is tied to the Messenger Webhooks and the Send API. You waffle around and figure you can isolate some of the logic that communicates to Messenger behind a transport interface. You create a second implementation of the same interface that talks to your chat bot through web sockets. Now you have created your own abstraction of an interface between your bot and a messaging platform.

We want our bot logic to be abstracted away from the individual messaging platforms as much as possible. The details of how to receive messages from the channel and send responses are details we don't want to concern ourselves with too much, unless we are the professionals building connectors into the various platforms. I don't think you would be reading this book if you were. You want to develop a bot, not the infrastructure. Lucky for us, the different bot frameworks in the market typically do all of this for us, as illustrated in Figure 1-12. The frameworks allow us to write a bot in a channel-agnostic manner and then connect to those channels by going through a few clicks and entering some data. These features are usually called *channels* or *channel integrations*.

As is the case with many generic frameworks, there are some edge cases that the framework does not support because the platform feature is either too new or platform specific. In such cases, the framework should allow us to communicate to the platform in its native format. The Bot Framework provides a mechanism for this.

In addition, our framework should be flexible enough to allow for us to create custom channel connectors. For example, if we desire to build a mobile app that provides a chat bot interface, the framework should allow us to do so. If our enterprise is using an instant messaging channel that is unsupported by Microsoft's Connector, we should be able to create one. Microsoft's Bot Framework allows for this level of integration via one of my favorite features: the Directline API.

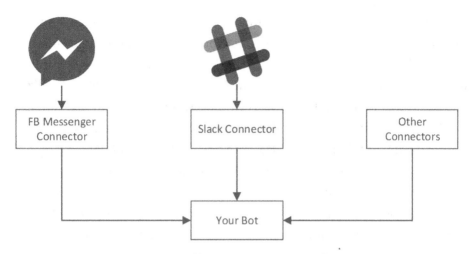

Figure 1-12. *Your bot should not be concerned with which channels it talks to. That should be abstracted away for you.*

We will cover channel and custom channel integrations in Chapters 9 and 10.

Conclusion

In this chapter, we took a quick look below the surface of the different components available to build bots. In my work, the Bot Framework has clearly won out against competitors that use a conversation as a service approach. The flexibility and control that the Bot Framework provides is a requirement for many enterprise scenarios. The Bot Framework also provides better and richer abstractions, deeper connector integration, and an open and diverse community. The Bot Framework teams has created an incredibly powerful suite that can be the foundation for any conversational bot. My team and I have been using the Bot Framework for almost two years and have found no reason to abandon the platform. In fact, the framework's approach to conversational engines and the connector architecture have proven resilient to any use cases we have thrown its way.

For these and many other reasons, this book revolves around using Microsoft's Bot Framework as the framework of choice. The framework is available for the C#/.NET and Node.js development platforms. For the purpose of this book, we will utilize the Node.js version. We will not utilize any additional tools like TypeScript or CoffeeScript. We simply use vanilla JavaScript to show how easy and straightforward it is to get started writing bots using the Bot Framework SDK for Node.js, aka Bot Builder.

Hype or not, the technology and techniques utilized to build bots are truly amazing. As part of this adventure, I want to make sure that we not only cover the basics of building bots but learn more about some of the underlying techniques and approaches. We will not be diving very deeply into these topics, but I'll cover enough to give the reader an introductory level understanding of how the intelligence in bots can be implemented to feel comfortable exploring more complex scenarios. In the interest of overall book focus, when I cover such topics, I will provide links and information for additional reading material to complement the content. I am not a data scientist, but I have done my best in introducing the relevant machine learning (ML) concepts.

We are about to embark on an exciting journey though the world of conversational design, natural language understanding, and machine learning as applied to chat bots. As we cover these topics and build bots, keep in mind that these techniques apply to everything from chat bots to voice assistant skills. With natural language and voice interfaces becoming more and more prevalent both at home and in the workplace, I guarantee you will apply these concepts in both current projects and future natural language apps. Let's get going!

CHAPTER 2

Chat Bot Natural Language Understanding

Before we jump into creating bots and fancy natural language models, we will take a quick detour into natural language understanding (NLU) and some of its machine learning (ML) underpinnings. We will be implementing some of these NLU concepts using Microsoft's Language Understanding Intelligence Service (LUIS) in the following chapter. Some other concepts are available for you to explore using other services (for instance, Microsoft's Cognitive Services) or Python/R ML tools. This chapter is meant to equip you with a quick-and-dirty introduction into the ML space as it pertains to natural language tasks. If you are familiar with these concepts, by all means, skip ahead to Chapter 3. Otherwise, we hope to impart a base-level understanding of the roots of NLU and how it can be applied to the field of bots. There is a great plethora of content on the Internet that goes into depth about all of these topics; we provide the appropriate references if you feel adventurous!

If we choose to develop an NLU-integrated chat bot, our day-to-day engineering will involve continuous interactions with systems that can make sense of what the user is saying. This is a nontrivial task. Consider using brute-force coding to understand free-text user input as related to

© Szymon Rozga 2018
S. Rozga, *Practical Bot Development*, https://doi.org/10.1007/978-1-4842-3540-9_2

our natural language controller thermostat. We introduced this use case in Chapter 1. We had four intents: PowerOn, PowerOff, SetMode, and SetTemperature. Let's consider the SetTemperature intent. How would you encode a system that understands that the user intends to set a temperature and which part of the user input represents the temperature?

We could use a regular expression that tries to match sentences like "set temperature to {temperature}," "set to {temperature}," and "set {temperature}." You test it out. You feel pretty good, and a tester comes along and says, "I want it to be 80 degrees." OK, no biggie. We add "I want it to be {temperature}." The next day someone comes along and says, "lower temperature by 2 degrees." We could add "lower temperature by {diff}" and "increase temperature by {diff}." But now we need to detect the word *lower* and *increase*. And how do we even account for variations of those words? And don't get us started on multiple commands such as "set to 68 during the day and 64 at night." Come to think of it, what temperature units are we talking about?

As we think through the interactions we want to support on the chat bot, we quickly notice that using the brute-force approach would result in quite a tedious system that, in the end, would not perform well given the fascinating and annoying inconsistencies of natural language communication. If we wanted to utilize a brute-force approach, the closest we can get, and still get some pretty good performance, is to use regular expressions. The Bot Framework supports this, as we will see in Chapter 5. If we use such an approach, assuming you are not a regular expression junkie, our interaction model would need to stay simple for maintenance reasons.

Natural language understanding (NLU) is a subset of the complex field of natural language processing (NLP) concerned with the machine comprehension of human language. NLU and NLP are inextricably tied to our understanding of AI, likely because we often correlate intelligence to communication skills. There is probably an underlying psychological nature to it as well; we think the bot is smarter if it understands what we are saying, regardless of our intelligence level and the complexity of our speech. In fact, we would probably be happiest with the kind of AI that could just understand what we are thinking, not what we say. But I digress.

Under that assumption, a command line is not intelligent because it requires commands to be in a specific format. Would we consider it intelligent if we could launch a Node.js script by asking the command line to "launch node...I'm not sure which file, though; can you help me out?." Using modern NLU techniques, we can build models that seem knowledgeable about certain specializations or tasks. Subsequently, on the face of it, a bot may seem somewhat intelligent. Is it?

The truth is that we have not yet developed the computational power and techniques to create an NLU system that matches human intelligence. A problem is said to be "AI hard" if it could be solved only if we could make computers as smart as humans. A proper NLU system that behaves and understands natural language input like a human is not yet within our grasp; but we can create narrow and clever systems that can understand a few things well enough to create a reasonable conversational experience.

Considering the hype surrounding ML and AI these days, it is important for us to set those expectations right from the beginning. One of the first things I always address with clients in our initial conversations about conversational intelligence is that there is a gap between expectations and reality. I like to say that anyone in the room will easily be able to defeat the bot by phrasing things in a way that a human may understand but the bot won't. There are limits to this technology, and there are limits in what it can do within the available budgets and timelines. That's OK. As long as we create a chat bot focused on certain tasks that make the lives on our users better, we're on the right path. And if we can delight our users by building some NLU into the chat bot, great!

Natural Language Machine Learning Background

The beginnings of the NLP field can be traced back to Alan Turing and, specifically, the Turing test,[1] a test to determine whether a machine can behave intelligently. In the test, an evaluator can ask questions of two participants. Responding as one of the participants is a human; a computer is the second participant. Based on the answers the evaluator receives from the two participants, if the evaluator cannot determine which participant is a human and which one is a computer, then it is said that the computer has passed the Turing test. Some systems have claimed to be able to pass the Turing test, but these announcements have been judged as premature.[2] There's a criticism that scripting a bot to try to trick a human to believe that it is human and understanding human input are two very different things. We are quite a few years from getting to passing the Turing test.

One of the most famous early successes in the NLP field was Eliza,[3] a simulation of a psychologist written by Joseph Weizenbaum. Written in the mid-1960s, it is a good example of a simple and seemingly intelligent bot. The bot was driven by a script that assigned values to inputs based on keywords and matched the scored input to an output, not dissimilar to recognizers in the Bot Framework. A JavaScript implementation may be found online; see Figure 2-1.[4] Many other similar systems were created, with varying levels of success.

---

[1]Turing Test: https://en.wikipedia.org/wiki/Turing_test

[2]Ask Ray | Response to announcement of chat bot Eugene Goostman passing the Turing test: http://www.kurzweilai.net/ask-ray-response-to-announcement-of-chatbot-eugene-goostman-passing-the-turing-test

[3]Eliza: https://en.wikipedia.org/wiki/ELIZA

[4]Elizabot: http://www.masswerk.at/elizabot/

Eliza

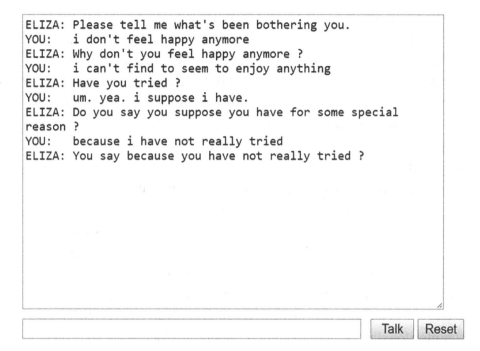

```
ELIZA: Please tell me what's been bothering you.
YOU:   i don't feel happy anymore
ELIZA: Why don't you feel happy anymore ?
YOU:   i can't find to seem to enjoy anything
ELIZA: Have you tried ?
YOU:   um. yea. i suppose i have.
ELIZA: Do you say you suppose you have for some special
reason ?
YOU:   because i have not really tried
ELIZA: You say because you have not really tried ?
```

Talk   Reset

Figure 2-1. *Sample interaction with JavaScript version of Eliza*

The NLU engines were generally rule based; they were encoded with structured representations of knowledge for the systems to use when processing user input. Around the 1980s, the field of machine learning started gaining ground. Machine learning is the process of having computers learn without being coded for the task—something seemingly closer to intelligence than the rule-based approach. For example, we briefly explored building a brute-force NLU engine and the tedious work of encoding with the various rules. Using machine learning, our system would not need to know anything about our domain and intent classifications ahead of time, though we can certainly start with a pretrained model. Instead, we would create an engine that we show sample inputs labeled with certain intent names. This is called the *training data set*. Based on the inputs and labeled intents, we train a model to identify the inputs as the presented labels. Once trained, a model is able to receive inputs it has not yet seen and assign scores to each intent. The more examples we train our model with, the better its performance. This is where the AI comes in: the net effect of training the model with high-quality data is that by using statistical models, the system can start making label predictions of inputs it has not yet encountered.

What was just described is a simplified version of what is known as supervised learning. The name comes from the fact that the input data is labeled. Supervised learning's performance can be quantitively analyzed quite well because we know the real labels and are able to compare them to the predicted labels to get a quantitative value, a technique known as *cross validation*. The type of tasks best suited for supervised learning are classification and regression problems. For a class C, classification is the task of determining whether an input i is or is not of class C; for example, is a photo one of a panda bear? Or we can go as far as given a set of classes S, determine the class of input i. Common algorithms for classification include support vector machines and decision trees. Figures 2-2, 2-3 and 2-4 illustrate a typical supervised learning scenario.

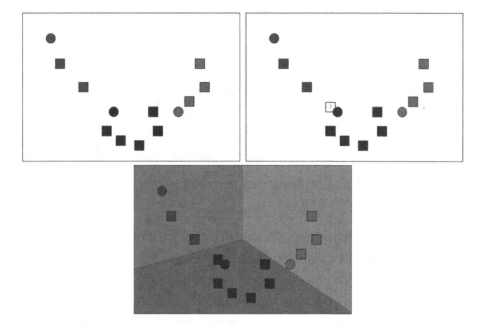

Figures 2-2, 2-3, 2-4. *A supervised learning example. Figure 2-2 is our training data, and we would like to ask the system to categorize the data point with the question mark in Figure 2-3. The classification algorithm will utilize the data points to figure out the boundaries based on the labeled data and then predict the label for the input data point (Figure 2-4).*

Regression is similar but is concerned with predicting continuous values. For example, say we have a data set of some weather features across airports. Maybe we have data for temperature, humidity, cloud cover, wind speed, rain quantity, and the number of flights canceled for that day for JFK in New York, San Francisco International, and O'Hare in Chicago. We could feed this data into a regression model and use it to estimate the number of cancellations given some hypothetical weather in New York, San Francisco, and Chicago.

There are other forms of machine learning besides supervised learning. Unsupervised learning is the task of making sense of unlabeled data, typically data clustering tasks as illustrated in Figures 2-5 and 2-6.

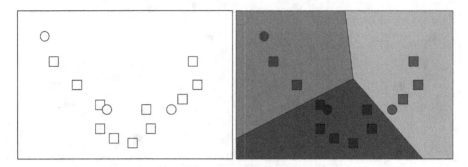

Figures 2-5 and 2-6. *Unsupervised learning in which an algorithm identifies three clusters of data*

Semisupervised learning is the idea of training a model with some labeled data and some unlabeled data. Reinforcement learning is the idea of a system learning by making observations and, based on said observations, making a decision that maximizes some reward function. If the decision yields a better reward, it is reinforced. Otherwise, the decision is penalized. More information about the different types of learning can be found elsewhere.[5]

There is a fascinating illustration of deep reinforcement learning on Stanford's CS pages.,[6] as shown in Figure 2-7. In this demo, an agent navigates a space and learns to navigate toward the red apples with positive reward and avoids the poisoned green apples.

[5]Machine Learning Explained: Understanding Supervised, Unsupervised, and Reinforcement Learning, Ronald Van Loon: https://www.datasciencecentral.com/profiles/blogs/machine-learning-explained-understanding-supervised-unsupervised

[6]Deep Reinforcement Learning Visualization: http://cs.stanford.edu/people/karpathy/convnetjs/demo/rldemo.html

State Visualizations

Left: Current input state (quite a useless thing to look at). **Right**: Average reward over time (this should go up as agent becomes better on average at collecting rewards)

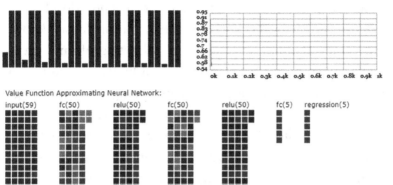

Value Function Approximating Neural Network:

input(59)   fc(50)   relu(50)   fc(50)   relu(50)   fc(5)   regression(5)

(Takes ~10 minutes to train with current settings. If you're impatient, scroll down and load an example pre-trained network from pre-filled JSON)

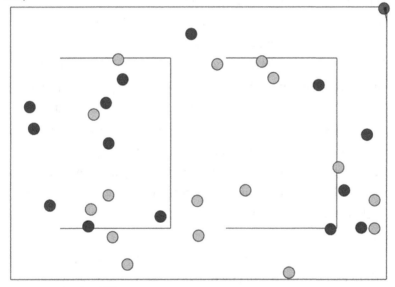

experience replay size: 1673
exploration epsilon: 1
age: 1675
average Q-learning loss: 0.17955135257684046
smooth-ish reward: 0.6003574188734979

Figure 2-7. *A visualization of a deep reinforcement learning algorithm*

37

An interesting point to highlight is that the general popular bot applications of NLU and NLP are quite superficial. In fact, there has been criticism to calling what Watson did on Jeopardy or what bots do NLU. As a *Wall Street Journal* article by Ray Kurzweil stated, Watson doesn't know it won Jeopardy. Understanding and classifying/extracting information are two different tasks. This is a fair criticism, but a well-built intent and entity model can prove useful when it comes to understanding human language in specific narrow contexts, which is exactly what chat bots do.

Aside from the intent classification problem, NLP concerns itself with tasks such as speech tagging, semantic analysis, translation, named entity recognition, automatic summarization, natural language generation, sentiment analysis, and many others. We will look into translation in Chapter 10 in the context of a multilingual bot.

In the 1980s, interest in artificial neural network (ANN) research was increasing. In the following decades, further research in the area yielded fascinating results. A simplistic view of a neuron in an ANN is to think of it as a simple function with N weights/inputs and one output. An ANN is a set of interconnected neurons. The neural network, as a unit, accepts a set of inputs and produces an output. The process of training a neural network is the process of setting the values of the weights on the neurons. Researchers have focused on analysis of many different types of neural networks. Deep learning is the process of training deep neutral networks, which are ANNs with many hidden layers between the input and output (Figure 2-8).

Google's Translate, AlphaGo, and Microsoft's Speech Recognition have all experienced positive results by utilizing deep neural networks. Deep learning's success is a result of research into the various connectivity architectures within the hidden layers. Some of the more popular architectures are convolutional neural networks (CNNs)[7] and recurrent

---

[7]Convolutional neural networks (CNNs): `http://ufldl.stanford.edu/tutorial/supervised/ConvolutionalNeuralNetwork/`

neural networks (RNNs).[8] Applications related to bots may include translation, text summarization, and language generation. There are many other resources for you to explore if you would like to go down the rabbit hole of how ANNs can be applied to natural language tasks.[9]

What is happening within the many ANN layers as the data goes back and forth between the neurons? It seems that no one is quite sure. Google's Translate, for example, has been observed creating an intermediate representation of language. Facebook's project to create AI that could negotiate with either other bots or human resulted in the AI creating its own shorthand and even lying. This has been written about as some indication that AI is taking over the world when, in reality, although these are fascinating and discussion-worthy behaviors, they are side effects of the training process. In the future, some of these side effects may become creepier and scarier as the complexity of the networks produce more unintended emergent behavior. For now, we are safe from an AI takeover.

The ease of developing deep learning models by using toolkits such as Microsoft's Cognitive Toolkit[10] and Google's Tensor Flow[11] is also a significant driver in the recent uptick of popularity of ANN models.

---

[8]Recurrent neural networks (RNNs) and associated architectures: https://en.wikipedia.org/wiki/Recurrent_neural_network

[9]Comparative Study of CNN and RNN for Natural Language Processing: https://arxiv.org/pdf/1702.01923.pdf

[10]Microsoft Cognitive Toolkit: https://www.microsoft.com/en-us/cognitive-toolkit/

[11]TensorFlow: https://www.tensorflow.org/

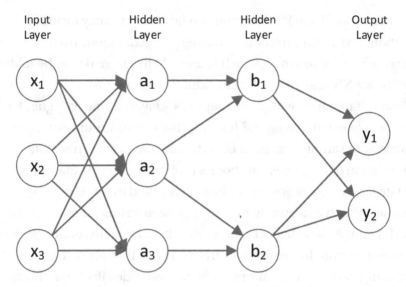

Figure 2-8. An ANN

Deep learning techniques are being utilized quite successfully in natural language processing tasks. In particular, speech recognition and translation have benefitted substantially from the introduction of deep learning. In fact, Microsoft Research has created speech recognition software "that recognizes conversations as well as professional human transcribers,"[12] and Google has decreased its translation algorithm's error rate by between 55 to 85 percent for certain language pairs by taking advantage of deep learning.[13] However, effectiveness in NLU tasks such as intent classification is not as strong as the deep learning hype may want it to be. The key insight here is that deep learning is another tool in the ML toolkit, not a silver bullet.

---

[12]Microsoft researchers achieve new conversational speech recognition milestone: https://www.microsoft.com/en-us/research/blog/microsoft-researchers-achieve-new-conversational-speech-recognition-milestone

[13]A Neural Network for Machine Translation, at Production Scale - https://research.googleblog.com/2016/09/a-neural-network-for-machine.html

Common NLP Tasks

In general, NLP deals with a whole multitude of problems, a subset of which are what we would consider NLU tasks. At a high level, the topics can be related to language syntax, semantics, and discourse analysis. Not every NLP task is immediately relevant to chat bot development; some of them are foundational to the more relevant higher-order features such as intent classification and entity extraction.

Syntax

Syntax tasks generally deal with issues corresponding to taking text input and breaking it up into its constituent parts. Many of these tasks are foundational and will not be directly used by a bot. Segmenting input into smaller units of speech, called *morphemes*, and building structures representing the speech in some grammar are two examples of this. Part of *speech tagging*, the process of tagging every word in user input with its part of speech (e.g., noun, verb, pronoun), could be used to refine user queries.

Semantics

Semantic tasks are related to finding meaning in natural language input. These tasks have real applications for chat bots and include the following:

- *Named entity extraction*: Given some text, determine which words map to names and what the type of name is (e.g., location, person). This is directly applicable to what we want chat bots to do.

- *Sentiment analysis*: Identify whether the contents of some text are overall positive, negative, or neutral. This can be utilized for determining user sentiment to bot responses, redirecting to a human agent, or in bot analytics understanding where users are tripping up and not reacting well to the bot.

- *Topic segmentation*: Given some text, break it into segments related to topics and extract those topics.

- *Relationship extraction*: This extracts the relationship between objects in text.

Discourse Analysis

Discourse analysis is the process of looking at larger natural language structures and making sense of them as a unit. In this area, we are interested in deriving meaning from context in a body of text. Automatic summarization is used to summarize a large body of content such as corporate financial statements. More relevant to chat bots is the concept of co-reference resolution. Co-reference resolution is the idea of determining what entity multiple words refer to. In the following input, the *I* refers to Szymon:

```
My name is Szymon. I am piling up cereal for my son.
```

Common Bot NLU Tasks

If we are planning on using NLU in our chat bot, there are several features to consider when evaluating a solution. The bare-bones basic functionality is the ability to recognize custom intents and entities. The following are some features to consider:

- *Multilanguage support*: The support of multiple languages in an NLU implementation speaks volumes about a serious undertaking of an NLU platform. Experience with optimizations for different languages can be a good indicator of the team's overall experience with NLU.

- *Ability to include prebuilt models*: A head start is always appreciated, and many systems will include many prebuilt intents and entities associated with a specific domain for you to start using.

- *Prebuilt entities*: There are many types of entities we would expect an existing system to be able to easily pull out for us, for example, numbers and date/time objects.

- *Entity types*: There should be an ability to specify different types of entities (lists versus nonlists come to mind).

- *Synonyms*: The system should accept the ability to show assign synonyms to entities.

- *Ongoing training via Active Learning*: The system should support the ability to utilize real user input as training data for the NLU models.

- *API* Although these tools will implement some sort of user interface for you to utilize to train the models, there should an API you can utilize to do so.

- *Export/Import*: The tool should allow you to import/ export models, preferably in an open text format like JSON.

An alternative approach to utilizing preexisting services would be to write your own. This is an advanced topic. If you are reading this book, chances are you do not possess the experience and knowledge to make it work. There are easy-to-use ML packages such as scikit-learn that may give the impression that creating something like this is easy, but the effort requires substantial optimizations, tuning, testing, and operationalization. Getting the right type of performance out of these general-purpose NLU systems takes a lot of time, effort, and expertise. If you are interested in how the technologies work, there are plenty of materials online for you to educate yourself.[14]

---

[14]Machine Learning, NLP: Text Classification using scikit-learn, python and NLTK: https://towardsdatascience.com/machine-learning-nlp-text-classification-using-scikit-learn-python-and-nltk-c52b92a7c73a

Cloud-Based NLU Systems

The great news from the space of cloud computing and the investment that the big technology firms are making into the ML as a service space is that the basic functionality for the tasks that we need for our bots are available as services. From a practical perspective, there are many benefits here: developers don't have to be concerned with selecting the best algorithms for our classification problem, there is no need to scale the implementation, there are existing efficient user interfaces and upgrades, and optimizations are seamless. If you are creating a chat bot and need the basic classification and entity extractions features, using a cloud-based service is the best option.

The field is very dynamic, and the features and focus of these systems change over time. At any rate, at the time of this writing, the following are the best options, in no particular order:

- *Microsoft's Language Understanding Intelligence Service (LUIS)*: This is the purest example of an LU system because it is completely independent from a conversation engine. LUIS allows the developer to add intents and entities, version the LUIS application, test the application before publishing, and finally publish to a test or production endpoint. In addition, it includes some very interesting active learning features.

- *Google's Dialogflow (Api.ai)*: Dialogflow, previously known as Api.ai, has been around for a while. It allows the developer to create NLU models and define conversions flows and calls to webhooks or cloud functions when certain conditions are met. The conversation is accessible via an API or via integrations to many messaging channels.

- *Amazon's Lex*: Amazon's Alexa has long allowed users to create intent classification and entity extraction models. With the introduction of Lex, Amazon brings a better user interface to NLU with bot development. Lex has a few channel integrations at the time of this writing and can be accessed via an API. Like Dialogflow, Lex allows developers to use an API to talk to the bot.

- *IBM Watson Conversation*: Yet another similar system, Watson Conversation allows the user to define intents, entities, and a cloud-based dialog. The conversation is accessible via an API. At the time of this writing, there are no prebuilt channel connectors; a broker must be written by the bot developer though samples exist.

- *Facebook's Wit.ai*: Wit.ai has been around for a while and includes an interface to define intents and entities. As of July 2017, it is refocusing on NLU and removing the bot engine pieces. Wit.ai is also being more closely integrated with the Facebook Messenger ecosystem.

For our NLU deep dive in the following chapter, we will utilize LUIS. Being a pure NLU system, LUIS has a significant advantage, especially when it comes to Bot Framework integration. Although there are not many benchmarks in the NLU space at this time, LUIS ranks among the top-performing NLU systems in the market.[15]

Enterprise Space

There are many other options in the enterprise space—really, too many to list. Some of the bigger company and product names you may run into

---

[15]Evaluating Natural Language Understanding Service for Conversational Question Answering Systems: http://www.sigdial.org/workshops/conference18/proceedings/pdf/SIGDIAL22.pdf

are IPsoft's Amelia and Nuance's Nina. Products in this space are generally advanced and contain years of enterprise-level investment. Some companies focus on IT or other process automation. Some companies focus on internal use cases. Some companies focus on specific verticals. And yet other companies focus entirely on prebuilt NLU models around specific use cases. In some products, we will write bot implementations via a proprietary language versus an open language.

In the end, the decision for enterprises is a classic buy versus build dilemma. Niche solutions may stay around for a while, but it is reasonable to assume that with the amount of investment IBM, Amazon, Microsoft, Google, and Facebook are throwing into this space, companies with less financial backing might be handicapped. Niche players that don't solve the general bot problem may certainly thrive, and I think we will find more companies creating and innovating in specialized NLU and bot solutions that are powered by the big tech company offerings.

Conclusion

We are truly seeing the democratization of AI in the NLU space. Years ago, bot developers would have to pick up the existing NLU and ML libraries to create a system that could be trained and used as readily and easily as the cloud options we have available these days. Now, it is incredibly easy to create a bot that integrates NLU, sentiment analysis, and coreferences. The firms' effort behind these systems isn't something to scoff at either; the largest technology companies are digging into this space to provide the tooling for their users to build conversational experiences for their own platforms. For you as a bot developer, this is great. It means competition will keep pushing for innovation in the space, and as research in the field progresses, improvements in classification, entity extraction and active learning will improve NLU systems' performance. Bot developers stand to gain from the increased pace of research and improved performance of all these NLP services.

CHAPTER 3

Language Understanding Intelligent Service (LUIS)

LUIS is an NLU system that my teams and I have used extensively and is a perfect learning tool to apply the important concepts of intent classification and entity extraction. You can access the system by going to `https://luis.ai`. Once you log in using a Microsoft account, you will be shown a page describing how to build a LUIS app. This is a good introduction to the different tasks we will be accomplishing in this chapter. Once you are done, click the *Create LUIS app* button near the bottom. You will be taken to a page with your LUIS applications. Click the *Create new app* button and enter a name; a LUIS app will be created for you where you can create a new model and train, test, and publish it for use via an API when ready.

In this chapter, we will create a LUIS app that lets us power a Calendar Concierge Bot. The Calendar Concierge Bot will be able to add, edit, and delete appointments; summarize our calendar; and find availability in a day. This task will take us on a tour of the various LUIS features. By the end of the chapter, we will have developed a LUIS app that not only can be used to create a useful bot but can constantly evolve and perform better.

© Szymon Rozga 2018
S. Rozga, *Practical Bot Development*, https://doi.org/10.1007/978-1-4842-3540-9_3

To start, let's create a new app in LUIS. When we click the *Create new app* button, we will get a pop up as in Figure 3-1. Fill out the Name and Description fields. LUIS not only works with English but supports other cultures as well. Different languages require different language models and optimizations. This selection informs LUIS which culture your app will be using so those optimizations can be utilized. At the time of this writing, LUIS supports Brazilian Portuguese, Chinese, Dutch, English, French, French Canadian, German, Italian, Japanese, Korean, Spanish, and Mexican Spanish. As the system matures, wider culture support may be introduced.

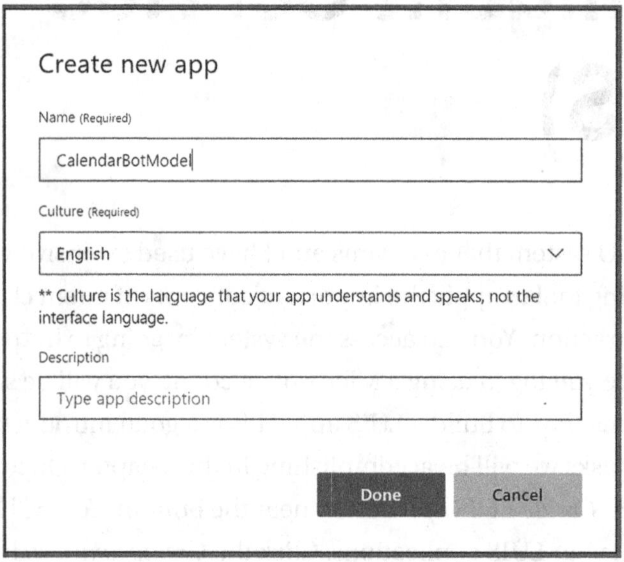

Create new app

Name (Required)

CalendarBotModel

Culture (Required)

English ⌄

** Culture is the language that your app understands and speaks, not the interface language.

Description

Type app description

Done   Cancel

Figure 3-1. *Creating a new LUIS app*

Once the app is created, you will be greeted by the Build section of the LUIS interface (Figure 3-2). As you can see, it is empty except for the None intent. We'll get into that once we start training intents. You will also see the Review Endpoint Utterances link. This is LUIS's active learning feature, which we will explore in subsequent sections.

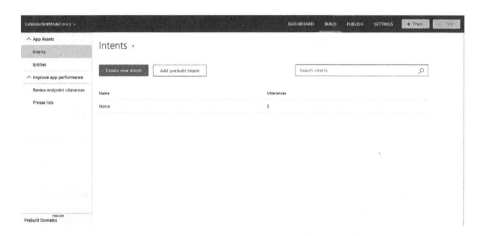

Figure 3-2. *LUIS Build section*

Note that as of the time of this writing, a LUIS application is limited to 500 intents, 30 entities, and 50 list entities. When LUIS was first released, the limits were closer to 10 intents and 10 entities. The latest up-to-date numbers can always be found here online.[1]

On the top of the page, you will see your app name, the active version, and links to the Dashboard, Build, Publish, and Settings sections of LUIS. We can also easily train and test the model right from within the interface. We will explore each of these LUIS sections as we build our calendar concierge app.

---

[1]LUIS Boundaries: `https://docs.microsoft.com/en-us/azure/cognitive-services/luis/luis-boundaries`

49

Classifying Intents

We covered the concepts of intent classification in the previous chapter, but this will be the first time we dive into it in practice. To reiterate, we would like to create a LUIS app that lets us add, edit, or delete calendar entries; display a summary of the calendar; and check availability in our calendar. We will create the following intents:

- AddCalendarEntry

- RemoveCalendarEntry

- EditCalendarEntry

- ShowCalendarSummary

- CheckAvailability

We left off within the Build section. In the left pane, we have selected the Intents item. There is one intent in the system: None. This intent is resolved whenever the user's input does not match any of the other intents. We could use this in our bot to tell the user that they are trying to ask questions outside of the bot's area of expertise and remind them what the bot is capable of.

A typical workflow for using LUIS is to add an intent and present LUIS with several sample utterances that represent the intent. This is exactly what we will do. Figure 3-3 illustrates the process of creating an intent. The UI allows us to enter the utterance in a free-text entry field. We enter a sample, press Enter, enter another sample, press Enter, and so forth. Once we add enough sample utterances, we click the Save button and we're done with the intent (Figure 3-4).

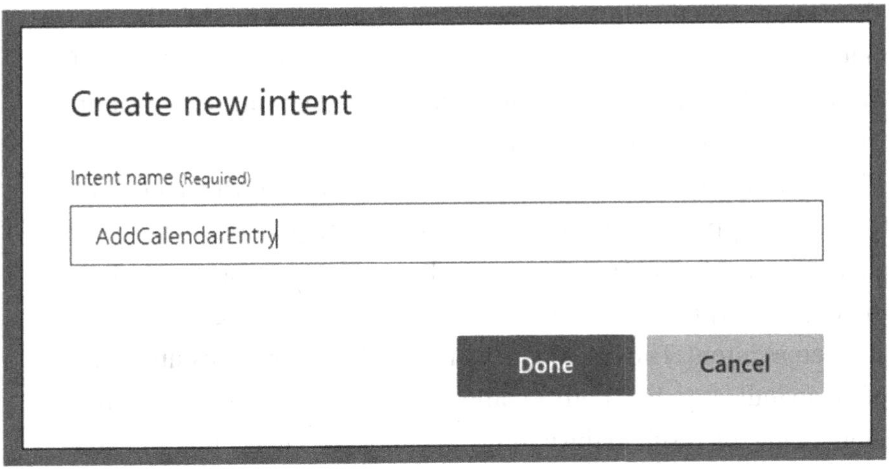

Create new intent

Intent name (Required)

AddCalendarEntry|

Done   Cancel

Figure 3-3. *Adding new LUIS intent*

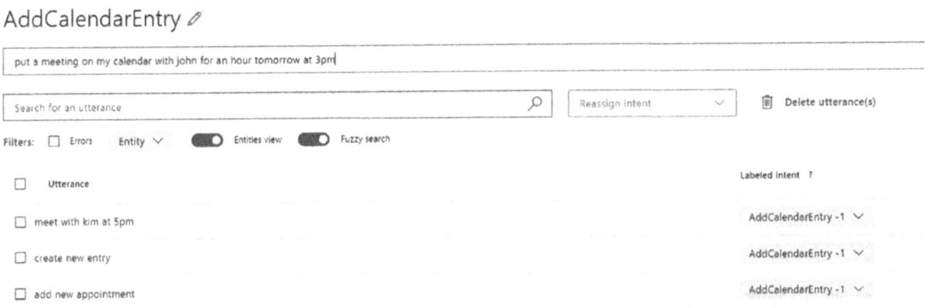

AddCalendarEntry ⌀

put a meeting on my calendar with john for an hour tomorrow at 3pm|

| Search for an utterance | 🔍 | Reassign intent | ⌄ | 🗑 Delete utterance(s) |

Filters: ☐ Errors   Entity ⌄   ⬤ Entities view   ⬤ Fuzzy search

☐	Utterance	Labeled Intent ?
☐	meet with kim at 5pm	AddCalendarEntry -1 ⌄
☐	create new entry	AddCalendarEntry -1 ⌄
☐	add new appointment	AddCalendarEntry -1 ⌄

Figure 3-4. *Adding utterances for AddCalendarEntry intent*

Note that the user interface allows us to search for utterances, delete utterances, reassign intents to utterances, and display the data in a few different formats. Feel free to explore this functionality as you go along.

Before we add the rest of the intents, let's see if we can train and test the application so far. Note that the Train button in the top right has a red indicator; this means the app has changes that have not yet been trained. Go ahead and click the Train button. Your request will be sent to the LUIS servers, and your app will be queued for training. You may notice a message that comes up informs you that LUIS is training your app

51

and "0/2 completed." The 2 is the number of classifier models that your application currently contains. One is for the None intent, and one is for AddCalendarEntry. When training is done, the Train button indicator will turn green to indicate that the app is up-to-date.

The intent interface also gives us information about which intent the latest trained app scores highest for each utterance (Figure 3-5). This piece of data is important because we can easily see when an application is trained to classify an utterance as one intent but assigns the highest score to a different intent. The discrepancy in the trained versus resulting intent is often an indicator that there is something in one or more models that is influencing the result in the wrong direction. We'll cover this and other scenarios in the *Troubleshooting* section of this chapter. For now, it appears all our utterances have been successfully trained to result in a score of 1 on the AddCalendarEntry intent and between 0.05 and 0.07 on the None intent (see Figure 3-6); these numbers may vary depending on your exact utterances and also changes made by the LUIS engineering team.

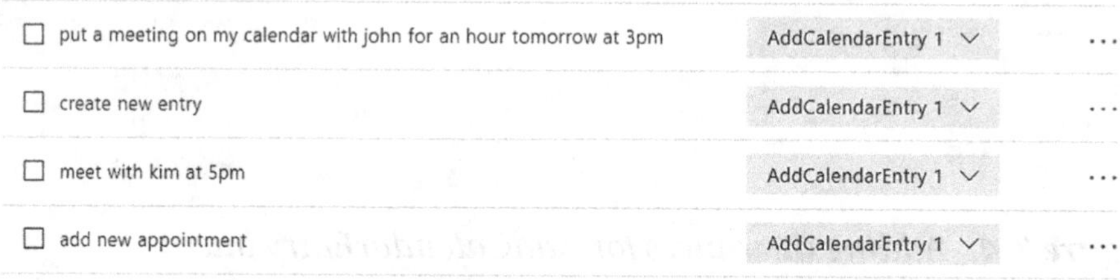

☐ put a meeting on my calendar with john for an hour tomorrow at 3pm	AddCalendarEntry 1 ∨	· · ·
☐ create new entry	AddCalendarEntry 1 ∨	· · ·
☐ meet with kim at 5pm	AddCalendarEntry 1 ∨	· · ·
☐ add new appointment	AddCalendarEntry 1 ∨	· · · ·

Figure 3-5. *Highest-scoring intents (also called predicted intents) for AddCalendarEntry intent*

rrow at 3pm	AddCalendarEntry 1 ∨	· · ·
	AddCalendarEntry 1	
	None 0.05	
	AddCalendarEntry 1 ∨	· · ·

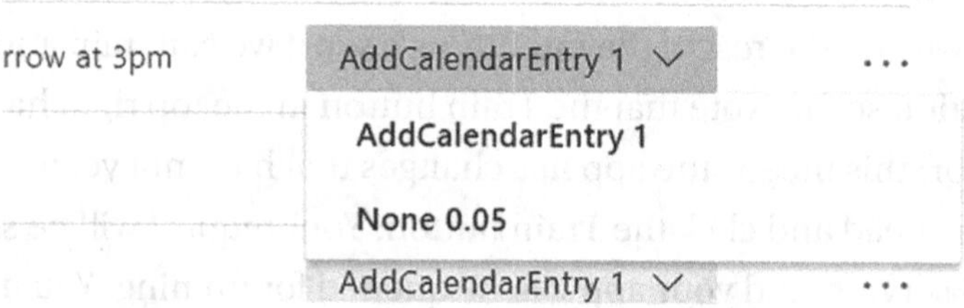

Figure 3-6. *Utterance score for each intent in our app*

Once trained, we can use the Test slide-out next to the Train button to test the models and see how they respond to different inputs (Figure 3-7). The *Batch testing panel* link allows a higher volume of testing to be performed. For our purposes, we will stick to the interactive mode.

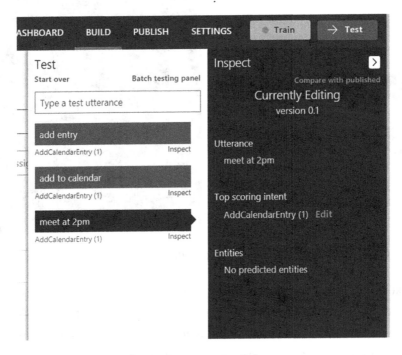

Figure 3-7. *Interactively testing our model*

The way LUIS functions is that it runs each input through all the models that were trained in the Training phase for our app. For each model, we receive a resulting score between 0 to 1 inclusive. The top-scoring intent is displayed prominently. Note that a score does not correspond to a probability. A score is dependent on the algorithm that is being used and usually represents some measure of the distance between the input to an intent's ideal form. If LUIS scores an input with similar scores for more than one intent, we probably have some additional training to do.

After training our app and testing it, it seems to perform well until we try to break it. Then, it quickly starts looking wrong. Figure 3-8 illustrates this point.

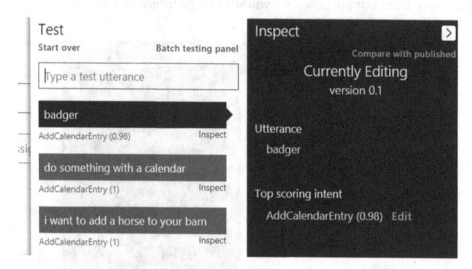

Figure 3-8. *Testing wacky and ridiculous inputs*

Yikes. This is not terribly surprising. We have trained one intent with a limited number of utterances. We provided zero sample utterances to the None intent. This is the kind of behavior an undertrained model will exhibit. Let's add some of these silly phrases to the None intent, train, and test again. You may try to add a few more nonsensical test cases like those in Figure 3-9. It should work better. We will not solve for all kinds of issues like this right now. This will take some time, dedication, and user feedback. But we should be aware that training the app what it should not know is as important as training an app what it should know.

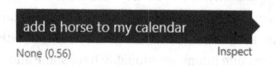

Figure 3-9. *We have made some progress!*

Next, we will add the remaining intents. Figure 3-10, Figure 3-11, Figure 3-12, and Figure 3-13 show some sample utterances for the CheckAvailability, EditCalendarEntry, DeleteCalendarEntry, and ShowCalendarSummary intents.

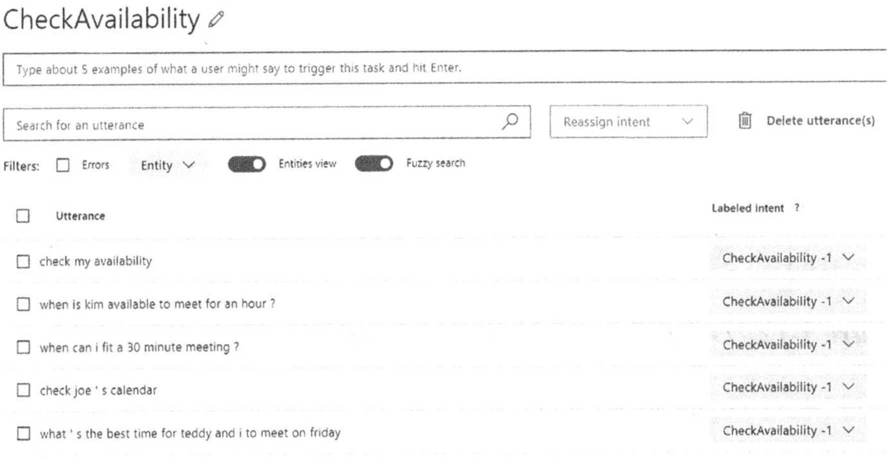

CheckAvailability ✎

	Utterance	Labeled Intent ?
☐	check my availability	CheckAvailability -1 ∨
☐	when is kim available to meet for an hour ?	CheckAvailability -1 ∨
☐	when can i fit a 30 minute meeting ?	CheckAvailability -1 ∨
☐	check joe ' s calendar	CheckAvailability -1 ∨
☐	what ' s the best time for teddy and i to meet on friday	CheckAvailability -1 ∨

Figure 3-10. *CheckAvailability intent sample utterances*

EditCalendarEntry ✎

	Utterance	Labeled Intent ?
☐	reschedule my 7am	EditCalendarEntry -1 ∨
☐	appointment with jeff needs to be moved to tomorrow 5pm	EditCalendarEntry -1 ∨
☐	change my meeting with kim to 2pm	EditCalendarEntry -1 ∨
☐	move my 1pm appointment to 3pm	EditCalendarEntry -1 ∨

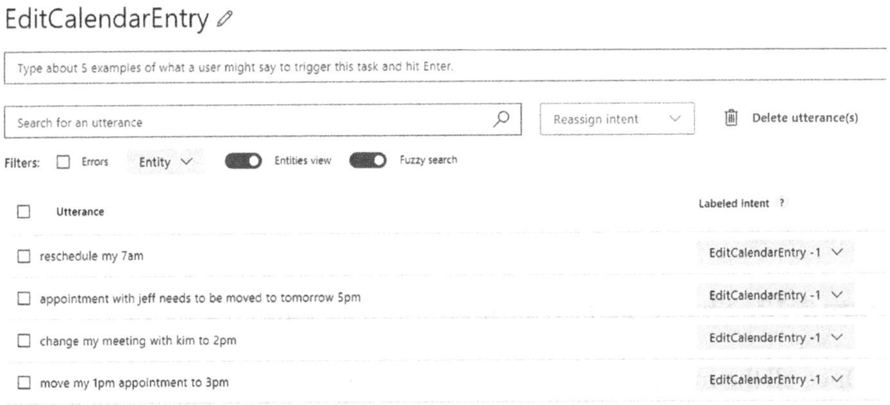

Figure 3-11. *EditCalendarEntry intent sample utterances*

DeleteCalendarEntry ✎

Type about 5 examples of what a user might say to trigger this task and hit Enter.

Search for an utterance 🔍	Reassign intent ⌄	🗑 Delete utterance(s)

Filters: ☐ Errors Entity ⌄ 🔘 Entities view 🔘 Fuzzy search

☐ Utterance	Labeled intent ?
☐ remove tuesday ' s meeting with joe	DeleteCalendarEntry -1 ⌄
☐ cancel friday ' s 1pm	DeleteCalendarEntry -1 ⌄
☐ cancel my appointment tomorrow at 5pm	DeleteCalendarEntry -1 ⌄
☐ cancel my 1pm meeting	DeleteCalendarEntry -1 ⌄
☐ remove meeting	DeleteCalendarEntry -1 ⌄
☐ cancel appointment	DeleteCalendarEntry -1 ⌄

Figure 3-12. *DeleteCalendarEntry intent sample utterances*

ShowCalendarSummary ✎

Type about 5 examples of what a user might say to trigger this task and hit Enter.

Search for an utterance 🔍	Reassign intent ⌄	🗑 Delete utterance(s)

Filters: ☐ Errors Entity ⌄ 🔘 Entities view 🔘 Fuzzy search

☐ Utterance	Labeled intent ?
☐ what ' s my meeting at 1pm about ?	ShowCalendarSummary -1 ⌄
☐ what am i doing on friday ?	ShowCalendarSummary -1 ⌄
☐ what do i have on my schedule today ?	ShowCalendarSummary -1 ⌄
☐ when am i meeting with kim ?	ShowCalendarSummary -1 ⌄
☐ show me event details for 7 / 28 meeting with jeff	ShowCalendarSummary -1 ⌄

Figure 3-13. *ShowCalendarSummary intent sample utterances*

Once all the intents are created and populated with sample utterances, we train and confirm that the predicted intents look accurate. You may note that although the top-scoring intent for each of the utterances is correct, the scores are rather low (Figure 3-14). This is an opportunity for us to train the app further. In fact, we can never assume that we can train an intent to be recognized with such a limited vocabulary and set of data. Getting NLU right requires patience, dedication, and thought. We will add more utterances to our app in an upcoming exercise.

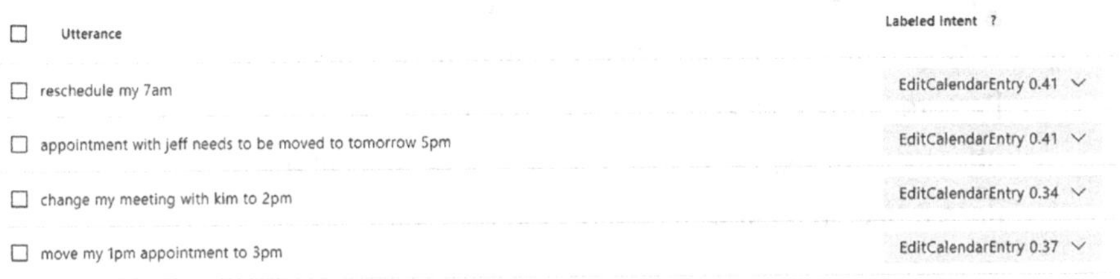

Utterance	Labeled Intent ?
reschedule my 7am	EditCalendarEntry 0.41 ∨
appointment with jeff needs to be moved to tomorrow 5pm	EditCalendarEntry 0.41 ∨
change my meeting with kim to 2pm	EditCalendarEntry 0.34 ∨
move my 1pm appointment to 3pm	EditCalendarEntry 0.37 ∨

Figure 3-14. *The scores are not looking great. This is an opportunity to further train.*

EXERCISE 3-1

Training LUIS Intents

The previous samples show some sample inputs into the intents we trained. Your task is to create a LUIS app, create the same set of intents, and train the app with enough utterance samples so that all intent scores are above 0.80.

- Create the following intents and enter at least ten sample utterances for each:

    - AddCalendarEntry

    - RemoveCalendarEntry

    - EditCalendarEntry

    - ShowCalendarSummary

    - CheckAvailability

- Add some more training to the None intent. Focus on inputs that either make no sense or make no sense in this application, such as "I like coffee." It makes sense but not for this application.

- Train the LUIS app and observe the predicated scores for each utterance by visiting the intent page. Use the interactive test tab as well.

- What are the scores? Are they higher than 0.80? Lower? Keep adding sample utterances to each intent to raise the score. Be sure to train the app every so often and reload the intent utterances to see the updated scores. How many utterances does it take to make you confident in your app?

Once you are done with these exercise, you will have built up the experience of training and testing LUIS intents.

Publishing Your Application

Obviously, we are not yet done developing our app. There are quite a few things missing and many details of LUIS we have not yet explored. We haven't seen any real user data yet either. But, we can develop both the LUIS app and the consuming application in parallel. The process of taking our trained app and making it accessible via HTTP is referred to as *publishing our app*.

On the top navigation strip for the app, next to the Build section, we can find the Publish section. When we click this, we are greeted with a page that allows us to deploy the LUIS application (Figure 3-15). LUIS allows us to publish the application in one of two deployment slots: staging or production. Staging is meant for usage when we are still developing and testing the LUIS app. The production slot is meant to be used by production apps. The idea behind the two slots is that you can have a previous stable version of the LUIS app deployed into production, while you work on new app features in the staging slot.

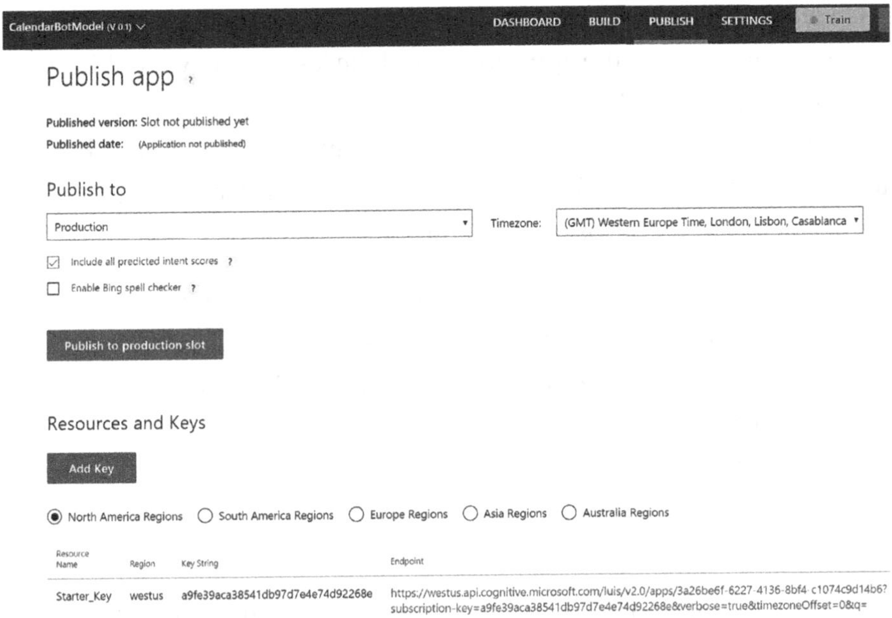

Figure 3-15. *LUIS Publish page*

We will go ahead and select the Staging slot from the "Publish to" drop-down. Once it's published, we can access the app via an HTTP endpoint.

Before we test the resulting endpoint using cURL, a command line tool to transfer data over HTTP (among many other protocols), you may have noticed that below the publish settings there is an Add Key button and a set of keys for several deployment regions. When accessing a LUIS app, we must provide a key, which is how LUIS can bill us for API usage. LUIS is deployed to several regions; a key must be associated with a region. Keys are created using Microsoft's Azure Portal. Azure is Microsoft's cloud services umbrella. We will utilize it to register and deploy a bot in Chapter 5. To associate a key with an app, we must use the Add Key button. Lucky for us, LUIS provides a free starter key to use against apps published in the Staging slot.

Once we publish to the Staging slot, a few things happened. We now have information about the app version and the last time it was published. The URL under Starter_Key is now functional. We may enable verbose results (something we will examine momentarily) or Bing spell check integration (which we will discuss later in this chapter) via URL query parameters. Let's take a closer look at the URL.

```
https://westus.api.cognitive.microsoft.com/luis/v2.0/
apps/3a26be6f-6227-4136-8bf4-c1074c9d14b6?
subscription-key=a9fe39aca38541db97d7e4e74d92268e&
staging=true&
verbose=true&
timezoneOffset=0&
q=
```

The first line of the URL is the service endpoint for the Azure Cognitive Services in the West US region and, specifically, our LUIS app. These are the query parameters that follow:

- The subscription key, in this case the Starter Key. This key can also be passed via the Ocp-Apim-Subscription-Key header.

- A flag indicating whether to use the Staging or Production slot. Not including this parameter assumes the Production slot.

- Verbose flag indicating whether to return all the intents and their scores or return only the top-scoring intent.

- Time zone offset to assist in temporal tagging datetime resolution, a topic we will dive into when exploring the built-in Datetime entity.

- q to indicate the user's query.

We can play with the API by making requests and seeing the responses by using curl. At its core, curl is a command-line tool to transfer data over a variety of protocols. We are going to use it to transfer data over HTTPS. You can find more information at https://curl.haxx.se/. The command we can utilize is as follows. Note that we pass the subscription key as an HTTP header.

```
curl -X GET -G -H "Ocp-Apim-Subscription-Key:
a9fe39aca38541db97d7e4e74d92268e" -d staging=true -d
verbose=true -d timezoneOffset=0 "https://westus.api.cognitive.
microsoft.com/luis/v2.0/apps/3a26be6f-6227-4136-8bf4-
c1074c9d14b6" --data-urlencode "q=hello world"
```

This query results in the following JSON. It gives us the score for each intent in our LUIS app.

```
{
  "query": "hello world",
  "topScoringIntent": {
    "intent": "None",
    "score": 0.24031198
  },
  "intents": [
    {
      "intent": "None",
      "score": 0.24031198
    },
    {
      "intent": "DeleteCalendarEntry",
      "score": 0.1572571
    },
    {
      "intent": "AddCalendarEntry",
```

```
      "score": 0.123305522
    },
    {
      "intent": "EditCalendarEntry",
      "score": 0.0837310851
    },
    {
      "intent": "CheckAvailability",
      "score": 0.07568088
    },
    {
      "intent": "ShowCalendarSummary",
      "score": 0.0100482805
    }
  ],
  "entities": []
}
```

You may be thinking, whoa, we just learned that we can have up to 500 intents, so the size of this response would be ridiculous. You would be quite correct thinking this (though gzip would certainly help here)! Setting the verbose query parameter to false results in a significantly more compact JSON listing.

```
{
  "query": "hello world",
  "topScoringIntent": {
    "intent": "None",
    "score": 0.24031198
  },
  "entities": []
}
```

Once we are ready to deploy into production, we would publish our LUIS app into the Production slot and remove the staging parameter from the URL request. The easiest way to accomplish this would be to simply have your development and test configuration files point at the Staging slot URL and the production configuration to point at the Production slot URL.

You are of course welcome to utilize any other HTTP tool you are comfortable with. In addition, Microsoft provides an easy-to-use console to test the LUIS API within the API documentation found online.[2]

EXERCISE 3-2

Publishing a LUIS App

You will now publish the LUIS App from Exercise 3-1 and access it via curl.

- Publish the LUIS app into the Staging slot as per the steps in the previous section.

- Use curl to get the JSON for predicted intents from the LUIS API for utterances you have entered as sample utterances and other utterances you can think of.

- Make sure the curl command uses your application ID and starter key.

The process of publishing an application into a slot is straightforward. Getting used to testing the HTTP endpoint using curl is important as you will commonly need to access the API to examine the results from LUIS.

---

[2]LUIS Endpoint API Documentation: https://westus.dev.cognitive. microsoft.com/docs/services/5819c76f40a6350ce09de1ac/operations/5819c 77140a63516d81aee78

Extracting Entities

So far, we have developed a simple intent-based LUIS application. But other than it being able to tell our bot a user's intent, we can't really do much with it. It is one thing for LUIS to give us information about the fact that the user wants to add a calendar entry, but it better to be able to tell us for what date and time, where, for how long, and with who. We could develop a bot that asks the user for all these details in a linear sequence whenever it sees an AddCalendarEntry. However, this is tedious and neglects the fact that users may very well present the bot with an utterance like this:

```
"add meeting with Huck tomorrow at 6pm"
```

It would be a bad user experience to ask the user to reenter all this data. The bot should immediately know what the datetime value of "tomorrow at 6pm" is and that "Huck" is someone who should be added to the invite.

Let's start with the basics. How do we make sure that "tomorrow at 6pm." "a week from now," and "next month" are machine readable? This is where entity recognition comes in. Lucky for us, LUIS comes equipped with many built-in entities that we can add to our application. By doing so, the datetime extraction will "just work."

If we go back into the Build section of the LUIS App and click the Entities header, we will encounter an empty list of entities (Figure 3-16). We can add three different types of entities. For now, we will simply add a prebuilt entity. We'll address normal entities and prebuilt domain entities in later sections.

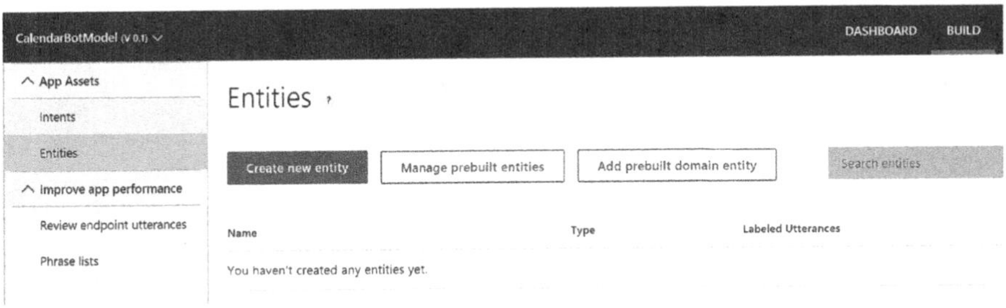

Figure 3-16. *Empty Entities page*

A prebuilt entity is a pretrained definition that can be recognized in utterances. The entity is automatically tagged in the input, and we cannot change how the prebuilt entities are recognized. There is a good amount of logic in them that we can utilize in our applications, and it is best to understand what Microsoft has built before building our own entities.

There are many different prebuilt entities. Not all entities are available across all supported cultures. The LUIS documentation provides details around which prebuilt entities are available across which cultures[3] (Figure 3-17).

---

[3]Pre-Built Entities Reference: https://docs.microsoft.com/en-us/azure/cognitive-services/luis/luis-reference-prebuilt-entities

Prebuilt entity	En-us	fr-FR	it-IT	es-ES	zh-CN	de-DE	pt-BR	ja-JP	ko-kr	fr-CA	es-MX	nl-NL
DatetimeV2	✓	✓	-	✓	✓	*	✓	-	-	-	-	-
Datetime	x	x	x	x	x	x	x	x	-	-	-	-
Number	✓	✓	✓	✓	✓	✓	✓	✓	-	-	-	-
Ordinal	✓	✓	✓	✓	✓	✓	✓	✓	-	-	-	-
Percentage	✓	✓	✓	✓	✓	✓	✓	✓	-	-	-	-
Temperature	✓	✓	✓	✓	✓	✓	✓	✓	-	-	-	-
Dimension	✓	✓	✓	✓	✓	✓	✓	✓	-	-	-	-
Money	✓	✓	✓	✓	✓	✓	✓	✓	-	-	-	-
Age	✓	✓	✓	✓	✓	✓	✓	✓	-	-	-	-
Geography	x	-	-	-	-	-	-	-	-	-	-	-
Encyclopedia	x	-	-	-	-	-	-	-	-	-	-	-
URL	✓	-	-	-	-	-	-	-	-	-	-	-
Email	✓	-	-	-	-	-	-	-	-	-	-	-
Phone number	✓	-	-	-	-	-	-	-	-	-	-	-

* = coming soon

x = See notes on Deprecated prebuilt entities

Figure 3-17. *LUIS built-in entity support across different cultures*

Some of these entities include what is called *value resolution*. Value resolution is the process of taking the text input and converting it into a value that can be interpreted by a computer. For example, "one hundred thousand" should resolve to 100000, and "next May 10th" should resolve to 05/10/2019 and so forth.

You may have noticed the JSON result from LUIS included an empty array called *entities*. This is the placeholder for all entities recognized in the user's input. A LUIS app can recognize any number of entities in an input. The format of each entity will be as follows:

```
{
    "entity": "[entity text]",
    "type": "[entity type]",
```

```
    "startIndex": [number],
    "endIndex": [number],
    "resolution": {
        "values": [
            {
                "value": "[machine readable string of resolved
                value]"
            }
        ]
    }
}
```

The resolution objects may include extra attributes, depending on which entity type was detected. Let's look at the different prebuilt entity types, what they allow us to do, and what the LUIS API result looks like.

Age, Dimension, Money, and Temperature

The age entity allows us to detect age expressions such as "five months old," "100 years," and "2 days old." The result object includes the value in number format and a unit argument, such as Day, Month, or Year.

```
{
    "entity": "five months old",
    "type": "builtin.age",
    "startIndex": 0,
    "endIndex": 14,
    "resolution": {
        "unit": "Month",
        "value": "5"
    }
}
```

Any length, weight, volume, and area measure can be detected using the Dimension entity. Inputs can vary from "10 miles" to "1 centimeter" to "50 square meters." Like the Age entity, the result resolution will include a value and a unit.

```
{
    "entity": "two milliliters",
    "type": "builtin.dimension",
    "startIndex": 0,
    "endIndex": 14,
    "resolution": {
        "unit": "Milliliter",
        "value": "2"
    }
}
```

The currency entity can help us detect currencies in use input. The resolution, yet again, includes a unit and value attribute.

```
{
    "entity": "12 yen",
    "type": "builtin.currency",
    "startIndex": 0,
    "endIndex": 5,
    "resolution": {
        "unit": "Japanese yen",
        "value": "12"
    }
}
```

The temperature entity helps us detect temperatures and includes a unit and value attribute in the resolution.

```
{
    "entity": "98 celsius",
    "type": "builtin.temperature",
    "startIndex": 0,
    "endIndex": 9,
    "resolution": {
        "unit": "C",
        "value": "98"
    }
}
```

DatetimeV2

DatetimeV2 is a powerful hierarchical entity that replaces the previous, you guessed it, datetime entity. A hierarchical entity defines categories and its members; it makes sense to use when certain entities are similar and closely related yet have different meanings. The datetimeV2 entity also attempts to resolve the datetime in machine-readable formats like TIMEX (which stands for "time expression"; TIMEX3 is part of TimeML) and the following formats: yyyy:MM:dd, HH:mm:ss, and yyyy:MM:dd HH:mm:ss (for date, time, and datetime, respectively). A basic example is illustrated below.

```
{
    "entity": "tomorrow at 5pm",
    "type": "builtin.datetimeV2.datetime",
    "startIndex": 0,
    "endIndex": 14,
```

```
    "resolution": {
        "values": [
            {
                "timex": "2018-02-18T17",
                "type": "datetime",
                "value": "2018-02-18 17:00:00"
            }
        ]
    }
}
```

The DatetimeV2 entity can detect various subtypes aside from the datetime subtype in the previous example. The following is a listing with sample responses.

This shows builtin.datetimeV2.date with phrases such as "yesterday," "next Monday," and "August 23, 2015":

```
{
    "entity": "yesterday",
    "type": "builtin.datetimeV2.date",
    "startIndex": 0,
    "endIndex": 8,
    "resolution": {
        "values": [
            {
                "timex": "2018-02-16",
                "type": "date",
                "value": "2018-02-16"
            }
        ]
    }
}
```

This shows builtin.datetimeV2.time with phrases such as "1pm," "5:43am," "8:00," or "half past eight in the morning":

```
{
    "entity": "half past eight in the morning",
    "type": "builtin.datetimeV2.time",
    "startIndex": 0,
    "endIndex": 29,
    "resolution": {
        "values": [
            {
                "timex": "T08:30",
                "type": "time",
                "value": "08:30:00"
            }
        ]
    }
}
```

This shows builtin.datetimeV2.daterange with phrases such as "next week," "last year," or "feb 1 until feb 20th":

```
{
    "entity": "next week",
    "type": "builtin.datetimeV2.daterange",
    "startIndex": 0,
    "endIndex": 8,
    "resolution": {
        "values": [
            {
                "timex": "2018-W08",
                "type": "daterange",
                "start": "2018-02-19",
```

```
                "end": "2018-02-26"
            }
        ]
    }
}
```

This shows building.datetimeV2.timerange with phrases such as "1 to 5p" and "1 to 5pm":

```
{
    "entity": "from 1 to 5pm",
    "type": "builtin.datetimeV2.timerange",
    "startIndex": 0,
    "endIndex": 12,
    "resolution": {
        "values": [
            {
                "timex": "(T13,T17,PT4H)",
                "type": "timerange",
                "start": "13:00:00",
                "end": "17:00:00"
            }
        ]
    }
}
```

This shows builtin.datetimeV2.datetimerange with phrases such as "tomorrow morning" or "last night":

```
{
    "entity": "tomorrow morning",
    "type": "builtin.datetimeV2.datetimerange",
    "startIndex": 0,
```

```
    "endIndex": 15,
    "resolution": {
        "values": [
            {
                "timex": "2018-02-19TMO",
                "type": "datetimerange",
                "start": "2018-02-19 08:00:00",
                "end": "2018-02-19 12:00:00"
            }
        ]
    }
}
```

This shows builtin.datetimeV2.duration with phrases such as "for an hour," "20 minutes," or "all day." The value is resolved in second units.

```
{
    "entity": "an hour",
    "type": "builtin.datetimeV2.duration",
    "startIndex": 0,
    "endIndex": 6,
    "resolution": {
        "values": [
            {
                "timex": "PT1H",
                "type": "duration",
                "value": "3600"
            }
        ]
    }
}
```

The builtin.datetimeV2.set type represents a set of dates and is detected by including phrases like "daily," "monthly," "every week," or "every Thursday." The resolution for this type is different in that there is no single value to represent a set. The timex resolution will be resolved in either of two ways. First, the timex string will follow the pattern P[n][u], where [n] is a number and [u] is the date unit like D for day, M for month, W for week, and Y for year. The meaning is "every [n] [u] units." P4W means every four weeks, and P2Y means every other year. The second timex resolution is a date pattern with Xs representing any value. For example, XXXX-10 means every October, and XXXX-WXX-6 means every Saturday of any week in the year.

```
{
    "entity": "daily",
    "type": "builtin.datetimeV2.set",
    "startIndex": 0,
    "endIndex": 4,
    "resolution": {
        "values": [
            {
                "timex": "P1D",
                "type": "set",
                "value": "not resolved"
            }
        ]
    }
}
{
    "entity": "every saturday",
    "type": "builtin.datetimeV2.set",
    "startIndex": 0,
    "endIndex": 13,
```

```
    "resolution": {
        "values": [
            {
                "timex": "XXXX-WXX-6",
                "type": "set",
                "value": "not resolved"
            }
        ]
    }
}
```

If there is ambiguity in the dates and/or times, LUIS will return multiple resolutions demonstrating the options. For example, ambiguity in dates means that if it is July 20 today and we enter an utterance of "July 21," the system will return July 21 of this and last year. Likewise, if your query does not specify a.m. or p.m., LUIS will return both times. You can see both cases here:

```
{
    "entity": "july 21",
    "type": "builtin.datetimeV2.date",
    "startIndex": 0,
    "endIndex": 6,
    "resolution": {
        "values": [
            {
                "timex": "XXXX-07-21",
                "type": "date",
                "value": "2017-07-21"
            },
            {
                "timex": "XXXX-07-21",
                "type": "date",
```

```
                    "value": "2018-07-21"
                }
            ]
        }
}
{
    "entity": "tomorrow at 5",
    "type": "builtin.datetimeV2.datetime",
    "startIndex": 0,
    "endIndex": 12,
    "resolution": {
        "values": [
            {
                "timex": "2018-02-19T05",
                "type": "datetime",
                "value": "2018-02-19 05:00:00"
            },
            {
                "timex": "2018-02-19T17",
                "type": "datetime",
                "value": "2018-02-19 17:00:00"
            }
        ]
    }
}
```

The Datetime V2 entity is powerful and really showcases some of the great LUIS NLU features.

E-mails, Phone Numbers, and URLs

These three types are all text-based. LUIS can identify when one of them exists in the user input. It is convenient to have this be done by LUIS as opposed to having to implement regular expression logic in our systems. We demonstrate the three types here:

```
{
    "entity": "srozga@bluemetal.com",
    "type": "builtin.email",
    "startIndex": 0,
    "endIndex": 19
}
{
    "entity": "212-222-1234",
    "type": "builtin.phonenumber",
    "startIndex": 0,
    "endIndex": 11
}
{
    "entity": "https://luis.ai",
    "type": "builtin.url",
    "startIndex": 0,
    "endIndex": 14
}
```

Number, Percentage, and Ordinal

LUIS can extract and resolve numbers and percentages for us as well. User input can be in either numerical or textual format. It even handles inputs like "thirty-eight and a half."

```
{
    "entity": "one hundred",
    "type": "builtin.number",
    "startIndex": 0,
    "endIndex": 10,
    "resolution": {
        "value": "100"
    }
}
{
    "entity": "52 percent",
    "type": "builtin.percentage",
    "startIndex": 0,
    "endIndex": 9,
    "resolution": {
        "value": "52%"
    }
}
```

The Ordinal entity allows us to identity ordinal numbers either in textual or numeric form.

```
{
    "entity": "second",
    "type": "builtin.ordinal",
    "startIndex": 0,
    "endIndex": 5,
    "resolution": {
        "value": "2"
    }
}
```

Entity Training

Let's go back into our application and apply some of what we just learned.
Being as we are writing an application related to calendars, the most
obvious prebuilt entity of choice for us is datetimeV2. On the Entities page,
click "Manage prebuilt entities" and select the datetimeV2, as shown in
Figure 3-18.

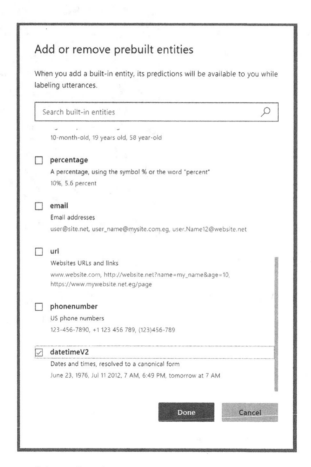

Figure 3-18. *Adding the datetimeV2 entity to the model*

After adding the entity, we should train our model. In the interactive testing UI, when we enter "add calendar entry tomorrow at 5pm," we should see the result in Figure 3-19.

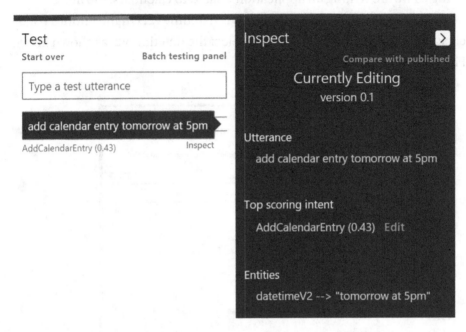

Figure 3-19. *The datetimeV2 entity is alive!*

That was easy. We publish the application to the Staging slot one more time. Using curl to run the same query, we receive the following JSON:

```
{
    "query": "add calendar entry tomorrow at 5pm",
    "topScoringIntent": {
        "intent": "AddCalendarEntry",
        "score": 0.42710492
```

```
    },
    "entities": [
        {
            "entity": "tomorrow at 5pm",
            "type": "builtin.datetimeV2.datetime",
            "startIndex": 19,
            "endIndex": 33,
            "resolution": {
                "values": [
                    {
                        "timex": "2018-02-19T17",
                        "type": "datetime",
                        "value": "2018-02-19 17:00:00"
                    }
                ]
            }
        }
    ]
}
```

Perfect. We can now utilize datetime entities in any of our intents. This is going to be relevant for us in all our application's intents, not just the AddCalendarEntry. In addition, we will go ahead and add the e-mail prebuilt entity, retrain, and publish to the Staging slot again. Now we can try an utterance like "meet with szymon.rozga@gmail.com at 5p tomorrow" to get the kind of result we have come to expect.

```
{
  "query": "meet with szymon.rozga@gmail.com at 5p tomorrow",
  "topScoringIntent": {
    "intent": "AddCalendarEntry",
    "score": 0.3665758
  },
  "entities": [
    {
      "entity": "szymon.rozga@gmail.com",
      "type": "builtin.email",
      "startIndex": 10,
      "endIndex": 31
    },
    {
      "entity": "5p tomorrow",
      "type": "builtin.datetimeV2.datetime",
      "startIndex": 36,
      "endIndex": 46,
      "resolution": {
        "values": [
          {
            "timex": "2018-02-19T17",
            "type": "datetime",
            "value": "2018-02-19 17:00:00"
          }
        ]
      }
    }
  ]
}
```

EXERCISE 3-3

Adding Datetime and E-mail Entity Support

In this exercise, you will enable prebuilt entities on the LUIS app you have been working on so far.

- Add the email and datetimev2 prebuilt entities into your application. Train your app.

- Go into your AddCalendarEntry intent and try to add several utterances with a datetime and e-mail expression in them. Note that LUIS highlights those entities for you.

- Publish the LUIS app into the Staging slot.

- Use curl to examine the resulting JSON.

Prebuilt entities are incredibly easy to use. As a further exercise, add some other prebuilt entities into your model to learn how they work and how they are picked up in different types of inputs. If you want to prevent LUIS from recognizing them, just remove them from your application's entities.

Custom Entities

Prebuilt entities can do a lot for our models without any extra training. It would be surprising if everything that we need could be provided by the existing prebuilt entities. In our example of a calendar app, calendar entries, by definition, include a few more attributes that we would be interested in.

For starters, we usually want to give meetings a subject (not only "Meet with Bob") and a location. Both would be arbitrary strings for meetings subjects and locations. How do we accomplish that?

LUIS gives us the ability to train custom entities to detect such concepts and extract their values from the users' inputs. This is where the power of the entity extraction algorithms really comes in; we show LUIS samples of when words should be identified as entities and when they should be ignored. The NLP algorithms consider context. For instance, given multiple samples of utterances, we can teach LUIS and ensure it doesn't confuse Starbucks with Starbuck, the character from Moby Dick.

There are four different types of custom entities that we can utilize in LUIS: simple, composite, hierarchical, and list. Let's examine each one.

Simple Entities

A simple custom entity is an entity such as a calendar entry subject or the prebuilt e-mail, phone number, and URL entities. One segment of the user input can be identified as an entity of said type based on its position in the utterance and the context of the words around it. LUIS makes it easy to create and train these types of entities. Let's create the calendar subject entity.

Let's say we want to be clear when we are telling the calendar bot about a subject name for the entry. Let's say that we want to accept inputs like "meet with Kim about mortgage application at 5pm." In this example, the subject will be "mortgage application." Let's get this in place.

Navigate to the Entities page and click the "Create new entity" button to create a new simple entity called Subject, as illustrated in Figure 3-20.

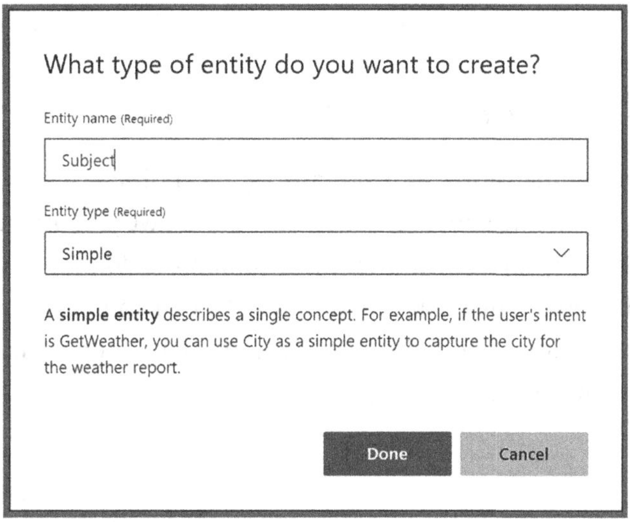

What type of entity do you want to create?

Entity name (Required)

Subject

Entity type (Required)

Simple   ⌄

A **simple entity** describes a single concept. For example, if the user's intent is GetWeather, you can use City as a simple entity to capture the city for the weather report.

Done   Cancel

Figure 3-20. *Creating a new simple entity*

Once you click Done, the entry is added to the list of entities in your application. The process of training an entity occurs in the same interface as training intents. Let's navigate into the AddCalendarEntry intent and add the utterance "meet with Kim about mortgage application at 5pm," as shown in Figure 3-21. Note that this is just a vanilla utterance and no entities are being identified.

☐   meet with kim about mortgage application at **datetimeV2**   AddCalendarEntry 0.67 ⌄

Figure 3-21. *Adding utterance. LUIS does not yet know about subjects.*

We now mouse over the *mortgage* and *application* words and notice that LUIS is allowing us to select the words. Click *mortgage* and then click *application* so LUIS has the phrase "mortgage application" selected. The pop-up will list all the custom entity types in your application. Select Subject. The utterance in LUIS should now look like Figure 3-22.

85

☐ meet with kim about Subject at datetimeV2   AddCalendarEntry 0.67 ∨

Figure 3-22. Entity highlighted and assigned

Save the utterance and train your app. At this point, LUIS won't be that great at identifying subjects quite yet. After all, we just provide one example, and entity identification is more difficult to do properly than intent classification. It needs more samples. We can enter a few more utterances in the utterances editor for the add calendar entry intent. A few samples are shown in Figure 3-23.

☐ meet about meaning of life   AddCalendarEntry 0.28 ∨

☐ add entry on mortgage app   AddCalendarEntry 0.44 ∨

☐ meet for coffee with kim at datetimeV2   AddCalendarEntry 0.92 ∨

Figure 3-23. Adding more utterances with subjects. None of them was identified after training LUIS with one sample.

Note that no subjects at all were identified. Let's reinforce the concept. It will take quite a few examples for the system to start recognizing the entity. I added more than ten utterances that had some type of subject somewhere in the utterance, as shown in Figure 3-24. Also, be sure to mark the subject of any utterances you may have added yourself. The process of what I call "bending LUIS to your will" can be more of an art than a science. The key point to remember is that there's going to be an inflection point at which the algorithms start realizing that something following a word is always an entity until some other key words, based on statistical inference. Think of a scale that you are slowly trying to tip into balance. Our utterances should be carefully crafted to ensure we're capturing as many variations as possible to show LUIS. Often, each variation will also need to include a few samples to really capture the essence of where within the context of an utterance the algorithm can find specific entities.

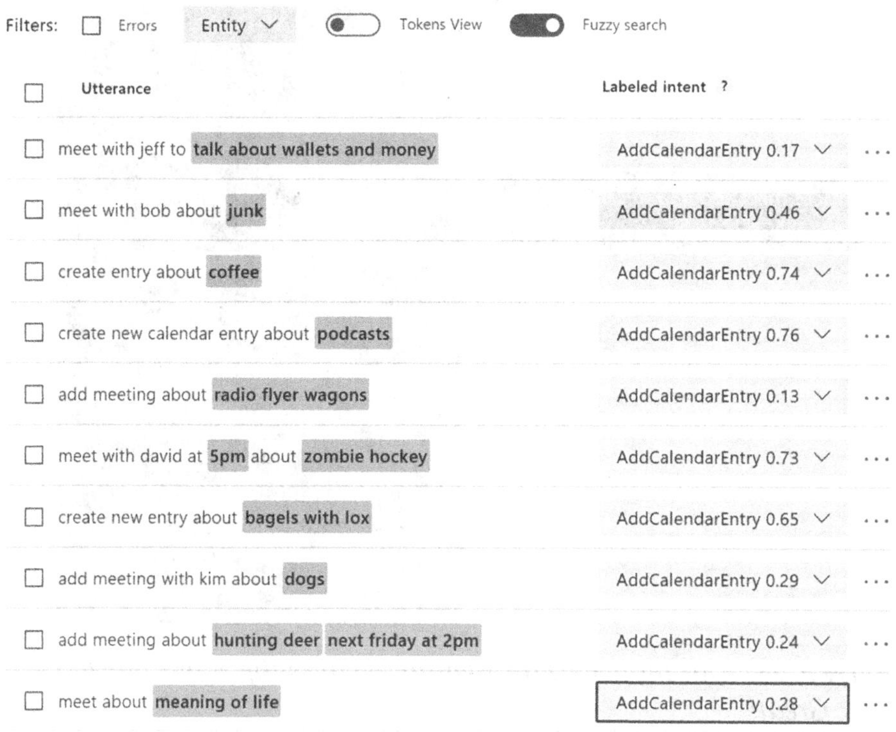

| Filters: ☐ Errors | Entity ⌄ | ◉ Tokens View | ◉ Fuzzy search |

☐	Utterance		Labeled intent ?
☐	meet with jeff to talk about wallets and money		AddCalendarEntry 0.17 ⌄ ⋯
☐	meet with bob about junk		AddCalendarEntry 0.46 ⌄ ⋯
☐	create entry about coffee		AddCalendarEntry 0.74 ⌄ ⋯
☐	create new calendar entry about podcasts		AddCalendarEntry 0.76 ⌄ ⋯
☐	add meeting about radio flyer wagons		AddCalendarEntry 0.13 ⌄ ⋯
☐	meet with david at 5pm about zombie hockey		AddCalendarEntry 0.73 ⌄ ⋯
☐	create new entry about bagels with lox		AddCalendarEntry 0.65 ⌄ ⋯
☐	add meeting with kim about dogs		AddCalendarEntry 0.29 ⌄ ⋯
☐	add meeting about hunting deer next friday at 2pm		AddCalendarEntry 0.24 ⌄ ⋯
☐	meet about meaning of life		AddCalendarEntry 0.28 ⌄ ⋯

Figure 3-24.   Training LUIS with many different flavors of subject utterances. Note that we change the toggle to the right of the Entity drop-down to Tokens View. This allows us to see which tokens are being identified as entities.

After training this data set, we see that the interactive testing tool is getting better at identifying the entity. I entered "hi let's meet about lawn care and harmonicas at 1:45p" (don't ask how I came up with that…) and received the result in Figure 3-25. We are making good progress. However, if we start entering inputs of different lengths and variations, LUIS may not identify the entities correctly. It just means we need to further train our entity model. We will leave this as an exercise to the reader.

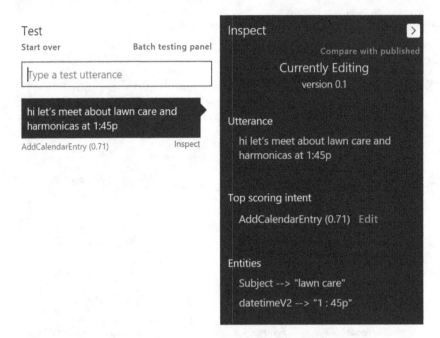

Figure 3-25. *Our model is now identifying the subject in some test cases. Great!*

We now have a good grasp of the calendar subject entity even though there are probably many cases that won't yet work. And truth be told, you won't be able to capture all the different types of ways users will ask things until you have a good testing phase. That's how LUIS app development goes. It is worth looking at the resulting JSON when this application is published.

```
{
  "query": "hi let's meet about lawn care and harmonicas at
  1:45pm",
  "topScoringIntent": {
    "intent": "AddCalendarEntry",
    "score": 0.8653278
  },
```

```
"entities": [
  {
    "entity": "1:45pm",
    "type": "builtin.datetimeV2.time",
    "startIndex": 48,
    "endIndex": 53,
    "resolution": {
      "values": [
        {
          "timex": "T13:45",
          "type": "time",
          "value": "13:45:00"
        }
      ]
    }
  },
  {
    "entity": "lawn care and harmonicas",
    "type": "Subject",
    "startIndex": 20,
    "endIndex": 43,
    "score": 0.587688446
  }
]
}
```

Note that the time entity is being identified as expected. The Subject entity comes back with the relevant entity value. It also comes back with a score. The score in this case is again a similar measure to intent scores; it's a measure of distance from the ideal entity. Unlike intents, LUIS will not return all your entities and their scores. LUIS will return only simple and hierarchical entities with scores above a threshold. For built-in entities, this score is hidden.

The nice thing about training the entity is that even though the samples with the entity are defined in the AddCalendarEntry intent, they carry over to other intents. Intents and entities are not tied directly to each other. I can say "cancel meeting about olympic hockey" and it works as shown in Figure 3-26.

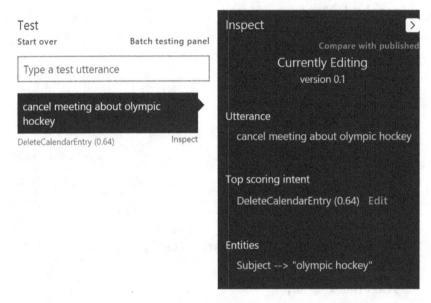

Figure 3-26. *Entity training within one intent can carry over to other intents*

Another observation is the lower score in terms of identifying the DeleteCalendarEntry intent. We've added many more utterances to the AddCalendarEntry intent, but DeleteCalendarEntry and EditCalendarEntry have much fewer examples. Take some time to improve that. Add some alternate phrasings and examples with our new Subject entity before we continue.

EXERCISE 3-4

Training the Subject Entity and Strengthening Our LUIS App

In this exercise, we will improve our LUIS app by training it to do some additional training.

- Add a Subject entity, as per the directions in the previous section.

- Add utterances into your intents to support the Subject entity. Train and test often to see your progress.

- Aim for at least 25 to 30 samples for LUIS to start. Make sure to convey multiple instances of different ways of expressing ideas.

- Ensure all your intents are getting your attention. Make sure every intent has 15 to 20 samples. Include entities in each intent.

- Train and publish the LUIS app into the Staging slot.

- Use curl to examine the resulting JSON.

Training custom entities, especially ones that are a bit vague in terms of positioning and context, can be challenging, but after some practice, you will start seeing patterns in LUIS's ability to extract them. Note things that need to be explicitly trained: number of words in the subject, subjects with the word *and*, subjects followed by datetime, and so forth. You may have noticed the explicit mention of number of samples. These are just starting points. An NLU system like LUIS gets better the more sample data it has. Do not overlook this point. If LUIS is not behaving the way you expect it, chances are it is not a LUIS performance problem but rather that your application needs more training.

The second entity we planned to add was the Location entity. Let's create a new simple custom entity and call it Location. Like the Subject entity, the location is going to be a free text entity, so we're going to need to train LUIS with many samples.

We're going to take a stab at this by adding utterances into the AddCalendarEntry intent again. We need to add utterances in these forms:

```
Meet with kim to talk about {Subject} at {Location}
Meet about {Subject} at {Location}
Add entry with teddy for {Subject} at {Location}
Add meeting at {Location}
Meet at {Location}
Meet in {Location} at {Subject}
```

You get it. You should also add datetime instances into these utterances. Training the location is going to be trickier as we are teaching LUIS to distinguish between a location and subject, two concepts that simply need a lot of data for LUIS to begin distinguishing since these are two free-text entities. In the end, I ended up adding more than 30 utterances that contained either just a location or a location combined with other entities. After that amount of training, we get decent performance. I can type "meet for dinner at the diner tomorrow at 8pm" and get the following JSON result:

```
{
    "query": "meet for dinner at the diner tomorrow at 8pm",
    "topScoringIntent": {
        "intent": "AddCalendarEntry",
        "score": 0.979418
    },
    "entities": [
        {
            "entity": "tomorrow at 8pm",
            "type": "builtin.datetimeV2.datetime",
```

```
        "startIndex": 29,
        "endIndex": 43,
        "resolution": {
            "values": [
                {
                    "timex": "2018-02-19T20",
                    "type": "datetime",
                    "value": "2018-02-19 20:00:00"
                }
            ]
        }
    },
    {

        "entity": "the diner tomorrow",
        "type": "Location",
        "startIndex": 19,
        "endIndex": 36,
        "score": 0.392795324

    },
    {

        "entity": "dinner",
        "type": "Subject",
        "startIndex": 9,
        "endIndex": 14,
        "score": 0.5891273

    }
    ]
}
```

We suggest you take some time to strengthen the entities even further. It would be a good experience to really gain an appreciation for the complexities and ambiguities in natural language and in training an NLU system like LUIS.

EXERCISE 3-5

Training the Location Entity

In this exercise, you will be adding the Location entity into your LUIS app. You will find that this will take a bit longer than the Subject entity by itself.

- Add a Subject entity, as per the directions in the previous section.

- Add utterances into your AddCalendarEntry to support the Location entity. Train and test often to see your progress.

- Aim to start with 35 to 40 samples for LUIS, probably more. As your intents support more entities, you may have to provide more samples to LUIS to properly distinguish. As you add utterances, constantly train and test to see how LUIS is learning. Make sure to use many variations and examples.

- Publish the LUIS app into the Staging slot.

- Use curl to examine the resulting JSON.

This exercise should have been a good experience in strengthening entity resolution when a single utterance contains many entities.

Composite Entities

Congratulations. The work we have done so far is a significant portion of what LUIS can accomplish. Using the intent classification and simple entity extraction techniques described, we can go off and work on our calendar application. Although we went over simple entities, we quickly ran into some complex NLU scenarios. Without a tool like LUIS, doing this kind of language recognition would be incredibly tedious and challenging.

There is another interesting scenario that comes up in natural language. Our model currently supports a user saying a phrase like this:

```
"Meet at Starbucks for coffee at 2pm"
```

What if the user wanted to add multiple calendar entries? What if the user wants to say something like the following utterance?

```
"Meet at trademark for lunch at noon and at Starbucks for
coffee at 2pm"
```

There's isn't anything not allowing a user to say that right now. If we've trained our app enough, it will certainly handle this input, and it will identify two Subject instances, two Location instances, and two datetime instances, as shown here:

```
{
    "query": "meet at culture for coffee at 11am and at the
    office for a code review at noon",
    "topScoringIntent": {
        "intent": "AddCalendarEntry",
        "score": 0.996190667
    },
    "entities": [
        {
            "entity": "11am",
            "type": "builtin.datetimeV2.time",
            "startIndex": 30,
            "endIndex": 33,
            "resolution": {
                "values": [
                    {
                        "timex": "T11",
                        "type": "time",
```

```
                    "value": "11:00:00"
                }
            ]
        }
    },
    {
        "entity": "noon",
        "type": "builtin.datetimeV2.time",
        "startIndex": 74,
        "endIndex": 77,
        "resolution": {
            "values": [
                {
                    "timex": "T12",
                    "type": "time",
                    "value": "12:00:00"
                }
            ]
        }
    },
    {
        "entity": "culture",
        "type": "Location",
        "startIndex": 8,
        "endIndex": 14,
        "score": 0.770069957
    },
    {
        "entity": "the office",
        "type": "Location",
        "startIndex": 42,
```

```
            "endIndex": 51,
            "score": 0.9432623
        },
        {
            "entity": "coffee",
            "type": "Subject",
            "startIndex": 20,
            "endIndex": 25,
            "score": 0.9667959
        },
        {
            "entity": "a code review",
            "type": "Subject",
            "startIndex": 57,
            "endIndex": 69,
            "score": 0.9293087
        }
    ]
}
```

And yet, parsing this using code would be quite challenging. How do we tell which entities should be grouped together? Which location goes with which subject? You should be able to use the startIndex property to figure it out I suppose, but that's not always as obvious.

Lucky for us, LUIS can group the entities into what are called *composite entities*. Rather than the messy result shown previously, LUIS will tell us which entities are part of which composite entity. This makes it way easier for us to know that there were two separate AddCalendar requests, one for 11 a.m. coffee at Culture and another one for a code review in the office at noon.

Composite entities can be created on the Entities page of LUIS. Figure 3-27 illustrates the process. Click the *Create new entity* button, enter a name for the entity, select the Composite entity type, and select the child entity types to be included as part of the new entity. We will use the name CalendarEntry to identify our composite entity.

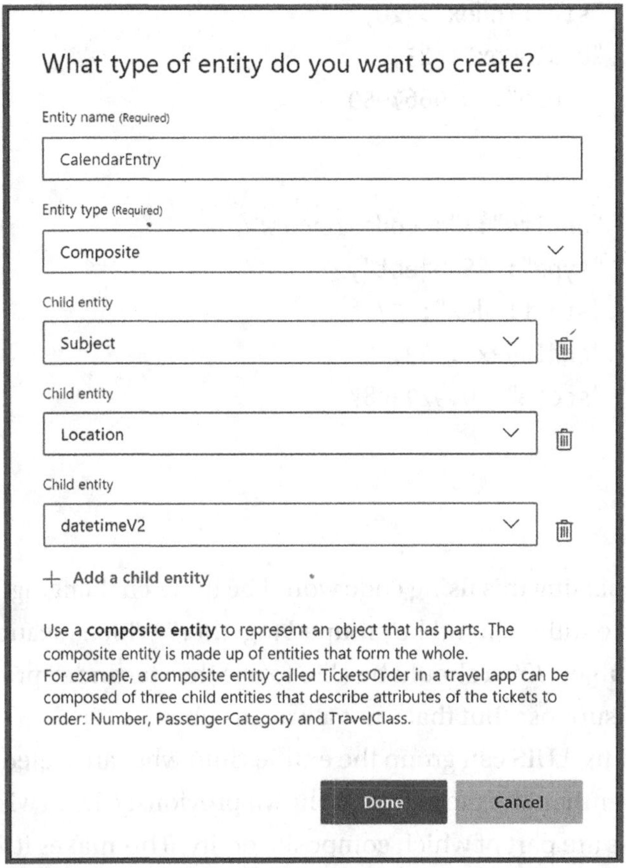

What type of entity do you want to create?

Entity name (Required)

CalendarEntry

Entity type (Required)

Composite

Child entity

Subject

Child entity

Location

Child entity

datetimeV2

+ Add a child entity

Use a **composite entity** to represent an object that has parts. The composite entity is made up of entities that form the whole.
For example, a composite entity called TicketsOrder in a travel app can be composed of three child entities that describe attributes of the tickets to order: Number, PassengerCategory and TravelClass.

Done   Cancel

Figure 3-27. Creating a new composite entity

Once it is created, we need to properly train LUIS to recognize it. Let's look at the AddCalendarEntry intent again. The easiest way to train LUIS would be to find all utterances that have the required three entities and wrap the entities into the composite entity. Figure 3-28 shows an example.

meet at **Location** for **Subject** **datetimeV2** and at **Location** for **Subject** at **datetimeV2**

Figure 3-28. *A "proper" CalendarEntry with a datetime, subject, and location. This is a perfect candidate to wrap in a composite entity.*

Click the first Location entity. A pop-up will appear asking you to relabel the entity or wrap it in a composite entity. Click *"Wrap in composite entity"* (Figure 3-29).

meet at **Location** for **Subject** **datetimeV2** and at **Location** for **Subject** at **datetimeV2**

meet for

Search or create composite

CalendarEntry

Figure 3-29. *Clicking the Location entity will allow us to wrap parts of the utterance in a composite entity*

We move our mouse over the Subject and datetimeV2 entities. Note the green underline expands to cover each entity (Figure 3-30). Click datetimeV2 so that it is included in the composite entity and click the CalendarEntry name.

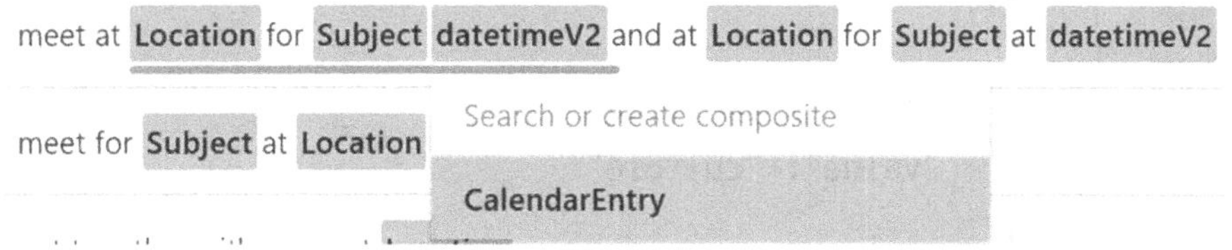

meet at **Location** for **Subject** **datetimeV2** and at **Location** for **Subject** at **datetimeV2**

meet for **Subject** at **Location**

Search or create composite

CalendarEntry

Figure 3-30. *Once the beginning of the composite entity is selected, it is a matter of showing LUIS where it ends*

Do the same for the second instance of the CalendarEntry entity. The result should look like Figure 3-31.

meet at `Location` for `Subject` `datetimeV2` and at `Location` for `Subject` at `datetimeV2`

Figure 3-31. *LUIS now has an example of how to wrap a composite entity*

We should do the same for any other utterance we can find that includes the three entities. Once we train and publish the app, LUIS should start extracting this composite entity. We only show the relevant API section here:

```
"compositeEntities": [
    {
        "parentType": "CalendarEntry",
        "value": "culture for coffee at 11am",
        "children": [
            {
                "type": "builtin.datetimeV2.time",
                "value": "11am"
            },
            {
                "type": "Subject",
                "value": "coffee"
            },
            {
                "type": "Location",
                "value": "culture"
            }
        ]
    },
```

```
{
    "parentType": "CalendarEntry",
    "value": "the office for a code review at noon",
    "children": [
        {
            "type": "builtin.datetimeV2.time",
            "value": "noon"
        },
        {
            "type": "Subject",
            "value": "a code review"
        },
        {
            "type": "Location",
            "value": "the office"
        }
    ]
}
]
```

EXERCISE 3-6

<u>Composite Entities</u>

In this exercise, you will add composite entities to your LUIS app.

- Create a composite entity called CalendarEntry, composed of datetimeV2, Subject, and Location entities.

- Train every utterance that has these three entities to recognize the composite entity.

- Train additional examples with multiple instances of the CalendarEntry composite entity. Remember, it takes time, dedication, and persistence to get it right.

- Publish the LUIS app into the Staging slot.

- Use curl to examine the resulting JSON.

Composite entities are a great feature to group entities into logical data objects. Composite entities allow us to encapsulate more complex expressions.

Hierarchical Entities

A hierarchical entity allows us to define a category of entities and its children. You can think of hierarchical entities as defining a parent/ subtype relationship between entities. We have run into this type before. Do you recall the Datetimev2 entity? It had seven subtypes such as daterange, set, and time.

LUIS allows us to easily create our own subtypes. Say we wanted to add support in our model to specify the calendar entry visibility as public or private. We could add support for utterances like this:

```
"create private entry for interview with competitor at
starbucks"
 "create invisible entry for interview with recruiter at
 trademark"
```

The words *private* or *invisible* here indicate the visibility field of the calendar. Why would we create a hierarchical entity as opposed to a simple entity? Can't we just look at the value of a Visibility property and determine whether it should be a private meeting or not? Yes and no. If the user sticks to those two words, yes. But remember, natural language is ambiguous and vague. Phrasings change. The user can say invisible, private, privately, hidden. It's the same with public. If we make assumptions about a closed set of options in our code, then we would have to change our code any time a new option shows up. The reason a hierarchical entity should be used as opposed to a simple one is that the statistical models of where in context the hierarchical entity appears is shared by the subtypes. Once that is identified, the step of identifying the child entity is essentially a classification problem. Making the entity hierarchical makes for better LUIS performance versus two simple entities. Not to mention, it's more efficient to have LUIS classify the meaning of an entity in the context of our application rather than writing code to do so.

Figure 3-32 illustrates the creation of a new hierarchical entity. We do this by visiting the Entities page, clicking "Create new entity," and selecting Hierarchical from the entity type drop-down. We give the parent entity a name and add the child entities. Once we click Done, it is a matter of going into the intent utterances and training LUIS. Let's go into AddCalendarEntry and add a few samples.

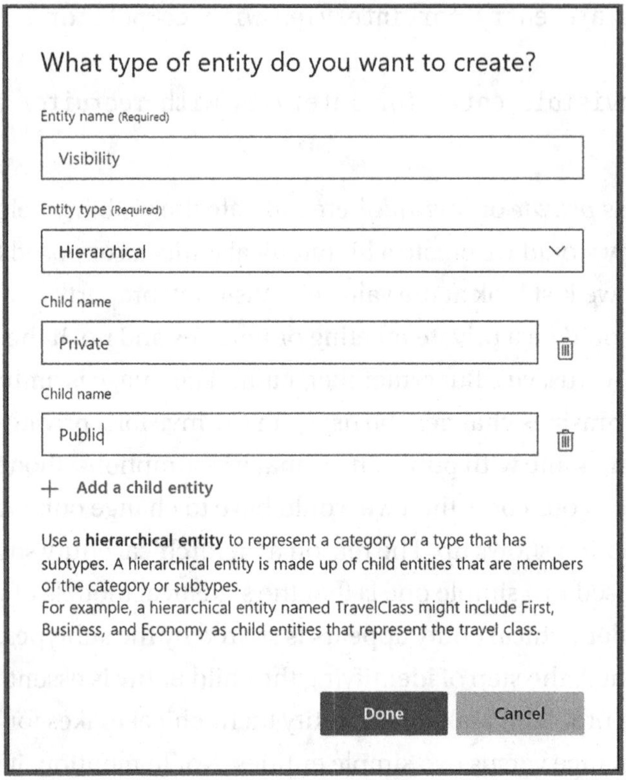

What type of entity do you want to create?

Entity name (Required)

Visibility

Entity type (Required)

Hierarchical   ∨

Child name

Private   🗑

Child name

Public   🗑

+   Add a child entity

Use a **hierarchical entity** to represent a category or a type that has subtypes. A hierarchical entity is made up of child entities that are members of the category or subtypes.
For example, a hierarchical entity named TravelClass might include First, Business, and Economy as child entities that represent the travel class.

Done   Cancel

Figure 3-32. *Creating a new hierarchical entity*

You may notice that one or two samples are not sufficient. We need to give LUIS a really good idea of where and how it may encounter the public and private visibility modifiers before it can start recognizing the entity in our inputs. The ten samples in Figure 3-33 were a good start.

meet Visibility::Private with recruiter at Location datetimeV2	AddCalendarEntry 0.99 ∨
create Visibility::Private meeting for datetimeV2 with teddy	AddCalendarEntry 0.99 ∨
create Visibility::Private meeting with teddy for little gym at datetimeV2	AddCalendarEntry 1 ∨
create Visibility::Public entry for Subject datetimeV2	AddCalendarEntry 1 ∨
create new Visibility::Public visible meeting with jeff to Subject	AddCalendarEntry 0.99 ∨
create Visibility::Private appointment with chelsea for Subject	AddCalendarEntry 0.99 ∨
create new Visibility::Private appointment with teddy	AddCalendarEntry 1 ∨
create new Visibility::Public meeting with kim	AddCalendarEntry 0.99 ∨

Figure 3-33. *Sample Visibility hierarchical entity utterances*

Once we train and publish, we can view the resulting JSON via curl, as shown here:

```
{
    "query": "create private meeting for tomorrow 6pm with teddy",
    "topScoringIntent": {
        "intent": "AddCalendarEntry",
        "score": 0.9856489
    },
    "entities": [
        {
            "entity": "tomorrow 6pm",
            "type": "builtin.datetimeV2.datetime",
            "startIndex": 27,
            "endIndex": 38,
            "resolution": {
                "values": [
                    {
                        "timex": "2018-02-19T18",
                        "type": "datetime",
```

```
                        "value": "2018-02-19 18:00:00"
                    }
                ]
            }
        },
        {
            "entity": "private",
            "type": "Visibility::Private",
            "startIndex": 7,
            "endIndex": 13,
            "score": 0.9018322
        }
    ]
}
{
    "query": "create public meeting with jeff",
    "topScoringIntent": {
        "intent": "AddCalendarEntry",
        "score": 0.975892961
    },
    "entities": [
        {
            "entity": "public",
            "type": "Visibility::Public",
            "startIndex": 7,
            "endIndex": 12,
            "score": 0.6018059
        }
    ]
}
```

List Entities

So far, the prebuilt, simple, composite, and hierarchical entities were all extracted from user input via machine learning techniques. Every time we added one of these entities and trained LUIS, you may have noticed the number of models being trained increased. Recall that a LUIS application is composed of one model per intent/entity. By now, we should be at ten models. Each of these is rebuilt any time we train our app.

List entities exist outside this machine learning world. A list entity is simply a collection of terms and synonyms for those terms. For example, if we want to identify cities, we can add an entry for New York that has the synonyms NY, The Big Apple, The City That Never Sleeps, Gotham, New Amsterdam, etc. LUIS will resolve any of these alternate names into New York.

Once a custom list entity type is created, we are redirected to a list entity editor in which we can enter the canonical term and the synonyms. This interface allows us to add new terms and their synonyms. It also makes recommendations to add extra terms that seem related to what we have added thus far. List entities are limited to 20,000 terms, including synonyms. We can have up to 50 list entities per application, so there is a lot of potential for LUIS-based term and synonym lookup features. Figure 3-34 shows a sample custom list entity definition.

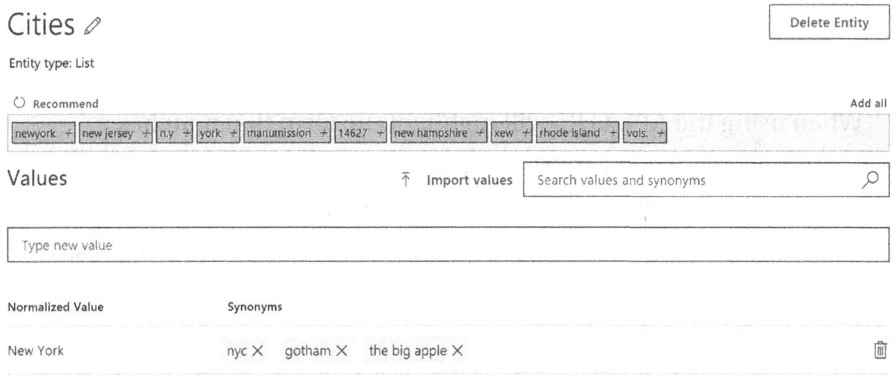

Figure 3-34. *LUIS List entity user interface*

Since list entities are not learned by LUIS, new values are not recognized based on context. If LUIS sees "Gotham," it identifies it as New York. If it sees "Gohtam," it does not. It is literally a lookup list.

```
{
    "query": "meet in the big apple",
    "topScoringIntent": {
        "intent": "AddCalendarEntry",
        "score": 0.943692744
    },
    "entities": [
        {
            "entity": "the big apple",
            "type": "Cities",
            "startIndex": 8,
            "endIndex": 20,
            "resolution": {
                "values": [
                    "New York"
                ]
            }
        }
    ]
}
```

When using the API, LUIS will highlight the term that matches a list entity type and will return the canonical name in the resolution values. This allows your consuming application to ignore all the possible synonyms for a term and execute logic based on the canonical names. List entities are powerful for situations where you know the set of possible values for terms ahead of time.

Regular Expressions Entities

LUIS allows us to create regular expression entities. These, like the list entities, are not based on context, but rather on a strict regular expression. For example, if we expected a knowledge base id to always be presented using the syntax *KB143230*, where the text *KB* is followed by 6 digits, we could create an entity with the regular expression *kb[0-9]{6,6}*. Once trained, the entity will always be identified if any user utterance segment matches this expression.

Prebuilt Domains

I hope you have gained an appreciation for some of the challenges of building NLU models. Machine learning tools allow us to get computers to start learning, but we need to be sure we are training them with a lot of good data. It takes years of day-to-day interactions for humans to be immersed in a language to be able to truly understand it. Yet, we assume that AI means that a computer will be able to pick up the concepts with ten samples. When it doesn't, sometimes we think to ourselves, "Oh, come on, you should know this by now!"

To help us on our journey, many of the NLU platforms provide what are called *prebuilt* models or domains. Essentially, the creators of LUIS and other platforms want to give us a head start with some domains that we can easily include in our application, train LUIS, and be off to the races. Some of LUIS's prebuilt models are shown in Figure 3-35.

Prebuilt domains

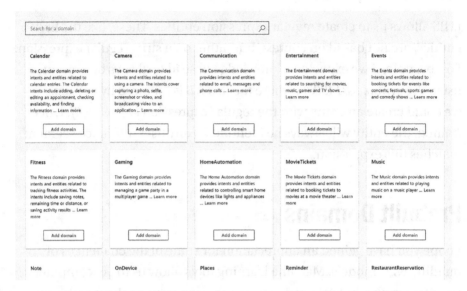

Figure 3-35. *Prebuilt domains*

We can find prebuilt domains in LUIS by navigating into the Build section and clicking the Prebuilt Domains link in the bottom left. At the time of this writing, this feature is still in Preview mode. That is the reason it is so isolated and why it is dynamic and may change by the time you read this. LUIS includes a variety of domains from Camera to Home Automation to Gaming to Music and even Calendar, which is similar to the app we have been working on in this chapter. In fact, we will do just that in Exercise 3-7. The "Learn more" text links to a page that describes in detail what intents and entities each domain pulls in and which domains are supported by which cultures.[4]

When we add a domain to your application, LUIS will add all the domain's intents and entities into our application, and they will count toward the application's maximums. At that point, we able to modify the

---

[4]LUIS Pre-built Domains: `https://docs.microsoft.com/en-us/azure/
cognitive-services/luis/luis-reference-prebuilt-domains`

intents and entities as we see fit. Sometimes you may want to get rid of certain intents or add new ones to complement the prebuilt ones. Other times we may need to train the system with more samples. We suggest the prebuilt domains are treated as starting points. Our goal is to extend them and build great experiences on top of them.

A Historical Point

LUIS has changed a lot over the years. Even over the course of writing this book, the system changed user interfaces and feature sets. LUIS used to have a Cortana app that anyone could tap into by utilizing a known app ID and using their subscription key. The Cortana app had many of the prebuilt intents and entities defined, but it was a closed system. You were not able to customize it or strengthen it to your liking in any way. Since then, Microsoft has gotten rid of this feature in favor of the prebuilt domains. However, the idea of openly sharing your model with others so they can call it using their own subscription key remains available and accessible via the Settings page.

EXERCISE 3-7

Utilizing Prebuilt Domains

In this exercise, you will utilize the prebuilt Calendar domain to create a LUIS app similar to the one we have built in this chapter.

- Create a new LUIS application.

- Navigate into the prebuilt domains section and add the Calendar domain.

- Train the application.

- Use the interactive testing user interface to examine the application's performance. How good is it at detecting intents and entities? How does it compare to the application we created both in terms of design and performance?

Prebuilt domains can be useful to get started with a domain, but LUIS requires diligent training to have a truly well-performing model.

Phrase Lists

So far, we have been exploring different techniques to create great models. We have the tools we need to make sure we can create a good conversational experience for our users. There are cases when we train LUIS that the model performance is not as good as we would like. Entities may not be getting recognized as well as we would like them to. Maybe we are building a LUIS app that deals specifically with internal terms that aren't exactly part of the culture your application is using. Maybe we haven't had a chance to train LUIS entities with every known possible value for an entity and list entities don't cut it because we want our entities to remain flexible.

One way to improve LUIS performance under these circumstances is to use phrase lists. Phrase lists are hints, rather than strict rules, that LUIS uses when training our app. They are not a silver bullet but can be very effective. A phrase list allows us to present to LUIS a category of words or phrases that are related to each other. This grouping is a hint to LUIS to treat the words in the category in a similar way. In the case of an entity value not being recognized properly, we could enter all the known possible values as a phrase list and mark the list as exchangeable, which indicates to LUIS that in the context of an entity, these values can be treated in the same way. If we are trying to improve LUIS's vocabulary with words it may not be familiar with, the phrase list would not be marked as nonexchangeable.

112

Let's say we wanted to improve our Calendar model's private visibility entity performance. After all, there are many ways of expressing that we want a private meeting. As a starting point, we could add a phrase list with all the different words we could expect the model to see. Figure 3-36 shows the LUIS user interface for working on a phrase list. You can get here by selecting the Phrase Lists item under the Build page and clicking *Create new phrase list.*

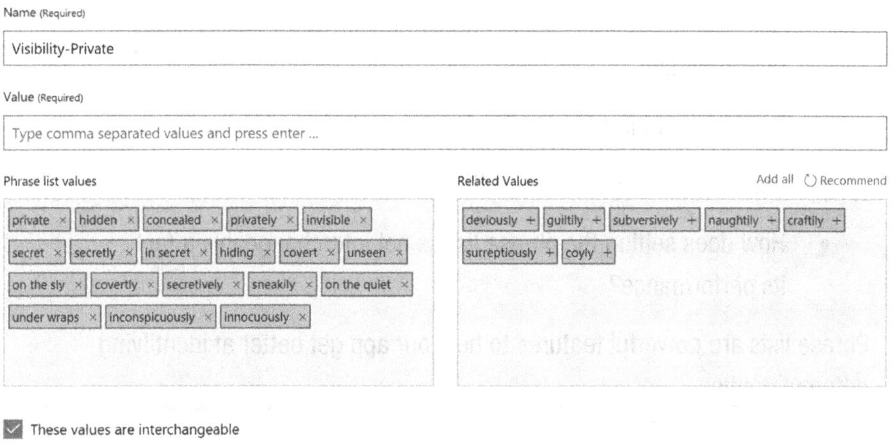

Figure 3-36. I may have gone overboard a bit. I blame the Related Values function.

A phrase list requires a name and some values. We enter the values one by one in the Value field. As we press Enter, it adds them to the *Phrase list values* field. The Related Values field contains synonyms automatically loaded by LUIS. We then select the checkbox to tell LUIS that the values are interchangeable.

Before training, let's try a few variations of the private meeting utterances without the phrase list enabled. If you try utterances like "Meet in private," "Meet in secret," or "Create a hidden meeting," LUIS does not recognize the entity. However, if we train the app with the phrase list, LUIS has no problem identifying the entity in those samples and many others.[5]

---

[5]Microsoft.Recognizers.Text: https://github.com/Microsoft/Recognizers-Text

---

EXERCISE 3-8

Training Features

In this exercise, you will improve our LUIS app by adding features.

- Add the Visibility hierarchical entity to your LUIS app.

- Add your own phrase list to improve the private visibility entity performance.

- Publish the LUIS app into the Staging slot.

- Use curl to examine the resulting JSON.

- How does setting the phrase list as not interchangeable affect its performance?

Phrase lists are powerful features to help our app get better at identifying different entities.

EXERCISE 3-9

Adding an Invitee Entity

You may have noticed that we have not spoken about how we capture meeting attendees, and so far, we have ignored this issue. In this exercise, we will address this.

- Add a new custom entity called Invitee.

- Go over every sample utterance so far and identify the invitee entity in the utterances.

- If it needs additional training, add more samples. Ensure to include samples where Invitee is the only entity or is one of many entities in an utterance.

- For bonus points, add the Invitee entity to the CalendarEntry composite entity.

- Train and make sure all intents and entities are still performing well.

- Publish the LUIS app into the Staging slot.

- Use curl to examine the resulting JSON.

If you have completed this exercise successfully, congratulations! You are getting darn good at using LUIS.

Active Learning

We've spent weeks training a model, we've gone through a round of testing, we've deployed the application into production, and we've switched our bot on. Now what? How do we know if the model is performing the best it can? How do we know whether some user has thrown unexpected input at the our application that breaks our bot and results in a bad user experience? Bug reports are one way for sure, but we would depend on getting that feedback. What if we could find out about these problems as soon as they occur? We can do so by taking advantage of LUIS's active learning abilities.

Recall that supervised learning is machine learning from labeled data, and unsupervised learning is machine learning from unlabeled data. Semisupervised learning lives somewhere in between. Active learning is a type of semisupervised learning in which the learner asks the supervisor to label new data samples. Based on the inputs that LUIS is seeing, it can ask you, the LUIS app trainer, for your assistance labeling data that is coming from your users. This improves model performance and over time makes our application more intelligent by using real user input as sample data.

You can access this functionality through the *Review endpoint utterances* link on the Build page (Figure 3-37). Throughout the training of the application, we've been utilizing the published application endpoint to test various utterances. LUIS bases its active leaning on the inputs against the endpoint, not the Interactive Test feature.

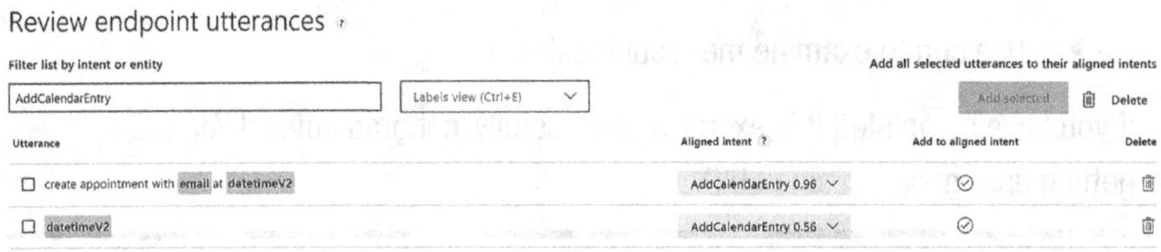

Review endpoint utterances

Filter list by intent or entity		Add all selected utterances to their aligned intents	
AddCalendarEntry	Labels view (Ctrl+E) ⌄	Add selected 🗑 Delete	
Utterance	**Aligned intent ?**	**Add to aligned intent**	**Delete**
☐ create appointment with email at datetimeV2	AddCalendarEntry 0.96 ⌄	⊘	🗑
☐ datetimeV2	AddCalendarEntry 0.56 ⌄	⊘	🗑

Figure 3-37. *The active learning interface*

The interface allows us to review past utterances and their top-scoring intent, referred to as the *aligned intent*. As trainers, we can add the utterance to the alignment intent, reassign to a different intent, or altogether get rid of the utterance. We can also zero in on specific intents or entities if we know there are problems with any of them.

Before adding the utterance to the aligned intent, we need to confirm that the utterance is correctly labeled and any entities are being correctly identified. We suggest that using this interface to improve LUIS application is a common practice for any team.

Dashboard Overview

Now that we have trained our application and utilized it for testing, it is well worth highlighting the data that the dashboard provides. The dashboard allows us to get a good glance at the overall app status, its usage, and the amount of data we have trained it with.

The very top provides information about the last time we trained and published the application, as per Figure 3-38. We can also get some metrics about the number of intents and entities we are using, the number of list entities we have, and how many total labeled utterances our application has so far.

App State

App Status			
	Last trained: Feb 16, 2018, 5:36:56 PM	Last published: Feb 19, 2018, 10:46:09 AM	
Intents	Entities	List Entities	Labeled Utterances
53	13	6	2045

Figure 3-38. Application status

The next section displays the kind of usage that the application is getting through the API. We can monitor the amount of endpoint hits for the last week up to the last year. This data is available only once an application is published to the production slot. This is illustrated in Figure 3-39.

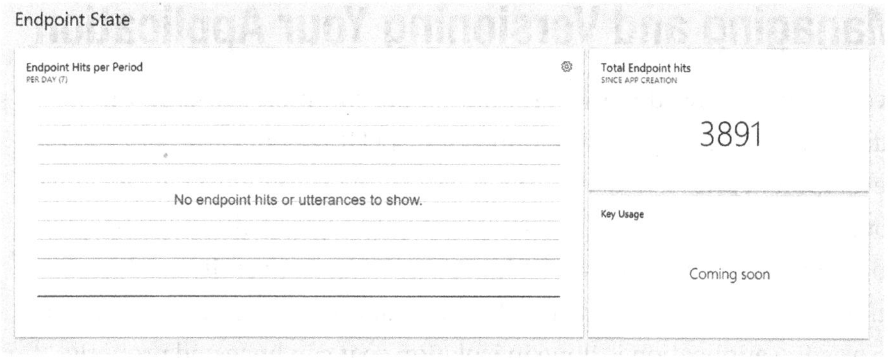

Endpoint State

Endpoint Hits per Period PER DAY (7)		Total Endpoint hits SINCE APP CREATION
		3891
No endpoint hits or utterances to show.		Key Usage
		Coming soon

Figure 3-39. API endpoint usage summary

Lastly, we are presented with an intent and entity breakdown, as shown in Figure 3-40. Here we see a distribution of the percentage of utterances used to train each intent. You can clearly see some of our intents contain significantly more sample utterances than others. It's the same for entities. The uneven distribution does not necessarily mean that an entity or intent needs more training.

117

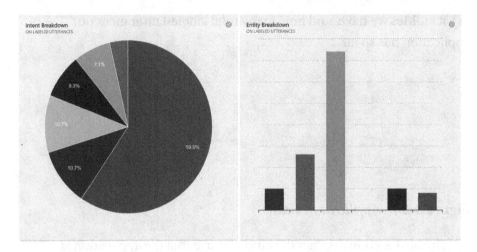

Figure 3-40. *Statistics around intent/entity utterance counts and distributions. Clicking an intent navigates to that intent's utterances page.*

Managing and Versioning Your Application

Everything we have done so far is part of the common workflow of adding samples, training, and publishing a LUIS application. During the development phase, this workflow is repeated over and over again. Once your application is in production, you should be careful about what you do to your app. The process of adding a new intent or entity can have unforeseen effects on the rest of the application, and it is best that editing an existing application is done in isolation so it can be tested properly.

We have experience with the concepts of the staging and production deployment slots. This certainly helps; we know that we can test changes without publishing to our production endpoints. A common rule is to have the Staging slot host the dev/test version of the application and the Production slot host the production version. Whenever a new application is ready for production, we move it from the Staging slot to the Production slot. But what if we make a mistake in our models? What if we need to roll the Production slot back? That is where versions come in.

LUIS allows you to create a named version of the application at any point in time. So far, by default we have been working on version 0.1. Once it is ready for production, we can publish it and clone it into a new version 0.2. At that point, you set the 0.2 version to Active. Now, the LUIS interface is editing version 0.2. If we accidentally publish version 0.2 into the production slot, we can easily go back to version 0.1 and publish that. Once version 0.2 is production ready, we deploy that into the Production slot and clone it into version 0.3 and set that version as the active version. And so forth. If at any point you deploy a version into the Production slot and need to revert, you set your LUIS active back to 0.2 and publish that version into the Production slot. The workflow is illustrated in Figure 3-41.

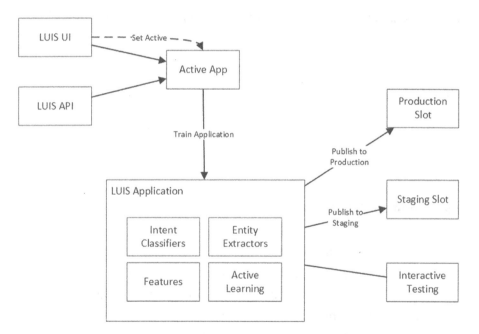

Figure 3-41.   *The LUIS development, training, testing, and publishing workflow*

We access the application version information through the Settings page. Figure 3-42 and Figure 3-43 show the interface plus what it looks like after cloning version 0.1 into 0.2.

Figure 3-42. *The versioning functionality on the Settings page*

Figure 3-43. *Version 0.1 was cloned into 0.2*

Note that after closing 0.1, it remains in the Staging slot, but 0.2 becomes the Active version. LUIS also doesn't allow for easy branching. If multiple users want to make changes to a single version, they cannot create a new version and then merge their changes using the user interface. One way to accomplish this would be to download the LUIS App JSON by clicking the Export Version button in Figure 3-42, utilizing a source control tool like Git to branch and merge, and finally, using the "Import new version" button to upload a new version from a JSON file.

The same page also allows us to add collaborators to the application. This is a great way to give access to other folks in your organization to assist in editing, training, and testing versions of the app. At the time of this writing, there are no fine-tuned audit controls; all collaborators can do anything with the application except add/remove other collaborators (Figure 3-44).

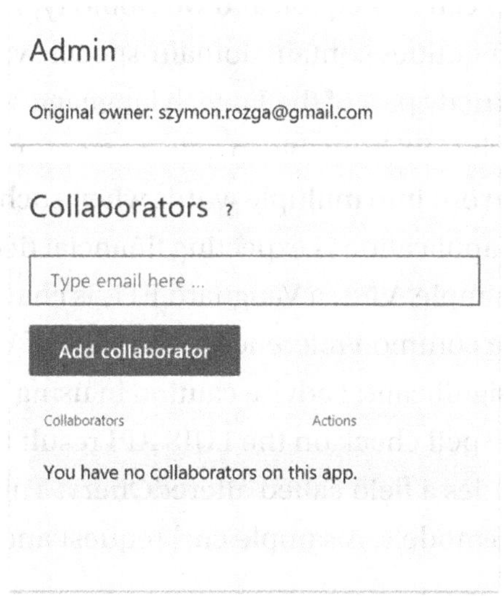

Figure 3-44. Adding collaborators to your LUIS application

Integrating with Spell Checking

One advanced feature in LUIS is the ability to integrate with a spell checker to automatically fix misspellings in user input. User input is, by its very nature, messy. Misspellings are immensely common. Combine that with the common usage of messaging apps, and you have a recipe for consistent misspelled input.

The spell checker integration runs the user query through Bing's Spell Checker service, gets a possibly altered query with misspellings fixed, and runs that altered query through LUIS. This feature is invoked by including the query parameters spellCheck and bing-spell-check-subscription-key. You can get a subscription key from the Azure Portal, which we will introduce in Chapter 5. We will also utilize the Spell Check API more directly in Chapter 10.

This functionality can be helpful, and we would typically recommend it with a caveat. If our entities contain domain-specific values or product names that are not strictly part of the English language, we may get an altered query in which LUIS is unable to detect an entity. For example, it may break up one word into multiple words when such behavior is unwanted. Or, if our application is expecting financial tickers, it may just change them. For example, VEA, a Vanguard ETF, is changed to VA. In the United States, that's a common reference to the state of Virginia. The loss of meaning is quite significant; I advise caution in using this feature.

The effect of the spell check on the LUIS API result is easy to spot. The result now includes a field called alteredQuery. This is the text passed into the LUIS models. A sample curl request and response JSON is presented here:

```
curl -X GET -G -H "Ocp-Apim-Subscription-Key:
a9fe39aca38541db97d7e4e74d92268e" -d staging=true -d
spellCheck=true -d bing-spell-check-subscription-key=c23d51fc
861b45c4b3401a6f8d37e47c -d verbose=true -d timezoneOffset=0
"https://westus.api.cognitive.microsoft.com/luis/v2.0/
apps/3a26be6f-6227-4136-8bf4-c1074c9d14b6" --data-urlencode
"q=add privtae meeting wth kim tomoorow at 5pm"
```

```
{
    "query": "add privtae meeting wth kim tomoorow at 5pm",
    "alteredQuery": "add private meeting with kim tomorrow
    at 5pm",
    "topScoringIntent": {
        "intent": "AddCalendarEntry",
        "score": 0.9612303
    },
    "entities": [
        {
            "entity": "tomorrow at 5pm",
            "type": "builtin.datetimeV2.datetime",
            "startIndex": 29,
            "endIndex": 43,
            "resolution": {
                "values": [
                    {
                        "timex": "2018-02-20T17",
                        "type": "datetime",
                        "value": "2018-02-20 17:00:00"
                    }
                ]
            }
        }
    ]
}
```

Import/Export Application

Any application built in LUIS can be exported into a JSON file and imported back into LUIS. The JSON file format is exactly what we would expect. There are elements that define which custom intents, custom entities, and prebuilt entities the application uses. There are additional elements to capture phrase lists. And, not surprisingly, there is a rather large segment describing all the sample utterances, their intent label, and the start and end index of any entities in the utterance. We can export the application by clicking Export App in the My Apps section of LUIS or Export Version in the Settings page, as per Figure 3-41.

Although the format of the exported application is specific to LUIS, it is easy to imagine how we could write code to interpret the data by other applications. From a governance perspective, it is good practice to export our applications and store the JSON in source control because the action of publishing an action is irreversible. This should not be an issue if our teams follow a strategy in which a publish into the Production slot implies the creation of a new application version, but mistakes do happen.

One of the most common questions we receive in our work with LUIS is "why we can't import an application into an existing application?" The reason is that this would be tantamount to a smart merge, especially where there are overlapping utterances with different intents or same name intents with completely different application connotations. Since every application has different semantics, this merge would be a nontrivial task. We suggest either utilizing Git to manage and merge application JSON code or creating custom code to merge using the LUIS Authoring API.

Using the LUIS Authoring API

When speaking about LUIS and its capabilities, the first question out of developers is, "can this be done via an API?" The answer is yes! The Authoring API allows us to perform all the tasks we have doing using the user interface via an API. The Authoring API is split into the following resources:

- *Apps*: Add, manage, remove, and publish applications.

- *Examples*: Upload a set of sample utterances into a specific version of your application.

- *Features*: Add, manage, or remove phrase or pattern features in a specific version of your application.

- *Models*: Add, manage or remove custom intent classifiers and entity extractors; add/remove prebuilt entities; add/remove prebuilt domain intents and entities.

- *Permissions*: Add, manage, and remove users in your application.

- *Train*: Queue application version for training and get the training status.

- *User*: Manage LUIS subscription keys and external keys in LUIS application.

- *Versions*: Add and remove versions; associate keys to versions; export, import, clone versions

The API is very rich and allows for training, custom active learning, and enables CI/CD type scenarios. The API Reference Docs[6] are a great place to learn about the API.

---

[6]LUIS Authoring API Reference Documentation: https://westus.dev.
cognitive.microsoft.com/docs/services/5890b47c39e2bb17b84a55ff

Troubleshooting Your Models

We have focused on LUIS itself and the process of creating applications by combining custom intent classifiers and custom entity extractors with prebuilt entities and prebuilt domains. Along the way, we have noticed some interesting behavior with the system. Machine learning is not perfect. We are all but guaranteed to run into strange scenarios where we are having trouble with our intents or entities. Here is a list of how we should approach troubleshooting LUIS issues:

- One of the most common problems is training the model without publishing it. Make sure that if you are testing the application using the Staging slot, that you publish it into the Staging slot. If you are calling your application's production slot, make sure the app is published. And ensure that you pass the staging flag as needed in your calls to the API.

- If intents are getting misclassified, provide more intent examples to the intents that are having problems. If problems persist, spend some time analyzing the intents themselves. Are they really two separate intents? Or is it really one intent and we need a custom entity to tell the difference? Also, make sure to train the None intent with some inputs that are truly irrelevant to your application. Test data is great for this purpose.

- If the application is having difficulty recognizing entities, consider the type of entity you are creating. There are entities that are usually a one-word modifier in the same place in an intent, like our Visibility entity. On the other hand, there are subtler entities that can be anywhere in the utterance usually prefixed and suffixed by some words. The former won't need as many sample utterances as the latter one. In general, entity recognition issues can be fixed by doing the following:

- Adding more utterance samples both in terms of different variations and multiple samples of the same variation.

- It is worth asking whether the entity should perhaps be a list entity. A good rule of thumb is, is this entity a lookup list? Or does the application need flexibility in how it identifies this type of entity?

- Consider using phrase lists to show LUIS what an entity may look like.

- Is LUIS getting confused between two entities? Are the entities similar with a slight variation based on context? If so, this may be a candidate for a hierarchical entity.

- Utilize composite entities if your users are trying to communicate higher-level concepts composed of multiple entities.

Building LUIS applications can be more of an art than science. You will sometimes spend a lot of time teaching LUIS the difference between some entities or where in a sentence an entity can appear. Be patient. Be thorough. And always think of the problem in statistical terms; the system needs to see enough samples to truly start understanding what's happening. As people, we can take our intelligence and language understanding for granted. In relative terms, it is quite amazing how quickly we can train a system like LUIS. Remember this as you work with LUIS or any other NLU system.

Conclusion

That was quite a lot of information! Congratulations, we are now equipped to start building our own NLU models using a tool like LUIS. To recap, we went through the exercise of creating an application by utilizing prebuilt entities, custom intents, and custom entities. We explored the power of the various prebuilt entities and dabbled a bit in the prebuilt domains that LUIS provides. We spent time training and testing our application, before publishing it into different types of slots and testing the API endpoints using curl. We optimized our application using phrase features and further improved it by using LUIS's active learning abilities. We explored versioning, collaborating, integrated spell check, exporting and importing of applications, using the authoring API, and common troubleshooting techniques in our LUIS applications.

I must reiterate that the concepts and techniques you just learned are all applicable to other NLU platforms. The process of training intents and entities and optimizing models is a powerful skill to have in your toolkit, whether for bots, voice assistants, or any other natural language interface. We are now ready to start thinking about how we build a bot. As we do, we'll keep checking back into this LUIS application as it gets consumed by our bot.

CHAPTER 4

Conversation Design

Although the technology allows us to develop a bot that behaves in just about any way, that doesn't mean we should. Users have certain expectations from their messaging communications such as acknowledgment of the message receipt, a quick response, and the ability to continue the conversation later. Although conversing with a bot is not the same as speaking with a human, messaging a friend is the closest analogous experience. Since users are still getting used to bots, it is reasonable to take those interactions as samples of how a bot should behave.

Successful bots can exhibit many types of behaviors, but there are some common patterns and flavors. That's not to say innovation has stagnated; not at all! These use cases are based on commonly observed patterns in the space given technology and budget constraints. The space is ripe for innovation, and the only question is, what are the limits of our collective imagination?

These common use cases also follow certain rules as to how they communicate with users. During my career, it was essential for me to internalize that most technology users don't use the technology the way that I do. I love the command line and its precision. Not being a native English speaker, the ambiguity of natural language has been troubling. But bots give users an ability to use this ambiguous natural language. As a result, there is a certain amount of self-restraint that bot developers need to exercise. It is easy for a developer to put together a bot experience that is more reminiscent of using a command line.

© Szymon Rozga 2018
S. Rozga, *Practical Bot Development*, https://doi.org/10.1007/978-1-4842-3540-9_4

Considering the limitations of natural language processing (NLP) and user expectations, it then becomes more important than ever to be careful about how the bot behaves when it doesn't understand things and when it's asking for feedback from the user. With a careful approach and a conscious choice of the type of responses we send our users, creating a delightful experience is within reach.

Common Use Cases

Developers are creating all sorts of conversational experiences. We can experience bots that specialize in tasks such as selling items, answering questions about products, sending order statuses, answering inquiries about orders, provisioning cloud infrastructure, searching over multiple data sources, sharing cat GIFs, and doing millions of other things.

At a high level, we will split the bots into two larger categories: consumer and enterprise. There is of course overlap in the subcategories but also some clear dividing lines.

Common Consumer Cases

Consumer bots are typically available via channels such as Facebook Messenger, Slack, and the other public messaging apps; web chat; voice interfaces; or even custom mobile apps when a custom interface is required. On the lower end of the quality scale, they are no more than toys. On the higher end, they can be impressive feats of design and engineering. Because of the general AI and bot fever we discussed in Chapter 1, many companies are deploying a bot along with their products. Atlassian, for example, has a Slackbot for its JIRA product. Even Amazon has a chat bot integrated into its mobile shopping app. You will also find brands dipping their toes into bots via Facebook Messenger. Facebook Pages makes it easy for a company to have an outward-facing public channel to talk to its customers via either public posts or Messenger. If it is Messenger, a human agent needs to log into the page inbox and reply to each message. A first step for many companies is to deploy a Messenger bot that replies to a few types of user queries, with the rest simply left for humans to reply to. Utility-wise, we are still trying to answer the question, what makes the most sense for users? The variety of bots in the space certainly points to that. The following are some broad categories of effective approaches.

FAQ Bot

An FAQ bot is typically the first entry into the bot and NLP space by teams taking the technology for a test run. It is an easy use case: let's take our existing FAQ and place it as a bot on Facebook Messenger or enterprise messaging. That way, the most typically asked questions can be caught by a bot before an employee spends time answering them. A simple text-based FAQ bot can turn into something quite interesting and aesthetically pleasing from a user perspective. An answer to a commonly asked question doesn't simply have to be a block of boring text. The answer can include further content such as images, videos, and links to additional content.

For example, consider a financial services bot that can answer different types of questions about financial topics. Within its response, it can embed additional suggested topics of interest as buttons. At that point, the user can look at related terms and their definitions. If there are websites that visually represent a concept, for example, the iron condor option investment strategy, those links can be included in the response for the user to click to get more information. Of course, our conversation design needs to balance all that content with possible user overload. The sweet spot in between can be effective at providing the user with a pleasant experience with the bot. Figure 4-1 is an example of Child Fund International's FAQ bot embedded into a web page.

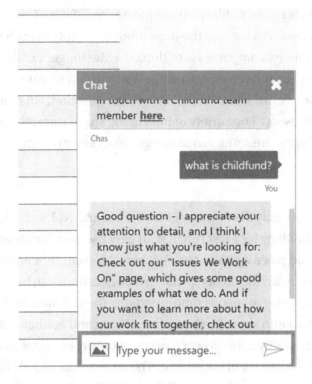

Figure 4-1. A basic FAQ bot in action

Task-Oriented Bot

A task-oriented bot is a virtual agent that can help users with a variety of tasks specific to a domain. These types of bots are sometimes called *concierge bots*. For example, JIRA's Slackbot (Figure 4-2) is task oriented. It can create tasks and assign tasks based on a conversation a team is having.

Figure 4-2. JIRA Slackbot

I once worked on a diabetes coach chat bot, which could help users who have Type 2 diabetes ask for meal and exercise advice personalized according to previous conversations and other data about the users. There are also financial services bots that connect to a trading account and update the user on their account balances and positions and even trade, like the TD Ameritrade bot (Figure 4-3). The Calendar LUIS app we developed in Chapter 3 is the base for a calendar task bot.

133

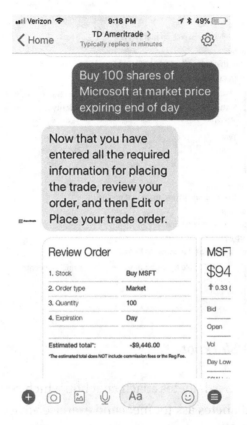

Figure 4-3. Trading stocks using the TD Ameritrade bot

Broadcast Bot

A broadcast bot is an interesting concept and is quite common. We can think of this as a bot that reaches out to the user without prompting, as opposed to the user contacting the bot first. In some bots, it is more a pattern to keep bots engaged. For example, different news bots, like the CNN bot on Facebook Messenger, will reach out daily with the biggest stories of the day.

A subset and more nuanced version of this can be seen in some celebrity bot implementations. Typically, these types of bots exist for fun. They adopt the personality of a celebrity and can talk to users about topics of interest, products, and other ways of interacting with the celebrity's branch. The bot can navigate you through a script of topics, send you videos and images, and maybe talk about products that the celebrity is endorsing. The conversation is almost entirely driven by the bot, instead of the user. It is an interesting storytelling device, but its success comes down to consistent fresh content. Figure 4-4 shows an example of Project Cali, a Snoop Dogg bot created for fun.

Figure 4-4. *Project Cali: a Snoop Dogg bot*

E-commerce Bot

Although not yet big in North America, bots are slowly starting to sell products to consumers. It is not a terribly challenging task from a technical perspective; the bigger challenge is getting users to use a messaging instead of apps or websites. The amount of e-commerce integration in these kinds of bots varies. For example, some bots provide the complete end-to-end shopping experience. Looking at clothing items (Figure 4-5) or flowers (Figure 4-6) through a bot is different from an online shopping experience. Some bots lean into this and provide quirky or innovative ways of figuring out what products to show the user to get the impulse buy!

Figure 4-5. *Louis Vuitton bot*

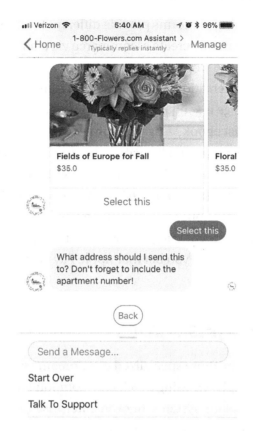

Figure 4-6. *The 1-800-Flowers.com Assistant*

We also run into experiences where the bot is responsible only for broadcasting a receipt for a purchase and order status updates, with a limited set of bot functionality. Everything else gets automatically routed to a human customer support representative. Although this kind of experience is not fully integrated e-commerce, it is a great first step into that journey and into getting customers acquainted with bots. In short, companies are embracing what is being called the *digitally driven consumer journey*, and bots are part of this strategy.[1]

---

[1]Brands Must Grasp the Digitally Driven Consumer Journey or Risk Becoming Prey: `www.adweek.com/digital/brands-must-grasp-the-digitally-driven-consumer-journey-or-risk-becoming-prey/`

Different messaging platforms provide different levels of payment support. We could certainly create e-commerce via a bot by providing a custom checkout page where the user can enter their payment information. The conversation is paused at this point. Once the payment is processed, a message is sent to the bot to continue the conversation. On the other hand, Facebook Messenger provides deeper integration with systems such as Stripe and PayPal. In that version, the payment experience stays completely within the Facebook Messenger app. From a user perspective, the less friction the better. And as users begin placing more trust in messaging apps to store their payment information, we will see more and more payment integrations like this. Apple has released its Business Chat[2] product and you bet that Apple Pay payments are fully integrated.[3]

Common Enterprise Cases

Enterprise bots may be more specialized to a domain or subject matter. They are typically deployed using a web chat component or integrated into enterprise messaging systems, or even enterprise Call Center and Interactive Voice Response (IVR) systems such as Cisco's Unified Communications Center. They can also be deployed on e-mail endpoints. The bots may be integrated with single sign-on solutions, powerful existing enterprise back ends, and knowledge management databases. Depending on the enterprise's practice, these will range from simple pilot bots to machine learning–driven large-scale deployments.

---

[2]Apple Business Chat: `https://developer.apple.com/business-chat/`
[3]Sending Apple Pay Payment Requests: `https://developer.apple.com/library/ content/documentation/General/Conceptual/MessagesIntegration/ SendingApplePayPaymentRequests.html#//apple_ref/doc/uid/ TP40017634-CH33-SW1`

Self-Service Bots

One of the most common use cases in an enterprise scenario is incident self-servicing. Enterprises have large knowledge bases that internal help desk agents use to communicate possible solutions to the user and guide them through the process of troubleshooting issues. Many of these step-by-step troubleshooting directions can be communicated to the user by a bot. For example, one of the most common queries to internal help desks is password reset. Companies could cut through a lot of volume and, frankly, money, if they were to handle such requests automatically. You could imagine an appliance manufacturer releasing a chat bot to assist in diagnosis and fixing issues before involving a service engineer.

The idea behind these self-service bots is that they can provide a variety of self-service content for the users, especially for the most common queries, and can even automate some of the common work that the customer support team is doing. These bots are usually integrated with live chat systems so that the user may initially be chatting to a bot but can be quickly rerouted into a live chat or phone conversation with a human customer service agent in case the bot's directions do not solve the problem.

Process Automation Bots

Robotic Process Automation (RPA) is a huge topic these days. Companies like IPsoft specialize in building bots and technology that can automate business and IT tasks.[4] In this context, bots are not necessarily chat bots but rather computer agents that perform the automation. These tasks can include everything from account provisioning, website automation and business processes automation. There are companies that focus on creating automation platforms, such as Automation Anywhere and UiPath. With machine learning these days being used for everything from contract

---

[4]IPSoft Amelia: `https://www.ipsoft.com/amelia/`

analysis to skin cancer diagnoses, chat bots can serve as an excellent front end into these processes. In an RPA scenario, the chat bot is more of an orchestrator rather than an automator. In addition, these bots may integrate into ticketing systems such as Remedy and ServiceNow to track its work.

In other instances, the chat bot is less visible to the user. For example, Slack is a great platform for bots that listen in to a team conversation and surface data as the right natural language arises. Bots that simply listen in to some natural language input and provide answers are a type of automation bot. Say, for example, a team of medical experts looks through text descriptions of procedures and is charged with translating them to insurance codes. That process can be automated by a machine learning algorithm that observes the team's behavior and results and can then take over the data.

Again, the actual brains behind the logic may not be inside the bot itself. There may be a separate system that implements the machine learning model for the insurance codes. Or, the automation code may be Python, PowerShell, or any other script. The bot serves as the front end to receive the natural language and orchestrate the automation (Figure 4-7).

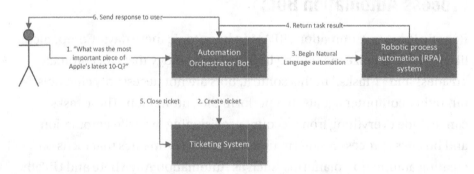

Figure 4-7. *A sample automation bot flow*

Knowledge Management Bots

Another type of enterprise bot is one that can solve natural language search problems across a variety of data sources. Many firms have huge knowledge repositories across disparate sets of systems. Being able to integrate with all those sources using natural language is important. There are interesting choices to make in these bots about which content to display to the user, in what format, and how to collect feedback on which content was the most useful given a query.

The bigger problems of natural language search that these projects try to solve are fascinating and beyond the scope of this book. This type of bot can be extremely interesting in a group conversation context, where the bot is querying articles, reports, white papers, and case studies as the group is having a conversation about topics of interest. The group's feedback to the bot during the search can further provide supervised learning data to improve the search experience even further.

Representing Conversations

How do we start developing a conversational chat bot? A good place is trying to graphically represent the conversation flow. What kinds of tasks can the chat bot handle? What intents and entities does it need to look for to achieve these goals? How does it help fill in missing data?

We will be referring to the conversation as a *graph*, which is a collection of nodes connected by edges. Figure 4-8 illustrates an undirected graph. Every node is connected to at least one other node in the graph. Each node represents a state of the conversation, and the edges represent a transition between states.

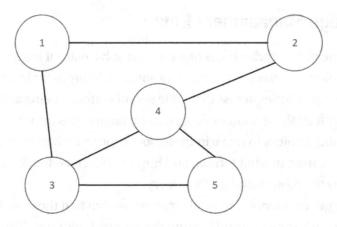

Figure 4-8. *An undirected graph*

We will use arrows in the edges to show the direction of flow. This is referred to as a *directed graph*. We start with the root node. The root node is the state of the beginning of the conversation. Using our Calendar bot as a sample, we know that our bot should support adding new entries, editing existing entries, removing entries, checking availability, and providing a summary of our calendar or an event. We can represent the bot as shown in Figure 4-9.

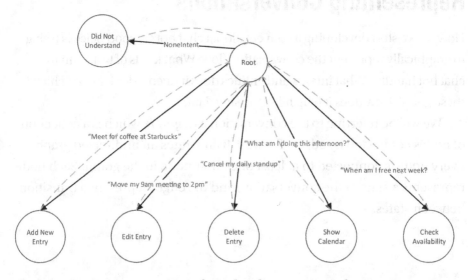

Figure 4-9. *Representation of a calendar concierge bot conversation*

Note that the conversation moves between states based on the user's utterance, which resolves to a LUIS intent. Each node along the conversation has built-in logic to resolve the entities and execute the correct logic for a state. After a state is done executing its logic, the conversation transfers back to the root node.

The transitions between states can be invoked either programmatically or by user input. For example, say our bot supports creating calendar appointments. Recall in Chapter 3 that we created a LUIS application that allows us to pass either several or no entities as part of an utterance to add a calendar entry. If our Add New Entry dialog did not receive information about a subject and invitee, as for example in the utterance "meet tomorrow at 2pm," we could elicit that information in another state. On the other hand, if the user uses an utterance that contains these entities, such as "meet with kim for coffee tomorrow at 2pm," we do not need to elicit this extra information. This conditional state transition is illustrated in Figure 4-10.

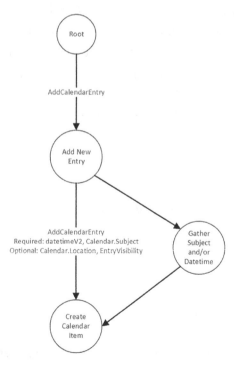

Figure 4-10. *Conditionally transfer to state based on user input*

The process of creating a conversation graph is usually referred to as *intent and entity mapping*; we model intent and entity combinations as transitions between state nodes.

Bot Responses

There are a variety of forms that a bot response to a user's query may take. Understanding the different options and how to best leverage them is key to any bot design. In the following sections we will dig into a number of concepts found amongst the various channels.

Building Blocks

We now understand how we can take user input and map it to bot states and function. We also understand how we can organize our bot code into various conversation states. The next step in our design is to figure out what the bot sends to the user in return. Bots can respond in a variety of ways. By default, we think of text or speech output. Most typically, we simply send back plain text. Some messaging channels support something more complex like Markdown or HTML. Markdown is a plain-text formatting syntax.[5] The following Markdown input translates to the formatted content in Figure 4-11:

```
# H1
# H2
Hello, my _name_ is **Szymon Rozga**
I like:
1. Bots
1. Dogs
1. Music
```

---

[5]Markdown: Syntax: https://daringfireball.net/projects/markdown/syntax

H1

H2

Hello, my *name* is **Szymon Rozga**

I like:

1. Bots
2. Dogs
3. Music

Figure 4-11. *A formatted markdown document*

Bot platforms can also support speech response. Many platforms also support the Speech Synthesis Markup Language (SSML) as a speech output format. SSML is a markup language that provides metadata about how speech should be constructed using elements such as pauses, breaks, changes of rate and pitch, and others. Here is a self-explanatory sample from the WC3 Recommendation[6]:

```
<?xml version="1.0"?>
<speak version="1.0" xmlns:="http://www.w3.org/2001/10/synthesis"
       xmlns:xsi="http://www.w3.org/2001/XMLSchema-instance"
       xsi:schemaLocation="http://www.w3.org/2001/10/synthesis
               http://www.w3.org/TR/speech-synthesis/
               synthesis.xsd"
       xml:lang="en-US">
  That is a <emphasis> big </emphasis> car!
  That is a <emphasis level="strong"> huge </emphasis>
  bank account!
</speak>
```

---

[6]Speech Synthesis Markup Language Version 1.1 WC3 Recommendation: https://www.w3.org/TR/speech-synthesis11/

Output to users does not always have to be text. We can use images and videos to communicate many ideas to our users. As part of any message sent back to the user, we may attach various content such as videos, audio files, and images. The specific supported formats will depend on the underlying operating system and channel. Some systems allow other file attachments as well, for instance XML files or a native format of some sort.

An alternative mechanism for presenting content to our users are cards. A card is typically a combination of an image, text, and optional buttons that serve as calls to action. Our YouTube Search bot from Chapter 1 (Figure 4-12) clearly displayed the video name, description, and a button to watch it in a set of cards.

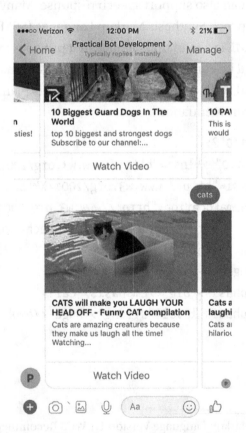

Figure 4-12. *Horizontal list of cards; also called a carousel*

This layout is called a *carousel*. It presents several cards side by side and gives the user the ability to swipe or scroll through the individual cards.

Buttons are typically sent as part of a card, but they can also be sent as stand-alone elements without an associate image. There are many types of buttons. The top three most popular buttons are used to open web pages, send a message back to the bot (IM back), or post a message back to the bot (post back). The difference between an IM back and a post back is that a post back message will not appear in the message history, whereas an IM back message would. Not all channels support both approaches, but the overall spirit of sending a message to the bot via a button click is widely supported.

Another type of button is a sign-in button. Sign-in buttons kick off an authentication or authorization flow via a login in a web view. Once the login is completed, the bot receives any necessary access tokens and can proceed with an authenticated session, as shown in Figure 4-13.

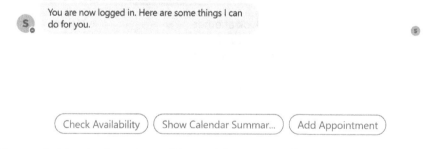

Figure 4-13. *Authenticated bot with suggested actions/quick replies*

All the content described previously is kept within a user's chat history. The carousels, the cards, the buttons, and, of course, all the text are available for the user to scroll through. There is one form of element that is displayed only in the context of the message that it is included in. That feature is suggested actions, also called *quick replies*. These buttons are presented on the bottom of the user interface until the user responds. These buttons are clear calls to actions and an indispensable tool for delightful conversational experiences. Figure 4-14 shows an example usage of suggested actions guiding users to video categories available in the TD Ameritrade bot.

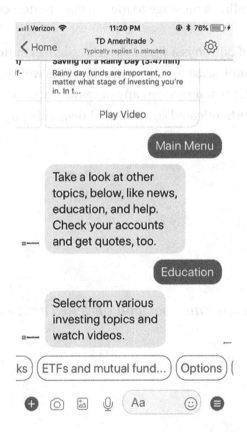

Figure 4-14. *Video category suggested action in the TD Ameritrade bot*

Authentication and Authorization in Bots

Let's be honest, no one is going to be sending a username and password to a bot chat window. This is a security risk. We do not want Facebook or Slack or any other channel to have our users' login credentials in their message history. At the end of the day, a bot is simply a web service, so using the standard OAuth or OpenID Connect flows is a natural fit.

The right approach is to utilize a sign-in card, which is a card that includes a button that opens a login web page for the user to enter their credentials (Figure 4-15).

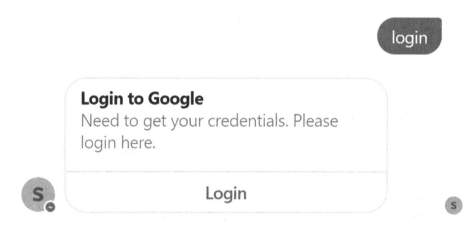

Figure 4-15. *A standard sign-in card*

Typically, this login page will be an OAuth page (Figure 4-16).

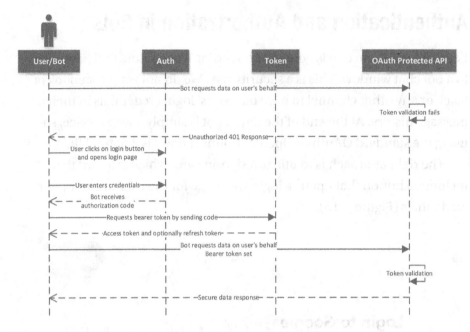

Figure 4-16. *OAuth authorization code flow*

OAuth 2.0[7] is a standard for token-based authorization over the Internet. There are several different types of authorization flows that are enabled by OAuth 2.0. A three-legged OAuth flow allows a resource owner (the user) to grant access to an application (the consumer) to an API (the service provider). In the context of a bot, it looks as follows:

- The user clicks a button to open a login page to a service in a web view for the third party and enters their username/password combination. The URI for this login page typically includes a client ID and a redirect URI. The redirect URI is an endpoint on our bot web service.

---

[7]OAuth 2.0 Documentation: https://oauth.net/2/

- Once the user logs in successfully, the service redirects the user back to the bot redirect URI. The bot redirect URI endpoint receives the authorization code. This is the user's grant to the application to use the service. The bot exchanges the authorization code for an access token (and an optional refresh token) from the token endpoint.

- The bot uses the access token when making requests to the service on behalf of the bot user.

- Typically, the access token is short lived, and the refresh token is longer lived. At any point, the bot can request a new access token from the token endpoint by posting the refresh token.

There is substantial documentation around the specifics of this and other OAuth flows. The RFC is a great starting point.[8] The key point is that a bot is a web service, and the complete OAuth flows can happen in an integrated manner. The only tricky part from a UX perspective is to ensure that the browser window automatically closes when the login is completed. The various channels approach this in slightly different ways. Although one can implement the entire flow manually, something we show off in Chapter 8, the Bot Framework does provide additional tools to facilitate this process.[9]

Specialized Cards

On platforms that support them, cards are a key component of the user experience. We covered the idea of a generic cards. Some channels provide several specialized cards. For instance, a receipt card (Figure 4-17) can be

---

[8]OAuth 2.0 RFC: `https://tools.ietf.org/html/rfc6749`

[9]`https://docs.microsoft.com/en-us/azure/bot-service/bot-builder-tutorial-authentication?view=azure-bot-service-3.0`

sent to communicate a purchase receipt with information such as totals, tax, payment confirmation, and so forth.

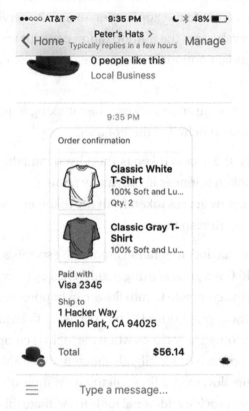

Figure 4-17. Messenger receipt template

In addition, Messenger gives developers the ability to utilize four air travel cards such as itinerary, boarding pass (Figure 4-18), check-in, and flight update.

Figure 4-18. *Messenger boarding pass template*

Tapping the boarding pass card shows a full-screen version with a QR code that can be utilized at the airport (Figure 4-19). Depending on which platform we target, there may be other templates for us to use. If they exist and match your use cases, use them. They provide a good, native user experience.

Figure 4-19. *Messenger boarding pass template details*

Another form of specialized card is one in which you use custom graphics. A common approach is to generate the custom graphics on a web service as the bot processes user input. In Chapter 11, we will build a simple custom graphics renderer using Headless Chrome to show how easily we can begin building custom graphics using HTML and JavaScript.

Lastly, Microsoft has introduced a new card format called *Adaptive Cards*.[10] Adaptive cards, which we will explode in Chapter 11, are a platform-agnostic manner to describe layouts of text, images, and input fields using a simple container-based layout engine. The Microsoft Bot channel connectors are then able to render the cards into platform-specific renderings. Adaptive Cards are a specialized version of the custom graphics approach integrated with logic to generate buttons and behavior in a card. It remains to be seen how many channels will end up supporting this format, but many of the Microsoft-owned channels already do.

Figure 4-20 shows an example of an HTML rendering of an Adaptive Card.

Figure 4-20. *Adaptive Card sample*

---

[10]Adaptive Cards: http://adaptivecards.io/

Figure 4-21 shows the rendering of an input form card on Microsoft's Teams app.

Figure 4-21. *Input form card sample*

Other Functions

Bots may include several other interesting pieces of functionality that can really make a bot experience shine. Some of these pieces of functionality are the following:

- *Proactive messaging*: A bot can reach out to a user asynchronously, triggered by an event other than an incoming message. If the bot stores a user's address (combination of service URLs and conversation and user IDs), it can utilize it to communicate to the user.

- *Human handoff*: In customer service scenarios and highly visible public-facing bot deployments, having a mechanism to seamlessly transfer the conversation from a bot to a human agent is a requirement for a successful bot.

- *Payments*: More and more platforms are opening their payment systems for easy conversational integration. Facebook Messenger has its Payments program with easy Stripe/PayPal integration. Microsoft provides easy Stripe integration for payments across the entire Windows ecosystem and the Bot Framework.

Conversational Experience Guidelines

There are some key guidelines that we should follow when developing a bot experience. Some of them may not apply to every type of bot or may be more relevant to consumer versus enterprise bots, but one should keep this list in mind at a minimum when designing bots.

Focus

As discussed in Chapters 1 and 2, there are limits to the technology and how intelligent a bot can be. Our bots should not try to get too clever; humans will always be able to break the bot in one way or another. For example, it is quite OK to handle greetings from the user like "hi" or "hello. We do not want to go down the rabbit hole of being handling every different type of greeting. Don't start creating specialized responses for "what's up?" versus "hi." If you are reading this book, you most likely don't have the budget that Microsoft or Google has (Figure 4-22). We are here to help with tasks, not general AI. It is OK to be honest about our bot's limitations.

Paul Boutin (Follow)
Writer with a tech background from MIT and Silicon Valley startups. AI, social media, interesting ideas of th...
Apr 19 · 4 min read

You're Not Facebook—Pick A Focus For Your Bot

A bot that does everything will be good at nothing.

Figure 4-22. *Good advice for building bots*

Don't Pretend the Bot Is a Human

We do not want our bots to end up in the uncanny valley.[11] That is, as with most, if not all, human-like objects, real humans will feel that something is not quite right, leading to strange and eerie feelings (Figure 4-23). We do not want our users to get those feelings. This goes hand in hand with representing your bot with human likeness. If you are representing your bot via an avatar, use an icon that clearly suggests a nonhuman entity. Siri and Cortana do this very well.

---

[11]Uncanny valley: why we find human-like robots and dolls so creepy: https://www.theguardian.com/commentisfree/2015/nov/13/robots-human-uncanny-valley

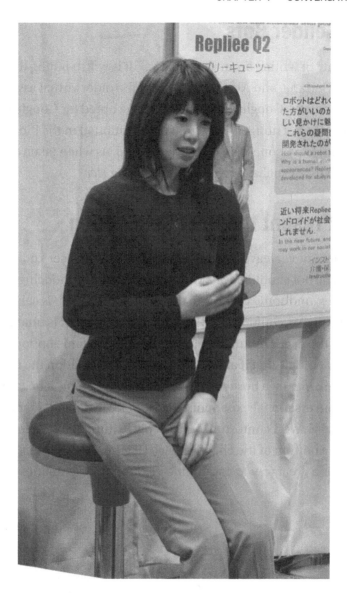

Figure 4-23. *We're definitely in the uncanny valley*

Do Not Gender Bots

There is plenty of writing around this topic.[12] It is worth noting that even though Siri, Cortana, and Alexa and some of the older virtual assistants have female names, Google and Facebook have opted for Google Assistant and M. This trend of nongendered bots has continued in the industry. Adopting female personas can quickly get weird, as when taken to the extreme with the sexualization of AI in the movie *Her*.

Always Present the Next Best Action

Our bot should never leave a user hanging without the user knowing what to do next. The bot should have a welcome message introducing itself, its capabilities, and some options to the user about what it is capable of. When the user is confused and asks for help or the bot is unable to recognize the user's input, the bot should suggest some options as well. The key point is that if at any point of the conversation the user is met by a blank message box with no suggested next steps, it becomes a confusing conversational experience. Facebook Messenger, Skype, and other channels have a contextual quick-reply feature that presents button options of the bottom of the chat interface (Figure 4-24). Presenting such suggestions is a great way to communicate our bot's capabilities and limitations.

---

[12]It took (only) six years for bots to start ditching outdated gender stereotypes: https://qz.com/1033587/it-took-only-six-years-for-bots-to-start-ditching-outdated-gender-stereotypes/

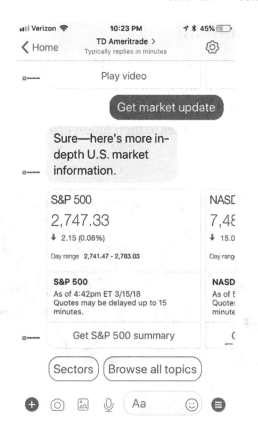

Figure 4-24. *Next best actions*

Have a Consistent Tone

Bots typically will end up getting a name and personality. Although I don't think gendered names make sense, your bot should have a personality and a consistent tone. Remember, these are brands speaking to your customers. Some bots are chatty. Others are less so. Some are formal. Others are more relaxed. Choose one for your bot and keep it consistent. And, although it is interesting technology, we should avoid using natural language generative models (machine learning algorithms that automatically generate responses) if we want to keep a brand-centric voice.

Utilize Rich Content

Bots provide us with the opportunity to utilize more than just text. We can format text and include images, videos, and audio files. We can render cards (Figure 4-25) and even create some custom graphics in your cards. We need to utilize those features to their fullest extent

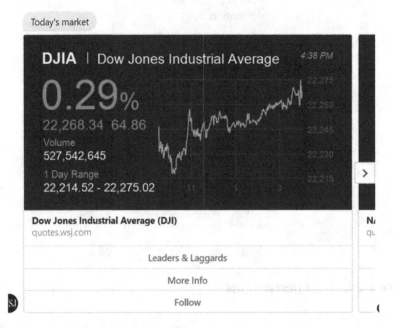

Figure 4-25. *Rich bot content is a good idea*

Be Forgiving

Natural language is tricky. Expect user inputs to be vague. Our bots should have conversational paths to confirm information or elicit missing data. If the user is expected to enter a number, we should parse any possible input but also be clear about the bot's expectations. If possible, provide some suggestions to the user of possible values they could enter by using a quick reply feature. The user will be pleased by such suggestions. There's nothing more frustrating than not knowing and not being instructed how to communicate to a bot.

Avoid Getting Stuck

At any point in our bot, the user should be able to change the conversation topic. Our bot should try to get stuck in a conversation context, unless absolutely necessary. For example, let's assume a calendar bot is asking the user for date. Our bot expects a string that resolves to a date. If the user enters "delete tomorrow's 9am appointment," our bot should handle the query gracefully instead of saying something like "I'm sorry that is not a date. Please enter a date in the format mm/dd/yyyy."

Don't Abuse Proactive Messaging

Bots give us an ability to reach out to user at any time, even without the bot seeing a message from the user. Do not abuse that privilege. In messaging applications, users get a notification any time they receive a message. There isn't an easier way to get removed from the messaging app than constantly sending reminders or trying to re-engage. Some channels have specific policies around this as well. Be a good citizen within the messaging channels.

Provide a Clear Path to Humans

If there is one thing that should be clear by now, it is that bots cannot understand everything. Even with a limited scope of functions, there are going to be questions and issues that the bot will not be able to handle. Our bots should have an ability to somehow connect users to a human agent, if relevant to the use case. Whether it is displaying a phone number with a case number or having seamless integration into a live chat system,

our bots should be clear in how our users can speak to humans for help
with their issues (Figure 4-26). For example, I once encountered a bot that
could answer frequently asked questions. I read a press release about the
bot, so I decided to try it. I started the conversation and got a message
about clicking a button. There were no buttons. I asked, "What can I do?" I
got redirected to a human agent. At this point, I couldn't do anything until
a human dealt with my case. I also had no indication of how long it would
take. Was their call center even open? Once the agent came around, I
spoke to them and got sent back to the bot. I had total silence, no buttons. I
said "Test." The next message I got was that I was getting transferred again.
At this point, I just quit. Don't make your users quit in frustration.

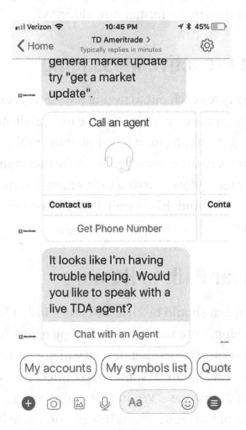

Figure 4-26. *Clear path to talking to a human*

Learn from Your Users

It is simple to use a conversational experience to collect data from users. It also easy to use user input in resolving conflicting intents from LUIS and then utilizing that data to train LUIS. Of course, the importance given to user input should be very different than the weight given to the utterances provided by a trainer. But if we have the data, we should use it to our advantage. Figure 4-27 shows an example of how we can implement such an approach. In the diagram we store user feedback into an active learning data store, and our active learning process determines how much of the same feedback it should observe before using the data point to train LUIS. Be careful with automated training based on user input. You do not want to go the way of Tay.[13]

Figure 4-27. *Implementing active learning*

There are more rules you may pick up on as you gain experience in this space across different messaging channels, but this list is a good starting point and something I suggest we follow on every chat bot project.

---

[13]Microsoft Silences its new AI Bot Tay: https://techcrunch.com/2016/03/24/microsoft-silences-its-new-a-i-bot-tay-after-twitter-users-teach-it-racism/

Conclusion

Conversation design is a rich field. We have numerous options for how we interact with users and how we communicate ideas in formats other than text. When developing bots, our approach should always be "do right by the user." A user's conversational experience can be very sensitive to tone, branding, verbosity, and overuse (you don't need to use a card for everything). Although in the early phases there are some key abstractions, such as cards, the space has developed to best handle bot-to-user interactions. As bots become more commonplace, these mechanisms will improve and increase in number. Microsoft's adaptive cards, for example, is a project that attempts to push the boundaries of what kind of functionality a bot can provide in conversation with users. My hope is that as bot become more and more commonplace, the messaging channels will support more and more types of behavior from bot cards.

We now have a good base understanding of the common operations bots perform and how they do so. The only remaining question is, how do we put all of this together in code? In the following chapter, we'll do just that and put these ideas into practice.

CHAPTER 5

Introducing the Microsoft Bot Framework

Microsoft's Bot Builder SDK comes in two flavors: C# and Node.js. As mentioned in Chapter 1, for the purposes of this book, we are going with the Node.js version. Node.js is a cross-platform JavaScript runtime; the fact that it is cross platform and based on a low barrier of entry language such as JavaScript means we can more easily show how easy it is to build bots using the technology. We stay within the confines of EcmaScript6; however, Bot Framework bots can be built using just about any flavor of JavaScript. The Bot Builder framework itself is written in TypeScript, a superset of JavaScript that includes optional static typing and can be compiled into JavaScript.

For this chapter, we should have an introductory-level knowledge of Node.js and npm (the node package manager). Code provided throughout the book will include the npm package definition, so we will need to run only two commands.

```
npm install
npm start
```

© Szymon Rozga 2018
S. Rozga, *Practical Bot Development*, https://doi.org/10.1007/978-1-4842-3540-9_5

Our aim in this chapter is to write a basic echo bot and deploy it to Facebook Messenger using Microsoft's channel connectors. Once we have the basic bot set up, we'll dive into the different concepts in the Bot Builder SDK that really allow us to write killer bots: waterfalls, dialogs, recognizers, sessions, cards, and much more. Let's go!

Microsoft Bot Builder SDK Basics

The core library we will be using to write the bot is called the Bot Builder SDK (https://github.com/Microsoft/BotBuilder). To get started, you will need to create a new node package and install the *botbuilder, dotenv-extended,* and *restify* packages. You can do so by creating a new directory and typing these commands:

```
npm init
npm install botbuilder dotenv-extended restify --save
```

Figure 5-1 shows the typical high-level bot architecture on a local machine. The idea is that the node app relies, principally, on two components. First, the Bot Builder SDK is the bot engine we use to build our bots. Second, all messages from any channel, either external to the machine or the Bot Framework Emulator from the developer machine, are sent to the bot via an HTTP endpoint. We use restify to listen to HTTP messages and to send those to the SDK.

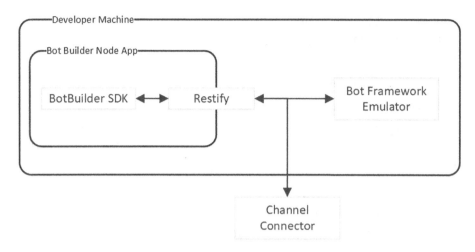

Figure 5-1. *Typical high-level bot architecture*

As an alternative to creating the package.json file manually, we can bootstrap this exercise using the *echo-bot* code provided with the book. The package.json for the *echo-bot* looks like this. Note that the *eslint* dependencies are purely for our development environment, so we can run a JavaScript linter[1] to check for stylistic and potential programmatic errors.

```
{
  "name": "practical-bot-development-echo-bot",
  "version": "1.0.0",
  "description": "Echo Bot from Chapter 1, Practical Bot
  Development",
  "scripts": {
    "start": "node app.js"
  },
```

---

[1]There are a few different linter options for JavaScript, namely, ESLint, JSLint, and JSHint. ESLint is one of the more extensible and powerful options. See https://eslint.org/.

```
  "author": "Szymon Rozga",
  "license": "MIT",
  "dependencies": {
    "botbuilder": "^3.9.0",
    "dotenv-extended": "^1.0.4",
    "restify": "^4.3.0"
  },
  "devDependencies": {
    "eslint": "^4.10.0",
    "eslint-config-google": "^0.9.1",
    "eslint-config-standard": "^10.2.1",
    "eslint-plugin-import": "^2.8.0",
    "eslint-plugin-node": "^5.2.1",
    "eslint-plugin-promise": "^3.6.0",
    "eslint-plugin-standard": "^3.0.1"
  }
}
```

The bot itself is defined in the app.js file. Note that the start script in the package definition specifies app.js as the entry point of our bot.

```
// load env variables
require('dotenv-extended').load();

const builder = require('botbuilder');
const restify = require('restify');

// setup our web server
const server = restify.createServer();
server.listen(process.env.port || process.env.PORT || 3978, ()
=> {
    console.log('%s listening to %s', server.name, server.url);
});
```

```
// initialize the chat bot
const connector = new builder.ChatConnector({
    appId: process.env.MICROSOFT_APP_ID,
    appPassword: process.env.MICROSOFT_APP_PASSWORD
});
server.post('/api/messages', connector.listen());

const bot = new builder.UniversalBot(connector, [
    (session) => {
        // for every message, send back the text prepended by echo:
        session.send('echo: ' + session.message.text);
    }
]);
```

Let's walk thought this code. We use a library called *dotenv* to load environment variables.

```
require('dotenv-extended').load();
```

The environment variables are loaded from a file called *.env* into the process.env JavaScript object. The *.env.defaults* file includes default environment variables and can be used to specify the values our Node.js requires. In this case, the file looks like this:

```
MICROSOFT_APP_ID=
MICROSOFT_APP_PASSWORD=
```

We require the *botbuilder* and *restify* libraries. Botbuilder is self-explanatory. Restify is used to run a web server endpoint for us.

```
const builder = require('botbuilder');
const restify = require('restify');
```

Now we set up our web server to listen for messages on port 3978.

```
const server = restify.createServer();
server.listen(process.env.port || process.env.PORT || 3978, () => {
    console.log('%s listening to %s', server.name, server.url);
});
```

Next, we create what is called a *chat connector*. In the context of the Bot Framework, the channel connectors are endpoints created and maintained by Microsoft that help translate messages from the native platform format to the Bot Builder SDK format. The *builder.ChatConnector* object knows how to receive HTTP messages from these connectors, pass them to the bot conversation engine, and send any outgoing messages back to the connectors, as in Figure 5-2.

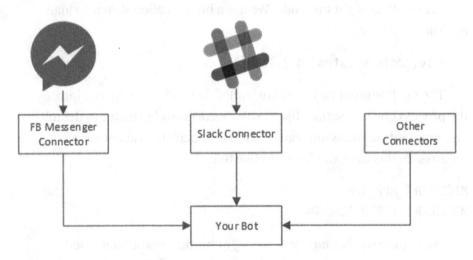

Figure 5-2. *Microsoft Bot Framework connectors*

The environment variables MICROSOFT_APP_ID and MICROSOFT_APP_PASSWORD are our bot's credentials. We will set them up in the Bot Framework at a later point when we create the Azure Bot Service registration with Azure. For now, we can leave those values blank because we don't care to secure our bot quite yet.

```
const connector = new builder.ChatConnector({
    appId: process.env.MICROSOFT_APP_ID,
    appPassword: process.env.MICROSOFT_APP_PASSWORD
});
```

Next we tell restify that any requests into the /api/messages endpoint, or, more specifically, http://localhost:3978/api/messages, should be handled by the function returned by connector.listen(). That is, we are allowing the Bot Framework to handle all incoming messages into that endpoint.

```
server.post('/api/messages', connector.listen());
```

Lastly, we create the *universal bot*. It is called a universal bot because it is not tied to any specific platform. It uses the connector for receiving and sending data. Any message that comes into the bot will be sent to the array of functions. For now, we have only one function. The function takes in a session object. This object contains data such as the message but also data about the user and conversation. The bot responds to the user by calling the *session.send* function.

```
const bot = new builder.UniversalBot(connector, [
    (session) => {
        // for every message, send back the text prepended by echo:
        session.send('echo: ' + session.message.text);
    }
]);
```

Notice that the Bot Builder SDK takes care of providing the right HTTP response to the incoming HTTP request. In practice, the internals will return an HTTP Accepted (202) if Bot Builder processes the code without a problem and will return an HTTP Internal Server Error (500) otherwise.

The content of our response is asynchronous, meaning that the response to the original request our bot receives does not contain any content. An incoming request, as we will see in the following chapter, includes a channel ID, the name of the connector such as *slack* or *facebook*, and a response URL where our bot sends messages. The URL typically looks like `https://facebook.botframework.com`. *Session.send* will send an HTTP POST request to the response URL.

We can run this bot by simply executing the following:

```
npm install
npm start
```

We will see some Node.js output in our console. There should be a server running on port 3978, on the path /api/messages. Depending on our local Node.js setup and the preexisting software on our machine, we may need to update to the latest version of the *node-gyp* package, a tool for compiling native addon tools.

How do we actually converse with the bot? We could try sending messages by using a command-line HTTP tool like curl, but we would have to host a response URL to see any responses. Additionally, we would need to add logic to obtain an access token to pass any security checks. Seems like too much work to simply test the bot.

Of course, we do not have to do any of this. Microsoft provides an emulator for us to test our bots. It is available at `https://emulator.botframework.com/` for download. The emulator supports Linux, Windows, and OS X (Figure 5-3).

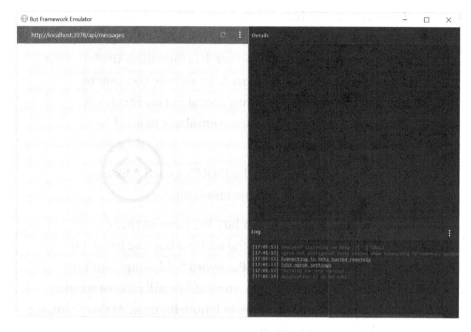

Figure 5-3. *Bot Framework Emulator*

Get ready because we will be using the emulator a lot. Here are some points we should be aware of:

- We can input our bot URL (`/api/messages`) into the address bar. The emulator also allows us to deal with bot security and specify the app ID/password. We'll get into that later.

- The log section shows us all the messages sent between the bot and emulator. We can see that the emulator opened a port to host a response URL. In this example, it is port 58462.

- The emulator log indicates when there is an update, so we are always running the latest and greatest version.

- There is some verbiage about ngrok. Ngrok is a reverse proxy that lets us tunnel requests from a public HTTPS endpoint into a local web server. It is incredibly useful when testing bot connectivity from remote computers, for example, if we want to run a local bot on Facebook Messenger. We can also use the emulator to send messages to remote bots.

- The details section shows the JSON for each message sent between the bot and the emulator.

Let's go ahead and connect to our bot. We enter `http://localhost:3978/api/messages` into the address bar and leave the Microsoft App ID and Microsoft App Password fields empty for now (Figure 5-4) since we haven't set up a *.env* file. We will receive security warnings in the console; these are fine to ignore for now. At this point, we are really to click the Connect button.

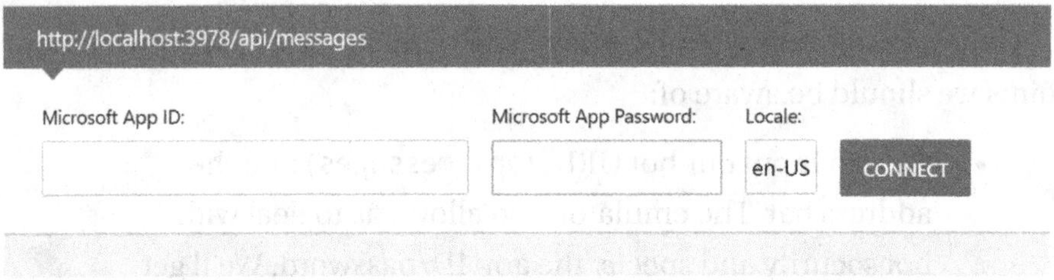

Figure 5-4. *Emulator connection UI*

We will see two messages appear in the emulator log. Both are of type *conversationUpdate* (Figure 5-5).

```
Log                                                                          ⋮

[17:01:13] Emulator listening on http://[::]:58462
[17:01:13] ngrok not configured (only needed when connecting to remotely hos
[17:01:13] Connecting to bots hosted remotely
[17:01:13] Edit ngrok settings
[17:01:13] Checking for new version...
[17:01:14] Application is up to date.
[17:02:10] -> POST 202 [conversationUpdate]
[17:02:10] -> POST 202 [conversationUpdate]
```

Figure 5-5. *conversationUpdate messages when establishing a connection from the emulator to our bot*

What does this mean? Each message between the bot and consuming connector (Emulator in this case) is called an *activity*, and each activity has a type. There are types like *message* or *typing*. If the activity is of type *message*, then it is literally a message between the bot and the user. A *typing* activity tells the connector to display a typing indicator. Previously, we saw the *conversationUpdate* type. This type indicates there is a change in the conversation; most commonly, users have joined or left the conversation. In a 1:1 conversation between a user and a bot, the user and bot will be the two members of a conversation. In a group chat scenario, the bot plus all the users would be part of the conversation. The message metadata will include information about which users joined or left the conversation. In fact, if we click the POST link for the two *conversationUpdate* activities, we find the JSON in the Details section. Here is the content for both messages:

```
{
    "type": "conversationUpdate",
    "membersAdded": [
        {
            "id": "default-user",
            "name": "User"
        }
```

```json
    ],
    "id": "hg71ma8cfj27",
    "channelId": "emulator",
    "timestamp": "2018-02-22T22:02:10.507Z",
    "localTimestamp": "2018-02-22T17:02:10-05:00",
    "recipient": {
        "id": "8k53ghlggkl2jl0a3",
        "name": "Bot"
    },
    "conversation": {
        "id": "mf24ln43lde3"
    },
    "serviceUrl": "http://localhost:58462"
}
{
    "type": "conversationUpdate",
    "membersAdded": [
        {
            "id": "8k53ghlggkl2jl0a3",
            "name": "Bot"
        }
    ],
    "id": "jfcdbhek0m4m",
    "channelId": "emulator",
    "timestamp": "2018-02-22T22:02:10.502Z",
    "localTimestamp": "2018-02-22T17:02:10-05:00",
    "recipient": {
        "id": "8k53ghlggkl2jl0a3",
        "name": "Bot"
    },
```

```
"conversation": {
    "id": "mf24ln43lde3"
},
"from": {
    "id": "default-user",
    "name": "User"
},
"serviceUrl": "http://localhost:58462"
}
```

Now, let's send a message to the bot with the text "echo!" and look at the Emulator logs (Figure 5-6). Note that if we do not set up an explicit bot storage implementation, we might get a warning like this: "Warning: The Bot Framework State API is not recommended for production environments, and may be deprecated in a future release." We will dive into this in the next chapter. Suffice it to say, it is strongly suggested that we use do not use the default bot storage. We can use the following code to replace it for now:

```
const inMemoryStorage = new builder.MemoryBotStorage();
bot.set('storage', inMemoryStorage);
```

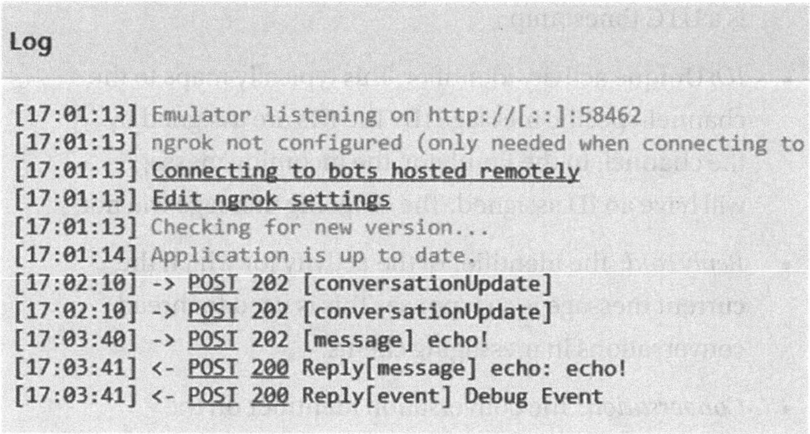

Figure 5-6. *It's alive!*

Aha! Our bot is alive. The emulator now contains a few more things. An incoming POST of type message with the text "echo!" and an outgoing POST of type message with the text "echo: echo!" and a POST with Debug Event data. Clicking the POST link will, again, display the JSON received or sent in this request. Note that both payloads are different, though underneath they utilize the same interface called IMessage. We will dig deeper into this in Chapter 6. Here is a list of some of the data that is part of either an incoming or outgoing message:

- *Sender info (id/name)*: The channel-specific identifier and username for the sender. If the message is from the user to bot, this is the user. In the reverse direction, the sender is the bot. The Bot Builder SDK takes care of populating this data. In our JSON, this is the *from* field.

- *Recipient info (id/name)*: The inverse of the sender info. This is the *recipient* field.

- *Timestamp*: The date and time when the message was sent. Typically, *timestamp* will be in UTC, and *localTimestamp* will be in the local time zone, though confusingly enough, the bot response's *localTimestamp* is a UTC timestamp.

- *ID*: Unique activity identifier. This typically maps to the channel-specific message ID. The IDs are assigned by the channel. In the Emulator, the incoming message will have an ID assigned. The outgoing message will not.

- *ReplyToId*: The identifier of the activity for which the current message is a response. This is used to thread conversations in messaging clients.

- *Conversation*: The conversation identifier on the platform.

- *Type*: The type of the activity. Possible values are message, conversationUpdate, contactRelationUpdate, typing, ping, deleteUserData, endOfConversation, event, and invoke.

- *Text*: The message's text.

- *TextFormat*: Text field format. Possible values are plain, markdown, and xml.

- *Attachments*: This is the structure through which the Bot Framework sends media attachments such as video, images, audio, or other types like hero cards. We can utilize this field for any kind of custom attachment type as well.

- *Text Local*: The user's language.

- *ChannelData*: Channel-specific data. For incoming messages, this may include the raw native message from a channel, for instance the native Facebook Messenger SendAPI. For outgoing messages, this would be a raw native message we want to pass through to the channel. This is typically used when the Microsoft channel connectors don't implement a specific type of message against a channel. We will explore some examples in Chapters 8 and 9.

- *ChannelId*: The messaging platform channel identifier.

- *ServiceUrl*: The endpoint to which the bot sends messages.

- *Entities*: A collection of data objects passed between the user and bot.

Let's examine the messages exchanged in more detail. The incoming message from the emulator looks as follows:

```
{
    "type": "message",
    "text": "echo!",
    "from": {
        "id": "default-user",
        "name": "User"
    },
    "locale": "en-US",
    "textFormat": "plain",
    "timestamp": "2018-02-22T22:03:40.871Z",
    "channelData": {
        "clientActivityId": "1519336929414.7950057585459784.0"
    },
    "entities": [
        {
            "type": "ClientCapabilities",
            "requiresBotState": true,
            "supportsTts": true,
            "supportsListening": true
        }
    ],
    "id": "50769feaaj9j",
    "channelId": "emulator",
    "localTimestamp": "2018-02-22T17:03:40-05:00",
    "recipient": {
        "id": "8k53ghlggkl2jl0a3",
        "name": "Bot"
    },
```

```
    "conversation": {
        "id": "mf24ln43lde3"
    },
    "serviceUrl": "http://localhost:58462"
}
```

There should be no surprises here. The response looks similar though a lot less verbose. This is typical. The incoming message will be populated by the channel connector with as much supporting data as possible. The response does not need to have all of this. One item of note is the fact that ID is not populated; the channel connector will typically take care of this for us.

```
{
    "type": "message",
    "text": "echo: echo!",
    "locale": "en-US",
    "localTimestamp": "2018-02-22T22:03:41.136Z",
    "from": {
        "id": "8k53ghlggkl2jl0a3",
        "name": "Bot"
    },
    "recipient": {
        "id": "default-user",
        "name": "User"
    },
    "inputHint": "acceptingInput",
    "id": null,
    "replyToId": "50769feaaj9j"
}
```

We also note the existence of the *inputHint* field, which is mostly relevant to a voice assistant system and is an indication to the messaging platform on the suggested state for the microphone. For example, *acceptingInput* would indicate the user may respond to a bot message, and *expectingInput* would indicate that a user response is expected right now.

Lastly, the Debug Event provides data on how the bot executed the request.

```
{
    "type": "event",
    "name": "debug",
    "value": [
        {
            "type": "log",
            "timestamp": 1519337020880,
            "level": "info",
            "msg": "UniversalBot(\"*\") routing \"echo!\" from
            \"emulator\"",
            "args": []
        },
        {
            "type": "log",
            "timestamp": 1519337020881,
            "level": "info",
            "msg": "Session.beginDialog(/)",
            "args": []
        },
        {
            "type": "log",
            "timestamp": 1519337020882,
            "level": "info",
            "msg": "waterfall() step 1 of 1",
            "args": []
        },
```

```
    {
        "type": "log",
        "timestamp": 1519337020882,
        "level": "info",
        "msg": "Session.send()",
        "args": []
    },
    {
        "type": "log",
        "timestamp": 1519337021136,
        "level": "info",
        "msg": "Session.sendBatch() sending 1 message(s)",
        "args": []
    }
],
"relatesTo": {
    "id": "50769feaaj9j",
    "channelId": "emulator",
    "user": {
        "id": "default-user",
        "name": "User"
    },
    "conversation": {
        "id": "mf24ln43lde3"
    },
    "bot": {
        "id": "8k53ghlggkl2jl0a3",
        "name": "Bot"
    },
    "serviceUrl": "http://localhost:58462"
},
```

```
    "text": "Debug Event",
    "localTimestamp": "2018-02-22T22:03:41.157Z",
    "from": {
        "id": "8k53ghlggkl2jloa3",
        "name": "Bot"
    },
    "recipient": {
        "id": "default-user",
        "name": "User"
    },
    "id": null,
    "replyToId": "50769feaaj9j"
}
```

Note, these are the same values as are printed in the bot console output. Again, if we did not override the default bot state, we would see more data here related to the deprecated code. The console output is shown here:

```
UniversalBot("*") routing "echo!" from "emulator"
Session.beginDialog(/)
/ - waterfall() step 1 of 1
/ - Session.send()
/ - Session.sendBatch() sending 1 message(s)
```

This output tracks how the user's request is executed and how it traverses the conversation dialogs. We will address this further in this chapter.

If we were to send more messages using the emulator, we would see the same type of output since this bot is very simple. As we gain more experience with features such as cards, we will benefit from using the Emulator and examining the JSON messages further. The protocol is a huge part of the Bot Framework's power: we should be as familiar with it as we can.

186

EXERCISE 5-1

Connecting to the Emulator

Retrieve the echo bot code and run it locally using *npm install* and *npm start*. Download the emulator and connect it to the bot.

1. Examine the request/response messages carefully.

2. Observe the behavior between the emulator and the bot.

3. Explore the emulator. Use the Settings menu to create new conversations or send system activity messages to the bot. How does it react? Can you write some code to handle any of these messages?

At the end of this exercise you should be familiar with running an unauthenticated local bot and connecting to it via the emulator.

Bot Framework End-to-End Setup

We now have a bot. How do we connect it to all these different channels? The Bot Framework makes this simple. Our goal here will be to register our bot and its endpoint with the Bot Framework through the Azure Portal and subscribe the bot to the Facebook Messenger channel.

There are a few things we will have to do. First, we have to create an Azure Bot service registration on the Azure Portal. We may need to create our first Azure Subscription. Part of this setup is using ngrok to allow the bot to be accessible from the Internet, so we should make sure that we have ngrok installed from here: `https://ngrok.com/`. Lastly, we will deploy the bot to Facebook Messenger. This means we need to create a Facebook page, a Facebook app, and Messenger and Webhook integrations, and connect all that back to the Bot Framework. There are quite a few steps, but once we become familiar with Azure and Facebook terminology, it is not that cumbersome. We will first quickly walk through the directions and then go back and explain what was done at each step.

Step 1: Connecting to Azure

Our first step is to log into the Azure Portal. If you have an Azure account, excellent. Skip ahead to step 2 if you have an Azure subscription already. If you do not, you are able to create a free developer account with a $200 30-day credit by going to `https://azure.microsoft.com/en-us/free/`.

Click "Start free." You will need to log in using a Microsoft or work account. If you have neither, you can easily create a Microsoft account at `https://account.microsoft.com/account`. Once you're authenticated, you will see a page like in Figure 5-7. This page will collect your personal information and verify your identity via a text message and a valid credit card. Don't be alarmed. The credit card is necessary to verify your identity. Chances are, you will not come even close to using the $200 credit, and if you do, you will not be charged; you will just not be able to use the services further. Much of what we use Azure for in this book can be accommodated via a free tier of the various Azure services.

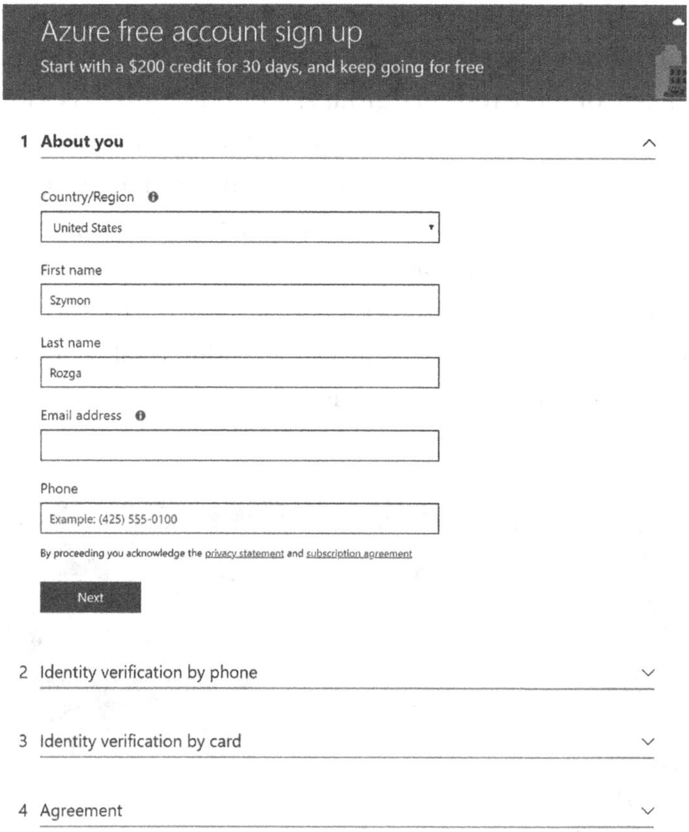

Azure free account sign up

Start with a $200 credit for 30 days, and keep going for free

1 **About you**   ∧

Country/Region ❶

| United States   ▾ |

First name

| Szymon |

Last name

| Rozga |

Email address ❶

| |

Phone

| Example: (425) 555-0100 |

By proceeding you acknowledge the privacy statement and subscription agreement

| Next |

2 Identity verification by phone   ∨

3 Identity verification by card   ∨

4 Agreement   ∨

Figure 5-7. *Azure sign-up page*

Once the process is done, you will be able to go into the Azure Portal at `https://portal.azure.com`. It looks something like Figure 5-8. On the top right, you will see the email address you signed up with and your directory name. For example, if my email were `szymon.rozga@aol.com` (it's not), then my directory name would be SZYMONROZGAAOL. If you were added into other directories, that menu would be a drop-down for you to select to which directory you are navigating.

An Azure account contains subscriptions. A subscription is a billing entity. If we navigate to `https://portal.azure.com/#blade/Microsoft_Azure_Billing/SubscriptionsBlade`, or the Subscriptions service in the portal, and we had just created the $200 trial account, we should see one subscription with the name Free Trial. Each Azure subscription can also contain one or more resource groups. A resource group is a logical container for resources, which are individual Azure services. All costs associated with resources in each resource group are charged against the payment method associated with the containing subscription. With the $200 trial account, services are automatically shut down when the combined costs reach the spending limit. If desired, the free account can be converted to a paid account that will accrue additional charges to your credit card (or alternative payment options).

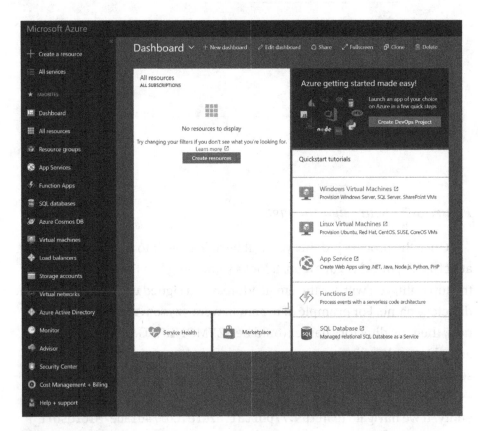

Figure 5-8. Empty Azure Portal

Step 2: Creating the Bot Registration

In the Azure Portal, click the "Create a resource" button in the top-left pane. In the Search the Marketplace text field, enter **azure bot**. You will get many results, but we are interested in the top three (Figure 5-9).

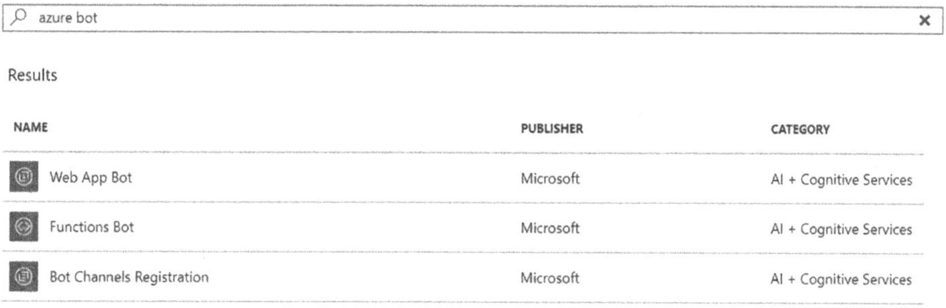

NAME	PUBLISHER	CATEGORY
Web App Bot	Microsoft	AI + Cognitive Services
Functions Bot	Microsoft	AI + Cognitive Services
Bot Channels Registration	Microsoft	AI + Cognitive Services

Figure 5-9. *Azure bot resources*

These are the three options:

- *Web App Bot*: A bot registration pointing to a web app deployed on Azure

- *Functions Bot*: A bot registration pointing to a bot running as an Azure function, one of Azure's serverless computing options

- *Bot Channels Registration*: A bot registration with no cloud-based back end

For our purposes, we will create a Bot Channels Registration bot, as we will keep on running the bot locally on our laptop. Click Bot Channels Registration and then click Create. As per Figure 5-10, enter a bot name, the name for the resource group that will contain this registration, and the resource location, namely, the Azure region that will host the registration. For Pricing Tier, select F0; this is the free option and sufficient for our needs. Leave the messaging endpoint empty for now and leave Application Insights selected to On. Application Insights is one of Microsoft's cloud telemetry and logging services. The Bot Framework uses this to store data

191

and analytics on your bot registration usage. By default, this will create the basic and free tier of Application Insights. Select as close a location to the Bot Channels Registration location as possible. Click Create when ready.

Figure 5-10. *Creating a new bot channel registration*

There is a progress indicator across the top of the portal, and we will receive a notification when the registration is ready. We can also navigate into the resource group by using the Resource Groups button on the left pane (Figure 5-11).

Figure 5-11. *The resources in our resource group*

Navigate into the bot channel registration and then navigate to the Settings blade (Figure 5-12). Note that Azure automatically populated the Application Insights identifiers and keys. These will be used to track analytics data for our bot. We will see one of the resulting analytics dashboards in Chapter 13.

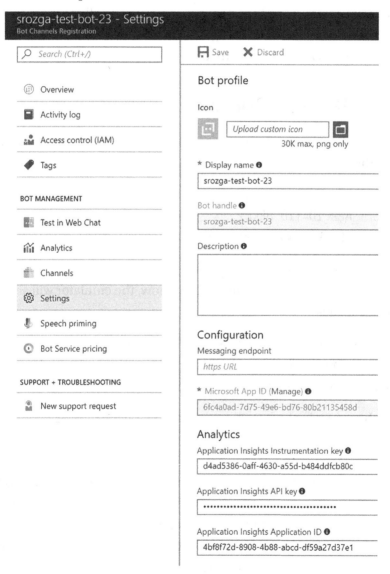

Figure 5-12. The Bot Channels Registration Settings blade

193

We will also be shown the Microsoft App ID. Take note of this value. Click the Manage link directly above it to navigate to the Microsoft Application Portal. This may ask for our login information once again because it is a separate site from Azure. Once we locate the newly created bot in the list of applications, click Generate New Password (in the Application Secrets section) and save the value; you will see it once only! Recall that we were seeing warnings that our bot was not secure in the bot console output? We will now fix that.

Step 3: Securing Our Bot

In the directory containing the echo bot code, create a file called .env and provide the Microsoft App ID and the password:

```
# Bot Framework Credentials
MICROSOFT_APP_ID={ID HERE}
MICROSOFT_APP_PASSWORD={PASSWORD HERE}
```

Shut down and restart the bot (npm start).

If we try to connect from the emulator now, the emulator will show the following log messages:

```
[08:00:16] -> POST 401 [conversationUpdate]
[08:00:16] Error: The bot's MSA appId or password is incorrect.
[08:00:16] Edit your bot's MSA info
```

The bot console output will contain the following message:

```
ERROR: ChatConnector: receive - no security token sent.
```

It seems a bit more secure now, right? We must enter the same app ID and password on the emulator side. Click the "Edit our bot's MSA (Microsoft Account) info" link, and enter the data into the emulator. If we try to connect using the emulator now, it will work fine. Send a message to the bot to confirm before continuing.

Step 4: Setting Up Remote Access

We could deploy the bot to Azure, connect the Facebook connector to that endpoint, and call it a day. But how do we develop or debug Facebook-specific features? The Bot Framework way is to run a local instance of the bot and connect a test Facebook page to the local bot for development.

To achieve this, run ngrok from the command line.

```
ngrok http 3978
```

We will be presented with the data in Figure 5-13. By default, ngrok assigns a random subdomain (paid ngrok versions allow you to specify a domain name). In this case, my URL is `https://cc6c5d5f.ngrok.io`. Note that the free version of ngrok provides a random subdomain each time we run it. We can get around this by either upgrading to a paid version or simply leaving the ngrok session up for as long as possible.

```
ngrok by @inconshreveable

Session Status                 online
Account                        Szymon Rozga (Plan: Pro)
Version                        2.2.8
Region                         United States (us)
Web Interface                  http://127.0.0.1:4041
Forwarding                     http://cc6c5d5f.ngrok.io -> localhost:3978
Forwarding                     https://cc6c5d5f.ngrok.io -> localhost:3978

Connections                    ttl      opn      rtl      rt5      p50      p90
                               0        0        0.00     0.00     0.00     0.00
```

Figure 5-13. *Ngrok forwarding HTTP/HTTPS requests to our local bot*

Let's see if this works. In the emulator, enter the ngrok URL followed by **/api/messages**. For instance, for the previous URL, the correct messaging endpoint is `https://cc6c5d5f.ngrok.io/api/messages`. Add the app ID and app password information into the emulator. Once you click Connect, the emulator should successfully connect to and chat with the bot.

Now, assign the same messaging endpoint URL in the Bot Channels Registration Settings blade, Figure 5-12. Next, navigate to the Test with Web Chat blade and try to send a message to the bot. It should work. You've connected your first channel to your bot (Figure 5-14)!

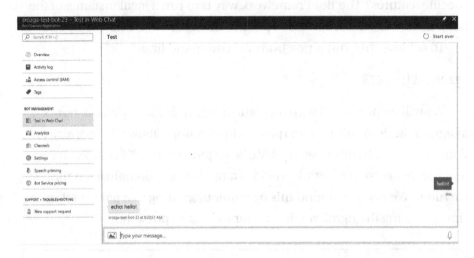

Figure 5-14. *It works! Our bot is connected to our first channel!*

Step 5: Connecting to Facebook Messenger

Pretty cool, right? The Bot Framework is almost completely integrated with our bot. We will now proceed to integrate our bot with Facebook Messenger. The Channels blade on the Bot Channels Registration gives us an ability to connect to the Microsoft-supported channels (Figure 5-15).

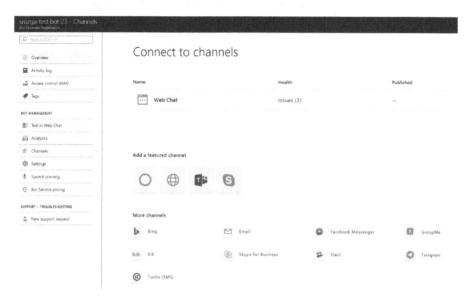

Figure 5-15. *Channel dashboard*

Click the Facebook Messenger button to go into the Messenger configuration screen (Figure 5-16). We are going to need to get four pieces of data from Facebook: page ID, app ID, app secret, and page access token. Lastly, we should take note of the callback URL and verify token. We will need these to set up connectivity between Facebook and the Bot Framework.

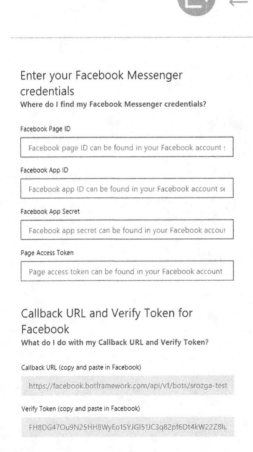

Figure 5-16. Facebook Messenger Bot Framework connector settings

Let's now set up the necessary Facebook assets. We must have a
Facebook account to complete the following tasks. Navigate to Facebook.
com and use the top-right drop-down menu to create a new page
(Figure 5-17). Facebook will ask for the type of page. For the purposes
of this example, we can select the Brand/Product type and App Page
subcategory.

Figure 5-17. *Creating a new Facebook page*

I created a page called Szymon Test Page. We can find the page ID by clicking to the About link on the left navigation pane (Figure 5-18). On the very bottom we will find the page ID. We need to copy that value into the Bot Framework Facebook Messenger channel configuration form (Figure 5-16).

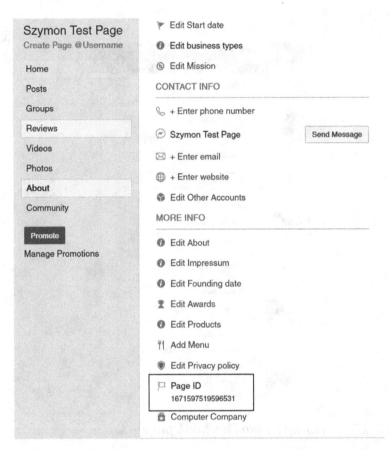

Figure 5-18. *Facebook Page About page, including the page ID*

Next, in a new browser tab or window, navigate to `https://developers.facebook.com`. If you have not yet done so, register for a developer account. Create a new app (Figure 5-19). Give it any name you like.

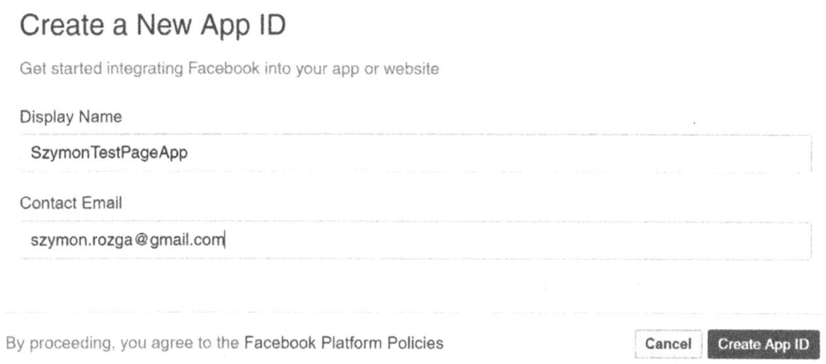

Create a New App ID
Get started integrating Facebook into your app or website
Display Name
SzymonTestPageApp
Contact Email
szymon.rozga@gmail.com
By proceeding, you agree to the Facebook Platform Policies
Cancel
Create App ID

***Figure 5-19.** Creating a new Facebook app*

Once you do, navigate to the Settings ➤ Basic page via the left sidebar menu and copy the Facebook app ID and app secret into the Bot Framework form (Figure 5-20).

SzymonTestPageApp
APP ID: 1972099883051321
OFF
Status: In Development
View Analytics
Dashboard
Settings
Basic
Advanced
Roles
App ID
1972099883051321
App Secret
••••••••
Show
Display Name
SzymonTestPageApp
Namespace

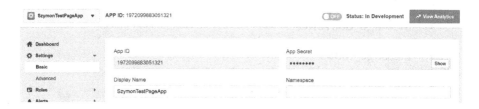

***Figure 5-20.** App ID and app secret*

Next, navigate to the Dashboard (from the link on the left sidebar) and set up the Messenger product. Scroll down the page until you get to the Token Generation section. Generate a page access token by selecting the page in the Token Generation section (Figure 5-21). Copy the token into the Bot Framework form within the Azure Portal.

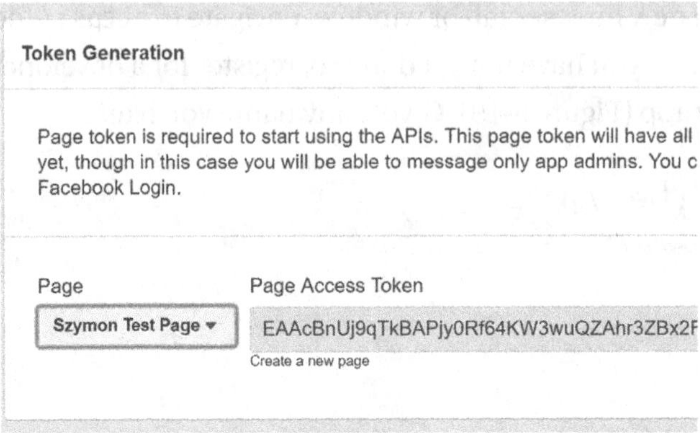

Token Generation

Page token is required to start using the APIs. This page token will have all
yet, though in this case you will be able to message only app admins. You c
Facebook Login.

Page	Page Access Token
Szymon Test Page ▼	EAAcBnUj9qTkBAPjy0Rf64KW3wuQZAhr3ZBx2F
Create a new page	

Figure 5-21. *Generating the page access token*

Next, scroll to the Webhooks section (just below the Token Generation
section of the Facebook App Dashboard) and click Setup Webhooks. You
will see a pop-up that asks you for a callback URL and the verify token.
Copy and paste both of those from the Configure Facebook Messenger
form in the Azure Portal.

In the Subscription Fields section, select the following fields:

- messages

- message_deliveries

- message_reads

- messaging_postbacks

- messaging_optins

- message_echoes

Click Verify and Save. Lastly, select the page you would like your bot
to subscribe to from the drop-down and click Subscribe. Your setup page
should look as shown in Figure 5-22.

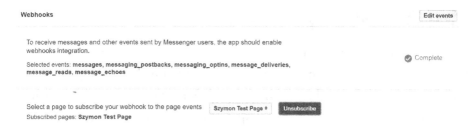

Webhooks   Edit events

To receive messages and other events sent by Messenger users, the app should enable
webhooks integration.   ✔ Complete

Selected events: **messages, messaging_postbacks, messaging_optins, message_deliveries,
message_reads, message_echoes**

Select a page to subscribe your webhook to the page events   Szymon Test Page ⬦   **Unsubscribe**
Subscribed pages: **Szymon Test Page**

Figure 5-22. *Subscribing to messages on our test page*

Make sure to save the Bot Framework configuration. That's it! You can
find the page in your Messenger contacts. You can send it a message, and
you should get it echoed back (Figure 5-23).

Figure 5-23. *Echo bot working in Messenger*

Step 6: Deploying to Azure

It would not be a complete tutorial if we did not deploy the code into the cloud. We will create a web app and deploy our Node.js app using Kudu ZipDeploy. Lastly, we will point the bot channel registration to the web app.

Go into your Azure resource group that we created in step 2 and create a new resource. Search for *web app*. Select Web App and not Web App Bot. The Web App Bot is a combination of a bot channel registration and an app service. We have no need for this combination since we have already created a bot channel registration.

When creating the web app, we will need to give it a name. Also ensure the correct resource group is selected (Figure 5-24). Azure will add it to our existing resource group and create a new app service plan for us. An app service plan is a container for web apps and similar compute resources; it defines the hardware on which our apps run as well as the costs. In Figure 5-24, we create a new app service plan and choose the Free pricing tier. Free is good.

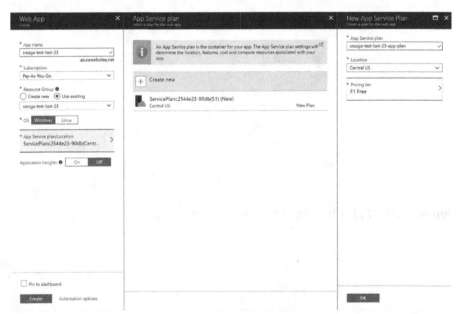

Figure 5-24. *Creating a new app service and app service plan*

Before we deploy our echo bot, we need to add two things. First, we add a response to the base URL endpoint to validate our bot was deployed. Add this code to the end of the app.js file:

```
server.get('/', (req, res, next) => {
    res.send(200, { "success": true });
    next();
});
```

Second, for a Windows-based Azure setup, we also need to include a custom web.config file to tell Internet Information Services (IIS)[2] how to run a Node app.[3]

```
<?xml version="1.0" encoding="utf-8"?
<!--
    This configuration file is required if iisnode is used to
    run node processes behind
    IIS or IIS Express.  For more information, visit:

    https://github.com/tjanczuk/iisnode/blob/master/src/
    samples/configuration/web.config
-->

<configuration>
  <system.webServer>
    <!-- Visit http://blogs.msdn.com/b/windowsazure/
    archive/2013/11/14/introduction-to-websockets-on-windows-
    azure-web-sites.aspx for more information on WebSocket
    support -->
```

---

[2]Internet Information Services (IIS) is Microsoft's rich and extensible web server. It runs all Azure Windows web apps. See https://www.iis.net/.

[3]Using a custom web.config for Node apps: https://github.com/projectkudu/kudu/wiki/Using-a-custom-web.config-for-Node-apps

```xml
<webSocket enabled="false" />
<handlers>
  <!-- Indicates that the server.js file is a node.js site
  to be handled by the iisnode module -->
  <add name="iisnode" path="app.js" verb="*"
  modules="iisnode"/>
</handlers>
<rewrite>
  <rules>
    <!-- Do not interfere with requests for node-inspector
    debugging -->
    <rule name="NodeInspector" patternSyntax="ECMAScript"
    stopProcessing="true">
      <match url="^app.js\/debug[\/]?" />
    </rule>

    <!-- First we consider whether the incoming URL matches
    a physical file in the /public folder -->
    <rule name="StaticContent">
      <action type="Rewrite" url="public{REQUEST_URI}"/>
    </rule>

    <!-- All other URLs are mapped to the node.js site
    entry point -->
    <rule name="DynamicContent">
      <conditions>
        <add input="{REQUEST_FILENAME}" matchType="IsFile"
        negate="True"/>
      </conditions>
      <action type="Rewrite" url="app.js"/>
    </rule>
  </rules>
</rewrite>
```

```
<!-- 'bin' directory has no special meaning in node.js and
apps can be placed in it -->
<security>
  <requestFiltering>
    <hiddenSegments>
      <remove segment="bin"/>
    </hiddenSegments>
  </requestFiltering>
</security>

<!-- Make sure error responses are left untouched -->
<httpErrors existingResponse="PassThrough" />

<!--
  You can control how Node is hosted within IIS using the
  following options:
    * watchedFiles: semi-colon separated list of files that
    will be watched for changes to restart the server
    * node_env: will be propagated to node as NODE_ENV
    environment variable
    * debuggingEnabled - controls whether the built-in
    debugger is enabled

  See https://github.com/tjanczuk/iisnode/blob/master/
  src/samples/configuration/web.config for a full list of
  options
  -->
  <!--<iisnode watchedFiles="web.config;*.js"/>-->
  </system.webServer>
</configuration>
```

Next, we visit our bot web app via the browser. In my case, I navigate to
https://srozga-test-bot-23.azurewebsites.net. There will be a default
"Your App Service app is up and running" page. Before we deploy, we
must zip the echo bot for transfer to Azure. We zip all the application files,
including the node-modules directory. We can use the following commands:

```
# Bash
zip -r echo-bot.zip .
```

```
# PowerShell
Compress-Archive -Path * -DestinationPath echo-bot.zip
```

Now that we have a zip file, we have two options as to how we deploy.
In option 1, we use a command line to deploy the bot by using the Kudu[4]
endpoint at https://{WEB_APP_NAME}.scm.azurewebsites.net. To enable
this, we must first visit the Deployment Credentials blade in the app service
(Figure 5-25) to set up a deployment username and password combination.

Figure 5-25. *Setting up deployment credentials*

---

[4]Kudu is the engine behind Azure web site deployment. It can also run outside of
Azure. See https://github.com/projectkudu/kudu/wiki.

Once done, we are ready to roll. Running the following curl command will kick off the deployment process:

```
curl -v POST -u srozga321 --data-binary @echo-bot.zip https://
srozga-test-bot-23.scm.azurewebsites.net/api/zipdeploy
```

Once you run this, curl will ask for the password that was provided in Figure 5-25. It will upload the zip and set up the app on the app service. Once done, make a request to your app's base URL, and you should see a 200 response with success set to true.

```
$ curl -X GET https://srozga-test-bot-23.azurewebsites.net
{"success":true}
```

The alternative way to deploy is to use the Kudu interface on the SCM website: `https://srozga-test-bot-23.scm.azurewebsites.net/ ZipDeploy`. You can simply drag and drop your zip file on the file listing in Figure 5-26.

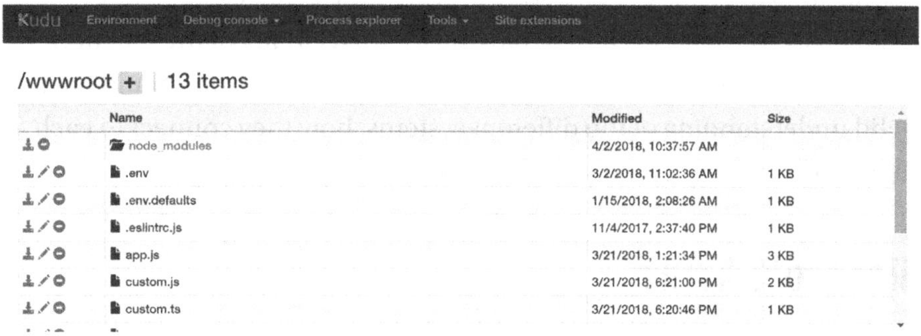

Figure 5-26. *Kudu ZipDeploy user interface*

There's one more step. Go into the Settings blade in the Bot Channels Registration entry and set the messages endpoint setting to your new app service (Figure 5-27). Make sure to click the Save button.

Figure 5-27. *Final update to the messaging endpoint*

Save and test on Web Chat and Messenger to your heart's content. Congratulations! We accomplished a lot! We now have a bot running on Azure using Node.js and the Microsoft Bot Framework talking to Web Chat and Facebook Messenger. Up next, we will dive into a description of what we just accomplished.

What Did We Just Do?

We went through quite a lot in the previous section. There are many moving parts in terms of registering and creating a bot, establishing connectivity to Facebook and deploying to Azure. Many of these action only need to be performed once, but as a bot developer you should have a solid understanding of the different systems, how they connect to each other and how they can be set up.

Microsoft Azure

Microsoft Azure is Microsoft's cloud platform. There are many types of resources ranging from infrastructure-as-a-service to platform-as-a-service and even software-as-a-service. We can provision new virtual machines as easily as creating new application services. We can create, modify, and edit resources using Azure PowerShell, Azure CLI (or the Cloud Shell), the Azure Portal (as we did in the example), or the Azure Resource Manager. The details of these are outside the scope of this book, and we refer you to the Microsoft online documentation for more information.

Bot Channels Registration Entry

When we create the bot channels registration, we are creating a global registration that can be used by all of the channel connectors to identify, authenticate, and communicate with our bot. Each connector, whether it communicates to Messenger, Slack, Web Chat, or Skype, knows about our bot, its Microsoft app ID/password, the messages endpoint, and other settings (Figure 5-28). The bot channels registration is the starting point for Bot Framework bots.

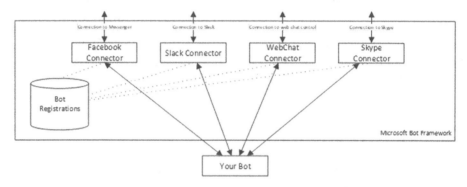

Figure 5-28. *Conceptual Bot Framework architecture*

We skipped the other two types of bot resources in Azure: Web App Bot and Functions Bot. A Web App Bot is exactly what we just set up; we provision a server to run bot app. Azure Functions is one of Azure's approaches to serverless computing. It allows us to host different code, or functions, in a cloud environment to be run on demand. We pay only for the resources we use. Azure scales the infrastructure dynamically based on load. Functions is a perfectly valid approach to bot development. For more complex scenarios, we need to be careful about architecting the function code for scale-out and multiserver deployment. For the purposes of this book, we do not utilize Functions Bots. However, we suggest you experiment with the topic as serverless computing is becoming more and more prominent.

Authentication

How do we ensure that only authorized channel connectors or applications can communicate with our bot? That's where the Microsoft app ID and app password come in. When a connector sends a message to our bot, it will include a token in the HTTP authorization header. Our bot must validate this token. When our bot sends outgoing messages to the connector, our bot must retrieve a valid token from Azure or the connector will reject the message.

The Bot Builder SDK provides all the code so that this process is transparent to the developer. The Bot Framework documentation describes the steps in both flows in detail: `https://docs.microsoft.com/en-us/bot-framework/rest-api/bot-framework-rest-connector-authentication`.

Connectivity and Ngrok

Although ngrok is not part of the Bot Framework, it is an indispensable part of our toolset. Ngrok is a reverse proxy that tunnels all requests through an externally accessible subdomain on ngrok.io to a port on our computer. The free version creates a new random subdomain each time we run it; the pro version allows us to have a static subdomain. Ngrok also exposes an HTTPS endpoint, which makes local development setup a breeze.

Typically, we will not typically experience any problems with Ngrok. If our ngrok is correctly configured, any issues could be narrowed down to either an external service or our bot.

Deploying to Facebook Messenger

Every platform is different, but we learned a bit about the intricacies of bots on Facebook. First, Facebook users interact with brands and companies using Facebook Pages. User requests on a page are typically responded to by a human who has enough access to the page to view and respond via the page's inbox. There are many enterprise live chat systems that connect to Facebook Pages and allow a team of customer service representatives to respond to users' queries in real time. With the Bot Framework's Facebook Messenger connector, we can now have a bot respond to those queries. We will discuss the idea of a bot handing a conversation over to an agent, known as *human handover*, in Chapter 13.

A bot on Facebook is a Facebook app that subscribes to messages coming into a Facebook page via web hooks. We registered the Bot Framework web hook endpoint that is called by Facebook when a message comes into our Facebook page. The bot channels registration page also provided the verify token that Facebook uses to make sure it is connecting to the right web hook. Azure's Bot Connectors need to know the Facebook app ID and app secret to verify the signature of each incoming message. We need the page access token to send a message back to a user in a chat with a page. We can find more details about Facebook's SendAPI and Messenger Webhooks in Facebook's documentation pages: `https://developers.facebook.com/docs/messenger-platform/reference/send-api/` and `https://developers.facebook.com/docs/messenger-platform/webhook/`.

Once all these things are in place, messages easily flow between Facebook and our bot. Although Facebook has some unique concepts like the page access tokens and specific names for webhook types, the overall idea behind what we did is similar to other channels. Generally, we will be creating an app on the platform and establishing a tie between that app and the Bot Framework endpoints. It is the Bot Framework's role to forward the messages to us.

213

Deploying to Azure

There are many approaches to deploying code to Azure. Kudu, the tool we used, allows us to deploy via a REST API. Kudu can also be configured to deploy from a git repo or other locations. There are also other tools that make deployment easier. If we were to write a bot using Microsoft's Visual Studio or Visual Studio Code, there are extensions that allow us to easily deploy our code into Azure. Again, this is a topic beyond the scope of this book. For our purposes of running a Node.js bot on a Linux app service, using the ZipDeploy REST API is sufficient.

Because we can develop our bot locally by use of the emulator and test a local bot on various channels by running ngrok, we do not deploy to Azure anymore throughout the rest of this book. If necessary, take down the web app instance so the subscription is not charged. Make sure to delete the app service plan; simply stopping the web app will not work.

Key Bot Builder SDK Concepts

It feels good to have worked through the details of getting a bot running via the emulator and Facebook Messenger, but the bot doesn't do anything useful! In this section, we will delve into the Bot Builder SDK for Node. js library. This is the focus for the rest of this chapter and the following chapter. For now, we will go over four foundational concepts of the Bot Builder SDK. Afterward, we show the skeleton code for a calendar bot conversation, based on the NLU work on LUIS from Chapter 3. This bot will know how to talk to users about many calendar tasks but will not integrate with any APIs quite yet. This is a common approach to demonstrate the conversation flow and how it may work without going through the entire back-end integration effort. Let's dive in.

Sessions and Messages

Session is an object that represents the current conversation and the operations that can be invoked on it. At the most basic level, we can use the Session object to send messages.

```
const bot = new builder.UniversalBot(connector, [
    session => {
        // for every message, send back the text prepended by
        echo:
        session.send('echo: ' + session.message.text);
    }
]);
```

Messages can include images, videos, files, and custom attachment types. Figure 5-29 shows the resulting message.

```
session => {
    session.send({
        text: 'hello',
        attachments: [{
            contentType: 'image/png',
            contentUrl: 'https://upload.wikimedia.org/
            wikipedia/commons/b/ba/New_York-Style_Pizza.png',
            name: 'image'
        }]
    });
}
```

Figure 5-29. *Sending an image*

We also can send a hero card. *Hero cards* are stand-alone containers that include an image, title, subtitle, and text plus an optional list of buttons. Figure 5-30 shows the resulting exchange.

```
let msg = new builder.Message(session);
msg.text = 'Pizzas!';
msg.attachmentLayout(builder.AttachmentLayout.carousel);
msg.attachments([
    new builder.HeroCard(session)
        .title('New York Style Pizza')
        .subtitle('the best')
        .text("Really, the best pizza in the world.")
        .images([builder.CardImage.create(session, 'https://
        upload.wikimedia.org/wikipedia/commons/b/ba/New_York-
        Style_Pizza.png')])
        .buttons([
```

```
                builder.CardAction.imBack(session, "I love New York
                Style Pizza!", "LOVE THIS")
            ]),
        new builder.HeroCard(session)
            .title('Chicago Style Pizza')
            .subtitle('not bad')
            .text("some people don't believe this is pizza.")
            .images([builder.CardImage.create(session, 'https://
            upload.wikimedia.org/wikipedia/commons/3/33/
            Ginoseastdeepdish.jpg')])
            .buttons([
                builder.CardAction.imBack(session, "I love Chicago
                Style Pizza!", "LOVE THIS")
            ]),
    ]);

session.send(msg);
```

Figure 5-30. *A sample pizza carousel*

217

This example introduces some new concepts. The hero card is just one type of card that the Bot Builder SDK supports. The following are other supported cards:

- *Adaptive card*: A flexible card with a combination of items including containers, buttons, input fields, speech, text, and images; not supported by all channels. We dive into adaptive cards in Chapter 11.

- *Animation card*: A card that supports animated GIFs or short videos.

- *Audio card*: A card to play audio.

- *Thumbnail card*: Similar to a hero card but with a smaller image size.

- *Receipt card*: Renders a receipt including common line items such as description, tax, totals, etc.

- *Sign in card*: A card to initiate a sign-in flow.

- *Video card*: A card to play videos.

Another interesting point is the attachment layout. By default, attachments are sent in a vertical list. We chose to use the carousel, a scrollable horizontal list, to provide a better experience for the user.

The buttons in this code use the IM Back action. This sends the button's value field ("I love New York Style Pizza!" or "I love Chicago Style Pizza!") as a text message to the bot when the LOVE THIS buttons are clicked. Other action types are described below. Each messaging platform has different levels of support for these types.

- *postBack*: Same as IM back, but the user doesn't see the message.

- *openUrl*: Opens a URL in a browser. This can be the default browser on the desktop or an in-app web view.

- *call*: Calls a phone number.

- *downloadFile*: Downloads a file to the user's device.

- *playAudio*: Plays an audio file.

- *playVideo*: Plays a video file.

- *showImage*: Shows an image in an image viewer.

We can also use the Session object to send speech consent in channels that support both written and spoken responses. We can either build a message object like we did in the carousel hero card sample or use a convenience method on the session. The input hint in the following code snippet tells the user interface whether the bot is expecting a response, accepting input, or not accepting input at all. For developers who have a background in voice assistant skill development, like for Amazon's Alexa, this should be a familiar concept.

```
const bot = new builder.UniversalBot(connector, [
    session => {
        session.say('this is just text that the user will
        see', 'hello', { inputHint: builder.InputHint.
        acceptingInput});
    }
]);
```

Session is also the object that helps us access relevant user conversation data. For example, we can store the last message the user sent to the bot inside the session's *privateConversationData* and utilize it later in the conversation as shown in the following sample (Figure 5-31):

```
session => {
    var lastMsg = session.privateConversationData.last;
    session.privateConversationData.last = session.message.text;
    if(lastMsg) {
```

```
        session.send(lastMsg);
    } else {
        session.send('i am memorizing what you are saying');
    }
}
```

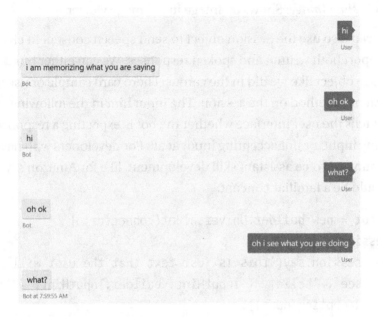

Figure 5-31. *Storing session data between messages*

The Bot Builder SDK makes it easy to store three types of data in the session object.

- *privateConversationData*: Private user data scoped to a conversation

- *conversationData*: Data for a conversation, shared between all users who are part of the conversation

- *userData*: Data for a user across all conversations on one channel

By default, these objects are all stored in memory, but we can easily provide an alternate storage service implementation. We will see an example in Chapter 6.

Waterfalls and Prompts

A *waterfall* is a sequence of functions that process incoming messages on a bot. The Universal Bot constructor takes an array of functions as a parameter. This is the waterfall. The Bot Builder SDK calls each function in succession, passing the result of the previous step into the current step. The most common use of this approach is to query the user for more information using a prompt. In the following code, we use a text prompt, but the Bot Builder SDK supports inputs such as numbers, dates, or multiple choice (Figure 5-32).

```
const bot = new builder.UniversalBot(connector, [
    session => {
        session.send('echo 1: ' + session.message.text);
        builder.Prompts.text(session, 'enter for another echo!');
    },
    (session, results) => {
        session.send('echo 2: ' + results.response);
    }
]);
```

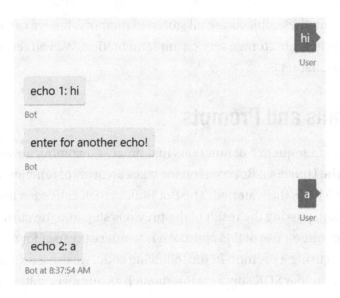

Figure 5-32. *Basic waterfall sample*

We can also advance the waterfall manually, using the next function, in which case the bot would not wait for additional input (Figure 5-33). This is useful in cases where the first step may conditionally ask for additional input. We will use this in our calendar bot code.

```
const bot = new builder.UniversalBot(connector, [
    (session, args, next) => {
        session.send('echo 1: ' + session.message.text);
        next({response: 'again!'});
    },
    (session, results, next) => {
        session.send('echo 2: ' + results.response);
    }
]);
```

Figure 5-33. Programmatic waterfall progression

The following is an even more complex data-gathering waterfall:

```
const bot = new builder.UniversalBot(connector, [
    session => {
        builder.Prompts.choice(session, "What do you want to
        do?", "add appointment|delete appointment", builder.
        ListStyle.button);
    },
    (session, results) => {
        session.privateConversationData.action = { type:
        results.response.index };
        builder.Prompts.time(session, "when?");
    },
    (session, results, next) => {
        session.privateConversationData.action.datetime =
        results.response.resolution.start;
        if (session.privateConversationData.action.type == 0) {
            builder.Prompts.text(session, "where?");
        } else {
            next({ response: null });
        }
    },
```

```
(session, results, next) => {
    session.privateConversationData.action.location =
    results.response;

    let summary = null;
    const dt = moment(session.privateConversationData.
    action.datetime).format('M/D/YYYY h:mm:ss a');

    if (session.privateConversationData.action.type ==  0) {
        summary = 'Add Appointment ' + dt + ' at location '
        + session.privateConversationData.action.location;
    } else {
        summary  = 'Delete appointment  ' + dt;
    }

    const action = session.privateConversationData.action;
    // do something with action
    session.endConversation(summary);
    }
]);
```

In this sample, we use a couple more types of prompts: Choice and Time. The Choice prompt asks the user to select an option. The prompt can render the choice using inline text (relevant in SMS scenarios for example) or buttons. The Time prompt uses the *chronos* Node.js library to parse a string representation of a datetime into a datetime object. An input like "tomorrow at 5pm" can resolve to a value that a computer can use.

Note that we use logic to skip certain waterfall steps. Specifically, if we are in the delete appointment branch, we do not need the event location. As such, we do not even ask for it. We take advantage of the *privateConversationData* object to the store action object, which represents the operation we will want to invoke against an API. Lastly, we use the *session.endConversation* method to finalize the conversation. This method will clear the user's state so that the next time the user interacts with the bot, it is as if the bot is seeing a new user.

Figure 5-34 shows the resulting conversation.

Figure 5-34. *Data gathering waterfall*

Dialogs

Let's bring this full circle with conversational design. In Chapter 4, we discussed how we can model a conversation using a graph of nodes we called *dialogs*. So far in this chapter, we have learned about waterfalls and how we can model a conversation in code.

We have also learned how we can utilize prompts to gather data from the user. Recall that prompts are simple mechanisms to collect data from users.

```
builder.Prompts.text(session, "where?");
```

Prompts are interesting. We call a function (*builder. Prompts.text*),
yielding the conversation to the prompt. Once a valid response is sent
by the user, the next step in our waterfall can access the prompt's result.
Figure 5-35 shows the overall process. From our waterfall's perspective, we
don't really know what the *Prompts.choice* call is doing, nor do we care. It is
listening for user input, doing some validation, reprompting on bad input,
and returning only a valid result, unless the user cancels. All that logic is
hidden from us.

Figure 5-35. *Conceptual transfer of control between dialogs*

This interaction is the same model as a programming function call.
The way a function call is typically implemented is using a stack. Examine
Figure 5-36 and the following code:

```
function f(a,b) { return a + b; }
```

When the function f is called, the function's arguments are pushed on
the top of the stack. The function's code then processes the stack. In this
example, the function adds the parameters. At the end, the only value left
at the top of the stack is the function's return value. The calling function
can then do whatever it wants with the return value.

Figure 5-36. Function calls on a stack

This is the way prompts work in a conversation. The generic concept in the Bot Builder SDK is a dialog. A prompt is a type of dialog. A dialog is nothing more than an encapsulation of conversation logic and is analogous to a function call. A dialog is initialized with some parameters. It receives input from the user, executing its own code or calling into other dialogs along the way, and can send responses back to the user. Once the dialog's purpose is accomplished, it returns a value to the calling dialog. In short, a calling dialog pushes a child dialog to the top of the stack. When the child dialog is done, it pops itself from the stack.

Let's go back to our Choice prompt example. In the dialog stack model, the Root dialog places the *Prompt.Choice* dialog on the top of the stack. After the dialog finishes executing, the resulting user input object is passed back down to the Root dialog. The Root dialog then does whatever it needs to do with the resulting object. The behavior over time is captured in Figure 5-37.

Figure 5-37. Dialogs on the dialog stack over time

We could take this concept even further. We could imagine a flow in our calendar bot in which adding a new calendar entry invokes a new dialog. Let's call it *AddCalendarEntry*. It then invokes a *Prompt.Time* dialog to gather the date and time of the event, and it invokes a *Prompt. Text* dialog to gather the event's subject. The *AddCalendarEntry* packages the collected data and creates a new calendar entry by calling some calendar API. Control is then returned to the Root dialog. We illustrate this in Figure 5-32. We could even have *AddCalendarEntry* call another dialog that encapsulates the logic to call the API if there was enough complexity in that process and we wanted to reuse the logic from other dialogs (Figure 5-38).

Figure 5-38. *A more complex dialog stack, illustrated over time*

Waterfalls and dialogs are the workhorses that translate a conversation design into actual working code. There are, of course, more details around them, and we'll get into those during the next chapters, but this is the magic behind the Bot Builder SDK. Its key value is an engine that can drive a conversation using the dialog abstractions. At each point during the conversation, the dialog stack and the supporting user and conversation data are stored. This means that depending on the conversation's storage implementation, the user may stop talking to the bot for days, come back, and the bot can pick up from where the user left off.

How do we apply some of these concepts? Revisiting the add and remove appointment waterfall sample, we can create a bot that, based on a Choice prompt, starts one of two dialogs: one to add a calendar entry or another to remove it. The dialogs have all the necessary logic to figure out which appointment to add or remove, resolve conflicts, prompt for user confirmation, and so forth.

```
const bot = new builder.UniversalBot(connector, [
    session => {
        builder.Prompts.choice(session, "What do you want to
        do?", "add appointment|delete appointment", builder.
        ListStyle.button);
    },
    (session, results) => {
        if (results.response.index == 0) {
            session.beginDialog('AddCalendarEntry');
        } else if (results.response.index == 1) {
            session.beginDialog('RemoveCalendarEntry');
        }
    },
    (session, results) => {
        session.send('excellent! we are done!');
    }
]);

bot.dialog('AddCalendarEntry', [
    (session, args) => {
        builder.Prompts.time(session, 'When should the
        appointment be added?');
    },
    (session, results) => {
        session.dialogData.time = results.response.resolution.
        start;
        builder.Prompts.text(session, 'What is the meeting
        subject?');
    },
    (session, results) => {
        session.dialogData.subject = results.response;
        builder.Prompts.text(session, 'Where should the meeting
        take place?');
```

```
    },
    (session, results) => {
        session.dialogData.location = results.response;

        // TODO: take the data and call an API to add the
        calendar entry

        session.endDialog('Your appointment has been added!');
    }]);
bot.dialog('RemoveCalendarEntry', [
    (session, args) => {
        builder.Prompts.time(session, 'Which time do you want
        to clear?');
    },
    (session, results) => {
        var time = results.response.resolution.start;
        // TODO: find the relevant appointment, resolve
        conflicts, confirm prompt, and delete
        session.endDialog('Your appointment has been
        removed!');
    }]);
```

We start a new dialog by calling the *session.beginDialog* method and
pass in the dialog name. We may also pass an optional argument object,
which would be accessible via the *args* parameter in the called dialog.
We use the *session.dialogData* object to store dialog state. We've run into
userData, privateConversationData, and *conversationData* before. Those
are scoped to the entire conversation. *DialogData,* however, is scoped
only to the lifetime of the current dialog instance. To end a dialog, we
call *session.endDialog.* This returns control to the next step in the root
waterfall. There is a method called session.endDialogWithResult that
allows us to pass data back to the calling dialog.

The conversation in Messenger ends up looking like Figure 5-39.

Figure 5-39. *A demonstration of an AddCalendarEntry dialog implementation*

This code has a few shortcomings. First, if we want to cancel either adding or deleting an appointment, there's no way to do that. Second, if we are the middle of adding an appointment and decide we want to delete an appointment, we cannot easily switch to the remove appointment dialog. We must finish the current dialog and then switch over. Third, but not essential, it would be nice to connect the bot to our LUIS model so users can interact with the bot using natural language. We'll address the first two points next and then follow with connecting to our LUIS models to really build some intelligence into the bot.

Invoking Dialogs

Let's continue with the following exercise. Say we want to allow the user to ask for help at any point in the conversation; this is a typical scenario. Sometimes the help will be contextual to the dialog. At other times, the help will be a global action, a bot behavior that can be accessed from anywhere within the conversation. The Bot Builder SDK allows us to insert both types of behaviors into our dialogs.

We introduce a simple help dialog.

```
bot.dialog('help', (session, args, next) => {
    session.endDialog("Hi, I am a calendar concierge bot. I can
    help you make and cancel appointments!");
})
.triggerAction({
    matches: /^help$/i
});
```

This code defines a new dialog with a global action handler that matches the "help" input. *TriggerAction* defines a global action. We are saying that the help dialog will be triggered globally whenever the user's input matches the regular expression ^help$. The ^ character denotes the start of a line, and the $ character denotes the end of a line. A problem arises, though. As we can see in Figure 5-40, it looks as if when we ask for help, our bot forgets we were in the add appointment dialog. In fact, the default behavior for global action matching is to replace the dialog on top of the stack. In other words, the add appointment dialog was removed and replaced with the help dialog.

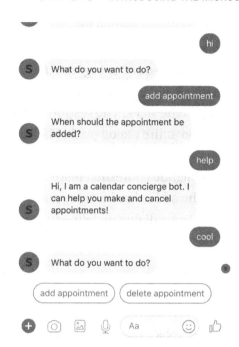

Figure 5-40. *Help cancels the previous dialog. Not good.*

We can override this behavior by implementing the *onSelectAction* callback.

```
bot.dialog('help', (session, args, next) => {
    session.endDialog("Hi, I am a calendar concierge bot. I can
    help you make and cancel appointments!");
})
.triggerAction({
    matches: /^help$/i,
    onSelectAction: (session, args, next) => {
        session.beginDialog(args.action, args);
    }
});
```

This brings up an interesting question: how can we affect the dialog stack? When we are working on a dialog flow and want to transition control over to another dialog, we can use either *beginDialog* or *replaceDialog*. replaceDialog replaces the dialog on top of the stack, and beginDialog pushes a dialog to the top of the stack. The session also has a method called *reset*, which resets the entire dialog stack. The default behavior is to reset the stack and push the new dialog on top.

What if we wanted to include contextual help? Let's create a new dialog to handle help for the add calendar entry dialog. We can use the *beginDialogAction* method on a dialog to define triggers that start new dialogs on top of the *AddCalendarEntry* dialog.

```
bot.dialog('AddCalendarEntry', [

    ...

])
    .beginDialogAction('AddCalendarEntryHelp',
    'AddCalendarEntryHelp', { matches: /^help$/ });
bot.dialog('AddCalendarEntryHelp', (session, args, next) => {
    let msg = "Add Calendar Entry Help: we need the time of
    the meeting, the subject and the location to create a new
    appointment for you.";
    session.endDialog(msg);
});
```

When we run this, we get the desired effect, as shown in Figure 5-41.

Figure 5-41. *Properly handling contextual actions*

We will dive deeper into actions and their behavior in the following chapter.

Recognizers

Recall we defined that the help dialog will be triggered via a regular expression. How does the Bot Builder SDK implement this? This is where recognizers come in. A recognizer is a piece of code that accepts incoming messages and determines what the user's intent was. A recognizer returns an intent name and a score. The intent and score can come from an NLU service like LUIS, but they do not have to.

By default, as seen in the previous examples, the only recognizer in our bot is a regular expression or plain-text matcher. It takes in a regular expression or a hard-coded string and matches it to the incoming message's text. We could utilize an explicit version of this recognizer by adding a *RegExpRecognizer* to our bot's list of recognizers. The following implementation states that if the user's input matches the provided regular expression, an intent called *HelpIntent* is resolved with a score of 1.0. Otherwise, the score is 0.0.

```
bot.recognizer(new builder.RegExpRecognizer('HelpIntent',
/^help$/i));

bot.dialog('help', (session, args, next) => {
    session.endDialog("Hi, I am a calendar concierge bot. I can
    help you make and cancel appointments!");
})
    .triggerAction({
        matches: 'HelpIntent',
        onSelectAction: (session, args, next) => {
            session.beginDialog(args.action, args);
        }
    });
```

Another thing that the recognizer model allows us to do is to create a custom recognizer that executes any code we want and resolves an intent with a score. Here's an example:

```
bot.recognizer({
    recognize: (context, done) => {
        var intent = { score: 0.0 };

        if (context.message.text) {
            if (context.message.text.toLowerCase().
            startsWith('help')) intent = { score: 1.0, intent:
            'HelpIntent' };
```

```
        }
        done(null, intent);
    }
});
```

Now this is quite a simple example, but our minds should be racing with the possibilities. For example, if the user's input is nontext media such as an image or video, we can write a custom recognizer that validates the media and responds accordingly.

The Bot Builder SDK allows us to register multiple recognizers to our bot. Whenever a message comes into the bot, each recognizer is invoked, and the recognizer with the highest score is deemed the winner. If two or more recognizers result in the same score, the recognizer that was registered first wins.

Lastly, this same mechanism can be used to connect our bot to LUIS, and in fact the Bot Builder SDK includes a recognizer for this very case. To do this, we take the endpoint URL for our LUIS application (perhaps the one we created in Chapter 3) and use it as a parameter to the *LuisRecognizer*.

```
bot.recognizer(new builder.LuisRecognizer('https://westus.api.
cognitive.microsoft.com/luis/v2.0/apps/{APP_ID}?subscription-
key={SUBSCRIPTION_KEY}}'));
```

Once we set this up, we add a *triggerAction* call for each intent we would like to handle globally, as we did with the help dialog. The strings passed as the "matches" member must correspond to our LUIS intent names.

```
bot.dialog('AddCalendarEntry', [
    ...
])
.beginDialogAction('AddCalendarEntryHelp',
'AddCalendarEntryHelp', { matches: /^help$/ })
```

```
.triggerAction({matches: 'AddCalendarEntry'});

bot.dialog('RemoveCalendarEntry', [
    ...
])
.triggerAction({matches: 'DeleteCalendarEntry'});
```

At this point, our bot conversation can navigate between the dialogs by using LUIS intents (Figure 5-42). LUIS's intent and entity objects are passed into the dialogs.

Figure 5-42. *Finally powered by our LUIS models!*

EXERCISE 5-2

Connecting Your Bot to LUIS

In this task you will connect a bot to the LUIS application you created in Chapter 3.

1. Create an empty bot and create a dialog to handle each type of intent created in Chapter 3. For each dialog, simply send a message with the dialog name.

2. Register the LUIS recognizer with your bot and confirm that it works.

3. The first method of every dialog waterfall is passed the session object and an args object. Use a debugger to explore the objects.[5] What is the structure of data from LUIS? Alternatively, send the JSON string representing the args object to the user.

Recognizers are a powerful feature in the Bot Builder SDK, allowing us to equip our bots with a variety of behaviors based on incoming messages.

Building a Simple Calendar Bot

Ideally the patterns around how we structure a conversation are becoming clear. The git repos provided with the book include a Calendar Concierge Bot that we build on throughout the remaining chapters in the book. Every chapter that makes changes to the bot has its own folder in the repo. The Chapter 5 folder includes the skeleton code that integrates with LUIS and sends back a message saying what the bot understood. Auth and API integration will be covered in Chapter 7. We add basic multilanguage support in Chapter 10, human handover in Chapter 12, and analytics integration in Chapter 13.

These are some of the questions that we intend to answer with the Chapter 5:

- In the context of Node, how do we structure a bot and its component dialogs?

- What is the general pattern of the code that interprets the data passed into dialogs?

---

[5]Debugging Node.js applications: `https://nodejs.org/en/docs/guides/debugging-getting-started/`. A rich IDE like VS Code makes it really easy: `https://code.visualstudio.com/docs/nodejs/nodejs-debugging`

- Although it is possible to create end-to-end tests with the Bot Builder SDK, in its current form, unit testing dialog logic is not the most straightforward task. How do we structure our code so that it can be unit tested as best as possible?

As we dive into the code and examine the different components, keep the following in mind:

- As the code is being built and tested, we will find that there are gaps in our LUIS applications. During the construction of this code, my model has changed a bit from what was produced in Chapter 3. These are not breaking changes but rather new utterances and entities. The code samples include this version of the model.

- We need to define the scope of each dialog. For example, the edit calendar entry dialog was repurposed to focus on moving appointments.

- We have created some helper classes that contain some of the trickiest logic, which is reading each type of entity from the LUIS results and translating them to objects that can be used in the dialogs. For example, many of our dialogs perform actions on the calendar based on datetimes or ranges and subject or invitee.

We take advantage of Bot Builder libraries to properly modularize the dialogs into libraries. Don't worry about this for now. It is simply a way to bundle dialog functionality. We will go over this concept in the next chapter. Start reviewing the code, and we'll dive into more Bot Builder details in the following chapter. The code is structured as follows:

- Constants and helpers

- Code that translates LUIS intents and entities into application objects

- Dialogs to support adding, moving, and removing an appointment; checking availability; and getting an agenda for the day

- Lastly, an app.js entry point that ties it all together

Conclusion

This was quite an introduction into the Bot Framework and Bot Builder SDK. We are now equipped to build basic bot experiences. The core concepts of creating bot channel registrations, connecting our bots to channel connectors, debugging using the Bot Framework Emulator and ngrok, and building bots using the Bot Builder SDK are the key pieces we need to understand to be productive. The Bot Builder SDK is a powerful library to assist us in the process. We introduced the core concepts from the SDK. Without getting too deep into the details of the SDK, we developed a chat bot that can interpret a large variety of natural language inputs that execute the use cases we aimed to support from Chapter 3. The only thing left to do is to pull in a calendar API and translate the LUIS intent and entity combinations into the right API calls.

Before we jump into this, we will dive deeper into the Bot Builder SDK to make sure we are selecting the correct approach in our final implementation.

CHAPTER 6

Diving into the Bot Builder SDK

In the previous chapter, we built a simple bot that can utilize an existing LUIS application and the Bot Builder SDK to enable a conversational flow for a calendar bot. As it stands, the bot is useless. It responds with text describing what it understood from user input, but it does not accomplish anything of substance. We're building up to connecting our bot to the Google Calendar API, but in the meantime, we need to figure out what tools the Bot Builder SDK provides at our disposal to create meaningful conversational experiences.

In this chapter, we will elaborate on some of the techniques we used in our Chapter 5 code and more thoroughly explore some of the Bot Builder SDK features. We will figure out how the SDK stores state, builds messages with rich content, builds actions and cards, and allows the framework to customize channel behavior, dialog behavior, and user action handling. Lastly, we will look at how we best group bot functionality into reusable components.

Conversation State

As mentioned throughout the previous chapters, a good conversational engine will store each user and conversation's state so that whenever a user communicates with the bot, the right state of the conversation flow is retrieved, and there is a coherent experience for the user. In the Bot Builder SDK, this state is, by default, stored in memory via the aptly named MemoryBotStorage. Historically, state was stored in a cloud endpoint; however, this has been deprecated. Every so often, we may run into a reference to the state service in some older documentation, so be aware that it no longer exists.

The state for every conversation is composed of three buckets accessible to bot developers. We introduced all of them in the previous chapter, but to reiterate they are as follows:

- *userData*: Data for a user across all conversations in a channel

- *privateConversationData*: Private user data scoped to a conversation

- *conversationData*: Data for a conversation, shared for any users who are part of the conversation

In addition, as a dialog is executing, we have access to its state object referred to as *dialogData*. Any time a message is received from a user, the Bot Builder SDK will retrieve the user's state from the state storage, populate the three data objects plus dialogData on the session object, and execute the logic for the current step in the conversation. Once all responses are sent out, the framework will save the state back into the state storage.

```
let entry = new et.EntityTranslator(session.dialogData.
addEntry);

if (!entry.hasDateTime) {
    entry.setEntity(results.response);
}

session.dialogData.addEntry = entry;
```

In some of the code from the previous chapter, there were instances where we had to re-create a custom object from dialogData and then store the object into the dialogData. The reason for this is that saving an object into the dialogData (or any of the other state containers) will turn the object into a vanilla JavaScript object, like using JSON.stringify would. Trying to invoke any method on session.dialogData.addEntry in the previous code, before resetting to a new object, would cause an error.

The storage mechanism is implemented by an interface called IBotStorage.

```
export interface IBotStorage {
    getData(context: IBotStorageContext, callback: (err: Error,
    data: IBotStorageData) => void): void;
    saveData(context: IBotStorageContext, data:
    IBotStorageData, callback?: (err: Error) => void): void;
}
```

The ChatConnector class that we instantiate when building a new instance of a bot installs the default MemoryBotStorage instance, which is a great option for development. The SDK allows us to provide our own implementation to replace the default functionality, something you will most likely want to do in a production deployment as this ensures that states are stored instead of being erased any time your instances restarts. For instance, Microsoft provides two additional implementations of the interface, a NoSQL implementation for Azure Cosmos DB[1] and an implementation for Azure Table Storage.[2] Both are Azure services available through the Azure Portal. You can find the two storage implementations in the botbuilder-azure node package, documented at https://github.com/Microsoft/BotBuilder-Azure. You are also able to write your own IBotStorage implementation and

---

[1]Azure Cosmos DB: https://azure.microsoft.com/en-us/services/cosmos-db/
[2]Azure Table Storage: https://azure.microsoft.com/en-us/services/storage/tables/

to register it with the SDK. Writing your own implementation is a matter of following the simple IBotStorage interface.

```
const bot = new builder.UniversalBot(connector, (session) => {
    // ... Bot code ...
})
.set('storage', storageImplementation);
```

Messages

In the previous chapter, our bot communicated to the user by sending text messages using either the session.send or session.endDialog method. This is fine, but it limits our bot a fair amount. A message between a bot and a user is composed of a variety of pieces of data that we ran into in the "Bot Builder SDK Basics" section in the previous chapter.

The Bot Builder IMessage interface defines what a message is really composed of.

```
interface IEvent {
    type: string;
    address: IAddress;
    agent?: string;
    source?: string;
    sourceEvent?: any;
    user?: IIdentity;
}

interface IMessage extends IEvent {
    timestamp?: string;           // UTC Time when message
                                  was sent (set by service)
    localTimestamp?: string;      // Local time when message
                                  was sent (set by client
                                  or bot, Ex: 2016-09-
                                  23T13:07:49.4714686-07:00)
```

```
summary?: string;                        // Text to be displayed by
                                         as fall-back and as short
                                         description of the message
                                         content in e.g. list of
                                         recent conversations
text?: string;                           // Message text
speak?: string;                          // Spoken message as
                                         Speech Synthesis Markup
                                         Language (SSML)
textLocale?: string;                     // Identified language of
                                         the message text.
attachments?: IAttachment[];             // This is placeholder
                                         for structured objects
                                         attached to this message
suggestedActions: ISuggestedActions; // Quick reply actions
                                         that can be suggested
                                         as part of the message
entities?: any[];                        // This property is
                                         intended to keep
                                         structured data objects
                                         intended for Client
                                         application e.g.:
                                         Contacts, Reservation,
                                         Booking, Tickets.
                                         Structure of these object
                                         objects should be known to
                                         Client application.
textFormat?: string;                     // Format of text fields
                                         [plain|markdown|xml]
                                         default:markdown
```

```
    attachmentLayout?: string;          // AttachmentLayout -
                                        hint for how to deal with
                                        multiple attachments
                                        Values: [list|carousel]
                                        default:list
    inputHint?: string;                 // Hint for clients to
                                        indicate if the bot is
                                        waiting for input or not.
    value?: any;                        // Open-ended value.
    name?: string;                      // Name of the operation
                                        to invoke or the name of
                                        the event.
    relatesTo?: IAddress;               // Reference to another
                                        conversation or message.
    code?: string;                      // Code indicating why the
                                        conversation has ended.
}
```

For this chapter, we will be most interested in the text, attachments, suggestedActions, and attachmentLayout as they form the basis of a good conversational UX.

To create a message object in code, we create a builder.Message object. At that point, you can assign the properties as per the following example. A message can then be passed into the session.send method.

```
const reply = new builder.Message(session)
    .text('Here are some results for you')
    .attachmentLayout(builder.AttachmentLayout.carousel)
    .attachments(cards);

session.send(reply);
```

Likewise, when a message comes into your bot, the session object contains a message object. Same interface. Same type of data. But, this time, it is coming in from the channel rather than from the bot.

```
const bot = new builder.UniversalBot(connector, [
    (session) => {
        const input = session.message.text;
    }]);
```

Note that IMessage inherits from IEvent, which means it has a type field. This field is set to message for an IMessage, but there are other events that may come from either the framework or a custom app.

Some of the other event types that the bot framework supports, based on channel support, are the following:

- *conversationUpdate*: Raised when a user has been added or removed from a conversation or some metadata about the conversation has changed; used for group chat management.

- *contactRelationUpdate*: Raised when the bot was either added or removed from a user's contact list.

- *typing*: Raised when a user is typing a message; not supported by all channels.

- *ping*: Raised to figure out if the bot endpoint is available.

- *deleteUserData*: Raised when the user requests to have their user data deleted.

- *endOfConversation*: Raised when a conversation has ended.

- *invoke*: Raised when a request is sent for the bot to perform some custom logic. For example, some channels may need to invoke a function on the bot and expect a response. The Bot Framework would send this request as an invoke request, expecting a synchronous HTTP reply. This is not a common scenario.

We can register a handler for each event type by using the *on* method on the UniversalBot. The resulting conversation with a bot that handles events can provide for more immersive conversational experiences for your users (Figure 6-1).

```
const bot = new builder.UniversalBot(connector, [
    (session) => {
    }
]);

bot.on('conversationUpdate', (data) => {
    if (data.membersAdded && data.membersAdded.length > 0) {
        if (data.address.bot.id === data.membersAdded[0].id)
        return;
        const name = data.membersAdded[0].name;
        const msg = new builder.Message().address(data.
        address);
        msg.text('Welcome to the conversation ' + name + '!');
        msg.textLocale('en-US');
        bot.send(msg);
    }
});

bot.on('typing', (data) => {
    const msg = new builder.Message().address(data.address);
```

```
msg.text('I see you typing... You\'ve got me hooked! Reel
me in!');
msg.textLocale('en-US');
bot.send(msg);
});
```

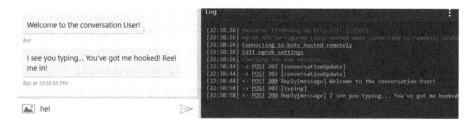

Figure 6-1. *A bot responding to typing and conversationUpdate*
events

Addresses and Proactive Messages

In the message interface, the address property uniquely represents a user
in a conversation. It looks like this:

```
interface IAddress {
    channelId: string;          // Unique identifier for
                                // channel
    user: IIdentity;            // User that sent or should
                                // receive the message
    bot?: IIdentity;            // Bot that either received
                                // or is sending the message
    conversation?: IIdentity;   // Represents the current
                                // conversation and tracks
                                // where replies should be
                                // routed to.
}
```

The importance behind an address is that we can use it to send a message proactively outside the scope of a dialog. For example, we could create a process that sends a message to a random address every five seconds. This message has zero effect on the user's dialog stack.

```
const addresses = {};

const bot = new builder.UniversalBot(connector, [
    (session) => {
        const userid = session.message.address.user.id;
        addresses[userid] = session.message.address;
        session.send('Give me a couple of seconds');
    }
]);

function getRandomInt(min, max) {
    return Math.floor(Math.random() * (max - min + 1)) + min;
}

setInterval(() => {
    const keys = Object.keys(addresses);
    if (keys.length == 0) return;
    const r = getRandomInt(0, keys.length-1);
    const addr = addresses[keys[r]];
    const msg = new builder.Message().address(addr).text('hello
from outside dialog stack!');
    bot.send(msg);
}, 5000);
```

If we did want to modify the dialog stack, perhaps by calling into a complex dialog operation, we can utilize the beginDialog method on the UniversalBot object.

```
setInterval(() => {
    var keys = Object.keys(addresses);
    if (keys.length == 0) return;
    var r = getRandomInt(0, keys.length-1);
    var addr = addresses[keys[r]];

    bot.beginDialog(addr, "dialogname", { arg: true});
}, 5000);
```

The significance of these concepts that we can have external events in disparate systems begin affecting the state of a user's conversation within the bot. We will see this applied in the context of OAuth web hooks in the next chapter.

Rich Content

Rich content can be sent to the user using the attachments functionality in the BotBuilder IMessage interface. In the Bot Builder SDK, an attachment is simply a name, content URL, and a MIME type.[3] A message in the Bot Builder SDK accepts zero or more attachments. It is up to the bot connectors to translate that message into something that the channel will understand. All types of messages and attachments are not supported by every channel. Be careful when creating attachments of various MIME types.

For example, to share an image, we can use the following code:

```
const bot = new builder.UniversalBot(connector, [
    (session) => {
        session.send({
            text: "Here, have an apple.",
            attachments: [
```

---

[3]MIME Types: https://developer.mozilla.org/en-US/docs/Web/HTTP/ Basics_of_HTTP/MIME_types

```
            {
                contentType: 'image/jpeg',
                contentUrl: 'https://upload.wikimedia.org/
                wikipedia/commons/thumb/1/15/Red_Apple.
                jpg/1200px-Red_Apple.jpg',
                name: 'Apple'
            }
        ]
    })
  }
]);
```

Figure 6-2 shows the resulting user interface in the emulator, and Figure 6-3 shows it in Facebook Messenger. We could imagine similar rendering in other platforms.

Figure 6-2. *Emulator image attachment*

Figure 6-3. *Facebook Messenger image attachment*

This code will send audio file attachments, which can be played right from within the messaging channel.

```
const bot = new builder.UniversalBot(connector, [
    (session) => {
        session.send({
            text: "Here, have some sound!",
            attachments: [
                {
                    contentType: 'audio/ogg',
                    contentUrl: 'https://upload.wikimedia.
                    org/wikipedia/en/f/f4/Free_as_a_
                    Bird_%28Beatles_song_-_sample%29.ogg',
                    name: 'Free as a bird'
                }
            ]
        })
    }
]);
```

Figure 6-4 shows the emulator, and Figure 6-5 shows Facebook Messenger ().

Figure 6-4. *An OGG sound file attachment in the Emulator*

Figure 6-5. *An OGG sound file attachment in Facebook Messenger*

Whoops! It seems like OGG[4] files are not supported. This is a good example of Bot Framework behavior when our bot sends an invalid message to Facebook or any other channel. We will investigate this further in the "Channel Errors" section later in this chapter. My console error log has this message:

```
Error: Request to 'https://facebook.botframework.com/v3/
conversations/1912213132125901-1946375382318514/activities/
mid.%24cAAbqN9VFI95k_ueUOVezaJiLWZXe' failed: [400] Bad Request
```

If we look at the error list in the Bot Framework Messenger Channels page, we should find another clue like in Figure 6-6.

---

[4]OGG Format, a free, open container format: https://en.wikipedia.org/wiki/Ogg

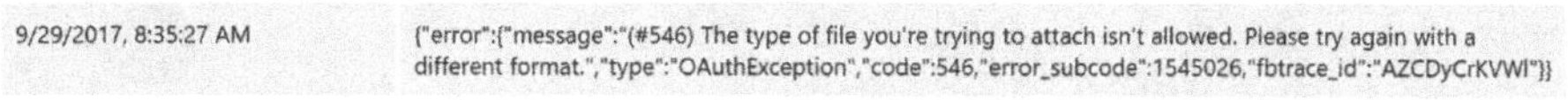

9/29/2017, 8:35:27 AM
{"error":{"message":"(#546) The type of file you're trying to attach isn't allowed. Please try again with a different format.","type":"OAuthException","code":546,"error_subcode":1545026,"fbtrace_id":"AZCDyCrKVWl"}}

Figure 6-6. *Bot Framework error for an OGG sound file on Messenger*

OK, so they make it somewhat easy to diagnose the problem. We know we must provide a different file format. Let's try an MP3.

```
const bot = new builder.UniversalBot(connector, [
    (session) => {
        session.send({
            text: "Ok have a vulture instead!",
            attachments: [
                {
                    contentType: 'audio/mp3',
                    contentUrl: 'http://static1.grsites.com/
                    archive/sounds/birds/birds004.mp3',
                    name: 'Vulture'
                }
            ]
        })
    }
]);
```

You can see the resulting Emulator and Facebook Messenger renderings in Figure 6-7 and Figure 6-8.

hi
User
Ok have a vulture instead!
Vulture
Bot at 8:46:15 AM

Figure 6-7. *Emulator MP3 file attachment*

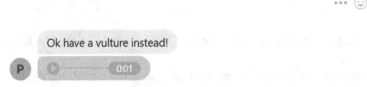

Figure 6-8. *Facebook Messenger MP3 file attachment*

The Emulator still produces a link, but Messenger has a built-in audio player you can utilize! The experience uploading a video is similar. Messenger will provide a built-in video player right within the conversation.

EXERCISE 6-1

Experimenting with Attachments

The goal of this exercise is to write a simple bot that can send different types of attachments to users and observe the behavior of the emulator and another channel, like Facebook Messenger.

1. Create a basic bot using the echo bot as a starting point.

2. From the bot function, send different types of attachments in your message such as JSON, XML, or file. Experiment with some types of rich media such as video. How does the emulator render these types of attachments? How about Messenger?

3. Try sending an image to the bot from the emulator. What data does the incoming message contain? Is this any different from when you send an image via Messenger?

Attachments are an easy way to share all kinds of rich content with your users. Use them wisely to create colorful and engaging conversational experiences.

Buttons

Bots can also send buttons to users. A button is a distinct call to action for a user to perform a task. Each button has a label associated with it, as well as a value. A button also has an action type, which will determine what the button does with the value when the button is clicked. The three most common types of actions are open URL, post back, and IM back. Open URL typically opens a web view within the messaging app or a new browser window in a desktop setting. Both post back and IM back send the value of the button as a message to the bot. The difference between the two is that clicking the post back should not display a message from the user in the chat history, whereas the IM back should. Not all channels implement both types of buttons.

```
const bot = new builder.UniversalBot(connector, [
    (session) => {

        const cardActions = [
            builder.CardAction.openUrl(session,
            'http://google.com', "Open Google"),
            builder.CardAction.imBack(session, "Hello!",
            "Im Back"),
            builder.CardAction.postBack(session, "Hello!",
            "Post Back")
        ];
        const card = new builder.HeroCard(session).
        buttons(cardActions);
```

```
        const msg = new builder.Message(session).text("sample
        actions").addAttachment(card);

        session.send(msg);
    }
]);
```

Note that in the previous code we used a CardAction object. A CardAction is an encapsulation of the data we discussed earlier: a type of action, a title, and value. The channel connectors will usually render a CardAction into a button on the individual platforms.

Figure 6-9 shows what running this code looks like in the emulator, and Figure 6-10 shows it in Facebook Messenger. If we click the Open Google button in the emulator, it opens the web page in your default browser. We first click Im Back, and then once we receive the response card, we click Post Back. Note that Im Back sent a message and the message appears in the chat history, whereas the Post Back button sent a message that the bot responds to, but the message does not appear in the chat history.

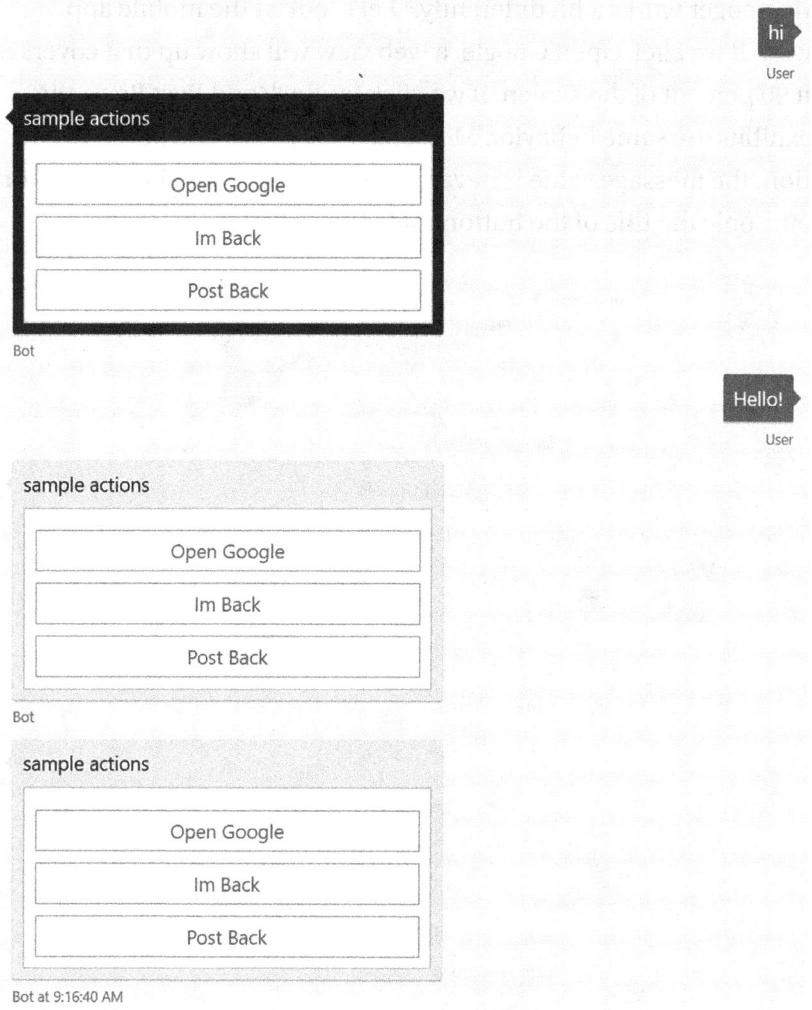

Figure 6-9. *A sampling of Bot Builder button behaviors in the emulator*

Messenger works a bit differently.[5] Let's look at the mobile app behavior. If we click Open Google, a web view will show up that covers about 90 percent of the screen. If we click Im Back and Post Back, the app exhibits the same behavior. Messenger only supports post back; in addition, the message value is never showed to the user. The chat history contains only the title of the button that was clicked.

Figure 6-10. *Sampling of button behaviors in Facebook Messenger*

---

[5]Facebook Messenger SendAPI Button Documentation:https://developers. facebook.com/docs/messenger-platform/send-messages/buttons

The Bot Builder SDK supports the following action types:

- *openUrl*: Opens a URL in a browser

- *imBack*: Sends a message to the bot from the user, which is visible to all conversation participants

- *postBack*: Sends a message to the bot from the user, which may not be visible to all conversation participants

- *call*: Places a call

- *playAudio*: Plays an audio file within the bot interface

- *playVideo*: Plays a video file within the bot interface

- *showImage*: Shows an image within the bot interface

- *downloadFile*: Downloads a file to the device

- *signin*: Kicks off an OAuth flow

Of course, not all channels support all types. In addition, channels may natively support other functionality that the Bot Builder SDK is not. For example, Figure 6-11 shows the documentation for actions Messenger supports through its button templates as of the time of this writing. We will look at utilizing native channel functionality later in this chapter.

- URL Button. Can be used to open a webpage in the in-app browser.
- Postback Button. Sends back developer-defined payload so you can perform an action or reply back.
- Call Button. Dials a phone number when tapped.
- Share Button. Opens a share dialog in Messenger enabling people to share message bubbles with friends.
- Buy Button. Opens a checkout dialog to enables purchases.
- Log In and Log Out buttons. Used in Account Linking flow intended to deliver page-scoped user id on web safely.

Figure 6-11. *Messenger button template types*

In the Bot Builder SDK, every card action can be created by using the static factory methods in the CardAction class. Here is the relevant code from the Bot Builder source:

```
CardAction.call = function (session, number, title) {
    return new CardAction(session).type('call').
    value(number).title(title || "Click to call");
};
CardAction.openUrl = function (session, url, title) {
    return new CardAction(session).type('openUrl').
    value(url).title(title || "Click to open website in
    your browser");
};
CardAction.openApp = function (session, url, title) {
    return new CardAction(session).type('openApp').
    value(url).title(title || "Click to open website in a
    webview");
};
CardAction.imBack = function (session, msg, title) {
    return new CardAction(session).type('imBack').
    value(msg).title(title || "Click to send response to
    bot");
};
CardAction.postBack = function (session, msg, title) {
    return new CardAction(session).type('postBack').
    value(msg).title(title || "Click to send response to
    bot");
};
CardAction.playAudio = function (session, url, title) {
    return new CardAction(session).type('playAudio').
    value(url).title(title || "Click to play audio file");
};
```

```
CardAction.playVideo = function (session, url, title) {
    return new CardAction(session).type('playVideo').
    value(url).title(title || "Click to play video");
};
CardAction.showImage = function (session, url, title) {
    return new CardAction(session).type('showImage').
    value(url).title(title || "Click to view image");
};
CardAction.downloadFile = function (session, url, title) {
    return new CardAction(session).type('downloadFile').
    value(url).title(title || "Click to download file");
};
```

Cards

Another type of Bot Builder attachment is the hero card. In our previous example with button actions, we conveniently ignored the fact that button actions need to be part of a hero card object, but what is that?

The term *hero card* originates from the racing world. The cards themselves are usually bigger than baseball cards and are designed to promote a race team, specifically the driver and sponsors. It would include photos, information about the driver and sponsors, contact information, and so on. But really the concept is reminiscent of typical baseball or Pokémon cards.

In the context of UX design, a card is an organized way of displaying images, text, and actions. Google brought cards to the masses when it introduced the world to its Material Design[6] on Android and the Web. Figure 6-12 shows two examples of card design from Google's Material Design documentation. Notice the distinct usage of images, titles, subtitles, and calls to action.

---

[6]Google Material Design: https://material.io/guidelines/

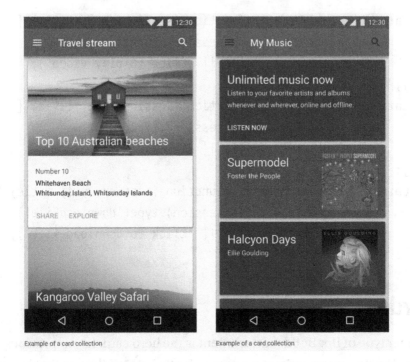

Example of a card collection · Example of a card collection

Figure 6-12. *Google's Material Design card samples*

In the context of bots, the term *hero card* refers to a grouping of an image with text, buttons for actions, and an optional default tap behavior. Different channels will call cards different things. Facebook loosely refers to them as *templates*. Other platforms just refer to the idea as attaching content to a message. At the end of the day, the UX concepts are the same.

In the Bot Builder SDK, we can create a card using the following code. We also show how this card renders in the emulator (Figure 6-13) and on Facebook Messenger (Figure 6-14).

```javascript
const bot = new builder.UniversalBot(connector, [
    (session) => {
        const cardActions = [
            builder.CardAction.openUrl(session, 'http://google.
            com', "Open Google"),
            builder.CardAction.imBack(session, "Hello!",
            "Im Back"),
            builder.CardAction.postBack(session, "Hello!",
            "Post Back")
        ];
        const card = new builder.HeroCard(session)
            .buttons(cardActions)
            .text('this is some text')
            .title('card title')
            .subtitle('card subtitle')
            .images([new builder.CardImage(session).
            url("https://bot-framework.azureedge.net/bot-
            icons-v1/bot-framework-default-7.png").toImage()])
            .tap(builder.CardAction.openUrl(session, "http://
            dev.botframework.com"));

        const msg = new builder.Message(session).text("sample
        actions").addAttachment(card);

        session.send(msg);
    }
]);
```

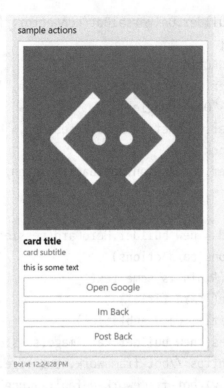

Figure 6-13. *A hero card as rendered by the emulator*

Figure 6-14. *Same hero card in Facebook Messenger*

Cards are a great way to communicate the results of a bot action invoked by the user. If you would like to display some data with an image and follow-up actions, there is no better way to do so than using cards. The fact that you get only a few different text fields, with limited formatting abilities, means that the UX resulting in this approach can be a bit limited. That is by design. For more complex visualizations and scenarios, you can either utilize adaptive cards or render custom graphics. We will explore both topics in Chapter 11.

The next question is, can we display cards side by side in a carousel style? Of course, we can. A message in the Bot Builder SDK has a property called *attachmentLayout*. We set this to carousel, add more cards, and we're done! The emulator (Figure 6-15) and Facebook Messenger (Figure 6-16) take care of laying the cards out in a friendly carousel format. The default attachmentLayout is a list. Using this layout, the cards would appear one below the other. It is not the most user-friendly approach.

269

```
const bot = new builder.UniversalBot(connector, [
    (session) => {
        const cardActions = [
            builder.CardAction.openUrl(session, 'http://google.
            com', "Open Google"),
            builder.CardAction.imBack(session, "Hello!",
            "Im Back"),
            builder.CardAction.postBack(session, "Hello!",
            "Post Back")
        ];

        const msg = new builder.Message(session).text("sample
        actions");

        for(let i=0;i<3;i++) {
            const card = new builder.HeroCard(session)
                .buttons(cardActions)
                .text('this is some text')
                .title('card title')
                .subtitle('card subtitle')
                .images([new builder.CardImage(session).
                url("https://bot-framework.azureedge.net/
                bot-icons-v1/bot-framework-default-7.png").
                toImage()])
                .tap(builder.CardAction.openUrl(session,
                "http://dev.botframework.com"));
            msg.addAttachment(card);
        }

        msg.attachmentLayout(builder.AttachmentLayout.carousel);

        session.send(msg);
    }
]);
```

Figure 6-15. *A hero card carousel in the emulator*

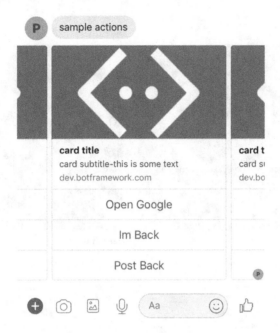

Figure 6-16. *Same hero card carousel on Messenger*

Cards can be a bit tricky because there are many ways of laying out buttons and images. Each platform has ever so slightly different rules. On some platforms, openUrl buttons (but not others) must point to an HTTPS address. There may also be rules that limit the number of buttons per card, number of cards in a carousel and image aspect ratios. Microsoft's Bot Framework will handle all this in the best way it can, but being aware of these limitations will help us debug our bots.

Suggested Actions

We've discussed suggested actions in the context of conversational design; they are message-context-specific actions that can be performed immediately after a message is received. If another message comes in, the context is lost, and the suggested actions disappear. This is in opposition to card actions, which stay on the card in the chat history pretty much forever.

The typical UX for suggested actions, also referred to as *quick replies*, is as a horizontally laid out list of buttons along the bottom of the screen.

The code for building suggested actions is similar to a hero card, except the only data we need is a collection of CardActions. The type of actions allowed in the suggested actions area will depend on the channel. Figure 6-17 and Figure 6-18 shows renderings on the emulator and Facebook Messenger, respectively.

```
msg.suggestedActions(new builder.SuggestedActions(session).
actions([
    builder.CardAction.postBack(session, "Option 1", "Option 1"),
    builder.CardAction.postBack(session, "Option 2", "Option 2"),
    builder.CardAction.postBack(session, "Option 3", "Option 3")
]));
```

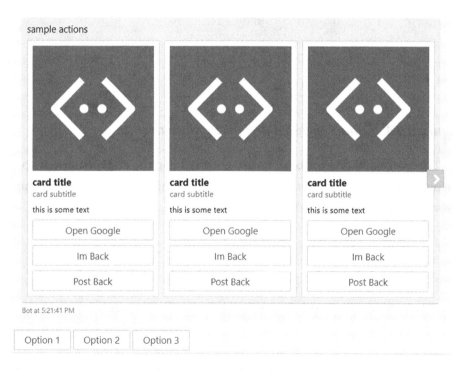

Figure 6-17. *Suggested actions rendered in the emulator*

Figure 6-18. *Same suggested actions in Messenger*

The suggested actions buttons are great to keep the conversation with the user going without asking the user to guess what they can type into the text message field.

EXERCISE 6-2

Cards and Suggested Actions

A dictionary and thesaurus are good inspirations for a good bot navigation experience. A user can input a word. The resulting card may show an image of the word and the definition. A button below may allow us to open a reference page, such as on `https://www.merriam-webster.com/`. The suggested actions could be a set of buttons of synonyms for the current word. Let's put this kind of interaction in place.

1. Create an account with and establish connectivity to `https://dictionaryapi.com`. This API will allow you to use the Dictionary and Thesaurus APIs.

2. Create a bot that can look up a word based on user input using the Dictionary API and responds with a hero card that includes the word and the definition text. Include a button that opens the word's page on the dictionary website.

3. Connect to the Thesaurus API to return the first ten synonyms as suggested actions.

4. As a bonus, use the Bing Image Search API to populate the image in the card. You can get an access key in Azure and use the following sample as a guide: `https://docs.microsoft.com/en-us/azure/cognitive-services/bing-image-search/image-search-sdk-node-quickstart`.

You now have experience connecting your bot to different APIs and translating those API responses into hero cards, buttons, and suggested actions. Well done!

Channel Errors

In the "Rich Content" section, we noted that when a bad request is sent by our bot to the Facebook Messenger connector, our bot will receive an HTTP error. This error was also printed out in the console output of the bot. It seems that the Facebook Bot connector is reporting an error from the Facebook APIs back to our bot. That is cool. The additional feature we saw was that the channel detail page in Azure also contained all those errors. Although minor, this is a powerful feature. It allows us to quickly see how many messages were rejected by the API and the error codes. The case we ran into, that a specific file type format was not supported, was just one of many possible errors. We would see errors if the message is malformed, if there are authentication issues, or if Facebook rejects the connector message for any other reason. Similar ideas apply to the other set of connectors. In general, the connectors are good at translating Bot Framework activities into something that will not be rejected by the channels, but it happens.

In general, if our bot sends a message to a Bot Framework connector and the message does not appear on the interface, chances are there was an issue with the interaction between the connector and channel, and this online error log will contain information about the failure.

Channel Data

We have mentioned several times that different channels may render messages differently or have different rules about certain items, such as the number of hero cards in a carousel or the number of buttons in a hero card. We have been showing examples of Messenger and emulator renderings, as those channels typically work well. Skype is another one that supports a lot of the Bot Builder features (which makes sense, as both are owned by Microsoft). Slack does not have as much rich support for these features, but its editable messages are a slick feature we will visit in Chapter 8.

For illustration purposes, Figure 6-19 is what the carousel with the suggested actions discussed earlier looks like in Slack.

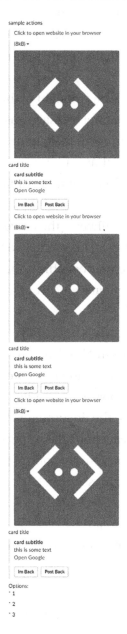

Figure 6-19. *Same Bot Builder object rendered in Slack*

That's not a carousel. There is no such concept in Slack! There are also no cards to speak of; it is just messages with attachments. The images are not clickable either; the default link is displayed above the image. Both the Im Back and Post Back buttons appear to do a post back. There is no concept of suggested actions/quick replies. You can find more information about the Slack Message format online.[7]

However, the team behind the Bot Builder SDK has thought of the issue where you may want to specify the exact native channel message, distinct from the default Bot Framework connector rendering for that channel. The solution is to provide a field on the Message object that contains the native channel JSON data for incoming messages and a field that may contain native channel JSON responses.

The terminology used in the Node SDK is sourceEvent (the C# version of Bot Builder refers to this concept as channelData). The sourceEvent in the Node SDK exists on the IEvent interface. Remember, this is the interface that IMessage implements as well. This means any event from a bot connector may include the raw channel JSON.

Let's look at a feature in Facebook Messenger that is not readily supported by the Bot Framework. By default, cards in Messenger require an image with a 1.91:1 aspect ratio.[8] The default conversion of a hero card by the connector utilizes this template. There is, however, the ability to utilize a 1:1 image ratio. There are other options in the documentation that are hidden by the Bot Framework. For example, Facebook has a specific flag around setting cards as sharable. Furthermore, you can control the size of the WebView invoked by an openURL button in Messenger. For now, we will stick to modifying the image aspect ratio.

For starters, let's see the code to send the same card we have been sending using the hero card object but using Facebook's native format:

---

[7]Slack Messages: https://api.slack.com/docs/messages

[8]Facebook Generic Template Reference: https://developers.facebook.com/docs/messenger-platform/send-messages/template/generic

```javascript
const bot = new builder.UniversalBot(connector, [
    (session) => {

        if (session.message.address.channelId == 'facebook') {
            const msg = new builder.Message(session);
            msg.sourceEvent({
                facebook: {
                    attachment: {
                        type: 'template',
                        payload: {
                            template_type: 'generic',
                            elements: [
                                {
                                    title: 'card title',
                                    subtitle: 'card subtitle',
                                    image_url: 'https://bot-
                                    framework.azureedge.net/
                                    bot-icons-v1/bot-framework-
                                    default-7.png',
                                    default_action: {
                                        type: 'web_url',
                                        url: 'http://dev.
                                        botframework.com',
                                        webview_height_ratio:
                                        'tall',
                                    },
                                    buttons: [
                                        {
                                            type: "web_url",
                                            url: "http://
                                            google.com",
```

```
                                                    title: "Open
                                                    Google"
                                            },
                                            {
                                                    type: 'postback',
                                                    title: 'Im Back',
                                                    payload: 'Hello!'
                                            },
                                            {
                                                    type: 'postback',
                                                    title: 'Post Back',
                                                    payload: 'Hello!'
                                            }
                                    ]
                            }
                    ],
                }
            }
        }
    });
    session.send(msg);
} else {
    session.send('this bot is unsupported outside of
    facebook!');
}
    }
});
```

The rendering (Figure 6-20) looks identical to the rendering using the hero card.

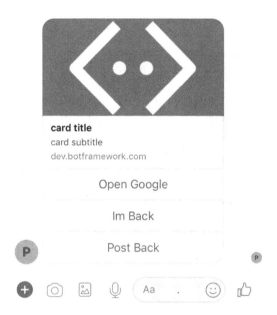

Figure 6-20. *Rendering a generic template in Messenger*

We set image_aspect_ratio to square, and now Facebook renders it as a square (Figure 6-21)!

```
const msg = new builder.Message(session);
msg.sourceEvent({
    facebook: {
        attachment: {
            type: 'template',
            payload: {
                template_type: 'generic',
                image_aspect_ratio: 'square',
                // more...
            }
        }
    }
});
session.send(msg);
```

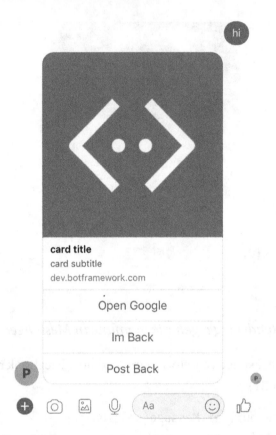

Figure 6-21. *Rendering a generic template with a square image on Messenger*

It's that easy! This is just a taste. In Chapter 8, we will explore using the Bot Framework to integrate with native Slack features.

Group Chat

Some types of bots are meant to be used in a group setting. In the context of Messenger, Twitter direct messages, or similar platforms, the interaction between a user and a bot is typically one on one. However, some channels, most notably Slack, are focused on collaboration. In such a context, the ability to converse with multiple users simultaneously becomes important. Giving your bot the ability to productively participate in a group conversation as well as to handle mention tags correctly is important.

Some channels will allow the bot to view every single message that is sent between users in a channel. Other channels will only send messages to the bot if it is mentioned (for example, "hey @szymonbot, write a book on bots will ya?").

If we are in a channel that allows our bot to see all messages in a group setting, our bot could monitor the conversation and silently execute code based on the discussion (because replying to every message on a group conversation is kind of annoying), or it could ignore everything that doesn't have a mention of the bot. It could also implement a combination of the two behaviors, where the bot is activated by a mention with a certain command and becomes chatty.

In the "Messages" section, we showed the interface for a message. We glossed over the entities list, but it becomes relevant here. One type of entity we may receive from a connector is mentions. The object includes the name and id of the mentioned user and looks as follows:

```
{
    mentioned: {
        id: '',
        name: ''
    },
    text: ''
};
```

Facebook does not support this type of entity, but Slack does. We will connect a bot to Slack in Chapter 8, but in the meantime, here is the code that could always reply in a direct messaging scenario but only reply in a group chat if it is mentioned:

```
const bot = new builder.UniversalBot(connector, [
    (session) => {
        const botMention = _.find(session.message.entities,
        function (e) { return e.type == 'mention' &&
        e.mentioned.id == session.message.address.bot.id; });

        if (session.message.address.conversation.isGroup &&
        botMention) {
            session.send('hello ' + session.message.user
            .name + '!');
        }
        else if (!session.message.address.conversation.isGroup) {
            // 1 on 1 session
            session.send('hello ' + session.message.user
            .name + '!');
        } else {
            // silently looking at non-mention messages
            // session.send('bein creepy...');
        }

        session.send(msg);
    }
]);
```

Figure 6-22 is what the experience looks like in Slack in a direct conversation.

Szymon Rozga 1:52 PM
hi there

PracticeBotDev APP 1:52 PM
hello srozga!

Figure 6-22. *Direct messaging a group chat–enabled bot in Slack*

Figure 6-23 shows the behavior in a group chat (excuse the overly original username srozga2).

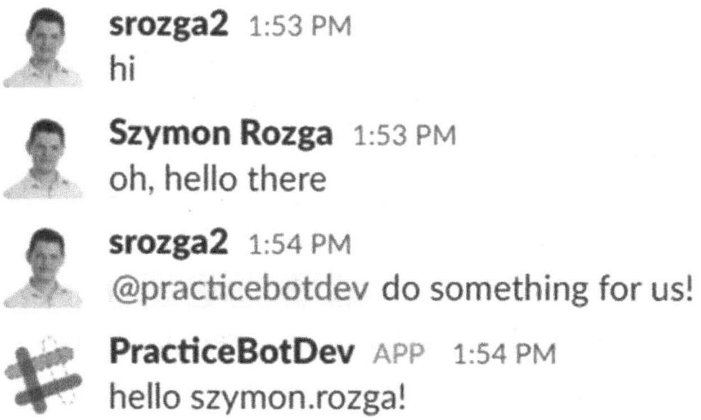

srozga2 1:53 PM
hi

Szymon Rozga 1:53 PM
oh, hello there

srozga2 1:54 PM
@practicebotdev do something for us!

PracticeBotDev APP 1:54 PM
hello szymon.rozga!

Figure 6-23. *Group chat–enabled bot ignoring messages without a mention*

Custom Dialogs

We have constructed our dialogs by using the bot.dialog(…) method. We also discussed the concept of a waterfall. In the calendar bot we started in the previous chapter, each of our dialogs was implemented via waterfalls: a set of steps that will execute in sequence. We can skip some steps or end the dialog before all steps are completed, but the idea of a predefined sequence is key. This logic is implemented by a class in the Bot Builder SDK called WaterfallDialog. If we look at the code behind the dialog(…) call, we will find this bit:

```
if (Array.isArray(dialog) || typeof dialog === 'function') {
    d = new WaterfallDialog(dialog);
} else {
    d = <any>dialog;
}
```

What if the conversation piece we would like to encode is not easily represented in a waterfall abstraction? What choices do we have? We can create a custom implementation of a dialog!

In the Bot Builder SDK, a dialog is a class that represents some interaction between the user and the bot. Dialogs can call other dialogs and accept return values from those child dialogs. They live on a dialog stack, not unlike a function call stack. Using the default waterfall helper hides some of these details; implementing a custom dialog brings us closer to the dialog stack reality. The abstract Dialog class from the Bot Builder is shown here:

```
export abstract class Dialog extends ActionSet {
    public begin<T>(session: Session, args?: T): void {
        this.replyReceived(session);
    }
```

```
abstract replyReceived(session: Session, recognizeResult?:
IRecognizeResult): void;

public dialogResumed<T>(session: Session, result:
IDialogResult<T>): void {
    if (result.error) {
        session.error(result.error);
    }
}

public recognize(context: IRecognizeDialogContext, cb:
(err: Error, result: IRecognizeResult) => void): void {
    cb(null, { score: 0.1 });
}
}
```

Dialog is just a class that we can inherit from that has four important methods.

- *Begin*: Called when the dialog is first placed on the stack.

- *ReplyReceived*: Called anytime a message arrives from a user.

- *DialogResumed*: Called when a child dialog ends and the current dialog becomes active again. One of the parameters received by the dialogResumed method is the child dialog's result object.

- *Recognize*: Allows us to add custom dialog recognition logic. By default, BotBuilder provides declarative methods to set up custom global or dialog-scoped recognition. However, if we would like to add further recognition logic, we can do so using this approach. We'll get more into this in the "Actions" section.

To illustrate the concepts, we create a BasicCustomDialog. Since Bot Builder is written in TypeScript,[9] a typed superset of JavaScript, we went ahead and wrote the subclass in TypeScript, compiled into JavaScript using the TypeScript Compiler (tsc), and then used it in app.js.

Let's look at the custom dialog's code. This happens to be TypeScript as it has a cleaner interface when using inheritance; the compiled JavaScript is shown later. When the dialog begins, it send the "begin" text. When it receives a message, it responds with the "reply received" text. If the user sent the "prompt" text, the dialog will ask the user for some text input. It would then receive the text input in the dialogResumed method, which prints that result. If the user had entered "done," the dialog finishes and returns to the root dialog.

```typescript
import  { Dialog, ResumeReason, IDialogResult, Session, Prompts
} from 'botbuilder'

export class BasicCustomDialog extends Dialog {
    constructor() {
        super();
    }

    // called when the dialog is invoked
    public begin<T>(session: Session, args?: T): void {
        session.send('begin');
    }

    // called any time a message is received
    public replyReceived(session: Session): void {
        session.send('reply received');
        if(session.message.text === 'prompt') {
            Prompts.text(session, 'please enter any text!');
```

---

[9]TypeScript: http://www.typescriptlang.org/

```
    } else if(session.message.text == 'done') {
        session.endDialog('dialog ending');
    } else {
        // no-op
    }
}

public dialogResumed(session: Session, result: any): void {
    session.send('dialog resumed with value: ' + result);
}
}
```

We use an instance of the dialog directly in app.js. In the default waterfall, we echo any message, except the "custom" input, which begins the custom dialog.

```
const bot = new builder.UniversalBot(connector, [
    (session) => {
        if(session.message.text === 'custom') {
            session.beginDialog('custom');
        } else {
            session.send('echo ' + session.message.text);
        }
    }
]);
const customDialogs = require('./customdialogs');
bot.dialog('custom', new customDialogs.BasicCustomDialog());
```

Figure 6-24 shows what a sample interaction looks like.

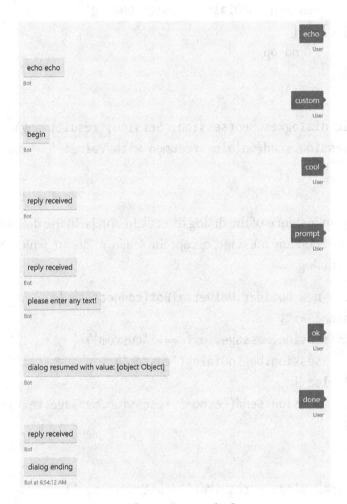

Figure 6-24. *Interacting with a custom dialog*

Incidentally, the Promps.text, Prompts.number, and other Prompt dialogs are all implemented as custom dialogs.

The compiled JavaScript for the custom dialog is shown next. It is a bit more challenging to reason about, but at the end of the day, it is standard ES5 JavaScript prototype inheritance.[10]

```
"use strict";
var __extends = (this && this.__extends) || (function () {
    var extendStatics = Object.setPrototypeOf ||
        ({ __proto__: [] } instanceof Array && function (d, b)
        { d.__proto__ = b; }) ||
        function (d, b) { for (var p in b) if
        (b.hasOwnProperty(p)) d[p] = b[p]; };
    return function (d, b) {
        extendStatics(d, b);
        function __() { this.constructor = d; }
        d.prototype = b === null ? Object.create(b) : (__.
        prototype = b.prototype, new __());
    };
})();
exports.__esModule = true;
var botbuilder_1 = require("botbuilder");
var BasicCustomDialog = /** @class */ (function (_super) {
    __extends(BasicCustomDialog, _super);
    function BasicCustomDialog() {
        return _super.call(this) || this;
    }
    // called when the dialog is invoked
    BasicCustomDialog.prototype.begin = function (session,
    args) {
        session.send('begin');
```

---

[10]Classical Inheritance in JavaScript ES5: https://eli.thegreenplace.net/2013/10/22/classical-inheritance-in-javascript-es5

```
    };
    // called any time a message is received
    BasicCustomDialog.prototype.replyReceived = function
    (session) {
        session.send('reply received');
        if (session.message.text === 'prompt') {
            botbuilder_1.Prompts.text(session, 'please enter
            any text!');
        }
        else if (session.message.text == 'done') {
            session.endDialog('dialog ending');
        }
        else {
            // no-op
        }
    };
    BasicCustomDialog.prototype.dialogResumed = function
    (session, result) {
        session.send('dialog resumed with value: ' + result);
    };
    return BasicCustomDialog;
}(botbuilder_1.Dialog));
exports.BasicCustomDialog = BasicCustomDialog;
```

EXERCISE 6-3

Implementing a Custom Prompts.number

As an exercise of the concept of a custom dialog, you will now create a custom Prompts.number dialog. This exercise is purely academic; it is interesting to know how framework-level behavior may be implemented.

1. Create a bot with a two-step waterfall that uses the standard Prompts.number to collect a numerical value and send the number back to the user in the second waterfall step. Note that you will be using the response field on the args parameter to the waterfall functions.

2. Create a custom dialog that collects user input until it receives a number. You can use parseFloat for the purposes of the exercise. When a valid number is received, call session. endDialogWithResult with an object of the same structure as the one returned by Prompts.number. If the user's input is invalid, return an error message and ask for a number again.

3. In your waterfall, instead of calling Prompts.number, call your new custom dialog. Your waterfall should still work!

4. As a bonus, add logic to your custom dialog to allow a maximum of five tries. After that, return a canceled result to your waterfall.

You now understand the building blocks of all dialogs in the Bot Builder SDK! We can use this knowledge to build just about any sort of interaction.

Actions

We now have a good idea of how powerful abstraction dialogs are and how the Bot Builder SDK manages the dialog stack. One of the key pieces of the framework that we do not have good insight into is how to link user actions to transformations of the dialog stack. At the most basic level, we can write code that simply calls beginDialog. But how do we make that determination based on user input? How can we hook that into the recognizers that we learned about in the previous chapter and specifically LUIS? That is what *actions* allow us to do.

The Bot Builder SDK contains six types of actions, with two being global and four scoped to a dialog. The two global actions are triggerAction and customAction. We've run into triggerAction before. It allows the bot to invoke a dialog when an intent is matched at any point during the conversation, assuming the intent does not match a dialog-scoped action beforehand. These are evaluated any time user input is received. The default behavior is to clear the entire dialog stack before the dialog is invoked.

```
lib.dialog(constants.dialogNames.AddCalendarEntry, [
    function (session, args, next) {
        ...
]).triggerAction({
    matches: constants.intentNames.AddCalendarEntry
});
```

Each of our main dialogs in our code in the calendar bot from the previous chapter uses the default triggerAction behavior, except for Help. The Help dialog is invoked *on top* of the dialog stack, so when it completes, we are back to whatever dialog the user was on to begin on. To achieve this effect, we override the onSelectAction method and specify the behavior we want.

```
lib.dialog(constants.dialogNames.Help, (session, args, next) => {
...
}).triggerAction({
    matches: constants.intentNames.Help,
    onSelectAction: (session, args, next) => {
        session.beginDialog(args.action, args);
    }
});
```

A customAction binds directly to the bot object, instead of a dialog. It allows us to bind a function to respond to user input. We don't get a chance to query the user for more information like a dialog implementation would. This is good for functionality that simply returns a message or performs some HTTP call based on user input. In fact, we could as far as to rewrite the Help dialog like this. The code looks straightforward, but we lose the encapsulation and extensibility of the dialog model. In other words, we no longer have the logic in its own dialog, with the ability to execute several steps, collect user input, or provide a result to the calling object.

```
lib.customAction({
    matches: constants.intentNames.Help,
    onSelectAction: (session, args, next) => {
        session.send("Hi, I am a calendar concierge bot. I
        can help you create, delete and move appointments. I
        can also tell you about your calendar and check your
        availability!");
    }
});
```

The four types of contextual actions are beginDialogAction, reloadAction, cancelAction, and endConversationAction. Let's examine each one.

BeginDialogAction creates an action that pushes a new dialog on the stack whenever the action is matched. Our contextual help dialogs in the calendar bot used this approach. We created two dialogs: one as the help for the AddCalendarEntry dialog and the second as a help for the RemoveCalendarEntry dialog.

```
// help message when help requested during the add calendar
entry dialog
lib.dialog(constants.dialogNames.AddCalendarEntryHelp,
(session, args, next) => {
    const msg = "To add an appointment, we gather the following
    information: time, subject and location. You can also
    simply say 'add appointment with Bob tomorrow at 2pm for an
    hour for coffee' and we'll take it from there!";
    session.endDialog(msg);
});
```

```
// help message when help requested during the remove calendar
entry dialog
lib.dialog(constants.dialogNames.RemoveCalendarEntryHelp,
(session, args, next) => {
    const msg = "You can remove any calendar either by subject
    or by time!";
    session.endDialog(msg);
});
```

Our AddCalendarEntry dialog can then bind the beginDialogAction to its appropriate help dialog.

```
lib.dialog(constants.dialogNames.AddCalendarEntry, [
    // code
]).beginDialogAction(constants.dialogNames.
AddCalendarEntryHelp, constants.dialogNames.
AddCalendarEntryHelp, { matches: constants.intentNames.Help })
.triggerAction({ matches: constants.intentNames.
AddCalendarEntry });
```

Note that the behavior of this action is the same as calling beginDialog manually. The new dialog is placed on top of the dialog stack, and the current dialog is continued when done.

The reloadAction call performs a replaceDialog. replaceDialog is a method on the session object that ends the current dialog and replaces it with an instance of a different dialog. The parent dialog does not get a result until the new dialog finishes. In practice, we can utilize this to restart an interaction or to switch into a more appropriate dialog in the middle of a flow.

Here is the code for the conversation (see Figure 6-25):

```
lib.dialog(constants.dialogNames.AddCalendarEntry, [
    // code
])
    .beginDialogAction(constants.dialogNames.
    AddCalendarEntryHelp, constants.dialogNames.
    AddCalendarEntryHelp, { matches: constants.intentNames.Help
    })
    .reloadAction('startOver', "Ok, let's start over...", {
    matches: /^restart$/i })
    .triggerAction({ matches: constants.intentNames.
    AddCalendarEntry });
```

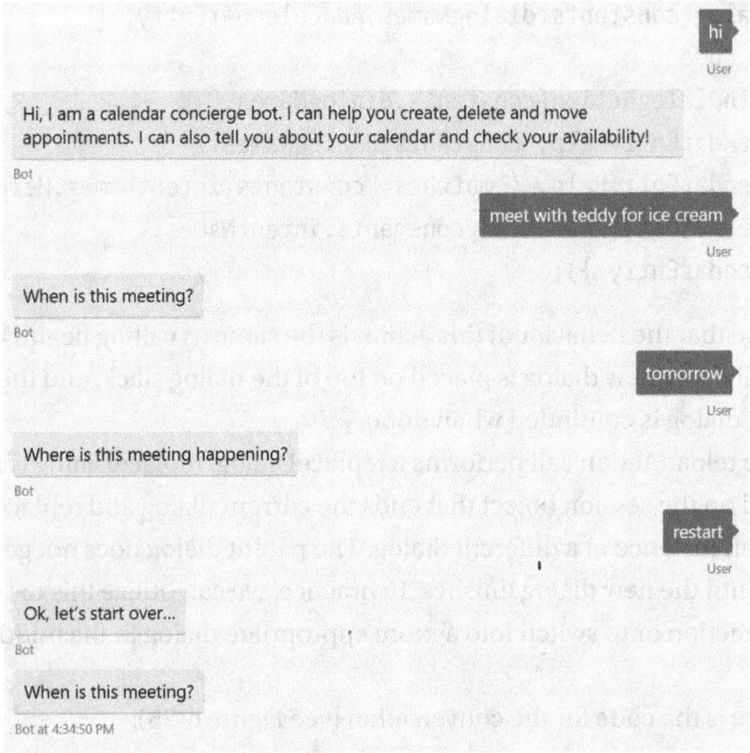

Figure 6-25. *Sample conversation triggering the reloadAction*

CancelAction allows us to cancel the current dialog. The parent dialog will receive a cancelled flag set to true in its resume handler. This allows the dialog to properly act on the cancellation. The code follows (the conversation visualization is shown in Figure 6-26):

```
lib.dialog(constants.dialogNames.AddCalendarEntry, [
    // code
])
    .beginDialogAction(constants.dialogNames.AddCalendarEntryHelp,
    constants.dialogNames.AddCalendarEntryHelp, { matches:
    constants.intentNames.Help })
```

```
.reloadAction('startOver', "Ok, let's start over...", {
matches: /^restart$/i })
.cancelAction('cancel', 'Cancelled.', { matches: /^cancel$/i})
.triggerAction({ matches: constants.intentNames.
AddCalendarEntry });
```

Figure 6-26. *Sample conversation triggering the cancelAction*

Lastly, the endConversationAction allows us to bind to the session. endConversation call. Ending a conversation implies that the entire dialog stack is cleared and that all the user and conversation data is removed from the state store. If a user starts messaging the bot again, a new conversation is created without any knowledge of the previous interactions. The code is as follows (Figure 6-27 shows the conversation visualization):

```
lib.dialog(constants.dialogNames.AddCalendarEntry, [
    // code
])
    .beginDialogAction(constants.dialogNames.AddCalendarEntryHelp,
    constants.dialogNames.AddCalendarEntryHelp, { matches:
    constants.intentNames.Help })
```

```
.reloadAction('startOver', "Ok, let's start over...", {
matches: /^restart$/i })
.cancelAction('cancel', 'Cancelled.', { matches:
/^cancel$/i})
.endConversationAction('end', "conversation over!", {
matches: /^end!$/i })
.triggerAction({ matches: constants.intentNames.
AddCalendarEntry });
```

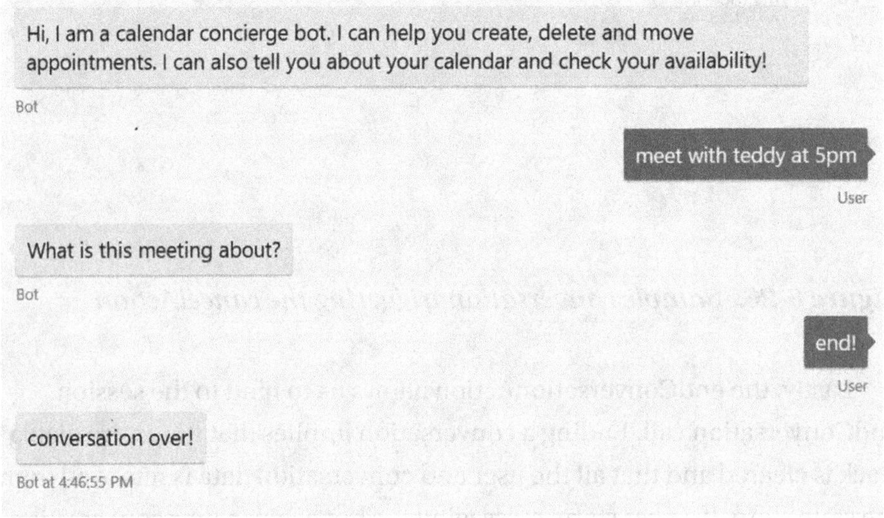

Hi, I am a calendar concierge bot. I can help you create, delete and move appointments. I can also tell you about your calendar and check your availability!

Bot

meet with teddy at 5pm

User

What is this meeting about?

Bot

end!

User

conversation over!

Bot at 4:46:55 PM

Figure 6-27. *A sample conversation triggering an endConversationAction*

Extra Notes on Actions

Recall from the previous chapter that each recognizer accepts a user input and returns an object with an intent text value and a score. We touched upon the fact that we can use recognizers that determine the intent from LUIS, that use regular expressions, or that implement any custom logic.

The *matches* object in each of the actions that we have created is a way for us to specify which recognizer intent an action is interested in. The matches object implements the following interface:

```
export interface IDialogActionOptions {
    matches?: RegExp|RegExp[]|string|string[];
    intentThreshold?: number;
    onFindAction?: (context: IFindActionRouteContext,
    callback: (err: Error | null, score: number, routeData?:
    IActionRouteData) => void) => void;
    onSelectAction?: (session: Session, args?: any, next?:
    Function) => void;
}
```

Here is what this object contains:

- Matches is the intent name or regular expression the action is looking for.

- intentThreshold is the minimum score a recognizer must assign to an intent for this action to get invoked.

- onFindAction allows us to invoke custom logic when an action is being checked for whether it should be triggered.

- onSelectAction allows you to customize the behavior for an action. For instance, use it if you don't want to clear the dialog stack but would rather place the dialog on top of the stack. We have seen this in action in our previous action samples.

In addition to this level of customization, the Bot Builder SDK has very specific rules around actions and their precedence. Recall that we've looked at global actions, dialog-scoped actions, and a possible recognize implementation on each dialog in our discussion on custom dialogs. The order of action resolution when a message arrives is as follows. First, the system tries to locate the current dialog's implementation of the recognize function. After that, the SDK looks at the dialog stack, starting from the current dialog all the way to the root dialog. If no action matches along that path, the global actions are queried. This order makes sure that actions closest to the current user experience are processed first. Keep this in mind as you design your bot interactions.

Libraries

Libraries are a way of packaging and distributing related bot dialogs, recognizers, and other functionality. Libraries can reference other libraries, resulting in bots with highly composed pieces of functionality. From the developer perspective, a library is simply a nicely packaged collection of dialogs, recognizers, and other Bot Builder objects with a name and, commonly, a set of helper methods to aid in invoking the dialogs and other library-specific features. In our Calendar Concierge Bot in Chapter 5, each dialog was part of a library related to a high-level bot feature. The app.js code loads all the modules and then installs them into the main bot via the bot.library call.

```
const helpModule = require('./dialogs/help');
const addEntryModule = require('./dialogs/addEntry');
const removeEntryModule = require('./dialogs/removeEntry');
const editEntryModule = require('./dialogs/editEntry');
const checkAvailabilityModule = require('./dialogs/
checkAvailability');
const summarizeModule = require('./dialogs/summarize');
```

```
const bot = new builder.UniversalBot(connector, [
    (session) => {
        // code
    }
]);

bot.library(addEntryModule.create());
bot.library(helpModule.create());
bot.library(removeEntryModule.create());
bot.library(editEntryModule.create());
bot.library(checkAvailabilityModule.create());
bot.library(summarizeModule.create());
```

This is library composition in action: UniversalBot is itself a subclass of Library. Our main UniversalBot library imports six other libraries. A reference to a dialog from any other context must be namespaced using the library name as a prefix. From the perspective of the root library or dialogs in the UniversalBot object, invoking any other library's dialog must use a qualified name in the format: libName:dialogName. This fully qualified dialog name referencing process is necessary only when crossing library boundaries. Within the context of the same library, the library prefix is not necessary.

A common pattern is to expose a helper method in your module that invokes library dialog. Think of it as library encapsulation; a library should not know anything about the internals of another library. For example, our help library exposes a method to do just that.

```
const lib = new builder.Library('help');

exports.help = (session) => {
    session.beginDialog('help:' + constants.dialogNames.Help);
};
```

Conclusion

Microsoft's Bot Builder SDK is a powerful bot construction library and conversation engine that helps us develop all types of asynchronous conversational experiences from simple back and forth to complex bots with a multitude of behaviors. The dialog abstraction is a powerful way of modeling a conversation. Recognizers define the mechanisms that our bot utilizes to translate user input into machine-readable intents. Actions map those recognizer results into operations on the dialog stack. A dialog is principally concerned with three things: what happens when it begins, what happens when a user's message is received, and what happens when a child dialog returns its result. Every dialog utilizes the bot context, called the *session*, to retrieve the user message and to create responses. A response may be composed of text, video, audio, or images. In addition, cards can produce richer and context-sensitive experiences. Suggested actions are responsible for keeping the user from guessing what to do next.

In the following chapter, we'll apply these concepts to integrate our bot with the Google Calendar API, and we'll take steps to creating a compelling first version of our calendar bot experience.

CHAPTER 7

Building an Integrated Bot Experience

So far, we have built a pretty good LUIS application that has been evolving over time. We also utilized the Bot Builder dialog engine that employs our natural language models, extracts the relevant intents and entities from user utterances, and contains conditional logic around many of the different permutations of inputs coming into the bot. But our code does not really do anything. How do we make it do something useful and real? Throughout the book, we've been exploring the idea of a calendar bot. This means we need to integrate with some kind of calendar API. For the purposes of this book, we're going to integrate with Google's Calendar API. After that is set up, we will explore how to integrate those calls into the bot flow. In this day and age of OAuth, we are not going to spend time collecting a user's name and password in our chat window. That would not be secure. Instead, we will implement a three-legged OAuth flow using the Google OAuth libraries. We'll then go ahead and make the changes in our code to support communication with the Google Calendar API. At the end of the chapter, we'll end up with a bot that we can use to create appointments and view entries in our calendar!

© Szymon Rozga 2018
S. Rozga, *Practical Bot Development*, https://doi.org/10.1007/978-1-4842-3540-9_7

Note, the code for this chapter is available as part of the code repository. Throughout the bot code and the code in this book, you'll find use of many libraries. One of the more used ones is Underscore. Underscore is a nifty library that provides a series of useful utility functions, especially around collections.

A Word on OAuth 2.0

This isn't a book about security, but understanding basic authentication and authorization mechanisms is essential to be a developer. OAuth 2.0 is a standard authorization protocol. The three-legged OAuth 2.0 flow allows third-party applications to access services on behalf of another entity. In our case, we will be accessing a user's Google Calendar data on behalf of that user. At the end of the three-legged OAuth flow, we end up with two tokens: an access token and a refresh token. The access token is included in requests to an API in the authorization HTTP header and provides data to the API declaring which user we are requesting data. Access tokens are typically short-lived to reduce the window during which a compromised access token can be utilized. When an access token expires, we can use the refresh token to receive a new access token.

To initiate the flow, we first redirect the user to a service that they can authenticate against, say, Google. Google presents an OAuth 2.0 login page where it authenticates the user and asks the user for their consent so that the bot can access the user's data from Google on their behalf. When authentication and consent are successful, Google sends an authorization code back into the bot's API, via what's known as the redirect URI. Finally, our bot requests the access and refresh tokens by presenting the authorization code to Google's token endpoint. Google's OAuth libraries will help us implement the three-legged flow in our calendar bot.

Setting Up Google APIs

Before we jump into it, we should set ourselves up to be able to use the Google APIs. Luckily, Google makes this quite easy via the Google Cloud Platform API console. Google Cloud Platform is Google's Azure or AWS; it is Google's one-stop shop for provisioning and managing different cloud services. To get started, we navigate to `https://console.cloud.google.com`. If this is our first time visiting the site, we will be asked to accept the terms of service. After that, we will be placed in the dashboard (Figure 7-1).

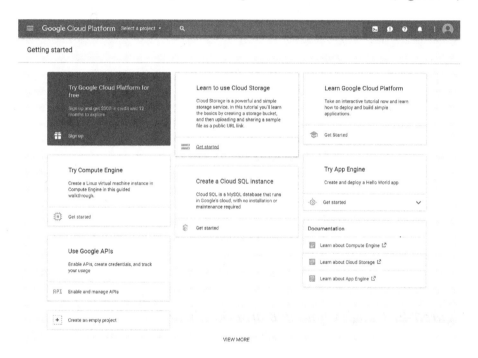

Figure 7-1. *Google Cloud Platform dashboard*

Our next steps are as follows. We will create a new project. Within that project, we will ask for access to the Calendar API. We will also give our project the ability to log in on behalf of users using OAuth2. Once done, we will receive a client ID and secret. Those two pieces of data, plus our redirect URI, are sufficient for us to use the Google API libraries within our bot.

Click the *Select a Project* drop-down. You'll be met with a pop-up that, if you have not used this console before, should be empty (Figure 7-2).

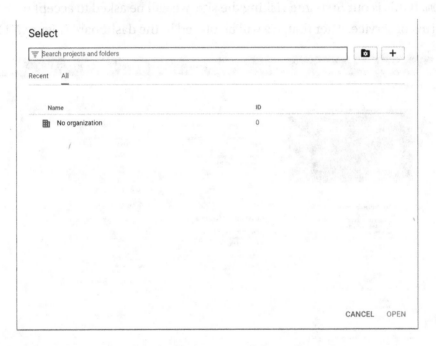

Figure 7-2.   *Google Cloud Platform Dashboard projects*

Click the + button to add a new project. Give the project a name. Once the project is created, we will be able to navigate to it through the *Select a Project* functionality (Figure 7-3). The project is also assigned an ID, prefixed by the project name.

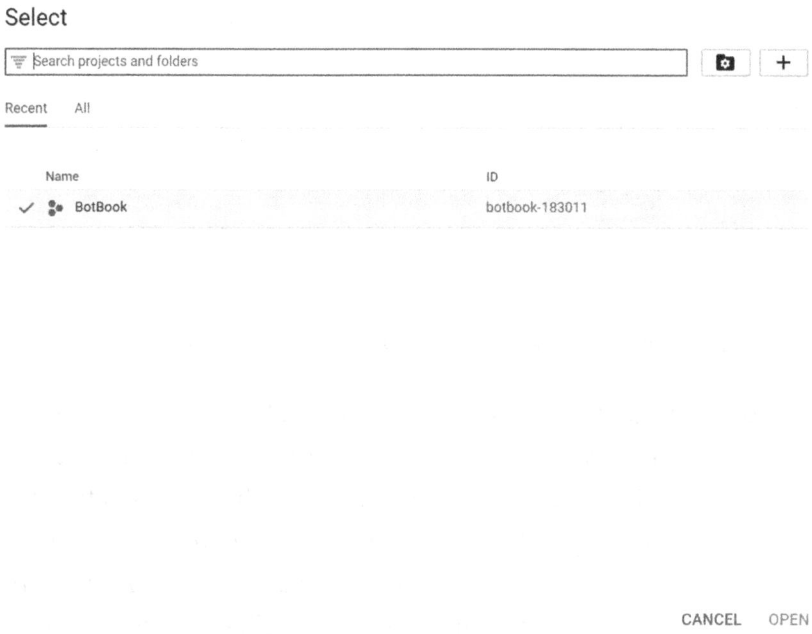

Select

Search projects and folders		📷	+

Recent   All

Name	ID
✓ BotBook	botbook-183011

CANCEL   OPEN

Figure 7-3. *Our project is created!*

When the open the project, we see the project dashboard, which initially looks intimidating (Figure 7-4). There are many things we can do here.

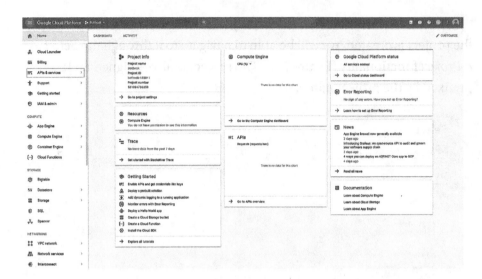

Figure 7-4. *There are many things to do with a project*

Let's begin by getting access to the Google Calendar API. We first click APIs & Services. We can find this link in the first few items on the left navigation pane. The page already has quite a few things populated. These are the default Google Cloud Platform services. Since we're not using them, we can disable each one. Once ready, we can click the *Enable APIs and Services* button. We search for Calendar and click Google Calendar API. Finally, we click the *Enable* button to add it to our project (Figure 7-5). We will receive a warning indicating that we may need credentials to use the API. No problem, we will do this next.

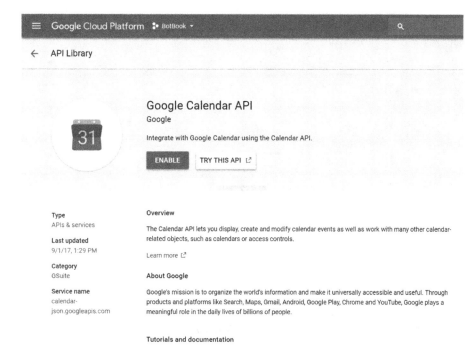

Figure 7-5. *Enabling the Calendar API for our project*

To set up authorization, we click the *Credentials* link on the left pane. We will be met with a prompt to create credentials. For our use case, in which we will be accessing the user's calendar, we need an OAuth Client ID[1] (Figure 7-6).

---

[1]Google Cloud Platform supports three types of credentials for their services. API keys are a way to identify a project and receive API access, quotas, and reports. An OAuth Client ID allows your application to make requests on behalf of a user. Lastly, service accounts allow applications to make requests on behalf of applications. You can find more information at `https://support.google.com/cloud/answer/6158857?hl=en`.

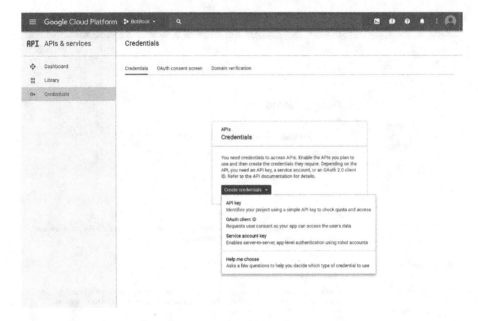

Figure 7-6. *Setting up our client credentials*

We will first be asked to set up the consent screen (Figure 7-7). This is the screen that the user will be shown when authenticating against Google. Most of us have probably encountered these types of screens across different web applications. For example, whenever we log into an app via Facebook, we will be presented with a page telling us that the app needs permission to read all your contact information and photos and even deepest secrets. This is Google's way of setting up a similar page. It asks for data such as the product name, logos, terms of service, privacy policy URLs, and so on. To test the functionality we minimally need a product name.

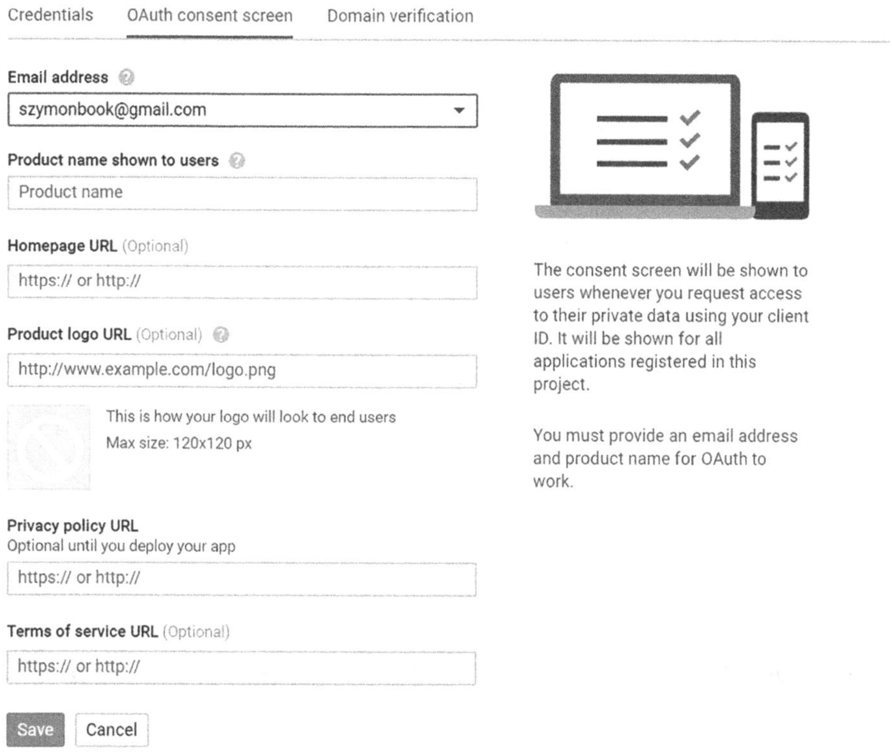

Credentials   OAuth consent screen   Domain verification

Email address ⓘ

szymonbook@gmail.com ▾

Product name shown to users ⓘ

Product name

Homepage URL (Optional)

https:// or http://

Product logo URL (Optional) ⓘ

http://www.example.com/logo.png

This is how your logo will look to end users
Max size: 120x120 px

Privacy policy URL
Optional until you deploy your app

https:// or http://

Terms of service URL (Optional)

https:// or http://

The consent screen will be shown to users whenever you request access to their private data using your client ID. It will be shown for all applications registered in this project.

You must provide an email address and product name for OAuth to work.

Save   Cancel

Figure 7-7.   OAuth consent configuration

At this point, we will be taken back to the *Create Client ID* function. As the Application Type setting, we should select *Web Application* and give our client a name and a redirect URI (Figure 7-8). We utilize our ngrok proxy URI (see Chapter 5 for more on ngrok). For local testing, we are free to enter a localhost address. For example, you can enter http:// localhost:3978.

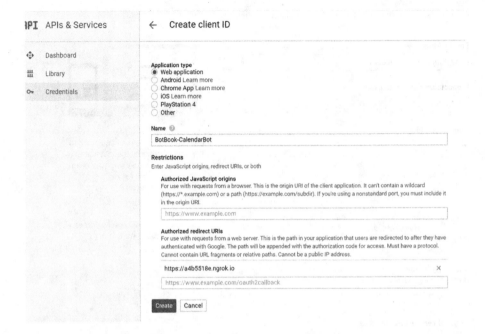

Figure 7-8. *Creating a new OAuth 2.0 Client ID and providing a redirect URI*

Once we click the *Create button,* we will receive a pop-up with the client ID and client secret (Figure 7-9). Copy them because we will need the values in our bot. If we lose the client ID and secret, we can always access them by navigating to the *Credentials* page for the project and selecting the entry we created in the OAuth 2.0 Client IDs.

←   Client ID for Web application   ⬇ DOWNLOAD JSON   ↻ RESET SECRET   🗑 DELETE

Client ID	693978449559-8t03j8064o6hfr1f8lh47s9gvc4afed4.apps.googleusercontent.com
Client secret	X6lzSlw500t0wmQQ2SpF6YV6
Creation date	Mar 28, 2018, 6:43:18 AM

Name ⊚

Calendar Bot Credentials

Restrictions

Enter JavaScript origins, redirect URIs, or both

Authorized JavaScript origins

For use with requests from a browser. This is the origin URI of the client application. It can't contain a wildcard (https://*.example.com) or a path (https://example.com/subdir). If you're using a nonstandard port, you must include it in the origin URI.

https://www.example.com

Authorized redirect URIs

For use with requests from a web server. This is the path in your application that users are redirected to after they have authenticated with Google. The path will be appended with the authorization code for access. Must have a protocol. Cannot contain URL fragments or relative paths. Cannot be a public IP address.

https://a4b5518e.ngrok.io/oauth2callback   ✕

https://www.example.com/oauth2callback

Figure 7-9. *We can always find a missing ID and secret*

At this point we are ready to hook our bot up to the Google OAuth2 provider.

Integrating Authentication with Bot Builder

We will need to install the *googleapis* node package as well as *crypto-js*, a library that lets us encrypt data. When we send the user to the OAuth login page, we also include a state in the URL. A state is simply a payload that our application can use to identify a user and their conversation. When Google sends back an authorization code as part of the OAuth 2.0 three-legged flow, it will also send back the state. The state parameter should be something recognizable to our API but very hard for a malicious actor to guess, such as a session hash or some other information we are interested in. Once we receive it from Google's auth page, we can continue the user's conversation using the data in the state parameter.

To mask the data from bad actors, we will encode this object as a
Base64 string. Base64 is an ASCII representation of binary data.[2] Since
a malicious actor could easily compromise this information by simply
decoding from Base64, we will use crypto-js to encrypt the state string.

First, let's install the two packages.

```
npm install googleapis crypto-js --save
```

Second, let's add three variables to our .env file representing the
client ID, secret, and redirect URI. We use the redirect URI we provided in
Figure 7-8 and the client ID and secret we received in Figure 7-9.

```
GOOGLE_OAUTH_CLIENT_ID=693978449559-8t03j806406hfr1f8lh47s9gvc4
afed4.apps.googleusercontent.com
GOOGLE_OAUTH_CLIENT_SECRET=X6lzSlw500t0wmQQ2SpF6YV6
GOOGLE_OAUTH_REDIRECT_URI=https://a4b5518e.ngrok.io
```

Third, we need to generate the URL to the login page and send a button
that can open this URL. The Google Auth APIs can do a lot of this for us.
We will do a few things in our code. First, we import the crypto-js and
googleapis packages. Next, we create an OAuth2 client instance including
our client data. The state that we will send as part of the login URL
contains the user's address. As shown in the previous chapter, an address
is sufficient to uniquely identify a user's conversation, and Bot Builder
contains the facilities to help us send messages to that user by simply
presenting the conversation address. We use crypto-js to encrypt the state,
using the ASE algorithm.[3] AES is a symmetric-key algorithm, which means
that the data is encrypted and decrypted using the same key or passphrase.
We add the passphrase into our .env file with the name AES_PASSPHRASE.

---

[2]Base64: https://en.wikipedia.org/wiki/Base64

[3]CryptoJS supports quite a few different hashing and cipher algorithms. The
full list can be found on the project's GitHub page at https://github.com/
jakubzapletal/crypto-js. You can find more information on the AES algorithm
at https://en.wikipedia.org/wiki/Advanced_Encryption_Standard.

```
GOOGLE_OAUTH_CLIENT_ID=693978449559-8t03j8064o6hfr1f8lh47s9gvc4
afed4.apps.googleusercontent.com
GOOGLE_OAUTH_CLIENT_SECRET=X6lzSlw500t0wmQQ2SpF6YV6
GOOGLE_OAUTH_REDIRECT_URI=https://a4b5518e.ngrok.io/
oauth2callback
AES_PASSPHRASE=BotsBotsBots!!!
```

Another thing to note is the *scopes* array. When requesting
authorization to the Google APIs, we specify to Google which APIs we are
looking for access to using scopes. We can think of each item in the scopes
array as a piece of data we want to access about the user from Google's
APIs. Of course, this array needs to be a subset of the APIs our Google
project may access to begin with. If we added a scope we did not enable for
our project earlier, the authorization process would fail.

```
const google = require('googleapis');
const OAuth2 = google.auth.OAuth2;
const CryptoJS = require('crypto-js');

const oauth2Client = getAuthClient();
const state = {
    address: session.message.address
};
const googleApiScopes = [
    'https://www.googleapis.com/auth/calendar'
];
const encryptedState = CryptoJS.AES.encrypt(JSON.
stringify(state), process.env.AES_PASSPHRASE).toString();
const authUrl = oauth2Client.generateAuthUrl({
    access_type: 'offline',
    scope: googleApiScopes,
    state: encryptedState
});
```

We also need to be able to send a button for the user to utilize to authorize the bot. We utilize the built-in SigninCard for this purpose.

```
const card = new builder.SigninCard(session).button('Login to
Google', authUrl).text('Need to get your credentials. Please
login here.');
const loginReply = new builder.Message(session)
    .attachmentLayout(builder.AttachmentLayout.carousel)
    .attachments([card]);
```

The emulator renders the SigninCard as per Figure 7-10.

Figure 7-10. *A SigninCard rendered in the Bot Framework emulator*

At this point we can click the Login button to log into Google and authorize our bot to access our data, but it would fail because we have not yet provided the code to handle the message from the return URI. We use the same approach to install a handler for the `https://a4b5518e.ngrok.io/oauth2callback` endpoint as we did to install the API messages endpoint. We also enable *restify.queryParser*, which will expose each parameter in the query string as a field in the req.query object. For example, a callback in the form *redirectUri?state=state&code=code* will result in a query object with two properties, state and code.

```
const server = restify.createServer();
server.use(restify.queryParser());
server.listen(process.env.port || process.env.PORT || 3978,
function () {
    console.log('%s listening to %s', server.name, server.url);
});

server.get('/oauth2callback', function (req, res, next) {
    const code = req.query.code;
    const encryptedState = req.query.state;

    ...
});
```

We read the authorization code from the callback and use the Google OAuth2 client to get the tokens from the token endpoint. The tokens JSON will look like the following data. Note that *expiry_date* is the datetime in milliseconds since the epoch.[4]

```
{

    "access_token": "ya29.GluMBfdm6hPy9QpmimJ5qjJpJXThL1y
    GcKHrOI7JCXQ46XdQaCDBcJzgp1gWcWFQNPTXjbBYoBp43BkEAyLi3
    ZPsR6wKCGlOYNCQIkeLEMdRTntTKIf5CE3wkolU",
    "refresh_token": "1/GClsgQh4BvHTxPdbQgwXtLW2hBza6FPLXDC9zBJ
    sKf4NK_N7AfItvO73kssh5VHq",
    "token_type": "Bearer",
    "expiry_date": 1522261726664
}
```

---

[4]UNIX Epoch Time is the number of milliseconds elapsed since January 1, 1970 00:00:00 UTC: https://en.wikipedia.org/wiki/Unix_time

Once we receive the tokens, we call *setCredentials* on the OAuth2 object, and it can now be used to access the Google Calendar API!

```
server.get('/oauth2callback', function (req, res, next) {
    const code = req.query.code;
    const encryptedState = req.query.state;

    const oauth2Client = new OAuth2(
        process.env.GOOGLE_OAUTH_CLIENT_ID,
        process.env.GOOGLE_OAUTH_CLIENT_SECRET,
        process.env.GOOGLE_OAUTH_REDIRECT_URI
    );

    res.contentType = 'json';
    oauth2Client.getToken(code, function (error, tokens) {
        if (!error) {
            oauth2Client.setCredentials(tokens);

            // We can now use the oauth2Client to call the
            calendar API

            next();
        } else {
            res.send(500, {
                status: 'error',
                error: error
            });
            next();
        }
    });
});
```

In the code location where we have access to the Calendar API, we can write code that gets a list of calendars that we own and prints out their names. Note that *calapi* in the following code is a helper object that wraps the Google Calendar API in JavaScript promises. The code is available in the chapter's code library.

```
calapi.listCalendars(oauth2Client).then(function (data) {
    const myCalendars = _.filter(data, p => p.accessRole ===
    'owner');
    console.log(_.map(myCalendars, p => p.summary));
});
```

This code results in the following console output, which is an unfortunate reminder of the rather lonely workout schedule that has not seen much action since I became a dad.

```
Array(5) ["BotCalendar", "Szymon Rozga", "Work", "Szymon WFH
Schedule", "Workout schedule"]
```

Fatherhood weight gain aside, this is great! We do have a few challenges. We need to store the users' OAuth tokens so we can access them any time the users message us. Where do we store them? This one is easy: private conversation data. How do we get access to that data dictionary in this context? We do this by passing the user's address to the *bot.loadSession* method.

Recall that we stored in the user's address into the encrypted state variable. We can decrypt that object by using the same passphrase we used to encrypt the data.

```
const state = JSON.parse(CryptoJS.AES.decrypt(encryptedState,
process.env.AES_PASSPHRASE).toString(CryptoJS.enc.Utf8));
```

After we receive the token, we can load the bot session from the address. At that point, we have a session object that has all the dialog methods such as *beginDialog* for us to use.

```
oauth2Client.getToken(code, function (error, tokens) {
    bot.loadSession(state.address, (sessionLoadError, session)
    => {
        if (!error && !sessionLoadError) {
            oauth2Client.setCredentials(tokens);

            calapi.listCalendars(oauth2Client).then(function
            (data) {
                const myCalendars = _.filter(data, p =>
                p.accessRole === 'owner');
                session.beginDialog('processUserCalendars', {
                tokens: tokens, calendars: myCalendars });

                res.send(200, {
                    status: 'success'
                });
                next();
            });

            // We can now use the oauth2Client to call the
            calendar API
        } else {
            res.send(500, {
                status: 'error',
                error: error
            });
            next();
        }
    });
});
```

The *processUserCalendars* dialog could look something like this. It sets the tokens into the private conversation data, lets the user know they are logged in, and displays the names of all of the client's calendars.

```
bot.dialog('processUserCalendars', (session, args) => {
    session.privateConversationData.userTokens = args.tokens;
    session.send('You are now logged in!');
    session.send('You own the following calendars. ' +
    _.map(args.calendars, p => p.summary).join(', '));
    session.endDialog();
});
```

The interaction would look like Figure 7-11.

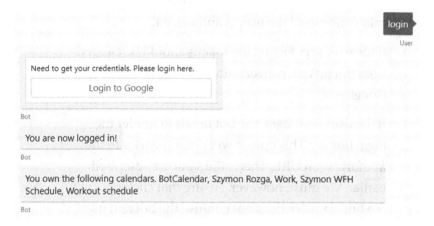

Figure 7-11. *Login flow integrated with a dialog*

Seamless Login Flow

We have successfully logged in and stored the access token, but we have
not yet demonstrated a seamless mechanism to redirect to a login flow
when a dialog requires our users to be logged in. More specifically, if in
the context of the calendar bot a user is not logged in and asks the bot to
add a new calendar entry, the bot should show the login button and then
continue with the Add Entry dialog once login is successful.

There are a few requirements to integrating with the existing dialog flow, listed here:

1. We want to allow users to message the bot with the text *login* or *logout* at any time and have the bot do the correct thing.

2. When a dialog that requires authorization begins, it needs to validate that the user authorization exists. If the auth does not exist, the login button should show up and block the user from continuing with said dialog until the user is authorized.

3. If the user says *logout*, the tokens should be cleared from the private conversation data and revoked with Google.

4. If the user says *login*, the bot needs to render the login button. This button will point the user to the authorization URL. This is the same as described earlier. We must, however, ensure that clicking the button twice does not confuse the bot and its understanding of the user's state.

We will naturally implement a *Login* dialog and a *Logout* dialog. Logout simply checks the existence of tokens in the conversation state. If we do not have the tokens, we are already logged out. If we do, we use Google's library to revoke the user's credentials.[5] The tokens are no longer valid.

```
function getAuthClientFromSession(session) {
    const auth = getAuthClient(session.privateConversation
    Data.tokens);
```

---

[5]OAuth Token Revocation: https://tools.ietf.org/html/rfc7009

```
    return auth;
};

function getAuthClient(tokens) {
    const auth = new OAuth2(
        process.env.GOOGLE_OAUTH_CLIENT_ID,
        process.env.GOOGLE_OAUTH_CLIENT_SECRET,
        process.env.GOOGLE_OAUTH_REDIRECT_URI
    );

    if (tokens) {
        auth.setCredentials(tokens);
    }
    return auth;
}

bot.dialog('LogoutDialog', [(session, args) => {
    if (!session.privateConversationData.tokens) {
        session.endDialog('You are already logged out!');
    } else {
        const client = getAuthClientFromSession(session);
        client.revokeCredentials();
        delete session.privateConversationData['tokens'];
        session.endDialog('You are now logged out!');
    }
}]).triggerAction({
    matches: /^logout$/i
});
```

Login is a waterfall dialog that begins an *EnsureCredentials* dialog before it gets to the next step. In the second step, it verifies whether it is logged in. See the following code. It does this by verifying that it receives the authenticated flag from the *EnsureCredentials* dialog. If yes, it simply lets the user know that she is logged in. Otherwise, an error is shown to the user.

Notice what we did here. We outsourced the logic of figuring out if we are logged in, logging in, and then sending the result back to a different dialog. As long as that dialog returns with an object with fields *authenticated* and, optionally, *error*, this just works. We will use the same technique to inject an authorization flow into any other dialog that requires it.

```
bot.dialog('LoginDialog', [(session, args) => {
    session.beginDialog(constants.dialogNames.Auth.
    EnsureCredentials);
}, (session, args) => {
    if (args.response.authenticated) {
        session.send('You are now logged in!');
    } else {
        session.endDialog('Failed with error: ' + args.
        response.error)
    }
}]).triggerAction({
    matches: /^login$/i
});
```

So, the most important question becomes, what does *EnsureCredentials* do? There are four cases that this code needs to handle. The first two are simple.

- What happens if a dialog requires credentials and the authorization is successful?

- What happens if a dialog requires credentials and the authorization fails?

  The second two are a bit more nuanced. Our question is specifically around what the bot should do if a dialog is not awaiting authorization but it comes in anyway. Or said differently, what happens if EnsureCredentials is not on top of the stack?

- What happens if the user clicks the login button outside the scope of a dialog that needs it and the authorization is successful?

- What happens if the user clicks the login button outside the scope of a dialog that needs it and the authorization fails?

We illustrate the flow for the first case in Figure 7-12. A dialog requests that we have the user's authorizations before continuing, like the *Login* dialog did in the previous code. The user is sent to the auth page. Once the auth page returns a successful authorization code, it sends a callback to our oauth2callback. Once we get the tokens, we call a *StoreTokens* dialog to store the tokens into the conversation data. That dialog will return a success message to *EnsureCredentials*. In turn, this returns a successful authentication message to the calling dialog.

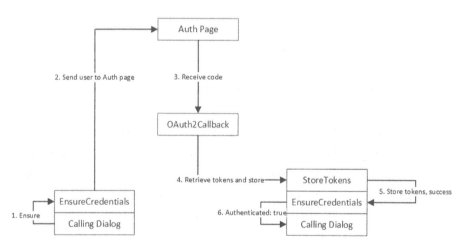

Figure 7-12. *Dialog requires authorization, successful authorization*

If an error occurs, the flow is similar except that we replace the *EnsureCredentials* dialog with the *Error* dialog. The *Error* dialog will then return a failed authenticate message to the calling dialog, which can

327

handle the error as it best sees fit (Figure 7-13). Recall, as we noted in Chapter 5, *replaceDialog* is a call that replaces the current dialog on top of the stack with an instance of another dialog. The calling dialog does not know, nor care, about this implementation detail.

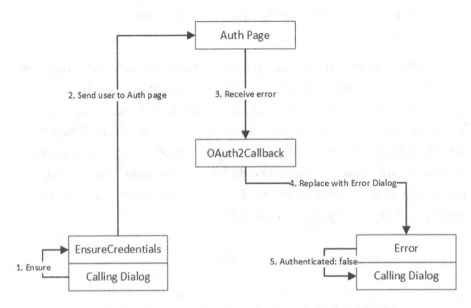

Figure 7-13. *Dialog requires authorization, failed authorization*

In the case that the user clicks the login button when a dialog is not expecting a reply and *EnsureCredentials* is not on top of the stack, the flow is slightly different. We want to display a success or failure message to the user if the authorization succeeds or fails. To achieve this, we will put a confirmation dialog, *AuthConfirmation*, on the stack before invoking the *StoreTokens* dialog (Figure 7-14).

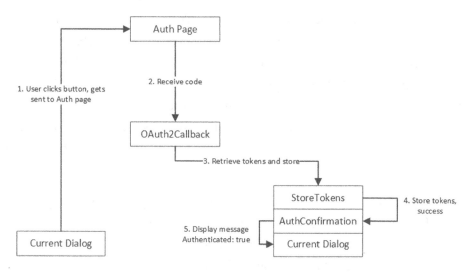

Figure 7-14. *User says login, successful authorization*

Likewise, in the case we receive an authorization error, we push the *AuthConfirmation* dialog on top of the stack, before pushing the *Error* dialog (Figure 7-15). This will ensure that the confirmation dialog displays the right type of message to the user.

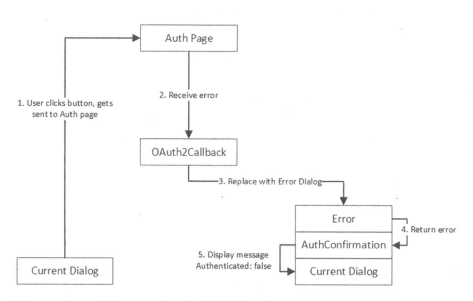

Figure 7-15. *User says login, failed authorization*

Let's see what the code for this looks like. The *Login* and *Logout* dialogs are done, but let's look at *EnsureCredentials*, *StoreTokens*, and *Error*.

EnsureCredentials is composed of two steps. First, if the user has a set of tokens defined, the dialog finishes passing a result indicating that the user is good to go. Otherwise, we create the auth URL and send a *SigninCard* to the user, just like we did in the previous section. The second step also executes in case 1. It simply tells the calling dialog that the user is authorized.

```
bot.dialog('EnsureCredentials', [(session, args) => {
    if(session.privateConversationData.tokens) {
        // if we have the tokens... we're good. if we have the
        tokens for too long and the tokens expired
        // we'd need to somehow handle it here.
        session.endDialogWithResult({ response: {
        authenticated: true } });
        return;
    }

    const oauth2Client = getAuthClient();
    const state = {
        address: session.message.address
    };
    const encryptedState = CryptoJS.AES.encrypt(JSON.
    stringify(state), process.env.AES_PASSPHRASE).toString();
    const authUrl = oauth2Client.generateAuthUrl({
        access_type: 'offline',
        scope: googleApiScopes,
        state: encryptedState
    });

    const card = new builder.HeroCard(session)
        .title('Login to Google')
```

```
    .text("Need to get your credentials. Please login
    here.")
    .buttons([
        builder.CardAction.openUrl(session, authUrl,
        'Login')
    ]);

const loginReply = new builder.Message(session)
    .attachmentLayout(builder.AttachmentLayout.carousel)
    .attachments([card]);

session.send(loginReply);
}, (session, args) => {
    session.endDialogWithResult({ response: { authenticated:
    true } });
}]);
```

StoreTokens and *Error* are similar. Both essentially return an authorization result to its parent dialog. In the case of *StoreTokens,* we also store the tokens into the conversation data.

```
bot.dialog('Error', [(session, args) => {
    session.endDialogWithResult({ response: { authenticated:
    false, error: args.error } });
}]);

bot.dialog('StoreTokens', function (session, args) {
    session.privateConversationData.tokens = args.tokens;
    session.privateConversationData.calendarId = args.
    calendarId;

    session.endDialogWithResult({ response: { authenticated:
true }});
});
```

Note that *EnsureCredentials* is going to consume the result of either of these two and simply pass it down to the calling dialog. It is up to the calling dialog to display a success or error message. There may not even be a success message; the calling dialog may just jump into its own steps.

That covers cases 1 and 2. To ensure cases 3 and 4 are covered, we need to implement this *AuthConfirmation* dialog. The role of this dialog is to display either a success or failure message. Recall that we place either an *Error* (case 3) or *StoreTokens* (case 4) dialog on top of *AuthConfirmation*. The idea is that *AuthConfirmation* will receive the name of the dialog to place on top of itself and then send the appropriate message to the user when it receives a result.

```
bod.dialog('AuthConfirmation', [
    (session, args) => {
        session.beginDialog(args.dialogName, args);
    },
    (session, args) => {
        if (args.response.authenticated) {
            session.endDialog('You are now logged in.')
        }
        else {
            session.endDialog('Error occurred while logging in.
            ' + args.response.error);
        }
    }
]);
```

Lastly, how do we change our endpoint callback code? Before we get there, we write a few helpers to invoke the different dialogs. We expose a function called *isInEnsure* that verifies whether we are getting into this piece of code from the *EnsureCredentials* dialog. This

will dictate whether we need the *AuthConfirmation. beginErrorDialog*
and *beginStoreTokensAndResume* both utilize this approach. Finally,
ensureLoggedIn is the function that each dialog that requires authorization
must call to kick off the flow.

```
function isInEnsure(session) {
    return _.find(session.dialogStack(), function (p) { return
    p.id.indexOf('EnsureCredentials') >= 0; }) != null;
}

const beginErrorDialog = (session, args) => {
    if (isInEnsure(session)) {
        session.replaceDialog('Error', args);
    }
    else {
        args.dialogName = 'Error';
        session.beginDialog('AuthConfirmation', args);
    }
};

const beginStoreTokensAndResume = (session, args) => {
    if (isInEnsure(session)) {
        session.beginDialog('StoreTokens', args);
    } else {
        args.dialogName = 'StoreTokens';
        session.beginDialog('AuthConfirmation', args);
    }
};

const ensureLoggedIn = (session) => {
    session.beginDialog('EnsureCredentials');
};
```

Finally, let's look at the callback. The code looks similar to our callback in the previous section, except we need to add the logic to begin the right dialogs. If we encounter any errors while loading our session object or we get an OAuth error, such as the user declining access to our bot, we redirect the user to the *Error* dialog. Otherwise, we use the authorization code from Google to get the tokens, set the credentials in the OAuth client, and call into the *StoreTokens* or *AuthConfirmation* dialog. The following code covers the four cases highlighted at the beginning of this section:

```
exports.oAuth2Callback = function (bot, req, res, next) {
    const code = req.query.code;
    const encryptedState = req.query.state;
    const oauthError = req.query.error;
    const state = JSON.parse(CryptoJS.AES.decrypt
    (encryptedState, process.env.AES_PASSPHRASE).
    toString(CryptoJS.enc.Utf8));
    const oauth2Client = getAuthClient();
    res.contentType = 'json';

    bot.loadSession(state.address, (sessionLoadError,
    session) => {
        if (sessionLoadError) {
            console.log('SessionLoadError:' +
            sessionLoadError);
            beginErrorDialog(session, { error: 'unable to load
            session' });
            res.send(401, {
                status: 'Unauthorized'
            });
        } else if (oauthError) {
            console.log('OAuthError:' + oauthError);
            beginErrorDialog(session, { error: 'Access Denied'
});
```

```javascript
            res.send(401, {
                status: 'Unauthorized'
            });
        } else {
            oauth2Client.getToken(code, (error, tokens) => {
                if (!error) {
                    oauth2Client.setCredentials(tokens);

                    res.send(200, {
                        status: 'success'
                    });
                    beginStoreTokensAndResume(session, {
                        tokens: tokens
                    });
                } else {
                    beginErrorDialog(session, {
                        error: error
                    });
                    res.send(500, {
                        status: 'error'
                    });
                }
            });
        }
        next();
    });
};
```

EXERCISE 7-1

Setting Up Google Auth with Gmail Access

The goal of this exercise to create a bot that allows a user to authorize against the Gmail API. Your goal is to follow these steps:

1. Set up a Google project and enable access to the Google Gmail API.

2. Create an OAuth client ID and secret.

3. Create a basic workflow in your bot that allows users to log into Google with the Gmail scope and store the tokens in the user's private conversation data.

At the end of this exercise, you will have created a bot that is ready to access the Gmail API on behalf of the bot user.

Integrating with the Google Calendar API

We are now ready to integrate with the Google Calendar API. There are a few things we should address first. Google Calendar allows users to have access to multiple calendars and, further, to have a different permission level for each calendar. In our bot, we assume that at any point we are querying or adding events into only one calendar, as flawed as that may seem. We could extend the LUIS application and bot to include the ability to specify a calendar for each utterance.

To handle this, we create a *PrimaryCalendar* dialog that allows users to set, reset, and retrieve their primary calendar. Similar to the *EnsureCredentials* dialog being called at the beginning of each dialog that requires authentication, we create a similar mechanism to guarantee that a calendar is set as primary.

Before we get there, let's talk about connecting to the Google Calendar API. The *googleapis* node package includes the Calendar APIs, among others. The API utilizes the following format:

```
API.Resource.Method(args, function (error, response) {
});
```

A calendar call would look as follows:

```
calendar.events.get({
    auth: auth,
    calendarId: calendarId,
    eventId: eventId
}, function (err, response) {
    // do stuff with the error and/or response
});
```

First, we will adapt this to the JavaScript Promise[6] pattern. Promises make it easy to work with asynchronous calls. A promise in JavaScript represents an eventual completion or failure of an operation, as well as its return value. It supports a *then* method that allows us to perform an action on the result and a *catch* method that allows us to perform an action on the error object. Promises can be chained: the result of a promise can be passed to another promise that produces a result that can get passed into another promise and so forth, resulting in code that look as follows:

```
promise1()
    .then(r1 => promise2(r2))
    .then(r2 => promise3(r2))
    .catch(err => console.log('Error in promise chain. ' + err));
```

---

[6]Mozilla Developer Network: Promise Object: https://developer.mozilla.org/en-US/docs/Web/JavaScript/Reference/Global_Objects/Promise

Our modified Google Calendar Promise API will look as follows:

```
gcalapi.getCalendar(auth, temp)
    .then(function (result) {
        // do something with result
    }).catch(function (err) {
        // do something with err
    });
```

We wrap all the necessary functions in a module called *calendar-api*. Some of the code is presented here:

```
const google = require('googleapis');
const calendar = google.calendar('v3');

function listEvents (auth, calendarId, start, end, subject) {
    const p = new Promise(function (resolve, reject) {
        calendar.events.list({
            auth: auth,
            calendarId: calendarId,
            timeMin: start.toISOString(),
            timeMax: end.toISOString(),
            q: subject
        }, function (err, response) {
            if (err) reject(err);
            resolve(response.items);
        });
    });
    return p;
}

function listCalendars (auth) {
    const p = new Promise(function (resolve, reject) {
        calendar.calendarList.list({
```

```
            auth: auth
        }, function (err, response) {
            if (err) reject(err);
            else resolve(response.items);
        });
    });
    return p;
};
```

With the API working, we now turn our focus to the *PrimaryCalendar* dialog. This dialog must handle several scenarios.

- What happens if a user sends utterances such as "get primary calendar" or "set primary calendar"? The former should return a card representation of the calendar, and the latter should allow the user to select a calendar card.

- What happens if a user logs in and a primary calendar isn't set? At that point, we automatically try to get the user to select a calendar.

- What happens if the user selects a calendar via the action button on the calendar card?

- What happens if the user selects a calendar by typing the calendar's name?

- What happens if the user tries to perform an action that requires a calendar to be set (such as adding a new appointment)?

The *PrimaryCalendar* dialog is a waterfall dialog with three steps. Step 1 ensures that the user is logged in by calling *EnsureCredentials*. Step 2 expects to receive a command from a user. We can either get our current primary calendar, set a calendar, or reset our calendar; thus, the three commands are get, set, or reset. Set calendar takes an optional calendar ID. If a calendar ID is not passed, the set command is treated equivalently to reset. Reset simply sends the user a list of all available calendars to which a user has write access to (another simplifying assumption).

The get case is handled by this code:

```
let temp = null;
if (calendarId) { temp = calendarId.entity; }
if (!temp) {
    temp = session.privateConversationData.calendarId;
}

gcalapi.getCalendar(auth, temp).then(result => {
    const msg = new builder.Message(session)
        .attachmentLayout(builder.AttachmentLayout.carousel)
        .attachments([utils.createCalendarCard
        (session, result)]);

    session.send(msg);
}).catch(err => {
    console.log(err);
    session.endDialog('No calendar found.');
});
```

The reset case sends the user a carousel of calendar cards. If the user enters a text input, the third step of the waterfall assumes that the input is a calendar name and sets the right calendar. If the input isn't recognized, an error message is sent.

```
handleReset(session, auth);

function handleReset (session, auth) {
    gcalapi.listCalendars(auth).then(result => {
        const myCalendars = _.filter(result, p => { return
        p.accessRole !== 'reader'; });
```

```
    const msg = new builder.Message(session)
        .attachmentLayout(builder.AttachmentLayout.
        carousel)
        .attachments(_.map(myCalendars, item => { return
        utils.createCalendarCard(session, item); }));

    builder.Prompts.text(session, msg);
}).catch(err => {
    console.log(err);
    session.endDialog('No calendar found.');
});
}
```

The *createCalendarCard* method simply sends a card with a title,
subtitle, and a button that sends the set calendar command. The button
posts back this value: *Set primary calendar to {calendarId}*.

```
function createCalendarCard (session, calendar) {
    const isPrimary = session.privateConversationData.
    calendarId === calendar.id;

    let subtitle = 'Your role: ' + calendar.accessRole;
    if (isPrimary) {
        subtitle = 'Primary\r\n' + subtitle;
    }
    let buttons = [];
    if (!isPrimary) {
        let btnval = 'Set primary calendar to ' + calendar.id;
        buttons = [builder.CardAction.postBack(session, btnval,
        'Set as primary')];
    }

    const heroCard = new builder.HeroCard(session)
        .title(calendar.summary)
        .subtitle(subtitle)
```

```
        .buttons(buttons);
    return heroCard;
};
```

This presents an interesting challenge. If a calendar card is sent in any context other than the *PrimaryCalendar* dialog, we need a full utterance like to resolve to a global action, which then invokes the *PrimaryCalendar* dialog. However, if we serve a card like this in the context of the primary calendar dialog, the button will still trigger the global action, therefore resetting our entire stack. We don't want to set different text based on which dialog created the card because these buttons remain in the chat history and can be clicked any time.

In addition, if the *PrimaryCalendar* dialog is invoked, we would like to ensure that it does not get rid of the current dialog. For example, if I am in the middle of adding an appointment, I should be able to switch calendars and come back to the right step in the process afterward.

We override the *triggerAction* and *selectAction* methods to ensure the right behavior. If another instance of the *PrimaryCalendar* dialog is on the stack, we replace it. Otherwise, we push the *PrimaryCalendar* dialog to the top of the stack.

```
.triggerAction({
    matches: constants.intentNames.PrimaryCalendar,
    onSelectAction: (session, args, next) => {
        if (_.find(session.dialogStack(), function (p) { return
        p.id.indexOf(constants.dialogNames.PrimaryCalendar)
        >= 0; }) != null) {
            session.replaceDialog(args.action, args);
        } else {
            session.beginDialog(args.action, args);
        }
    }
});
```

If a *PrimaryCalendar* dialog is invoked while the user is within another instance of the *PrimaryCalendar* dialog, we replace the top dialog with another instance of the PrimaryCalendar dialog. In reality, and bear with me here, this will occur only in the reset command, and it will actually replace the builder.Prompts.text dialog that we invoke in *handleReset*.

So, in essence we end up with a *PrimaryCalendar* dialog waiting for a response object that can now come from another *PrimaryCalendar* dialog. We can have the topmost instance return a flag when it is done so that the other instance simply exits when the third step resumes. Here is the final waterfall step to illustrate this logic:

```
function (session, args) {
    // if we have a response from another primary calendar
    dialog, we simply finish up!
    if (args.response.calendarSet) {
        session.endDialog({ response: { calendarSet: true } });
        return;
    }

    // else we try to match the user text input to a calendar
    name
    var name = session.message.text;
    var auth = authModule.getAuthClientFromSession(session);

    // we try to find the calendar with a summary that matches
    the user's input.
    gcalapi.listCalendars(auth).then(function (result) {
        var myCalendars = _.filter(result, function (p) {
        return p.accessRole != 'reader'; });
        var calendar = _.find(myCalendars, function (item)
        { return item.summary.toUpperCase() === name.
        toUpperCase(); });
        if (calendar == null) {
```

```
            session.send('No such calendar found.');
            session.replaceDialog(constants.dialogNames.
            PrimaryCalendar);
        }
        else {
            session.privateConversationData.calendarId =
            result.id;
            var card = utils.createCalendarCard(session, result);
            var msg = new builder.Message(session)
                .attachmentLayout(builder.AttachmentLayout.
                carousel)
                .attachments([card])
                .text('Primary calendar set!');
            session.send(msg);
            session.endDialog({ response: { calendarSet: true }
            });
        }
    }).catch(function (err) {
        console.log(err);
        session.endDialog('No calendar found.');
    });
}
```

The set action is less complex. If we receive a calendar ID along with
the user message, we simply set that message and send back a card of the
calendar. If we do not receive a calendar ID, we assume the same behavior
as reset.

```
let temp = null;
if (calendarId) { temp = calendarId.entity; }
if (!temp) {
    handleReset(session, auth);
} else {
```

```
gcalapi.getCalendar(auth, temp).then(result => {
    session.privateConversationData.calendarId = result.id;
    const card = utils.createCalendarCard(session, result);
    const msg = new builder.Message(session)
        .attachmentLayout(builder.AttachmentLayout.
        carousel)
        .attachments([card])
        .text('Primary calendar set!');
    session.send(msg);
    session.endDialog({ response: { calendarSet: true } });
}).catch(err => {
    console.log(err);
    session.endDialog('this calendar does not exist');
    // this calendar id doesn't exist...
});
}
```

That was a lot to process, but it is a good illustration of some the dialog gymnastics that need to occur to ensure a consistent and comprehensive conversational experience. In the following section, we will integrate the authentication and primary calendar flows into the dialogs we developed in Chapter 6 and connect the logic to calls into the Google Calendar API.

Implementing the Bot Functionality

At this point, we are ready to connect our bot code to the Google Calendar API. Our code doesn't change too much from its Chapter 5 state. These are the main changes to our dialogs:

- We must ensure that the user is logged in.
- We must ensure a primary calendar is set.
- Utilize the Google Calendar APIs to finally make things happen!

Let's start with the first two items. We have created the
EnsureCredentials and *PrimaryCalendar* dialogs for this very purpose.
In the provided code, our *authModule* and *primaryCalendarModule*
modules contain a couple of helpers to call the *EnsureCredentials* and
PrimaryCalendar dialogs. Each of our functions can utilize the helpers to
ensure that the credentials and the primary calendar are set.

This is too much responsibility for those dialogs. We would have to
add two steps into every single dialog. Instead, let's create a dialog that can
evaluate all the prechecks in the correct order and simply pass one result
to the calling dialog. Here's how we would achieve this. We create a dialog
called *PreCheck*. This dialog will make the necessary checks and return
a response object with an error set if there is an error as well as a flag
indicating which check failed.

```
bot.dialog('PreCheck', [
    function (session, args) {
        authModule.ensureLoggedIn(session);
    },
    function (session, args) {
        if (!args.response.authenticated) {
            session.endDialogWithResult({ response: { error:
            'You must authenticate to continue.', error_auth:
            true } });
        } else {
            primaryCalendarModule.ensurePrimaryCalendar
            (session);
        }
    },
    function (session, args, next) {
        if (session.privateConversationData.calendarId)
        session.endDialogWithResult({ response: { } });
```

```
    else session.endDialogWithResult({ response: { error:
    'You must set a primary calendar to continue.', error_
    calendar: true } });
  }
]);
```

Any dialog that needs auth and a primary calendar to be set only needs to invoke the *PreCheck* dialog and ensure there was no error. Here is an example from the *ShowCalendarSummary* dialog in the sample code. Note that the first step in the waterfall calls *PreCheck,* and the second step ensures all prechecks successfully passed.

```
lib.dialog(constants.dialogNames.ShowCalendarSummary, [
    function (session, args) {
        g = args.intent;
        prechecksModule.ensurePrechecks(session);
    },
    function (session, args, next) {
        if (args.response.error) {
            session.endDialog(args.response.error);
            return;
        }
        next();
    },
    function (session, args, next) {
        // do stuff
    }
]).triggerAction({ matches: constants.intentNames.
ShowCalendarSummary });
```

So that's it for the first two items. At this point, all that is left is the third one; we need to implement the actual integration with the Google Calendar API. The following is the example of what the third step of the

ShowCalendarSummary dialog looks like. Notice that we gather the datetimeV2 entities to figure out what time period we need to retrieve events for, we optionally use the *Subject* entity to filter out calendar items, and we build a carousel of event cards, ordered by date. The *createEventCard* method creates a HeroCard object for every Google Calendar API event object.

The implementation of the remaining dialogs is available in the calendar-bot-buildup repository included with the book.

```
function (session, args, next) {
    var auth = authModule.getAuthClientFromSession(session);
    var entry = new et.EntityTranslator();
    et.EntityTranslatorUtils.attachSummaryEntities(entry,
    session.dialogData.intent.entities);
    var start = null;
    var end = null;

    if (entry.hasRange) {
        if (entry.isDateTimeEntityDateBased) {
            start = moment(entry.range.start).
            startOf('day');
            end = moment(entry.range.end).endOf('day');
        } else {
            start = moment(entry.range.start);
            end = moment(entry.range.end);
        }
    } else if (entry.hasDateTime) {
        if (entry.isDateTimeEntityDateBased) {
            start = moment(entry.dateTime).startOf('day');
            end = moment(entry.dateTime).endOf('day');
        } else {
            start = moment(entry.dateTime).add(-1, 'h');
```

```
            end = moment(entry.dateTime).add(1, 'h');
    }
}
else {
    session.endDialog("Sorry I don't know what you
    mean");
    return;
}

var p = gcalapi.listEvents(auth, session.
privateConversationData.calendarId, start, end);
p.then(function (events) {

    var evs = _.sortBy(events, function (p) {
        if (p.start.date) {
            return moment(p.start.date).add(-1, 's').
            valueOf();
        } else if (p.start.dateTime) {
            return moment(p.start.dateTime).valueOf();
        }
    });

    // should also potentially filter by subject
    evs = _.filter(evs, function(p) {
        if(!entry.hasSubject) return true;

        var containsSubject = entry.subject.
        toLowerCase().indexOf(entry.subject.
        toLowerCase()) >= 0;
        return containsSubject;
    });

    var eventmsg = new builder.Message(session);
    if (evs.length > 1) {
```

```
                    eventmsg.text('Here is what I found...');
            } else if (evs.length == 1) {
                eventmsg.text('Here is the event I found.');
            } else {
                eventmsg.text('Seems you have nothing going on
                then. What a sad existence you lead.');
            }

            if (evs.length >= 1) {
                var cards = _.map(evs, function (p) {
                    return utils.createEventCard(session, p);
                });

                                        eventmsg.attachmentLayout
                                        (builder.AttachmentLayout.
                                        carousel);
                eventmsg.attachments(cards);
            }

            session.send(eventmsg);
            session.endDialog();
        });
    }

function createEventCard(session, event) {

    var start, end, subtitle;
    if (!event.start.date) {
        start = moment(event.start.dateTime);
        end = moment(event.end.dateTime);

        var diffInMinutes = end.diff(start, "m");
        var diffInHours = end.diff(start, "h");

        var duration = diffInMinutes + ' minutes';
```

```javascript
        if (diffInHours >= 1) {
            var hrs = Math.floor(diffInHours);
            var mins = diffInMinutes - (hrs * 60);

            if (mins == 0) {
                duration = hrs + 'hrs';
            } else {
                duration = hrs + (hrs > 1 ? 'hrs ' : 'hr ') +
                (mins < 10 ? ('0' + mins) : mins) + 'mins';
            }
        }
        subtitle = 'At ' + start.format('L LT') + ' for ' +
        duration;
    } else {
        start = moment(event.start.date);
        end = moment(event.end.date);

        var diffInDays = end.diff(start, 'd');
        subtitle = 'All Day ' + start.format('L') +
        (diffInDays > 1 ? end.format('L') : '');
    }

    var heroCard = new builder.HeroCard(session)
        .title(event.summary)
        .subtitle(subtitle)
        .buttons([
            builder.CardAction.openUrl(session, event.htmlLink,
            'Open Google Calendar'),
            builder.CardAction.postBack(session, 'Delete event
            with id ' + event.id, 'Delete')
        ]);
    return heroCard;
};
```

Integrating with the Gmail API

Although you are welcome to follow the code in the previous section and then use the code provided with the book to put together a calendar bot, the goal of this exercise is to create a bot that can send emails from the user's Gmail account. This way, you can exercise your authentication logic from Exercise 7-1 and integrate with a client API you have not seen before.

1. Taking your code from Exercise 7-1 as a starting point, create a bot that contain two dialogs, one for sending mail and one for viewing unread messages. There is no need to create a LUIS application (though you are certainly free to work on that). Use keywords like *send* and *list* to invoke the dialogs.

2. For the send operation, create a dialog called *SendMail.* This dialog should collect an email address, a title, and message body text. Ensure the dialog is integrated with an auth flow.

3. Integrate with the Gmail client library to send an email using the user's access tokens collected during the auth flow. Use the documentation here for the messages.send API call: `https://developers.google.com/gmail/api/v1/reference/users/messages/send`.

4. For the list operation, create a dialog called *ListMail.* This dialog should get all unread mail from the user's inbox using the user's access tokens collected during the auth flow. Use the documentation here for the messages.list API call: `https://developers.google.com/gmail/api/v1/reference/users/messages/list`.

5.   Render the list of unread messages as a carousel. Display the
     title, date received, and a button to open the email message
     in a web browser. You can find the reference for the messages
     object here: `https://developers.google.com/gmail/`
     `api/v1/reference/users/messages#resource`.
     The URL for a message is `https://mail.google.com/`
     `mail/#inbox/{MESSAGE_ID}`.

If you succeeded in creating this bot, congratulations! This is not the easiest
of exercises, but the results is well worth it. You now have the skills to create
a bot, integrate it with an OAuth flow, use a third-party API to make your bot
functional, and render items as cards. Great work!

Conclusion

Building bots is both easy and challenging. It is easy to set up a basic bot
with some simple commands. It is easy to get user utterances and execute
code based on them. It is, however, quite challenging to get the user
experience just right. As we have observed, the challenges in developing
bots are twofold.

First, we need to make sense of the many permutations of natural
language utterances. Our users can say the same things in numerous ways
with nuanced variations. The LUIS application we've built for this book are
a good start, but there are many other ways of expressing the same ideas.
We'll need to exercise judgment on when we say that a LUIS application
is good enough. Bot testing is where a lot of this kind of evaluation occurs.
Once we unleash a set of users on your bot, we will see how users end
up using your bot and what type of inputs and behaviors they expect to
be handled. This is the data we need to improve our natural language
understanding and decide what features to build next. We will cover
analytics tools that help with this task in Chapter 13.

Second, it is important to spend time on the overall conversations experience. Although this is not the focus of this book, a proper experience is key to our bots' success. We did spend some time thinking around how to ensure that the user is logged in before we proceed into dialogs with any actions against the Calendar API. This is an example of the type of behaviors and flows that need to be thought through as we develop a bot. A more naïve bot may simply send the user an error saying they need to log in first, after which the user would have to repeat their input. A better implementation is the redirection through dialogs that we created in this chapter. Lucky for us, the Bot Builder SDK and its dialog model help us describe these complex flows in code.

We now have the skills and experience to develop complex and amazing bot experiences, with all types of API integrations. This is the real combined power of LUIS and the Microsoft Bot Framework!

CHAPTER 8

Extending Channel Functionality

We have spent a substantial amount of time so far discussing NLU systems, conversational experiences, and how we can develop bots in a generic manner using a common format via the Bot Builder SDK. The Bot Builder SDK lets us get up and running quickly. This is part of why it is such a powerful abstraction. But frankly, a lot of the innovation in the space is coming from the various messaging platforms. For example, Slack is leading the pack in terms of collaboration software. Slack's ability to edit messages, allowing for interactive workflows, is very powerful.

In this chapter, we will explore the ability to invoke native functionality from within a Bot Framework bot. We will learn to invoke Slack's feature to transform simple text-based workflows into rich button and menu-based experiences. Along the way, we will sign up for a Slack integration, connect our bot to our Slack workspace, and then use native Slack calls to create a compelling and straightforward workflow. Let's dive in.

Deeper Slack Integration

Slack is a rich platform that allows close collaboration among different members of internal and external teams. The interface is simple, yet the messaging framework is quite different from something like Facebook

Messenger. For example, although there is a facility called *attachments* that results in a user interface similar to cards, it is not treated in the same way. There are no carousels, and there are no requirements around aspect ratios for images.

A message in Slack is simply a JSON object with a text property, where the text can have special sequences that reference users, channels, or teams. These references, called *@mentions*, are text strings like *@channel*, which notifies all users in a channel to pay attention to a message. Other examples are *@here* and *@everyone*. A message can include up to 20 attachments. An attachment is simply an object that provides additional context to the message. The JSON object looks as follows:

```
{
    "attachments": [
        {
            "fallback": "Required plain-text summary of the
            attachment.",
            "color": "#36a64f",
            "pretext": "Optional text that appears above the
            attachment block",
            "author_name": "Bobby Tables",
            "author_link": "http://flickr.com/bobby/",
            "author_icon": "http://flickr.com/icons/bobby.jpg",
            "title": "Slack API Documentation",
            "title_link": "https://api.slack.com/",
            "text": "Optional text that appears within the
            attachment",
```

```
        "fields": [
            {
                "title": "Priority",
                "value": "High",
                "short": false
            }
        ],
        "image_url": "http://my-website.com/path/to/image.
        jpg",
        "thumb_url": "http://example.com/path/to/thumb.png",
        "footer": "Slack API",
        "footer_icon": "https://platform.slack-edge.com/
        img/default_application_icon.png",
        "ts": 123456789
    }
  ]
}
```

Like a *HeroCard*, we can include title, text, and images. In addition, there are various other parameters we can provide to Slack. We can include references to a message author, data fields or theme colors.

To aid in the nuances of attachments, Slack includes a Message Builder (Figure 8-1), which can be used to visualize how a JSON object will render in the Slack user interface.

1. Enter your message as JSON

```
1  {
2      "attachments": [
3          {
4              "fallback": "Required plain-text summary of the attachment.",
5              "color": "#36a64f",
6              "pretext": "Optional text that appears above the attachment block",
7              "author_name": "Bobby Tables",
8              "author_link": "http://flickr.com/bobby/",
9              "author_icon": "http://flickr.com/icons/bobby.jpg",
10             "title": "Slack API Documentation"
```

Examples: Basic formatting | Attachments | Message buttons

2. Preview your message

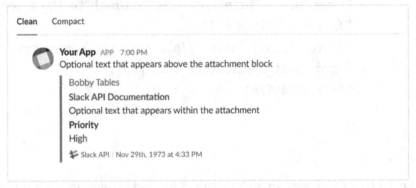

Figure 8-1. *Slack Message Builder and preview*

Slack also provides best practices documentation for messages.[1] Among the advice on the site is to use as few attachments as makes sense for our application (Figure 8-2).

Don't get too attached

Don't use an attachment when regular message text will suffice, and don't send multiple attachments when a single attachment will do.

And never ever (ever!) send more than 20 attachments.

Figure 8-2. *Good direction...*

---

[1]Slack Message guidelines: https://api.slack.com/docs/message-guidelines

Unfortunately, this does not seem to be the way that the Bot Framework works. In fact, the Slack Bot channel connector renders a *HeroCard* object as multiple attachments (Figure 8-3).

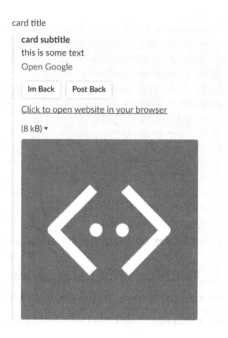

Figure 8-3. *Except that the Slack guidelines are not fully respected by the Slack Bot channel connector*

It's a small detail, but it just does not look good. The default styling for an image and buttons is to render the buttons below the image (Figure 8-4). Unfortunately, the rendering is violating the direction provided by Slack.

Message with image attachment

Figure 8-4. *What a well-formed attached could look like*

Naturally, this is the kind of detail the Bot Framework team will most likely support in the future. Until then, if there is a mismatch in terms of the type of interface we want to render and what the platform supports, we can drop into the native JSON to achieve our goals.

Slack also includes a few features that we have no way of accessing as first-class citizens in the bot service. Slack supports ephemeral messages, which are messages that are visible to only one user in a group setting. The Bot Builder SDK does not provide an easy way to achieve this. Furthermore, Slack supports the idea of interactive messages, which are messages with buttons and menus that users can act on. Even better, a user's action can trigger an update to the message rendering! A message can include buttons as a way to gather data from the user (as shown in Figures 8-3 and 8-4), or a message can include menus to select an option (Figure 8-5).

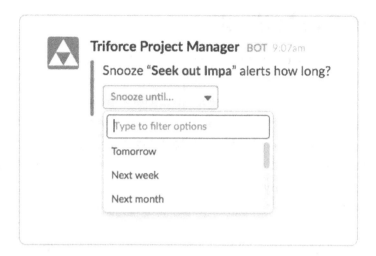

Figure 8-5. *A Slack menu*

In this section, we will explore how to achieve the interactive message effect by integrating closely via native messages.

First, we will integrate our bot with a Slack workspace. Second, we will create a one-step interactive message. Third, we'll create a multistep interactive message that provides a rich, Slack-native data-gathering experience.

Before we continue, let's go over a few ground rules. This chapter is not intended to give you a deep dive into Slack's Messaging APIs and features. We encourage you to read about these on your own; Slack has very rich documentation on the subject. What we do want to show is how we can leverage the bot service to provide that deeper integration with Slack. You may ask, why not just develop a native Slackbot using Slack's Node Developer Kit? You certainly can, but there are two big reasons for using the Bot Builder library. One, you get the dialog and conversation engine to help guide a user through a conversation, and two, if you are exposing an experience on multiple messaging channels, one codebase enables code reuse.

Connecting to Slack

Let's assume you have never used Slack. We will first need to create a
Slack workspace. A workspace is simply a Slack environment for a team to
collaborate in. We can create these for free. There are some limitations, but
free teams remain very functional and will certainly allow us to develop
and demo Slack bots. Go to `https://slack.com/create` to create a
workspace. Slack will ask for an email (Figure 8-6) and send a confirmation
code to verify our identity.

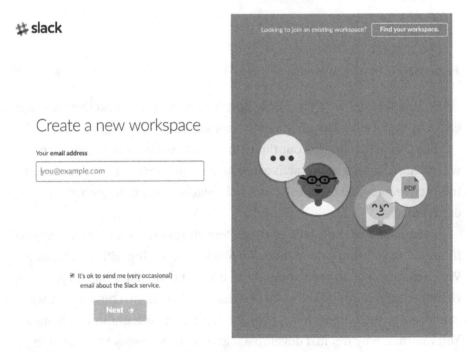

Figure 8-6. *Creating a new Slack workspace*

Once we enter the confirmation code, it will ask us for our name,
password, (group) workspace name, target audience, and workspace
URL. We can send invitations to the workspace, but we will skip this for
now. We will not be redirected to the workspace. For the purposes of this
demo, mine is `https://srozgaslacksample.slack.com`.

At this point, we should integrate the bot service and Slack. In our Bot Service entry on Azure, click the Slack channel. We'll be greeted with the Slack Configuration screen (Figure 8-7).

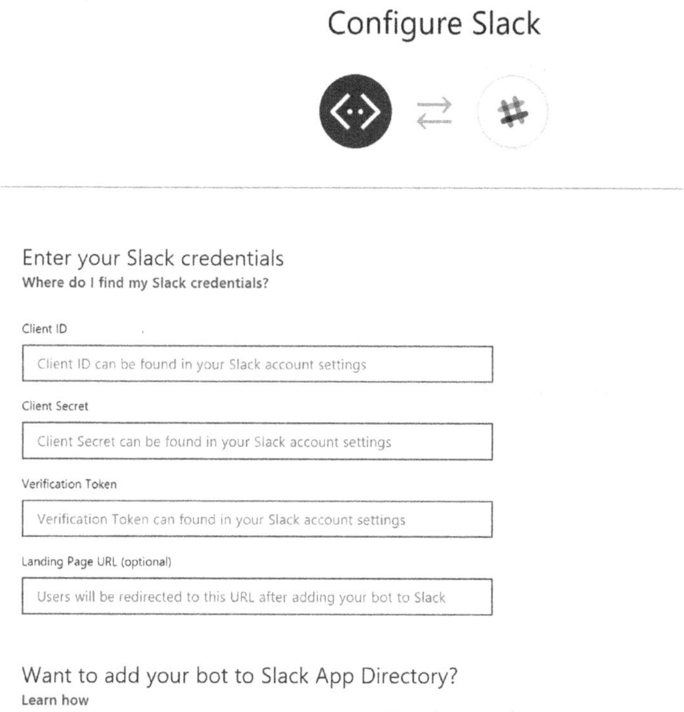

Configure Slack

Enter your Slack credentials
Where do I find my Slack credentials?

Client ID

Client ID can be found in your Slack account settings

Client Secret

Client Secret can be found in your Slack account settings

Verification Token

Verification Token can found in your Slack account settings

Landing Page URL (optional)

Users will be redirected to this URL after adding your bot to Slack

Want to add your bot to Slack App Directory?
Learn how

Figure 8-7. *Configuring our bot's Slack integration*

The interface is like the Facebook Messenger channel configuration interface but asks for differrent data. We will need three pieces of information from Slack: the client ID, the client secret, and the verification token.

Log into Slack and create a new app at `https://api.slack.com/apps`. Enter an app name and select the development workspace that we just created (Figure 8-8). Lastly click the *Create App* button.

Figure 8-8. *Creating a Slack app*

Once the app is created, we will be redirected to the app page. Click *Permissions* to set up a redirect URL (Figure 8-9). You will be taken to a page called *OAuth & Permissions*.

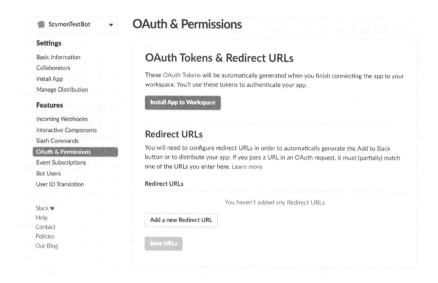

Figure 8-9. *Setting up the bot service redirect URI*

Click *Add a new Redirect URL* and enter **https://slack.botframework.com**. Next select the *Bot Users* item in the left sidebar, and add a user for the bot. This allows us to assign a username to the bot and indicate whether it should always appear online (Figure 8-10).

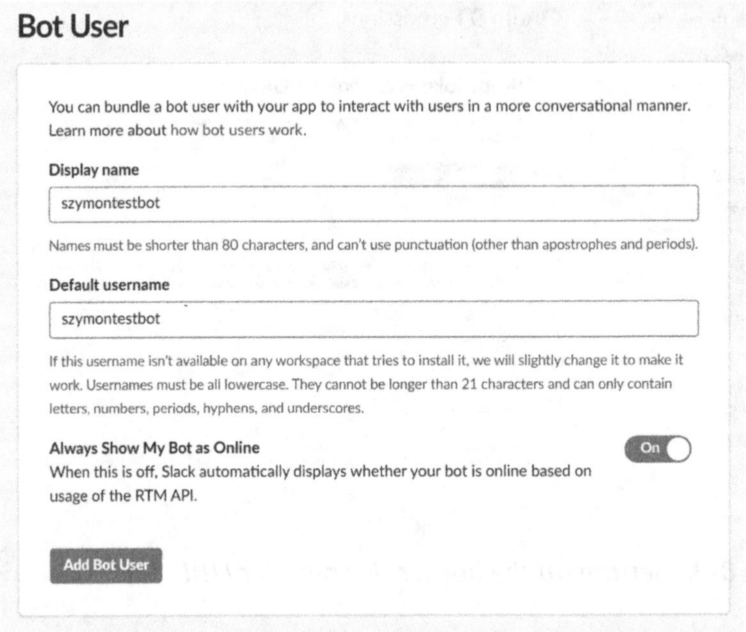

Bot User

You can bundle a bot user with your app to interact with users in a more conversational manner. Learn more about how bot users work.

Display name

szymontestbot

Names must be shorter than 80 characters, and can't use punctuation (other than apostrophes and periods).

Default username

szymontestbot

If this username isn't available on any workspace that tries to install it, we will slightly change it to make it work. Usernames must be all lowercase. They cannot be longer than 21 characters and can only contain letters, numbers, periods, hyphens, and underscores.

Always Show My Bot as Online   On
When this is off, Slack automatically displays whether your bot is online based on usage of the RTM API.

Add Bot User

Figure 8-10. *Creating a bot user that represents a bot in a channel*

Next, we will subscribe to several events that will be sent to the bot service web hooks. This will ensure that the bot service can properly send the relevant Slack events into our bot. Navigate to *Event Subscriptions*, enable events via the toggle at the right, and enter **https://slack. botframework.com/api/Events/{YourBotHandle}** as the request URL. A bot handle was assigned to our bot channel registration in Chapter 5 and can be found in the Settings blade. Once entered, Slack will establish connectivity to the endpoint. Lastly, under *Subscribe to Bot Events* (not *Workspace Events!*) add the following events:

- member_joined_channel

- member_left_channel

- message.channels

- message.groups

- message.im

- message.mpim

Figure 8-11 shows the resulting configuration.

Figure 8-11. *Subscribing our bot to Slack events*

We also need to enable interactive components to support receiving a message with a menu, button, or interactive dialog. Select *Interactive Components* from the left menu, click *Enable Interactive Messages*, and enter the following request URL: **https://slack.botframework.com/api/Actions** (Figure 8-12). Click *Enable Interactive Components* and save the changes.

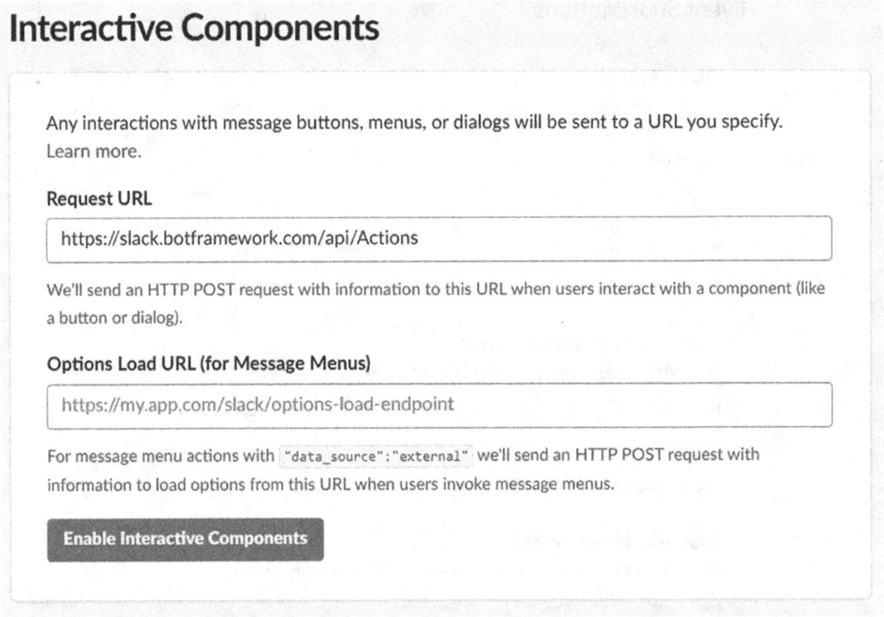

Interactive Components

Any interactions with message buttons, menus, or dialogs will be sent to a URL you specify. Learn more.

Request URL

https://slack.botframework.com/api/Actions

We'll send an HTTP POST request with information to this URL when users interact with a component (like a button or dialog).

Options Load URL (for Message Menus)

https://my.app.com/slack/options-load-endpoint

For message menu actions with `"data_source":"external"` we'll send an HTTP POST request with information to load options from this URL when users invoke message menus.

Enable Interactive Components

Figure 8-12. *Enabling interactive components in our bot. That means buttons and menus!*

Lastly, we extract the credentials from the App Credentials section (accessible via the Basic Information menu item) and enter the client ID, client secret, and verification token into the Configure Slack screen within the Channels blade of your bot channels registration in the Azure Portal. Once submitted, you will be asked to log into your Slack workspace and verify the app. After authorization, your bot will appear in your Slack workspace interface (under the Apps category), and you will be able to communicate with it (Figure 8-13).

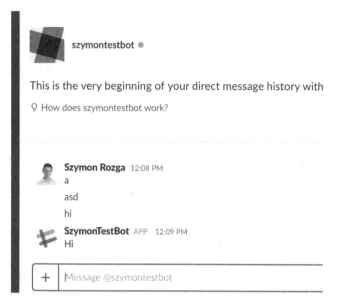

Figure 8-13. *We've connected to the Azure bot service*

Remember to run ngrok! You can tell I forgot to run my ngrok in Figure 8-13.

EXERCISE 8-1

Basic Slack Integration and Message Rendering

The goal of this exercise is to connect a bot into Slack so you can get familiar with Slack as a messaging and bot platform. Your goal is to take the calendar bot you created in the Chapters 5 and 7 and deploy it to Slack. Once deployed, you may examine how the different elements are rendered in Slack versus the emulator or Facebook Messenger.

1. Create a test Slack workspace.

2. Connect your Azure Bot service bot to the workspace by following the steps in the previous section.

3. Confirm you can communicate with your bot via Slack.

4. Test the bot and answer the following questions: How does the
    bot render the sign-in button? How does the bot render the
    primary card selection cards? How does the bot behave in a
    multi-user conversation (you may need to add a new test user
    to the workspace)?

Great work. You are now able to connect an existing bot to Slack, and you are
learning about Slack, its message, and attachments.

Experimenting with the Slack APIs

We just send a message to Slack using the Bot Builder SDK and the
Bot Framework, but we can also access the Slack APIs directly. We are
interested in several Slack API methods.[2]

- *Chat.postMessage*: Posts a new message into a Slack
  channel

- *Chat.update*: Updates an existing message in Slack

- *Chat.postEphemeral*: Posts a new ephemeral message,
  one visible to only one user, into a Slack channel

- *Chat.delete*: Deletes a Slack message

To invoke any of these, we need an access token. For example,
assuming we have a token, we could use the following Node.js code to
create a new message:

```
function postMessage(token, channel, text, attachments) {
    return new Promise((resolve, reject) => {
        let client = restify.createJsonClient({
```

---

[2]Slack API Methods: https://api.slack.com/methods

```
        url: 'https://slack.com/api/chat.postMessage',
        headers: {
            Authorization: 'Bearer ' + token
        }
    });
    client.post('',
        {
            channel: channel,
            text: text,
            attachments: attachments
        },
        function (err, req, res, obj) {
            if (err) {
                console.log('%j', err);
                reject(err);
                return;
            }
            console.log('%d -> %j', res.statusCode,
            res.headers);
            console.log('%j', obj);
            resolve(obj);
        });
    });
}
```

A natural question is how do we obtain the token? If we examine the message coming in from the bot service channel connector, we notice that we have all that information at our disposal. The full incoming message from Slack looks like this:

```
{
    "type": "message",
    "timestamp": "2017-11-23T17:27:13.5973326Z",
```

```
"text": "hi",
"attachments": [],
"entities": [],
"sourceEvent": {
    "SlackMessage": {
        "token": "ffffffffffffffffffffffff",
        "team_id": "T84FFFFF",
        "api_app_id": "A84SFFFFF",
        "event": {
            "type": "message",
            "user": "U85MFFFFF",
            "text": "hi",
            "ts": "1511458033.000193",
            "channel": "D85TN0231",
            "event_ts": "1511458033.000193"
        },
        "type": "event_callback",
        "event_id": "Ev84PDKPCK",
        "event_time": 1511458033,
        "authed_users": [
            "U84A79YTB"
        ]
    },
    "ApiToken": "xxxxxxxxxxxxxxxxxxxxxxxxxxxxxxxxxxxx"
},
"address": {
    "id": "ffffffffffffffffffffffffffffffffffff",
    "channelId": "slack",
    "user": {
        "id": "U85M9EQJ2:T84V64ML5",
        "name": "szymon.rozga"
    },
```

```
        "conversation": {
            "isGroup": false,
            "id": "B84SQJLLU:T84V64ML5:D85TN0231"
        },
        "bot": {
            "id": "B84SQJLLU:T84V64ML5",
            "name": "szymontestbot"
        },
        "serviceUrl": "https://slack.botframework.com"
    },
    "source": "slack",
    "agent": "botbuilder",
    "user": {
        "id": "U85M9EQJ2:T84V64ML5",
        "name": "szymon.rozga"
    }
}
```

Note that the *sourceEvent* includes an *ApiToken* and a *SlackMessage* with all the details about which channel the bot is in and the user from which the original message originated. In this example, the channel is D85TN0231, and the user is U85M9EQJ2. Further, we can find the IDs for the team, the bot, the bot user, and the app. An incoming message doesn't really have an ID in Slack; each message has a unique-per-channel timestamp referred to as *ts*.

So, once we have the first message from a user, we can easily respond either by using the Bot Builder's *session.send* method or by using the *chat. postMessage* endpoint directly (Figure 8-14). Of course, *session.send* is doing all the token work for us underneath the covers by calling to the Slack channel connector, which then calls *chat.postMessage*.

```
const bot = new builder.UniversalBot(connector, [
    session => {
        let token = session.message.sourceEvent.ApiToken;
        let channel = session.message.sourceEvent.SlackMessage.
        event.channel;

        postMessage(token, channel, 'POST!');
    }
]);
```

Figure 8-14. Responding using a native Slack call

postMessage does not really get us anything better than *session.send,*
except that *chat.postMessage* returns the message's native *ts* value, whereas
session.send does not. Very cool. That means we can now update the
message! We define an *updateMessage* method as follows:

```
function updateMessage(token, channel, ts, text, attachments) {
    return new Promise((resolve, reject) => {
        let client = restify.createJsonClient({
            url: 'https://slack.com/api/chat.update',
            headers: {
                Authorization: 'Bearer ' + token
            }
        });
        client.post('',
            {
                channel: channel,
                ts: ts,
```

```
                    text: text,
                    attachments: attachments
                },
                function (err, req, res, obj) {
                    if (err) {
                        console.log('%j', err);
                        reject(err);
                        return;
                    }
                    console.log('%d -> %j', res.statusCode,
                    res.headers);
                    console.log('%j', obj);
                    resolve(obj);
                });
        });
    });
};
```

Now we can write code to send a message and update it whenever any other response comes in (see Figure 8-15, Figure 8-16, and Figure 8-17).

```
let msgts = null;

const bot = new builder.UniversalBot(connector, [
    session => {
        let token = session.message.sourceEvent.ApiToken;
        let channel = session.message.sourceEvent.SlackMessage.
        event.channel;
        let user = session.message.sourceEvent.SlackMessage.
        event.user;

        if (msgts) {
            updateMessage(token, channel, msgts, '<@' + user +
            '> said ' + session.message.text);
        } else {
```

```
        postMessage(token, channel, 'A placeholder...').
        then(r => {
            msgts = r.ts;
        });
    }
  }
]);
```

hi

 SzymonTestBot APP   9:26 PM
A placeholder...

Figure 8-15. *So far so good...*

hi

 SzymonTestBot APP   9:26 PM
@Szymon Rozga said hello

 Szymon Rozga 9:26 PM
hello

Figure 8-16. *Seems to be working...*

hi

 SzymonTestBot APP   9:26 PM
@Szymon Rozga said what?

 Szymon Rozga 9:26 PM
hello
what?

Figure 8-17. *Exactly as designed*

Now this is a contrived example, but it illustrates our ability to call a *postMessage* followed by an update to modify the contents of a message. There are some rules around what exactly update can do, but we leave reading that documentation[3] as an exercise to the developer.

Another example of what we can accomplish with the APIs is posting and removing ephemeral messages. An ephemeral message is visible only to the recipient of the message. The bot can, for example, give feedback to a user without displaying the result in the channel until all the necessary data has been gathered. Although a slightly different interaction model, the *giphy*[4] Slash command is a great example of this model.

Using /*giphy* allows us to search for any text and brings up a few GIF options in an ephemeral message. You may have to enable the integration first, before utilizing it. Once we decide which one we want to use and click Send, the GIF is sent to the channel on our behalf (Figure 8-18, Figure 8-19, and Figure 8-20).

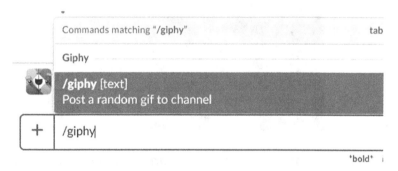

Figure 8-18. *Invoking the /giphy Slash command*

---

[3]Slack API chat.update: `https://api.slack.com/methods/chat.update`
[4]Giphy for Slack: `https://get.slack.help/hc/en-us/`
 `articles/204714258-Giphy-for-Slack`

377

Figure 8-19. *A preview of a cool mom mean girls GIF*

Figure 8-20. *I've now immortalized in Slack conversation the 2004 cult classic Mean Girls by using /giphy mean girls*

We could use the *postEphemeral* message to give feedback to only certain users. And, of course, delete gives us the ability to delete old messages from the bot. From a usability perspective, the delete feature is not interesting. It is a better experience to update a message with a correction or to notify the user that a message has been deleted, rather than to simply get rid of it without any explanation.

Simple Interactive Message

Slack allows us to instrument better conversational experiences using what are known as interactive messages.[5] An interactive message is a message that includes the usual message data plus buttons and menus. In addition, as users interact with the user interface elements, the message can change to reflect that.

Here is an example: the bot would send a message asking for approval, and when the user clicks the yes or no button, our bot modifies the message to reflect the selection (Figure 8-21, Figure 8-22, and Figure 8-23).

Figure 8-21. *A simple interactive message*

Figure 8-22. *Request approved*

Figure 8-23. *Request was not approved*

---

[5]Slack Interactive Messages: https://api.slack.com/interactive-messages

Certainly, we can orchestrate this type of behavior using *postMessage* and *updateMessage*, but there's an easier and more integrated way to do it. First, we define a dialog called *simpleflow* that uses a Choice Prompt to send a message with buttons.

```
const bot = new builder.UniversalBot(connector, [
    session => {
        session.beginDialog('simpleflow');
    },
    session => {
        session.send('done!!!');
        session.endConversation();
    }
]);

bot.dialog('simpleflow',
[
    (session, arg) =>{
        builder.Prompts.choice(session, 'A request for access
        to /SYS13/ABD has come in. Do you want to approve?',
        'Yes|No');
    },
    ... // next code snippet goes here
]);
```

Then we handle the response to the button click by making a POST request to a response_url.

```
(session, arg) =>{
    let r = arg.response.entity;
    let responseUrl = session.message.sourceEvent.Payload.
    response_url;
    let token = session.message.sourceEvent.Payload.token;
```

```javascript
let client = restify.createJsonClient({
    url: responseUrl
});
let userId = session.message.sourceEvent.Payload.user.id;

let attachment ={
    color: 'danger',
    text: 'Rejected by <@' + userId + '>'
};
if (r === 'No'){} else if (r === 'Yes'){
    attachment ={
        color: 'good',
        text: 'Approved by <@' + userId + '>'
    };
}

client.post('',
{
    token: token,
    text: 'Request for access to /SYS13/ABD',
    attachments: [attachment
    ]
}, function (err, req, res, obj){
    if (err) console.log('Error -> %j', err);
    console.log('%d -> %j', res.statusCode, res.headers);
    console.log('%j', obj);
    session.endDialog();
});
}
```

A few things are happening here. First, we grab the response from Slack, which is resolved to the entity value. Second, we grab what's known as the response_url from the Slack message. A response_url is a URL that allows us to modify the interactive message that a user just responded to or to create a new message in the channel. Next, we grab the token that authorizes us to send POST requests to the response_url. Lastly, we POST to the response_url with the updated message.

We will get into more details around interactive message structure, but let's discuss user experience. When developing a bot that utilizes this functionality, we have to make a decision: when the bot presents an interactive message, does the user have to answer it immediately, or can the interactive message remain in the history while the user and bot discuss other topics? In the latter case, at any time later in the conversation, the user could scroll back up and click a button to complete the action. The previous sample utilizes the former approach; that is the way Bot Builder prompts work. Figure 8-24 shows what this looks like if the user doesn't respond to the message.

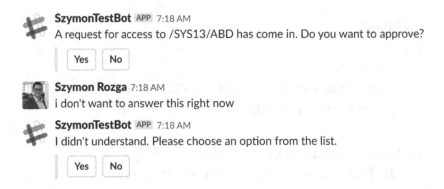

Figure 8-24. *Hmm...seems I have two sets of buttons to answer the same question*

OK, we have the two set of buttons. That makes sense. If we click either the *Yes* or *No* button, that message will be modified per Figure 8-25. The dialog finished, and the second step of the bot waterfall sends the "done!!!" message. However, the conversation is left in a weird state; it appears as if the original request is still open.

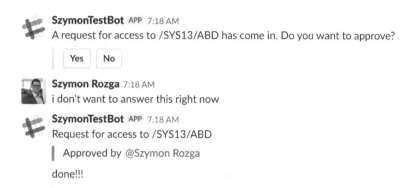

Figure 8-25. *Shouldn't the first message update as well?*

Now, the dialog stack no longer contains the choice prompt on top of the stack. This means that if we click the *Yes* or *No* button in the upper message, we will run into a problem because our code is not expecting that type of response (Figure 8-26). In fact, we will receive yet another prompt because the bot once again calls *beginDialog*. Having multiple unresolved interaction messages without the ability to resolve all of them is bad UX.

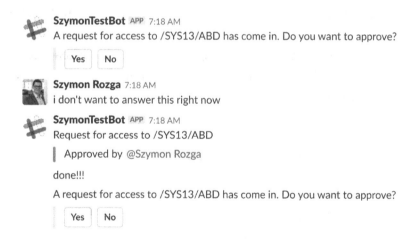

Figure 8-26. *Oh, that makes no sense...*

The experience can get complicated quickly. That's the problem with rendering buttons on any platform: the buttons stay in the chat history and can be clicked any time. Our role as developers is to make sure the bot can handle the buttons and their payloads at any time.

Here is one approach to solve the previous problem. We leave the default behavior as is, but we create a custom recognizer that handles interactive message inputs and redirects the message to a dialog that tells the user that the action has expired, if these inputs are not expected. Let's start with the dialog. It will read the response_url for the interactive message and simply post a "Sorry, this action has expired." message to it. The dialog is invoked when the bot resolves the intent *practicalbot.expire*. A naming convention like that allows us to draw a distinction between LUIS intents and intents internal to the bot.

```
bot.dialog('remove_action',
[
    (session, arg) =>{
        let responseUrl = session.message.sourceEvent.Payload.
        response_url;
        let token = session.message.sourceEvent.Payload.token;
        let client = restify.createJsonClient({
            url: responseUrl
        });

        client.post('',
        {
            token: token,
            text: 'Sorry, this action has expired.'
        }, function (err, req, res, obj){
            if (err) console.log('Error -> %j', err);
            console.log('%d -> %j', res.statusCode, res.
            headers);
            console.log('%j', obj);
```

```
        session.endDialog();
    });
  }
]).triggerAction({ matches: 'practicalbot.expire'
});
```

The custom recognizer would look like this:

```
bot.recognizer({
    recognize: function (context, done){
        let intent = { score: 0.0 };
        if (context.message.sourceEvent &&
            context.message.sourceEvent.Payload &&
            context.message.sourceEvent.Payload.response_url)
        {
            intent = { score: 1.0, intent: 'practicalbot.
            expire' };
        }
        done(null, intent);
    }
});
```

In short, we are saying that if our dialog cannot explicitly handle an action response from the user, the global *practicalbot.expire* intent will be hit. In that case, we simply tell the user that the action has expired. The net effect can be seen in Figure 8-27 and Figure 8-28. We first get into the scenario where we have two interaction messages asking us for Yes or No input. We approve the second one. In Figure 8-28, we click Yes on the first button set.

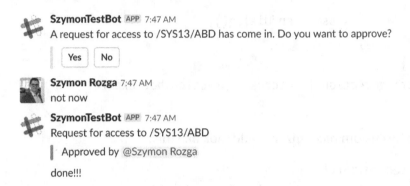

Figure 8-27. *OK, back to this scenario*

Figure 8-28. *It works. We can now act of older interactive messages without creating UX chaos.*

There are a couple of caveats we should mention. First, if you tried responding to the prompt using text instead of clicking a button, the code provided would fail. Why is this? Slack does not send a Payload object with details about the message interaction. It would just be considered text input, and we would not have a way to properly update the message to be *approved* or *rejected*. One way of dealing with this is to simply require button inputs instead of text input. Another way is to accept it but send the confirmation as a new message. Here is the code with that behavior with the resulting conversation after responding with a text message in Figure 8-29:

```
(session, arg) => {
    let r = arg.response.entity;
    let userId = null;
    const isTextMessage = session.message.sourceEvent.
    SlackMessage; // this means we receive a slack message
    if (isTextMessage) {
        userId = session.message.sourceEvent.SlackMessage.
        event.user;
    } else {
        userId = session.message.sourceEvent.Payload.user.id;
    }
    Let attachment = {
        color: 'danger',
        text: 'Rejected by <@' + userId + '>'
    };
    if (r === 'No') {

    } else if (r === 'Yes') {
        attachment = {
            color: 'good',
            text: 'Approved by <@' + userId + '>'
        };
    }

    if (isTextMessage) {
        // if we got a text message, reply using
        // session.send with the confirmation message
        let msg = new builder.Message(session).
        sourceEvent({
            'slack': {
                text: 'Request for access to /SYS13/ABD',
                attachments: [attachment]
```

```
            }
        });
        session.send(msg);
    } else {
        let responseUrl = session.message.sourceEvent.
        Payload.response_url;
        let token = session.message.sourceEvent.Payload.
        token;
        let client = restify.createJsonClient({
            url: responseUrl
        });

        client.post('', {
            token: token,
            text: 'Request for access to /SYS13/ABD',
            attachments: [attachment]
        }, function (err, req, res, obj) {
            if (err) console.log('Error -> %j', err);
            console.log('%d -> %j', res.statusCode,
            res.headers);
            console.log('%j', obj);
            session.endDialog();
        });
    }
}
}
```

Figure 8-29. *We can now handle text responses as well*

The second caveat is that in the previous example we use the choice prompt that blocks the conversation until a yes or no response is sent by the user. We want to avoid this behavior so that the user can continue working with the bot without necessarily having to answer the prompt immediately. A better approach would be to install a global recognizer that is able to map interactive message responses to intents that, in turn, map to dialogs that fulfill certain actions. We will be looking at this in Exercise 8-2.

EXERCISE 8-2

Exploring Nonblocking Interactive Messages in Slack

In the previous section we explored how we can utilize the choice prompt to ask the user for input using an interactive message. In this exercise, you will create a custom recognizer to map interactive message responses to dialogs. The dialogs will contain logic to update the interactive messages by using the response_url provided by Slack.

1. Create a universal bot that begins a dialog called *sendExpenseApproval.*

2. Create a dialog called *sendExpenseApproval*. The dialog should create a random expense object with four fields: *ID*, *user*, *type*, *amount*. This object would represent the fact that *user* spent $*amount* on an item of type *type*. ID should just be a random unique identifier. For example, create an object representing the fact that Szymon spent $60 on a taxi ride or that Bob spent $20 on a case of flavored sparkling water. After generating the random expense, send a hero card to the user summarizing the expense and two buttons with the labels *Approve* and *Reject*. After sending the response using *session.send*, end the dialog.

3. At this point, the bot doesn't do anything. Modify the Approve and Reject buttons in the hero card so that the value sent to the bot is Approved request with id {ID} and Reject request with id {ID}.

4. Create a custom recognizer to match these patterns and extract the ID. Your custom recognizer should return the intent *ApproveRequestIntent* or *RejectRequestIntent* based on the input. Make sure to include the ID in the resulting recognizer object.

5. Create two dialogs, one called *ApproveRequestDialog* and one called *RejectRequestDialog*. Use *triggerAction* to connect the · dialogs to the corresponding intents.

6. Ensure the two dialogs send the correct approved or rejected response to the response_url so that the original hero card is updated.

The technique used in this exercise to handle all the interactive messages globally is powerful and extensible. You can easily add more message types, intents, and dialogs for any future behavior. In practice, you may end up with a mix of blocking and nonblocking messages. You are now equipped to handle both styles.

Multistep Experience

In the previous section, we created a single-step interactive message. We will continue our exploration of interactive messages on Slack with a more complex, multistep interaction. Let's say we want to guide the user through a multistep process of selecting a type of pizza, some ingredients, and a size. We will build the experience using a multistep interactive message. The code for this section is included in the book's git repos; we will share the most relevant bits in the following pages.

Our experience will look as follows. The bot will first ask the user for a sauce type for their pizza (Figure 8-30).

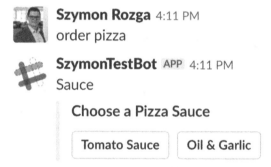

Figure 8-30.   What pizza sauce would you like?

If the user responds tomato sauce, our limited bot will ask the user to select one of two types of pies: regular or pepperoni (Figure 8-31).

Figure 8-31.   Pizza type options with tomato sauce

If the user had selected the Oil & Garlic sauce, they would get a different set of options (Figure 8-32).

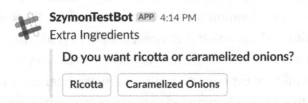

Figure 8-32. *Extra ingredient options for an Oil & Garlic base pizza*

The last step requires the user to select a size. We render a menu for this step (Figure 8-33).

Figure 8-33. *Which size would you like?*

Once done, the message will turn into a summary of the order (Figure 8-34).

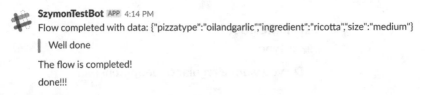

Figure 8-34. *User order summary*

As an exercise, we will utilize the native Slack APIs. The Bot Builder SDK needs a dialog step to explicitly use prompts to proceed from one step to the next. Since we will be using the Slack API directly, we will have a one-step waterfall dialog. This means the same function will be called over and over until a different global action is recognized or our dialog calls *endDialog*.

You'll recall that in the previous example, we took advantage of Bot Builder's prompts to send buttons back and collect the results back to logic in our bot. One of the things that the Bot Framework abstracts for us is that sending a prompt to a user actually sends a Slack message with an attachment that includes a set of actions where each button is a different action. When the user taps or clicks a button, a callback is made into our bot with a callback ID to identify the action.

For example, if we send this message to Slack, it will render a message that looks like Figure 8-31.

```
pizzatype: {
    text: 'Sauce',
    attachments: [
        {
            callback_id: 'pizzatype',
            title: 'Choose a Pizza Sauce',
            actions: [
                {
                    name: 'regular',
                    value: 'regular',
                    text: 'Tomato Sauce',
                    type: 'button'
                },
                {
                    name: 'step2b',
                    value: 'oilandgarlic',
                    text: 'Oil & Garlic',
```

```
                    type: 'button'
                }
            ]
        }
    ]
}
```

When either button is clicked, our bot will receive a message with a callback ID of *pizzatype* and the selected value. Here is the relevant JSON fragment of the message we receive when we click Tomato Sauce:

```
"sourceEvent": {
    "Payload": {
        "type": "interactive_message",
        "actions": [
            {
                "name": "regular",
                "type": "button",
                "value": "regular"
            }
        ],
        "callback_id": "pizzatype",
        ...
    },
    "ApiToken": "xxxxxxxxxxxxxxxxxxxxxxxxxxxxxxxxxxxxx"
}
```

So, the logic to figure out whether we are getting a callback of a type is easy. In fact, the code is similar to our recognizer code shown earlier. We create an *isCallbackResponse* function that can tell us whether a message is a callback and, optionally, whether it is a callback of a certain type.

```
const isCallbackResponse = function (context, callbackId){
    const msg = context.message;
```

```
    let result = msg.sourceEvent &&
        msg.sourceEvent.Payload &&
        msg.sourceEvent.Payload.response_url;

    if (callbackId){
        result = result && msg.sourceEvent.Payload.callback_id
        === callbackId;
    }
    return result;
};
```

We can then configure our recognizer to use this function instead.

```
bot.recognizer({
    recognize: function (context, done) {
        let intent = { score: 0.0 };
        if (isCallbackResponse(context)) {
            intent = { score: 1.0, intent: 'practicalbot.
            expire' };
        }
        done(null, intent);
    }
});
```

Now we can build a dialog that is able to walk users through a process.
We first declare the messages that we will send for each step. We will send
one of five messages:

- The first message to select a pizza type

- Based on the pizza type selected, one of two ingredient
  selections

- A selection for the pizza size

- A final confirmation message

Here is the JSON we use:

```
exports.multiStepData = {
    pizzatype: {
        text: 'Sauce',
        attachments: [
            {
                callback_id: 'pizzatype',
                title: 'Choose a Pizza Sauce',
                actions: [
                    {
                        name: 'regular',
                        value: 'regular',
                        text: 'Tomato Sauce',
                        type: 'button'
                    },
                    {
                        name: 'step2b',
                        value: 'oilandgarlic',
                        text: 'Oil & Garlic',
                        type: 'button'
                    }
                ]
            }
        ]
    },
    regular: {
        text: 'Pizza Type',
        attachments: [
            {
                callback_id: 'ingredient',
```

```
            title: 'Do you want a regular or pepperoni
            pie?',
            actions: [
                {
                    name: 'regular',
                    value: 'regular',
                    text: 'Regular',
                    type: 'button'
                },
                {
                    name: 'pepperoni',
                    value: 'pepperoni',
                    text: 'Pepperoni',
                    type: 'button'
                }

            ]
        }
    ]
},
oilandgarlic: {
    text: 'Extra Ingredients',
    attachments: [
        {
            callback_id: 'ingredient',
            title: 'Do you want ricotta or caramelized
            onions?',
            actions: [
                {
                    name: 'ricotta',
                    value: 'ricotta',
                    text: 'Ricotta',
```

```
                        type: 'button'
                },
                {
                        name: 'carmelizedonions',
                        value: 'carmelizedonions',
                        text: 'Caramelized Onions',
                        type: 'button'
                }

            ]
        }
    ]
},
collectsize: {
    text: 'Size',
    attachments: [
            {
                text: 'Which size would you like?',
                callback_id: 'finish',
                actions: [

                    {
                        name: 'size_list',
                        text: 'Pick a pizza size...',
                        type: 'select',
                        options: [
                            {
                                text: 'Small',
                                value: 'small'
                            },
                            {
                                text: 'Medium',
                                value: 'medium'
```

```
                },
                {
                    text: 'Large',
                    value: 'large'
                }
            ]
        }
    ]
}
]
},
finish: {
    attachments: [{
        color: 'good',
        text: 'Well done'
    }]
}
};
```

We then create a waterflow dialog with one step. If the message
we receive from the user is not a callback, we send the first step using
postMessage.

```
let apiToken = session.message.sourceEvent.ApiToken;
let channel = session.message.sourceEvent.SlackMessage.event.
channel;
let user = session.message.sourceEvent.SlackMessage.event.user;
let typemsg = multiFlowSteps.pizzatype;

session.privateConversationData.workflowData ={};
postMessage(apiToken, channel, typemsg.text, typemsg.
attachments).then(function (){
    console.log('created message');
});
```

Otherwise, if the message is a callback, we determine the callback type, get the data passed in the message (which is slightly different depending on whether it is coming from a button press or a menu), save the response data appropriately, and respond with the next relevant message. We track that state using *privateConversationData*. One caveat is that we need to explicitly save the state.

```
session.save();
```

Typically, the state would be saved as part of the *session.send* call. Since we don't use this mechanism anymore because we are using the Slack API directly, we'll call it explicitly at the end of our method. We detect if the user says "quit" to exit the flow. Here's what the entire method looks like:

```
(session, arg, next) => {
    if (session.message.text === 'quit') {
        session.endDialog();
        return;
    }

    if (isCallbackResponse(session)) {
        let responseUrl = session.message.sourceEvent.Payload.
        response_url;
        let token = session.message.sourceEvent.Payload.token;
        console.log(JSON.stringify(session.message));
        let client = restify.createJsonClient({
            url: responseUrl
        });

        let text = '';
        let attachments = [];

        let val = null;
        const payload = session.message.sourceEvent.Payload;
        const callbackChannel = payload.channel.id;
```

```
if (payload.actions && payload.actions.length > 0) {
    val = payload.actions[0].value;
    if (!val) {
        val = payload.actions[0].selected_options[0].
        value;
    }
}

if (isCallbackResponse(session, 'pizzatype')) {
    session.privateConversationData.workflowData.
    pizzatype = val;
    let ingredientStep = multiFlowSteps[val
    ];
    text = ingredientStep.text;
    attachments = ingredientStep.attachments;
}
else if (isCallbackResponse(session, 'ingredient')) {
    session.privateConversationData.workflowData.
    ingredient = val;
    var ingredientstep = multiFlowSteps.collectsize;
    text = ingredientstep.text;
    attachments = ingredientstep.attachments;
}
else if (isCallbackResponse(session, 'finish')) {
    session.privateConversationData.workflowData.size =
    val;
    text = 'Flow completed with data: ' + JSON.
    stringify(session.privateConversationData.
    workflowData);
    attachments = multiFlowSteps.finish.attachments;
}

client.post('',
```

```
            {
                token: token,
                text: text,
                attachments: attachments
            }, function (err, req, res, obj) {
                if (err) console.log('Error -> %j', err);
                console.log('%d -> %j', res.statusCode, res.
                headers);
                console.log('%j', obj);
                if (isCallbackResponse(session, 'finish')) {
                    session.send('The flow is completed!');
                    session.endDialog();
                    return;
                }
            });
    } else {
        let apiToken = session.message.sourceEvent.ApiToken;
        let channel = session.message.sourceEvent.SlackMessage.
        event.channel;
        let user = session.message.sourceEvent.SlackMessage.
        event.user;
        // we are beginning the flow... so we send an ephemeral
        message
        let typemsg = multiFlowSteps.pizzatype;

        session.privateConversationData.workflowData = {};
        postMessage(apiToken, channel, typemsg.text, typemsg.
        attachments).then(function () {
            console.log('created message');
        });
    }
    session.save();
}
```

After writing all that code, let us see what happens (Figure 8-35 and 8-36).

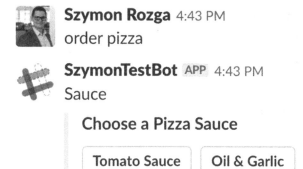

Szymon Rozga 4:43 PM
order pizza

SzymonTestBot APP 4:43 PM
Sauce

Choose a Pizza Sauce

| Tomato Sauce | Oil & Garlic |

Figure 8-35. *So far so good*

Szymon Rozga 4:43 PM
order pizza

SzymonTestBot APP 4:43 PM
Sorry, this action has expired.

Figure 8-36. *Yikes!*

So, what happened? As it turns out, the recognizer we previously created to reject interactive message responses when they were not expected kicked in and told us the action is expired. It seems that the prompt code pre-empted the global recognizer, whereas if we use a waterfall dialog, there is no way for us to control the recognition process.

In Chapter 6, when we discussed custom dialogs, we briefly touched on a method called *recognize*. This method allows us to indicate to the Bot Builder SDK that we want our current dialog to be first in line in interpreting a user message. In this case, we have specific callbacks coming in from Slack. This is a great use case for the recognize feature. But how do we access it? Turns out, we can create a custom subclass of *WaterfallDialog* and define a custom *recognize* implementation.

```
class WaterfallWithRecognizeDialog extends builder.
WaterfallDialog {
    constructor(callbackId, steps) {
        super(steps);
        this.callbackId = callbackId;
    }

    recognize(context, done) {
        var cb = this.callbackId;

        if (_.isFunction(this.callbackId)) {
            cb = this.callbackId();
            // callback can be a function that returns an ID
        }
        if (!_.isArray(cb)) cb = [cb]; // or a list of IDs

        let intent = { score: 0.0 };

        // lastly we evaluate each ID to see if it matches the
        message.
        // if yes, handle within this dialog
        for (var i = 0; i < cb.length; i++) {
            if (isCallbackResponse(context, cb[i])) {
                intent = { score: 1.0 };
                break;
            }
        }

        done(null, intent);
    }
}
```

In short, *recognize* is called any time a message comes in. We resolve
the supported callbacks in the dialog from the *this.callbackId* object. We

support a single callback value, an array of callback values, or a function that returns callback values. If the callback is of any of the supported callback IDs, we return a score of 1.0, which means that our dialog will handle the message. Otherwise, we pass a score of 0.0. This means these callbacks will go up to the global recognizers, as discussed in Chapter 6. Any other callback ID will be considered expired.

We can easily use this class as follows:

```
bot.dialog('multi-step-flow', new WaterfallWithRecognizeDialog(
['pizzatype', 'ingredient', 'finish'], [
    ...
]));
```

If we run the code now, we get the same resulting flow as in Figures 8-30 through 8-33.

EXERCISE 8-3

Interactive Messages

In this exercise, you will create a multistep interactive flow to support a bot that could filter clothing products. The goal will be to utilize a similar approach to the previous section to guide the user through a multistep data input process.

1. Create a universal bot with two steps. The first step calls a dialog called *filterClothing*, and the second step prints the dialog's result to the console and ends the conversation.

2. Follow the structure of the latest section to create a multistep interactive message dialog called *filterClothing*. Collect three pieces of data to filter a hypothetical clothing collection: garment type, size, and color. Exclusively use menus.

3. Make sure to utilize HTTP requests against response_url to
    update the interactive message.

You are now well-versed in exercising the Slack API for multistep interactive
messages, one of the cooler Slack features.

Conclusion

The code demonstrated in this chapter is just scratching the surface of
the integration possibilities between our Bot Builder bots and different
channels. Although we have deliberately focused on Slack use cases, we
hope it is clear there are plenty opportunities to reuse our bot code across
a spectrum of different experiences both generic and platform-specific in
nature.

The powerful abstractions of dialogs, state, and recognizers can be
applied across all channels, even when using native mechanisms to invoke
the dialogs. We have not yet explored creating a connector for a custom
channel. We will examine this in the next chapter.

CHAPTER 9

Creating a New Channel Connector

It should now be clear that integrating all kinds of channels with built-in bot service support is feasible. The Bot Builder SDK designers were aware that not every single feature of every channel can be handled by the bot service and kept the SDK flexible to support extensibility.

The bot service supports quite a few channels, but what if our bot needs to support a channel like the Twitter Direct Messages API? What if we need to integrate with a live chat platform that integrates directly with Facebook Messenger and we cannot utilize the Bot Framework Facebook channel connector? The bot service includes support for SMS via Twilio, but what if we want to extend it to Twilio's Voice APIs so we can literally talk to our bot?

All of this is possible via a facility offered by Microsoft called the Direct Line API. In this chapter, we will walk through what this is, how to build a custom web chat interface that communicates with our bot, and finally how to hook our bot into Twilio's Voice APIs. By the end of the chapter, we will be calling a phone number, speaking to our bot, and listening to it respond to us!

© Szymon Rozga 2018
S. Rozga, *Practical Bot Development*, https://doi.org/10.1007/978-1-4842-3540-9_9

The Direct Line API

If you explored the channels section in your bot service entry, you may
have run into something called Direct Line. The Direct Line channel is
simply a way for us to call into the bot via an easy-to-use API from client
applications that do not have the ability to host a webhook to receive
responses. That was a mouthful. Let's review. Typically, as per Figure 9-1,
a channel communicates to our bot by calling into the bot's messages
endpoint. The incoming message is processed by the bot. As responses
are created, our bot sends message to the channel's response URL with
the response messages. Recall that the incoming message includes a
serviceUrl. This is where the response HTTP endpoint resides. If we were
to write a custom client app, such as a mobile app, this URL must be
an endpoint hosted by the client application on the user's phone. This
asynchronous model is quite powerful; there are no restrictions around
when a message must come back, if ever, and how many messages need
to come back. The downside, of course, is that our client app needs to
host a web server. This is a nonstarter with many environments. Can one
even host an HTTP server on an iOS device?

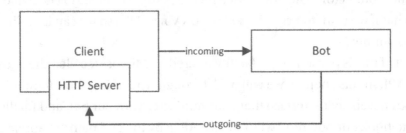

*Figure 9-1. Interaction between a client application and an Bot
Framework bot*

The solution offered by Microsoft is to create a channel that encapsulates an HTTP server for us. Direct Line can easily post messages into our bot and provides an interface for our client application to poll for any responses sent by the bot back to the user. Microsoft's Direct Line API, currently in its third version, also supports WebSockets,[1] so developers do not need to use a polling mechanism. Figure 9-2 presents the general design.

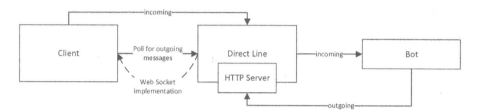

Figure 9-2. *Direct Line obviating the need for the client to host an HTTP server*

The Direct Line channel is also convenient because it handles bot authentication for us. We only need to pass a Direct Line key as the Bearer token into the Direct Line channel.

The Direct Line v3 API contains the following operations around conversations:

- *StartConversation*: Begins a new conversation with the bot. The bot will receive the necessary messages to indicate that a new conversation is starting.

- *GetConversation*: Gets details around an existing conversation including a streamUrl that the client can use to connect via WebSocket.

- *GetActivities*: Gets all the activities exchanged between the bot and the user. This provides an optional ability to pass a watermark to only get activities after the watermark.

---

[1]WebSocket Protocol: `https://en.wikipedia.org/wiki/WebSocket`

- *PostActivity*: Sends a new activity from the user to the bot.

- *UploadFile*: Uploads a file from the user to the bot.

The API also contains two authentication methods.

We can access the Direct Line API with a shared Direct Line secret. However, if a malicious actor obtains the key, he can do start any number of new conversations with our bot as a new or known user. If we are only doing server-to-server communication, this should not be a huge risk, provided we correctly manage the key. However, if we want a client application to talk to the API, we need another solution. Direct Line provides two token endpoints for us to use.

- *Generate token*: `POST /v3/directline/tokens/generate`

- *Refresh token*: `POST /v3/directline/tokens/refresh`

The Generate endpoint generates a token to be used for one and only one conversation. The response also includes an *expires_in* field. If there is a need to extend the timeline, the API provides the Refresh endpoint to refresh the token for another *expires_in* value at a time. At the time of this writing, the value of *expires_in* is 30 minutes.

The API is invoked as REST calls to the following endpoints (all hosted at `https://directline.botframework.com`):

- *Start Conversation*: `POST /v3/conversations`

- *Get Conversation*: `GET /v3/conversations/{conversationId}?watermark={watermark}`

- *GetActivities*: `GET /v3/conversations/{conversationId}/activities?watermark={watermark}`

- *PostActivity*: `POST /v3/conversations/{conversationId}/activities`

- *UploadFile*: `POST /v3/conversations/{conversationId}?userId={userId}`

You can find more details about the Direct Line API in the online documentation.[2]

Custom Web Chat Interface

There are many Direct Line samples online; one in the context of a console node app can be found here: `https://github.com/Microsoft/BotBuilder-Samples/tree/master/Node/core-DirectLine/DirectLineClient`.

We'll take this code as a template and create a custom web chat interface to discuss connecting to a bot from a client application. Although the Bot Builder SDK already includes a componentized version of a web chat,[3] building it ourselves will be great experience with Direct Line.

First, we need to enable Direct Line. In our bot's Channels blade, click the Direct Line button (Figure 9-3) to get to the Direct Line configuration screen.

Figure 9-3. *The Direct Line channel icon*

---

[2]Key Concepts in the Bot Framework Direct Line API: `https://docs.microsoft.com/en-us/azure/bot-service/rest-api/bot-framework-rest-direct-line-3-0-concepts`

[3]The Bot Framework WebChat is a React component. The code can be extended to provide different rendering behavior or to change the control's styling. You can find more information at `https://github.com/Microsoft/BotFramework-WebChat`.

411

We can create multiple keys to authenticate our client against Direct Line. In this example, we will simply use the Default Site keys (Figure 9-4).

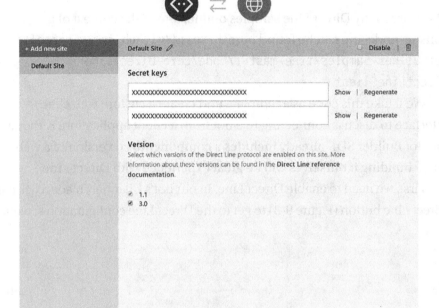

Figure 9-4. The Direct Line configuration interface

Now that we have the keys ready, we will create a node package that contains a bot and a simple jQuery-enabled web page to illustrate how to wire the bot together with a client app. The full code for the following work is included as part of our git repo.

We will create a basic bot that can respond to some simple input, so we will create an index.html page that hosts our web chat component. The bot's .env file should include the MICROSOFT_APP_ID and MICROSOFT_APP_PASSWORD values as usual. We also add DL_KEY, which is the value of our shared Direct Line key from Figure 9-4. When the page opens, the code will fetch a token from the bot so that we do not expose the secret to the client. This requires implementing endpoints on our bot.

To get started, set up an empty bot with our typical dependencies. The basic conversation code is shown next. We support some silly things such as "hello," "quit," "meaning of life," "where's waldo," and "apple." If the input doesn't match any of these, we default with the dismissive "oh, that's cool."

```
const bot = new builder.UniversalBot(connector, [
    session => {
        session.beginDialog('sampleConversation');
    },
    session => {
        session.send('conversation over');
        session.endConversation();
    }
]);

bot.dialog('sampleConversation', [
    (session, arg) => {
        console.log(JSON.stringify(session.message));

        if (session.message.text.indexOf('hello') >= 0 ||
        session.message.text.indexOf('hi') >= 0)
            session.send('hey!');
        else if (session.message.text === 'quit') {
            session.send('ok, we\'re done');
            return;
        } else if (session.message.text.indexOf('meaning of
        life') >= 0) {
            session.send('42');
        } else if (session.message.text.indexOf('waldo') >= 0) {
            session.send('not here');
        } else if (session.message.text === 'apple') {
```

```
            session.send({
                text: "Here, have an apple.",
                attachments: [
                    {
                        contentType: 'image/jpeg',
                        contentUrl: 'https://upload.wikimedia.
                        org/wikipedia/commons/thumb/1/15/Red_
                        Apple.jpg/1200px-Red_Apple.jpg',
                        name: 'Apple'
                    }
                ]
            });
        }
        else {
            session.send('oh that\'s cool');
        }
    }
]);
```

Second, we want to create a web chat page index.html page that includes jQuery and Bootstrap from a CDN.

```
server.get(/\/?.*/, restify.serveStatic({
    directory: './app',
    default: 'index.html'
}))
```

Our index.html provides a simple user experience. We will have a chat client container with two elements: a chat history view that will render any messages between the user and the bot and a text entry box. We'll assume that pressing the Return key sends the message. For the chat history, we will insert chat entry elements and use CSS and JavaScript to size and position the entry elements correctly. We will use the messaging paradigm of messages from the user being on the left and messages from the other party on the right.

```html
<!doctype html>
<html lang="en">
    <head>
        <title>Direct Line Test</title>
        <link rel="stylesheet" href="https://stackpath.
        bootstrapcdn.com/bootstrap/4.0.0/css/bootstrap.min.css"
        type="text/css" />

        <link rel="stylesheet" href="app/chat.css" type="text/
        css" />
    </head>

    <body>
        <script src="https://code.jquery.com/jquery-3.3.1.min.
        js" integrity="sha256-FgpCb/KJQlLNfOu91ta32o/
        NMZxltwRo8QtmkMRdAu8=" crossorigin="anonymous">
        </script>
        <script src="https://stackpath.bootstrapcdn.com/
        bootstrap/4.0.0/js/bootstrap.min.js"></script>

        <script src="app/chat.js"></script>

        <h1>Sample Direct Line Interface</h1>

        <div class="chat-client">
            <div class="chat-history">

            </div>
            <div class="chat-controls">
                <input type="text" class="chat-text-entry" />
            </div>
        </div>
    </body>
</html>
```

The chat.css style sheet looks as follows:

```css
body {
    font-family: Helvetica, Arial, sans-serif;
    margin: 10px;
}

.chat-client {
    max-width: 600px;
    margin: 20px;
    font-size: 16px;
}

.chat-history {
    border: 1px solid lightgray;
    height: 400px;
    overflow-x: hidden;
    overflow-y: scroll;
}

.chat-controls {
    height: 20px;
}

.chat-img {
    background-size: contain;
    height: 160px;
    max-width: 400px;
}

.chat-text-entry {
    width: 100%;
    border: 1px solid lightgray;
    padding: 5px;
}
```

```css
.chat-entry-container {
    position: relative;
    margin: 5px;
    min-height: 40px;
}

.chat-entry {
    color: #666666;
    position: absolute;
    padding: 10px;
    min-width: 10px;
    max-width: 400px;
    overflow-y: auto;
    word-wrap: break-word;
    border-radius: 10px;
}
.chat-from-bot {
    right: 10px;
    background-color: #2198F4;
    border: 1px solid #2198F4;
    color: white;
    text-align:right;
}
.chat-from-user {
    background-color: #E5E4E9;
    border: 1px solid #E5E4E9;
}
```

Our client-side logic lives in chat.js. In this file, we declare a few functions to help us call the necessary Direct Line endpoints.

```js
const pollInterval = 1000;
const user = 'user';
```

417

```
const baseUrl = 'https://directline.botframework.com/v3/
directline';
const conversations = baseUrl + '/conversations';

function startConversation(token) {
    // POST to conversations endpoint
    return $.ajax({
        url: conversations,
        type: 'POST',
        data: {},
        datatype: 'json',
        headers: {
            'authorization': 'Bearer ' + token
        }
    });
}

function postActivity(token, conversationId, activity) {
    // POST to conversations endpoint
    const url = conversations + '/' + conversationId +
    '/activities';

    return $.ajax({
        url: url,
        type: 'POST',
        data: JSON.stringify(activity),
        contentType: 'application/json; charset=utf-8',
        datatype: 'json',
        headers: {
            'authorization': 'Bearer ' + token
        }
    });
}
```

```javascript
function getActivities(token, conversationId, watermark) {
    // GET activities from conversations endpoint
    let url = conversations + '/' + conversationId +
    '/activities';
    if (watermark) {
        url = url + '?watermark=' + watermark;
    }

    return $.ajax({
        url: url,
        type: 'GET',
        data: {},
        datatype: 'json',
        headers: {
            'authorization': 'Bearer ' + token
        }
    });
}

function getToken() {
    return $.getJSON('/api/token').then(function (data) {
        // we need to refresh the token every 30 minutes at
        most.
        // we'll try to do it every 25 minutes to be sure
        window.setInterval(function () {
            console.log('refreshing token');
            refreshToken(data.token);
        }, 1000 * 60 * 25);
        return data.token;
    });
}
```

```
function refreshToken(token) {
    return $.ajax({
        url: '/api/token/refresh',
        type: 'POST',
        data: token,
        datatype: 'json',
        contentType: 'text/plain'
    });
}
```

To support the *getToken*() and *refreshToken*() client-side functions, we expose two endpoints on the bot. /api/token generates a new token, and /api/token/refresh accepts a token as input and refreshes it, extending its lifetime.

```
server.use(restify.bodyParser({ mapParams: false }));
server.get('/api/token', (req, res, next) => {
    // make a request to get a token from the secret key
    const jsonClient = restify.createStringClient({ url:
    'https://directline.botframework.com/v3/directline/tokens/
    generate' });
    jsonClient.post({
        path: '',
        headers: {
            authorization: 'Bearer ' + process.env.DL_KEY
        }
    }, null, function (_err, _req, _res, _data) {
        let jsonData = JSON.parse(_data);
        console.log('%d -> %j', _res.statusCode, _res.headers);
        console.log('%s', _data);
        res.send(200, {
            token: jsonData.token
        });
```

```
        next();
    });
});

server.post('/api/token/refresh', (req, res, next) => {
    // make a request to get a token from the secret key
    const token = req.body;
    const jsonClient = restify.createStringClient({ url:
    'https://directline.botframework.com/v3/directline/tokens/
    refresh' });
    jsonClient.post({
        path: '',
        headers: {
            authorization: 'Bearer ' + token
        }
    }, null, function (_err, _req, _res, _data) {
        let jsonData = JSON.parse(_data);
        console.log('%d -> %j', _res.statusCode, _res.headers);
        console.log('%s', _data);
        res.send(200, {
            success: true
        });
        next();
    });
});
```

When the page is loaded on the browser, we start a conversation, fetch a token for it, and listen for incoming messages.

```
getToken().then(function (token){
    startConversation(token)
        .then(function (response){
            return response.conversationId;
        })
```

```
        .then(function (conversationId){
            sendMessagesFromInputBox(conversationId, token);
            pollMessages(conversationId, token);
    });
});
```

Here is what *sendMessagesFromInputBox* looks like:

```
function sendMessagesFromInputBox(conversationId, token) {
    $('.chat-text-entry').keypress(function (event) {
        if (event.which === 13) {
            const input = $('.chat-text-entry').val();
            if (input === '') return;

            const newEntry = buildUserEntry(input);
            scrollToBottomOfChat();

            $('.chat-text-entry').val('');

            postActivity(token, conversationId, {
                textFormat: 'plain',
                text: input,
                type: 'message',
                from: {
                    id: user,
                    name: user
                }
            }).catch(function (err) {
                $('.chat-history').remove(newEntry);
                console.error('Error sending message:', err);
            });
        }
    });
}
```

```
function buildUserEntry(input) {
    const c = $('<div/>');
    c.addClass('chat-entry-container');
    const entry = $('<div/>');
    entry.addClass('chat-entry');
    entry.addClass('chat-from-user');
    entry.text(input);
    c.append(entry);
    $('.chat-history').append(c);

    const h = entry.height();
    entry.parent().height(h);
    return c;
}

function scrollToBottomOfChat() {
    const el = $('.chat-history');
    el.scrollTop(el[0].scrollHeight);
}
```

The code listens to a Return key press on the textbox. If the user input
is not empty, it sends the message to the bot and adds the user's message
to the chat history. If the message to the bot fails for any reason, the user's
message is removed from the chat history. We also make sure that the chat
history control scrolls to the bottom so the newest messages are visible. On
the receiving end, we poll Direct Line for messages. Here is the supporting
code:

```
function pollMessages(conversationId, token) {
    console.log('Starting polling message for conversationId: '
    + conversationId);
    let watermark = null;
    setInterval(function () {
```

```
        getActivities(token, conversationId, watermark)
            .then(function (response) {
                watermark = response.watermark;
                return response.activities;
            })
            .then(insertMessages);
    }, pollInterval);
}

function insertMessages(activities) {
    if (activities && activities.length) {
        activities = activities.filter(function (m) { return
        m.from.id !== user });
        if (activities.length) {
            activities.forEach(function (a) {
                buildBotEntry(a);
            });
            scrollToBottomOfChat();
        }
    }
}

function buildBotEntry(activity) {
    const c = $('<div/>');
    c.addClass('chat-entry-container');
    const entry = $('<div/>');
    entry.addClass('chat-entry');
    entry.addClass('chat-from-bot');
    entry.text(activity.text);

    if (activity.attachments) {
        activity.attachments.forEach(function (attachment) {
            switch (attachment.contentType) {
```

```
                case 'application/vnd.microsoft.card.hero':
                    console.log('hero card rendering not
                    supported');
                    // renderHeroCard(attachment, entry);
                    break;

                case 'image/png':
                case 'image/jpeg':
                    console.log('Opening the requested image '
                    + attachment.contentUrl);
                    entry.append("<div class='chat-img'
                    style='background-size: cover; background-
                    image: url(" + attachment.contentUrl + ")'
                    />");
                    break;
            }
        });
    }

    c.append(entry);
    $('.chat-history').append(c);

    const h = entry.height();
    entry.parent().height(h);
}
```

Notice that Direct Line API returns all messages between the user and bot, so we must filter out anything sent by the user since we already appended those when the message was initially sent. Beyond that, we have custom logic to support image attachments.

```
entry.append("<div class='chat-img' style='background-size:
cover; background-image: url(" + attachment.contentUrl + ")'
/>");
```

We could extend that piece to support hero (we have a switch case for this in our code already, but we have not implemented a *renderHeroCard* function) or adaptive cards, audio attachments, or any other kind of custom rendering our application needs.

A quick note: since we are using the Direct Line API and a custom client application, we have the option of defining custom attachments. Thus, if our bot has a need of rendering some application user interface within the web chat, we could specify this rendering logic by using our own attachment. The code in *buildBotEntry* would simply know how to do so.

If we build the bot and run it on localhost:3978, we can access our web chat by pointing the browser to http://localhost:3978. The interface looks plain when we run it as Figure 9-5. Figure 9-6 shows the conversation after a few interactions with our bot working as intended!

Sample Direct Line Interface

Figure 9-5. *Plain empty chat interface*

Sample Direct Line Interface

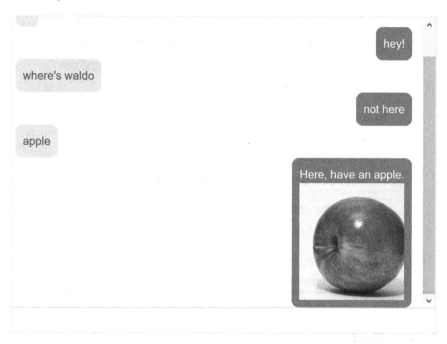

Figure 9-6. *Oh, wait, there we go! That's pretty cool*

EXERCISE 9-1

Node Console Interface

For this exercise, you will create a bot with some basic commands that return text and create a command-line interface to communicate with it. The goal will be to utilize both a polling client and a web sockets client and compare the performance.

1. Create a simple bot that can respond to several user utterance options with text. Ensure the bot works as expected by using the emulator.

2. Configure your bot to accept Direct Line input on the bot channel registration Channels blade.

3. Write a node command-line app that listens to user's console input and sends the input to Direct Line when the user presses Return.

4. For incoming messages, write the code to poll for messages and print them out on the screen. Poll every 1 to 2 seconds. Use the console app to send multiple messages to the bot and see how fast it responds.

5. As a second exercise, write code that utilizes the streamUrl to initialize a new WebSocket connection. You can use the *ws* Node.js package, documented here: `https://github.com/websockets/ws`. Print incoming messages to the screen.

6. How does the performance of the polling solution compare to the WebSocket option?

You are now well versed in integrating with the Direct Line API. If you are developing custom channel adapters, this is the place to start.

Voice Bots

OK, so we have a lot of flexibility with the Bot Framework. There is one more area around channels we planned to address, and that's custom channel implementations. Say, for example, you are building a bot for a client, and everything is going well and on schedule. On a Friday afternoon, the client comes by and asks you, "Hey, Ms. Bot Developer, can a user call an 800 number to talk to our bot?"

Well, uh, sure I suppose anything is possible with enough time and money, but how do we get started? Something very similar happened to me once, and my initial reaction was "No way, this is crazy. There's too many issues. Voice is not the same as chat." Some of these reservations remain; reusing a bot between a messaging and voice channel is a tricky area that requires a lot of care because the two interfaces are quite different. Of course, that doesn't mean we are not going to try!

As it turns out, Twilio is a solid and easy-to-use provider of voice calls and SMS APIs. Lucky for us, not too long ago, Twilio added speech recognition to its platform, and it can now translate a user's voice into text. In the future, intent recognition will be integrated into the system. In the meantime, what is there now should be sufficient for our purposes. In fact, the Bot Framework is already integrated into SMS via Twilio; maybe one day we'll have full voice support as well.

Twilio

Before we get jump into the bot code, let's talk a bit about Twilio and how it works. One of Twilio's products is called Programmable Voice. Any time a call comes into a registered phone number, a Twilio server will send a message to a developer-defined endpoint. The endpoint must respond informing Twilio the actions it should perform, for example, speak an utterance, dial another number into the call, gather data, pause, etc. Anytime an interaction occurs, such as Twilio gathering user input via speech recognition, Twilio calls into this endpoint to receive its instructions on what to do next. This is good for us. It means our code does not need to know anything about phone calls. It's just APIs!

The way that we instruct Twilio what to do is via an XML markup language called TwiML.[4] A sample is shown here:

```xml
<?xml version="1.0" encoding="UTF-8"?
<Response>
    <Say voice="woman">Please leave a message after the tone.
    </Say>
    <Record maxLength="20" />
</Response>
```

---

[4]TwiML documentation: https://www.twilio.com/docs/api/twiml

In this context, the XML elements named *Say* and *Record* are called *verbs*. Twilio includes a total of 13 verbs at the time of this writing.

- *Say*: Speak text to the caller

- *Play*: Play an audio file for the caller

- *Dial*: Add another party to the call

- *Record*: Record the caller's voice

- *Gather*: Collect digits the caller types on their keypad, or translate voice into text

- *SMS*: Send an SMS message during a phone call

- *Hangup*: Hang up the call

- *Enqueue*: Add the caller to a queue of callers

- *Leave*: Remove a caller from a queue of callers

- *Redirect*: Redirect call flow to a different TwiML document

- *Pause*: Wait before executing more instructions

- *Reject*: Decline an incoming call without being billed

- *Message*: Send an MMS or SMS message reply

Your TwiML response can have one or multiple verbs. Some verbs can be nested for specific behaviors on the system. If your TwiML document contains multiple verbs, Twilio will execute each verb one after another in sequential order. For example, we could create the following TwiML document:

```
<?xml version="1.0" encoding="UTF-8"?
<!-- page located at http://example.com/complex_gather.xml -->
<Response>
    <Gather action="/process_gather.php" method="GET">
```

```
    <Say>
        Please enter your account number,
        followed by the pound sign
    </Say>
  </Gather>
  <Say>We didn't receive any input. Goodbye!</Say>
</Response>
```

This document will start by trying to gather user input. It will first prompt the user to enter their account number, followed by the pound sign. The nested behavior of *Say* within a *Gather* means that the user can speak their response before the *Say* speech content is done. This is a great feature for returning users. If the *Gather* verb results in no user input, Twilio proceeds to the next element, which is a *Say* element notifying the user that Twilio did not receive a response. At this point, since there are no more verbs, the phone call ends.

There are detailed documentation and samples for each verb, and as we would expect, a full-fledged TwiML application can get complex. As with all user interfaces, there are many details. For our purposes, we will create a basic integration so that we can talk to the same bot that we just created for our custom web chat.

Integrating Our Bot with Twilio

We will begin by registering our app with Twilio. First, we need to create a trial account with Twilio. Visit www.twilio.com and click *Sign Up*. Fill out the form with the relevant information, as per Figure 9-7. Once you do, you'll enter your phone number and a verification code.

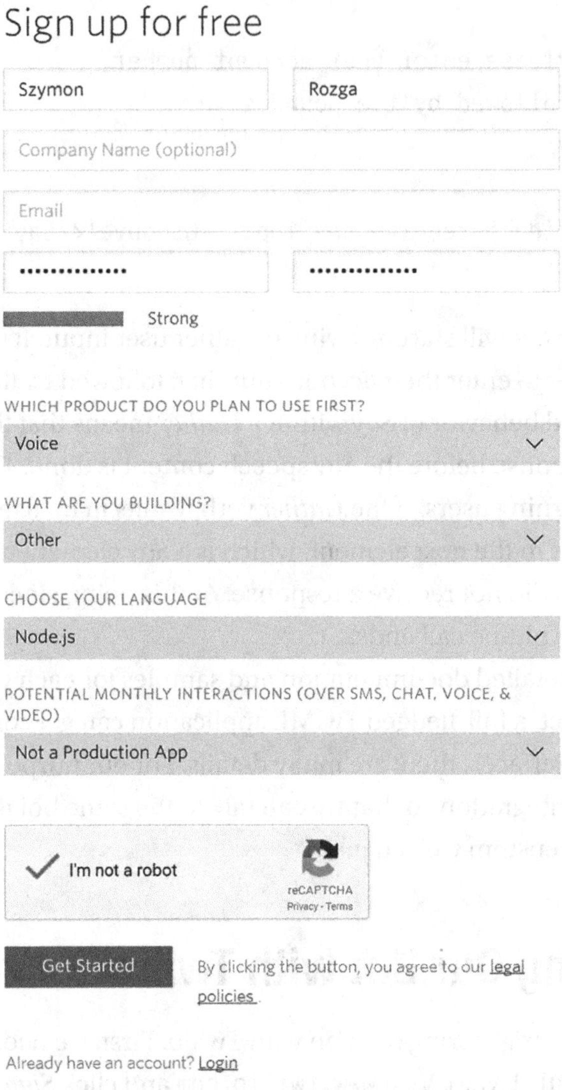

Sign up for free

Szymon	Rozga

Company Name (optional)

Email

••••••••••••••	••••••••••••••

▬▬▬▬▬▬▬ Strong

WHICH PRODUCT DO YOU PLAN TO USE FIRST?

Voice ⌄

WHAT ARE YOU BUILDING?

Other ⌄

CHOOSE YOUR LANGUAGE

Node.js ⌄

POTENTIAL MONTHLY INTERACTIONS (OVER SMS, CHAT, VOICE, & VIDEO)

Not a Production App ⌄

✓ I'm not a robot   reCAPTCHA
                      Privacy - Terms

Get Started   By clicking the button, you agree to our legal
               policies

Already have an account? Login

Figure 9-7. *Signing up for a Twilio account*

Twilio will next ask for our project name. Feel free to provide something more interesting than the name in Figure 9-8.

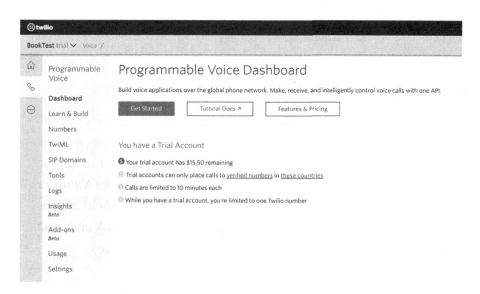

Figure 9-8. *Creating a new Twilio project*

We will be redirected to the Twilio dashboard (Figure 9-9).

Figure 9-9. *The Twilio project dashboard*

Our next task is for us to set up a phone number and point it at our bot. Click the *Numbers* navigation item in the left pane, and we will be taken to the *Phone Numbers* dashboard (Figure 9-10).

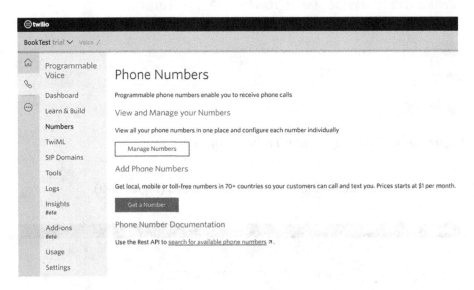

Figure 9-10. *Let's get a phone number for our project!*

Click *Get a Number*. Twilio will assign a number to you. Since we're just testing, any number will do. You may also buy a toll-free number or transfer one from a different service.[5] Afterward, click *Manage Numbers* and then click the number you were just assigned. Find the field for the URL to contact on incoming calls and copy in your bot's ngrok endpoint (Figure 9-11). We will create this endpoint in the coming pages.

---

[5]Buying a toll-free number from Twilio: `https://support.twilio.com/hc/en-us/articles/223183168-Buying-a-toll-free-number-with-Twilio`

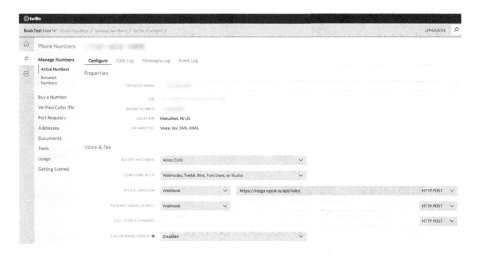

Figure 9-11. *Configuring the endpoint Twilio will send a message to on an incoming call*

Now, any time that anyone calls that number, our endpoint will receive an HTTP POST request with all the information relevant to the call. We will be able to accept this call and respond using TwiML documents like the ones we previously discussed.

OK, so what now? In our bot code, we can add the /api/voice endpoint to start accepting calls. For now, we simply added a log but return no response. Let's see what kind of data we get from Twilio.

```
server.post('/api/voice', (req, res, next) => {
    console.log('%j', req.body);
});

{
    "Called": "+1xxxxxxxxxx",
    "ToState": "NJ",
    "CallerCountry": "US",
    "Direction": "inbound",
    "CallerState": "NY",
```

```
    "ToZip": "07050",
    "CallSid": "xxxxxxxxxxxxxxxxxxxxxx",
    "To": "+1xxxxxxxxxx",
    "CallerZip": "10003",
    "ToCountry": "US",
    "ApiVersion": "2010-04-01",
    "CalledZip": "07050",
    "CalledCity": "ORANGE",
    "CallStatus": "ringing",
    "From": "+1xxxxxxxxxx",
    "AccountSid": "xxxxxxxxxxxxxxxxxxxxxx",
    "CalledCountry": "US",
    "CallerCity": "MANHATTAN",
    "Caller": "+1xxxxxxxxxx",
    "FromCountry": "US",
    "ToCity": "ORANGE",
    "FromCity": "MANHATTAN",
    "CalledState": "NJ",
    "FromZip": "10003",
    "FromState": "NY"
}
```

Twilio sends some interesting data. Since we get the caller number, we can easily use that as the user ID in interactions with our bot. Let's create a response to the API call. Let's first install the Twilio node API.

```
npm install twilio --save
```

We can then import the relevant types into our node app.

```
const twilio = require('twilio');
const VoiceResponse = twilio.twiml.VoiceResponse;
```

VoiceResponse is a convenient type that helps generate the response XML. Here is a sample of how we can return a basic TwiML response:

```
server.post('/api/voice', (req, res, next) => {
    let twiml = new VoiceResponse();

    twiml.say('Hi, I\'m Direct Line bot!', { voice: 'Alice' });

    let response = twiml.toString();

    res.writeHead(200, {
        'Content-Length': Buffer.byteLength(response),
        'Content-Type': 'text/html'
    });
    res.write(response);
    next();
});
```

Now, when we call the phone number provided by Twilio, after a disclaimer, we should see a request to our API endpoint, and a female voice should speak to us over the phone and then hang up. Congratulations! You've established connectivity!

It is not a great experience when our bot hangs up pretty much immediately, but we can improve on that. First, let's gather some input from the user.

The *Gather* verb includes several different options, but we are mainly concerned with the fact that *Gather* can be used to accept either voice or dual-tone multi-frequency (DTMF) signals from the user's phone. DTMF are just the signals sent when you press a key on your phone. That is how a phone system can reliably gather information such as a credit card number without the user speaking it. For the purposes of this example, we are solely concerned with collecting speech.

Here is a *Gather* sample, like what we will be using:

```xml
<?xml version="1.0" encoding="UTF-8"?>
<Response>
    <Gather input="speech" action="/api/voice/gather"
    method="POST">
        <Say>
            Tell me what's on your mind
        </Say>
    </Gather>
    <Say>We didn't receive any input. Goodbye!</Say>
</Response>
```

This snippet tells Twilio to gather speech from the user and for Twilio to send the recognized speech using a POST to /api/voice/gather. That's it! *Gather* has many other options around timeouts and sending partial speech recognition results as well, but those are unnecessary for our purposes.[6]

Let's establish an echo Twilio integration. We extend our code for /api/voice to include the Gather verb and then create the endpoint for /api/voice/gather that echoes back what the user said and gathers more information, establishing a virtually endless conversation loop.

```javascript
server.post('/api/voice', (req, res, next) => {
    let twiml = new VoiceResponse();

    twiml.say('Hi, I\'m Direct Line bot!', { voice: 'Alice' });
    let gather = twiml.gather({ input: 'speech', method:
    'POST', action: '/api/voice/gather' });
    gather.say('Tell me what is on your mind', { voice: 'Alice' });

    let response = twiml.toString();
```

---

[6]Twilio Gather Verb: https://www.twilio.com/docs/voice/twiml/gather

```
        res.writeHead(200, {
            'Content-Length': Buffer.byteLength(response),
            'Content-Type': 'text/html'
        });
        res.write(response);
        next();
});

server.post('/api/voice/gather', (req, res, next) => {
    let twiml = new VoiceResponse();
    const input = req.body.SpeechResult;
    twiml.say('Oh hey! That is so interesting. ' + input, {
    voice: 'Alice' });
    let gather = twiml.gather({ input: 'speech', method:
    'POST', action: '/api/voice/gather' });
    gather.say('Tell me what is on your mind', { voice: 'Alice'
});

    let response = twiml.toString();

    res.writeHead(200, {
        'Content-Length': Buffer.byteLength(response),
        'Content-Type': 'text/html'
    });
    res.write(response);
    next();
});
```

Go ahead and run this code in your bot. Call the phone number. Talk
to you bot. That's cool, right? Great. It's not useful, but we've establish
a working conversation loop between a Twilio phone conversation and
our bot.

Lastly, let's integrate this into our bot by using Direct Line. Before we jump into the code, we write a few functions to help our bot invoke Direct Line.

```
const baseUrl = 'https://directline.botframework.com/v3/
directline';
const conversations = baseUrl + '/conversations';

function startConversation (token) {
    return new Promise((resolve, reject) => {
        let client = restify.createJsonClient({
            url: conversations,
            headers: {
                'Authorization': 'Bearer ' + token
            }
        });

        client.post('', {},
            function (err, req, res, obj) {
                if (err) {
                    console.log('%j', err);
                    reject(err);
                    return;
                }
                console.log('%d -> %j', res.statusCode,
                res.headers);
                console.log('%j', obj);
                resolve(obj);
            });
    });
}

function postActivity (token, conversationId, activity) {
    // POST to conversations endpoint
```

```
    const url = conversations + '/' + conversationId + '/
    activities';
    return new Promise((resolve, reject) => {
        let client = restify.createJsonClient({
            url: url,
            headers: {
                'Authorization': 'Bearer ' + token
            }
        });

        client.post('', activity,
            function (err, req, res, obj) {
                if (err) {
                    console.log('%j', err);
                    reject(err);
                    return;
                }
                console.log('%d -> %j', res.statusCode,
                res.headers);
                console.log('%j', obj);
                resolve(obj);
            });
    });
}

function getActivities (token, conversationId, watermark) {
    // GET activities from conversations endpoint
    let url = conversations + '/' + conversationId + '/
    activities';
    if (watermark) {
        url = url + '?watermark=' + watermark;
    }
```

```
    return new Promise((resolve, reject) => {
        let client = restify.createJsonClient({
            url: url,
            headers: {
                'Authorization': 'Bearer ' + token
            }
        });

        client.get('',
            function (err, req, res, obj) {
                if (err) {
                    console.log('%j', err);
                    reject(err);
                    return;
                }
                console.log('%d -> %j', res.statusCode,
                res.headers);
                console.log('%j', obj);
                resolve(obj);
            });
    });
}
```

We will extract the creation and sending of the TwiML response into
its own function called *buildAndSendTwimlResponse*. We have added a bit
more structure into the act of listening to input and, if none is received, to
ask for input again before hanging up.

```
function buildAndSendTwimlResponse(req, res, next, userId,
text) {
    const twiml = new VoiceResponse();

    twiml.say(text, { voice: 'Alice' });
```

```
twiml.gather({ input: 'speech', action: '/api/voice/
gather', method: 'POST' });
twiml.say('I didn\'t quite catch that. Please try again.',
{ voice: 'Alice' });
twiml.gather({ input: 'speech', action: '/api/voice/
gather', method: 'POST' });
twiml.say('Ok, call back anytime!');
twiml.hangup();

const response = twiml.toString();
console.log(response);

res.writeHead(200, {
    'Content-Length': Buffer.byteLength(response),
    'Content-Type': 'text/html'
});
res.write(response);
next();
}
```

When a call first starts, we need to create a Direct Line conversation for our bot to use. We also need to cache the mapping of user ID (caller phone number) to conversation ID. We do so in a local JavaScript object (*cachedConversations*). If we were to scale this service out to multiple servers, this approach will break; we can get around this by utilizing a cache such as Redis.

```
server.post('/api/voice', (req, res, next) => {
    let userId = req.body.Caller;
    console.log('starting convo for user id %s', userId);

    startConversation(process.env.DL_KEY).then(conv => {
        cachedConversations[userId] = { id: conv.
        conversationId, watermark: null, lastAccessed:
        moment().format() };
```

```
        console.log('%j', cachedConversations);
        buildAndSendTwimlResponse(req, res, next, userId,
        'Hello! Welcome to Direct Line bot!');
    });
});
```

The code for the *Gather* element should retrieve the conversation ID, get the user input, send the activity to the bot via the Direct Line API, and then wait for the response to come back before sending it back to Twilio as TwiML. Since we need to poll for the new messages, we need to use *setInterval* until we get a response from the bot. The code doesn't include any kind of timeout, but we should certainly consider it in case something goes wrong with the bot. We also only support one response from the bot per message. Voice interactions are not a place to exercise a bot's ability to send multiple responses asynchronously, although we could certainly try. One approach would be to include custom channel data communicating the number of messages expected to return or to wait a predefined number of seconds and then send all messages back.

```
server.post('/api/voice/gather', (req, res, next) => {
    const input = req.body.SpeechResult;
    let userId = req.body.Caller;
    console.log('user id: %s | input: %s', userId, input);
    let conv = cachedConversations[userId];
    console.log('got convo: %j', conv);
    conv.lastAccessed = moment().format();

    postActivity(process.env.DL_KEY, conv.id, {
        from: { id: userId, name: userId },
        type: 'message',
        text: input
    }).then(() => {
        console.log('posted activity to bot with input %s',
        input);
```

```
    console.log('setting interval');
    let interval = setInterval(function () {
        console.log('getting activities...');
        getActivities(process.env.DL_KEY, conv.id, conv.
        watermark).then(activitiesResponse => {
            console.log("%j", activitiesResponse);
            let temp = _.filter(activitiesResponse.
            activities, (m) => m.from.id !== userId);
            if (temp.length > 0) {
                clearInterval(interval);
                let responseActivity = temp[0];
                console.log('got response %j',
                responseActivity);

                conv.watermark = activitiesResponse.
                watermark;
                buildAndSendTwimlResponse(req, res, next,
                userId, responseActivity.text);
                conv.lastAccessed = moment().format();
            } else {
                console.log('no activities for you...');
            }
        });
    }, 500);
  });
});
```

If you run this, you should now be able to talk to the same bot that we exposed via our webchat via Twilio!

EXERCISE 9-2

Twilio Voice Integration

The goal of this exercise is to create a bot and call it by integrating with Twilio.

1. Sign up for a trial Twilio account and get a testing phone number.

2. Enter your bot voice endpoint for Twilio to use when your phone number receives a call.

3. Integrate the voice endpoint with a Direct Line call into your bot. Return the first reply you receive from your bot.

4. Explore Twilio's voice dashboard. The dashboard provides information about each call and, more importantly, a functionality to view all errors and warnings. If your bot appears to be working correctly but the phone call to your bot fails, the "Errors & Warnings" section is a great place to start investigating what may have happened.

5. Add the *Gather* verb into your response so the user can have a conversation with the bot. How long of a conversation can you have before the novelty of a dumb bot wears off and you want to implement something meaningful?

6. Substitute the polling mechanism for a WebSocket, like you did in Exercise 9-1. Does it help with this solution?

7. Play around a bit with Twilio's speech recognition. How good is it? How good is it at recognizing your name? How easily can it be broken?

8. Applying speech recognition to arbitrary voice data is challenging enough as it is, not to mention when applied to phone quality voice data. Twilio's *Gather* verb allows for hints[7] to prime the speech recognition engine[8] with a vocabulary of words or phrases. Typically, this improves the voice recognition performance. Go ahead and add some hints that contain words supported by your bot. Does the speech recognition behave any better?

You just created your own voice-enabled chat bot and experimented with some interesting Twilio features. You can use similar techniques to create connectors for just about any other channel.

Integrating with SSML

Recall that systems like Google Assistant and Amazon's Alexa support voice output via Speech Synthesis Markup Language (SSML). Using this markup language, developers can specify tone, speed, emphasis, and pauses in the bot's voice responses. Unfortunately, Twilio does not support SSML at the time of this writing. Lucky for us, Microsoft has some APIs that can convert text to speech using SSML.

One such APIs is Microsoft's Bing Speech API.[9] This service provides both speech-to-text and text-to-speech functionality. For the text-to-speech functionality, we provide an SSML document and receive an audio file in response. We have some control over the output format, though for our sample we will receive a wave file. Once we have the file, we can utilize the *Play* verb to play the audio to the phone call. Let's see how this works.

---

[7]TwiML Gather Verb Hints Attribute: `https://www.twilio.com/docs/voice/twiml/gather#attributes-hints`

[8]Speech Priming in the Context of a Bot Framework Bot: `https://docs.microsoft.com/en-us/azure/bot-service/bot-service-manage-speech-priming`

[9]Bing Speech API: `https://azure.microsoft.com/en-us/services/cognitive-services/speech/`

We'll first pull in the *bing-speechclient-api* Node.js package.

```
npm install --save bingspeech-api-client
```

A sample *Play* TwiML document looks like this:

```
<?xml version="1.0" encoding="UTF-8"?
<Response>
    <Play loop="10">https://api.twilio.com/cowbell.mp3</Play>
</Response>
```

Twilio accepts a URI in the *Play* verb. As such, we will need to save the output from the Bing Speech API to a file on the file system and generate a URI that Twilio can use to retrieve the audio file. We are going to write all output audio files into a directory called audio. We will also set up a new *restify* route to retrieve those files.

First, let's create our function to generate the audio file and store it in the right location. Given some text, we want to return a URI for the calling function to utilize. We will use an MD5 hash of the text as the identifier for the audio file.

```
npm install md5 --save
```

This is what the code looks like to generate an audio file and save it locally. There are two prerequisites. First, we need to generate an API key to utilize Microsoft's Bing Speech API. We can achieve this by creating a new Bing Speech API resource in the Azure Portal. There is a free plan version of this API. Once we have the key, we add it to the .env file and name it MICROSOFT_BING_SPEECH_KEY. Second, we add our base ngrok URI to the .env file as BASE_URI.

```
const md5 = require('md5');
const BingSpeechClient = require('bingspeech-api-client').
BingSpeechClient;
const fs = require('fs');
```

```
const bing = new BingSpeechClient(process.env.MICROSOFT_BING_
SPEECH_KEY);
function generateAudio (text) {
    const id = md5(text);
    const file = 'public\\audio\\' + id + '.wav';
    const resultingUri = process.env.BASE_URI + '/audio/' + id
    + '.wav';

    if (!fs.existsSync('public')) fs.mkdirSync('public');
    if (!fs.existsSync('public/audio')) fs.mkdirSync('public/
    audio');

    return bing.synthesize(text).then(result => {
        const wstream = fs.createWriteStream(file);
        wstream.write(result.wave);

        console.log('created %s', resultingUri);
        return resultingUri;
    });
}
```

To test this, we create a test endpoint that creates an audio file and
responds with the URI. We could then use the browser to point at the URI
and download the resulting sound file. The following SSML is borrowed
from Google's SSML documentation, and I've added the current time using
Date().getTime() so that we generate a unique MD5 each time.

```
server.get('/api/audio-test', (req, res, next) => {
    const sample = 'Here are <say-as interpret-
    as="characters">SSML</say-as> samples. I can pause <break
    time="3s"/>.' +
        'I can speak in cardinals. Your number is <say-as
        interpret-as="cardinal">10</say-as>.' +
```

```
        'Or I can even speak in digits. The digits for ten are
        <say-as interpret-as="characters">10</say-as>.' +
        'I can also substitute phrases, like the <sub
        alias="World Wide Web Consortium">W3C</sub>.' +
        'Finally, I can speak a paragraph with two sentences.' +
        '<p><s>This is sentence one.</s><s>This is sentence
        two.</s></p>';

    generateAudio(sample + ' ' + new Date().getTime()).then(uri
    => {
        res.send(200, {
            uri: uri
        });
        next();
    });
});
```

If we invoke the URL from curl, we get the following result. The audio file referenced by the URI is clearly a speech synthesis of the SSML document.

```
$ curl https://botbook.ngrok.io/api/audio-test
{"uri":"https://botbook.ngrok.io/audio/1ce776f3560e54064979c4eb
69bbc308.wav"}
```

Finally, we integrate this into our code. We change the *buildAndSendTwimlResponse* function to generate the audio files for any text we send. We also make a change in the *generateAudio* function to use any previously generated audio files based on the MD5 hash. That means we'll have to generate only one audio file per input.

```
function buildAndSendTwimlResponse(req, res, next, userId, text) {
    const twiml = new VoiceResponse();

    Promise.all(
```

```
[
    generateAudio(text),
    generateAudio('I didn\'t quite catch that. Please
    try again.'),
    generateAudio('Ok, call back anytime!')]).then(
uri => {
    let msgUri = uri[0];
    let firstNotCaughtUri = uri[1];
    let goodbyeUri = uri[2];

    twiml.play(msgUri);
    twiml.gather({ input: 'speech', action: '/api/
    voice/gather', method: 'POST' });

    twiml.play(firstNotCaughtUri);
    twiml.gather({ input: 'speech', action: '/api/
    voice/gather', method: 'POST' });

    twiml.play(goodbyeUri);
    twiml.hangup();

    const response = twiml.toString();
    console.log(response);

    res.writeHead(200, {
        'Content-Length': Buffer.byteLength(response),
        'Content-Type': 'text/html'
    });
    res.write(response);
    next();
});
}
```

```
function generateAudio (text) {
    const id = md5(text);
    const file = 'public\\audio\\' + id + '.wav';
    const resultingUri = process.env.BASE_URI + '/audio/' + id
    + '.wav';

    if (!fs.existsSync('public')) fs.mkdirSync('public');
    if (!fs.existsSync('public/audio')) fs.mkdirSync('public/
    audio');

    if (fs.existsSync(file)) {
        return Promise.resolve(resultingUri);
    }

    return bing.synthesize(text).then(result => {
        const wstream = fs.createWriteStream(file);
        wstream.write(result.wave);

        console.log('created %s', resultingUri);
        return resultingUri;
    });
}
```

Final Touches

We are almost done. One thing we have not yet done is to have the bot respond with SSML, instead of using the text. We do not utilize all the speech features from the Bot Builder. As shown in Chapter 6, we could have each message populate the *inputHint* to assist in determining which TwiML verbs should be used and even to consolidate multiple response from the bot. We stick to simply populating the *speak* field in each message with the appropriate SSML. We must also modify our connector code to use the *speak* field, instead of the *text* field.

```
bot.dialog('sampleConversation', [
    (session, arg) => {
        console.log(JSON.stringify(session.message));

        if (session.message.text.toLowerCase().indexOf('hello')
        >= 0 || session.message.text.indexOf('hi') >= 0)
            session.send({
                text: 'hey!',
                speak: '<emphasis level="strong">really like</
                emphasis> hey!</emphasis>'
            });
        else if (session.message.text.toLowerCase() === 'quit') {
            session.send({
                text: 'ok, we\'re done!',
                speak: 'ok, we\'re done',
                sourceEvent: {
                    hangup: true
                }
            });
            session.endDialog();
            return;
        } else if (session.message.text.toLowerCase().indexOf('
        meaning of life') >= 0) {
            session.send({
                text: '42',
                speak: 'It is quite clear that the meaning
                of life is <break time="2s" /><emphasis
                level="strong">42</emphasis>'
            });
        } else if (session.message.text.toLowerCase().
        indexOf('waldo') >= 0) {
            session.send({
```

```
            text: 'not here',
            speak: '<emphasis level="strong">Definitely</
            emphasis> not here'
        });
    } else if (session.message.text.toLowerCase() ===
    'apple') {
        session.send({
            text: "Here, have an apple.",
            speak: "Apples are delicious!",
            attachments: [
                {
                    contentType: 'image/jpeg',
                    contentUrl: 'https://upload.wikimedia.
                    org/wikipedia/commons/thumb/1/15/Red_
                    Apple.jpg/1200px-Red_Apple.jpg',
                    name: 'Apple'
                }
            ]
        });
    }
    else {
        session.send({ text: 'oh that\'s cool', speak: 'oh
        that\'s cool' });
    }
    }
]);
```

Note that we also added an extra metadata control field. The response to input *quit* includes a field called *hangup,* set to true. This is an indicator to our connector to include the *Hangup* verb. We create a function called *buildAndSendHangup* to generate that response.

```
function buildAndSendHangup(req, res, next) {
    const twiml = new VoiceResponse();

    Promise.all([generateAudio('Ok, call back anytime!')]).
    then(
        (uri) => {
            twiml.play(uri[0]);
            twiml.hangup();

            const response = twiml.toString();
            console.log(response);

            res.writeHead(200, {
                'Content-Length': Buffer.byteLength(response),
                'Content-Type': 'text/html'
            });
            res.write(response);
            next();
        });
}
```

We modify the /api/voice/gather handler to use the speak property and interpret the *hangup* field correctly.

```
server.post('/api/voice/gather', (req, res, next) => {
    const input = req.body.SpeechResult;
    let userId = req.body.Caller;
    console.log('user id: %s | input: %s', userId, input);

    let conv = cachedConversations[userId];
    console.log('got convo: %j', conv);
    conv.lastAccessed = moment().format();

    postActivity(process.env.DL_KEY, conv.id, {
```

```
    from: { id: userId, name: userId }, // required (from.
    name is optional)
    type: 'message',
    text: input
}).then(() => {
    console.log('posted activity to bot with input %s',
    input);

    console.log('setting interval');
    let interval = setInterval(function () {
        console.log('getting activities...');
        getActivities(process.env.DL_KEY, conv.id, conv.
        watermark).then(activitiesResponse => {
            console.log("%j", activitiesResponse);
            let temp = _.filter(activitiesResponse.
            activities, (m) => m.from.id !== userId);
            if (temp.length > 0) {
                clearInterval(interval);
                let responseActivity = temp[0];
                console.log('got response %j',
                responseActivity);

                conv.watermark = activitiesResponse.
                watermark;
                if (responseActivity.channelData &&
                responseActivity.channelData.hangup) {
                    buildAndSendHangup(req, res, next);
                } else {
                    buildAndSendTwimlResponse(req, res,
                    next, userId, responseActivity.speak);
                    conv.lastAccessed = moment().format();
                }
```

```
        } else {
            console.log('no activities for you...');
        }
    });
}, 500);
});
});
```

Now we can call and have a great conversation with a witty bot that pauses before saying the meaning of life is 42 and places emphasis on the fact that Waldo is *definitely* not where the bot is!

Conclusion

Direct Line is a powerful feature and is the main interface for calling into our bot from a client app. Having the ability to consider other channels as sort of a client app is how we can create custom channel connectors. One of the more interesting tasks we accomplished in this chapter was adding SSML support to our bot integration. This kind of integration is just a taste of the intelligence that we can begin building into our bot experience. The Bing Speech API that we utilized is just one of numerous Microsoft APIs known as the Cognitive Services APIs. In the next chapter, we'll look at applying other APIs in that family to tasks we may encounter in the bot space.

CHAPTER 10

Making the Chat Bot Smarter

In the previous chapter, we spent time connecting our chat bot's Speech Synthesis Markup Language (SSML) output into a cloud-based text-to-speech engine to give our chat bot as human a voice as possible. The Bing Speech API that we utilized is an example of what is collectively being called *cognitive services*. These are typically services that enable more natural human-like interactions with applications. Originally, Microsoft referred to these as Project Oxford.[1] These days, the suite of APIs is now branded as Azure Cognitive Services.

At a more technical level, these are services that allow easy access to machine learning (ML) algorithms that perform cognitive-type tasks, for example, speech recognition, speech synthesis, spell-checking, auto-correction, recommendation engines, decision engines, and visual object recognition. LUIS, which we explored in depth in Chapter 3, is another example of an Azure Cognitive Service. Microsoft is obviously not the only player in this space. IBM has many similar services under its Watson umbrella. Google's Cloud Platform includes similar services on the Google stack.

---

[1]Original Project Oxford blog announcement: `https://blogs.microsoft.com/ ai/microsofts-project-oxford-helps-developers-build-more-intelligent- apps/`

© Szymon Rozga 2018
S. Rozga, *Practical Bot Development*, https://doi.org/10.1007/978-1-4842-3540-9_10

This ML-as-a-service approach is extremely convenient for many tasks. Although it may not be appropriate from a latency and cost perspective for all workloads, for many it just makes sense to use for prototyping, pilot and production deployments. In this chapter, we will explore a few of Microsoft's Azure Cognitive Services at our disposal. This is not meant to be an exhaustive treatment of the subject but rather an introduction to the type of services that may be of interest to chat bot developers.

In either case, it is worth exploring these services to understand what is being offered, to learn what types of technologies can be applied to our business problems applications, and, most importantly, to engender our chat bots with some relevant intelligence.

Before we jump in, please note that all the cognitive services can be provisioned by using the Azure Portal at `https://portal.azure.com`. Adding the desired service resource into a resource group will allow us to get an access key. For example, when we try to add a "bing spell check" resource into the "book test" resource group, we can select Bing Spell Check v7 API (Figure 10-1).

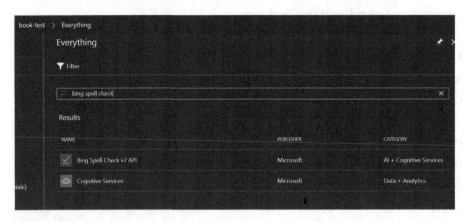

Figure 10-1. *Adding the Bing Spell Check v7 API in Azure*

After we give the service a name and select the pricing tier (Figure 10-2), we can see the access keys. There are typically two access keys available for us to use (Figure 10-3). Having two keys allows for easy key rotation.

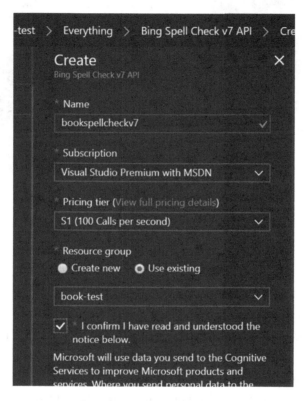

Figure 10-2. *Creating the Bing Spell Check v7 API resource*

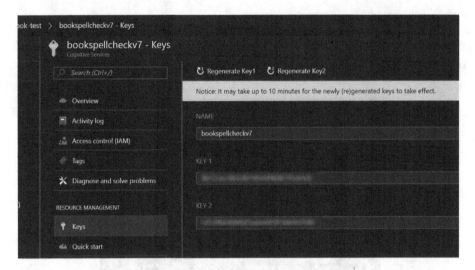

Figure 10-3. *Finding the access keys for the Bing Spell Check v7 API resource*

This process works similarly for the rest of the services; no advanced level of knowledge of the portal is needed to get started.

When the services were first being developed in public preview, most were offered free. As the services moved from preview into general availability, tiered pricing models were established. Lucky for us, most of the services still have a free tier that permits a substantial amount of usage. For example, LUIS allows us to call the endpoint 10,000 times per month for free. We can use the Translator Text API to translate 2,000,000 characters per month free. You can find more pricing details for all the services at `https://azure.microsoft.com/en-us/pricing/details/ cognitive-services/`.

Spell-Checking

One feature for any application that deals with user-generated text input is spell-checking. We would like an engine that is flexible and can handle common spelling issues such as dealing with slang, handling proper name errors within a context, figuring out word breaks, and spotting errors with homophones. Additionally, the engine should be continually updated with new entities such as brands and popular cultural expressions. That is no small feat, yet Microsoft offers its Spell Check API that does just that.

Microsoft's Bing Spell Check API provides two spell-checker modes: *Proof* and *Spell*. *Proof* is designed for document spell-checking including capitalization and punctuation suggestions to help with document authoring (the type of spell checking you may find in Microsoft Word). *Spell* is designed for correcting the spelling in web searches. Microsoft claims the *Spell* mode to be more aggressive as it is designed to optimize for search results.[2] The context of chat bots is closer to a web search than drafting long documents, so *Spell* is probably the better choice.

We will begin with the basics, passing the mode, the culture for which we want to spell check (referred to as the *market*), and the text itself. We also have the option of adding the context before and after the input text. In many scenarios, context can be important and relevant for the spell checker. You can find more details in the API reference documentation.[3]

To demonstrate the APIs usage, we will create a basic chat bot that simply passes the user input through the spell-checker and responds by modifying the user's input with suggested improvements that have a score higher than 0.5. The bot will first prompt for the user to select the spell-check mode. At that point, any input will be sent to the Spell Check API using the selected mode. Finally, we can send the message "exit" at any time to return to the main menu and select the mode again. This is basic, but it will illustrate interacting with the API. You can find the code for this bot under the `chapter10-spell-check-bot` folder in the book's GitHub repo.

·

---

[2]More information about the Bing Spell Check API: `https://azure.microsoft.com/en-us/services/cognitive-services/spell-check/`

[3]Bing Spell Check API V7 API documentation: `https://docs.microsoft.com/en-us/rest/api/cognitiveservices/bing-spell-check-api-v7-reference`

We first create the Bing Spell Check v7 API resource in Azure, so we can get a key. Although we could write our own client library to use with the service, we will use a Node.js package called *cognitive-services*[4] that includes client implementations for most of Microsoft's cognitive services.

```
npm install cognitive-services --save

const cognitiveServices = require('cognitive-services');
```

We set up our UniversalBot as usual. We add the Spell Check API key into our .env file and call the field *SC_KEY*.

```
const welcomeMsg = 'Say \'proof\' or \'spell\' to select spell
check mode';
const bot = new builder.UniversalBot(connector, [
    (session, arg, next) => {
        if (session.message.text === 'proof') {
            session.beginDialog('spell-check-dialog', { mode:
            'proof' });
        } else if (session.message.text === 'spell') {
            session.beginDialog('spell-check-dialog', { mode:
            'spell' });
        } else {
            session.send(welcomeMsg);
        }
    },
    session => {
        session.send(welcomeMsg);
    }
]);
const inMemoryStorage = new builder.MemoryBotStorage();
bot.set('storage', inMemoryStorage);
```

---

[4]Node.js cognitive-services package and Cognitive Service API support listing: https://www.npmjs.com/package/cognitive-services

Next, we create a dialog called *spell-check-dialog*. In this code we send a request to the Spell Check API any time a new message is sent by the user. When we receive the result, we replace the segments flagged as problematic with a suggested correction that has a score greater or equal to 0.5. Why 0.5? It is a bit of an arbitrary decision, and it is suggested to modify the score threshold and input option to find the best values for your application.

```
bot.dialog('spell-check-dialog', [
    (session, arg) => {
        session.dialogData.mode = arg.mode;
        builder.Prompts.text(session, 'Enter your input text.
        Say \'exit\' to reconfigure mode.');
    },
    (session, arg) => {
        session.sendTyping();

        const text = arg.response;

        if (text === 'exit') {
            session.endDialog('ok, done.');
            return;
        }

        spellCheck(text, session.dialogData.mode).
        then(resultText => {
            session.send(resultText);
            session.replaceDialog('spell-check-dialog', { mode:
            session.dialogData.mode });
        });
    }
]);
```

We define the *spellCheck* function to call the Bing Spell Check API and replace misspelled words with the suggested correction.

```
function spellCheck(text, mode) {
    const parameters = {
        mkt: 'en-US',
        mode: mode,
        text: text
    };

    const spellCheckClient = new cognitiveServices.
    bingSpellCheckV7({
        apiKey: process.env.SC_KEY
    })

    return spellCheckClient.spellCheck({
        parameters
    }).then(response => {
        console.log(response); // we do this so we can easily
        inspect the resulting object
        const resultText = applySpellCheck(text, response.
        flaggedTokens);
        return resultText;
    });
}

function applySpellCheck(originalText, possibleProblems) {
    let tempText = originalText;
    let diff = 0;
```

```
for (let i = 0; i < possibleProblems.length; i++) {
    const problemToken = possibleProblems[i];
    const offset = problemToken.offset;
    const originalTokenLength = problemToken.token.length;

    const suggestionObj = problemToken.suggestions[0];
    if (suggestionObj.score < .5) {
        continue;
    }

    const suggestion = suggestionObj.suggestion;
    const lengthDiff = suggestion.length -
    originalTokenLength;

    tempText = tempText.substring(0, offset + diff) +
    suggestion + tempText.substring(offset + diff +
    originalTokenLength);

    diff += lengthDiff;
}

return tempText;
}
```

Figure 10-4 shows the resulting conversation.

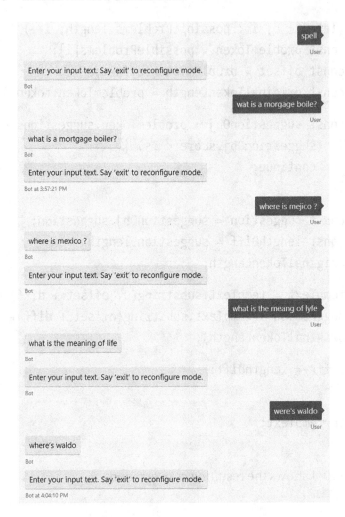

Figure 10-4. Spell-checker bot in action

It works well! Another approach is to always run input through the spell-checker before it even reaches the dialog stack. We can do this by installing custom middleware in the bot. The idea behind middleware is to be able to add logic into the pipeline that the Bot Builder uses to process every incoming and outgoing message. The structure of a middleware object is as follows. The method *bot.use* adds the middleware object to Bot Builder's pipeline.

468

```
bot.use({
    receive: function (event, next) {
        logicOnIncoming(event);
        next();
    },
    send: function (event, next) {
        logicOnOutgoing(event);
        next();
    }
});
```

We could create the following middleware using our previously defined code. We spell-check incoming input, overwriting the input with the autocorrected text. We do not define any logic on outgoing messages.

```
bot.use({
    receive: function (event, next) {
        if (event.type === 'message') {
            spellCheck(event.text, 'spell').then(resultText => {
                event.text = resultText;
                next();
            });
        }
    },
    send: function (event, next) {
        next();
    }
});
```

That's it! Now our dialog can be so much simpler!

```
bot.dialog('middleware-dialog', [
    (session, arg) => {
        let text = session.message.text;
        session.send(text);
    }
]);
```

The resulting conversation looks something like Figure 10-5.

Figure 10-5. *Spell-checking using the middleware approach*

In Chapter 3 we explored the options the Language Understanding Intelligence Service (LUIS) offers when it comes to spell-checking. As mentioned previously, LUIS is another one of Microsoft's cognitive services; it is an NLU system that allows us to classify intents and extract named entities. One of the tasks it can accomplish is to integrate with the Bing Spell Check API and run the spell-checked query (versus the raw input) through the NLU models. The benefit to this approach is that our LUIS app does not need to be trained with misspelled words. The disadvantage is that our scenario may include domain-specific language that the spell-checker does not recognize but our LUIS model does.

The approach of using middleware to completely change the user's input so that the bot never sees the raw input is not something we recommend. Minimally, we should be logging the raw input and raw output. If enabling spell-checking on LUIS itself yields problematic behaviors in our model, we could move some of that logic into our bot. One option would be to wrap the LUIS recognizer around a custom spell-check LUIS recognizer. In this custom recognizer, you would have logic to ensure that spell-checker never modifies a certain vocabulary subset. In effect, we would be performing a partial spell-check.

Sentiment

In the first chapter, we demonstrated a bot that can respond to the sentiment it detects from the user's input (Figure 10-6). Basic sentiment analysis can be simply implemented using lookups of "good" and "bad" words.

Figure 10-6. *A bot that can respond to sentiment*

Obviously, this approach has limitations such as not considering the word's context. If we were to develop our own lookups, we would need to make sure the list keeps up-to-date as cultural norms change. More advanced approaches use machine learning classification techniques to create a sentiment function to score an utterance's sentiment. Microsoft offers an ML algorithm based on a large corpus of text prelabeled with sentiment.

Microsoft's sentiment analysis is part of its Text Analytics API. The service offers three main functions: sentiment analysis, key phrase extraction, and language detection. We will first focus on sentiment analysis.

The API allows us to send one or more text strings and receive a response with one or more numeric scores between 0 and 1, where 0 is negative sentiment and 1 is positive. Here is an example (and you can tell my son woke me up way too early with this one):

```
{
    "documents": [
        {
            "id": "1",
            "language": "en",
            "text": "i hate early mornings"
        }
    ]
}
```

Here is the result:

```
{
    "documents": [
        {
            "score": 0.073260486125946045,
            "id": "1"
        }
    ],
    "errors": []
}
```

Sentiment analysis has some interesting applications in the chat bot space. We can utilize the data after the fact in analytics reports to see which features challenge users the most. Or, we can utilize the live sentiment score to automatically transfer the conversation to a human agent to immediately address a user's concern or frustration.

Supporting Multiple Languages

Supporting multiple languages in a chat bot is a complex topic in and of itself that we cannot fully cover in the scope of this book. Nevertheless, we demonstrate how to update the calendar bot we have been working on throughout the book to support multiple languages by using the Text Analytics and Translator APIs. The code can be found under the chapter10-calendar-bot folder of the book's GitHub repo. We are going to approach this task as follows:

- Anytime a user sends a message to the bot, our chat bot will use the Text Analytics API to identify the user's language.

- If the language is English, continue as normal. If not, translate the utterance into English.

- Run the English phrase through LUIS.

- On the way out, if the user's language was English, continue as normal. Otherwise, translate the bot's response into the user's language before sending to user.

In essence, we are using English as an intermediary language to provide LUIS support. This approach isn't foolproof. There are reasons LUIS supports multiple cultures, like the many nuances and cultural variations in language. A direct literal translation without extra context may not make sense. And in fact, we may want to support completely different ways of saying things in one language than in English. A correct approach to the problem is to develop detailed LUIS applications for each culture for which we want to provide first-class support, use those applications based on language detection, and use the Translator API and intermediary English only when we don't have LUIS support for a language. Or maybe we even avoid the Translator API altogether because of the possible issues with translation.

Although we do not use this approach in the following example, since we can control the bot's text output, we could provide those static strings localized across all languages we want to support (instead of using translation services). We could fall back on automatic translation for anything not explicitly scripted.

From a technology perspective, we must make a choice of when the translation is going to occur. For example, is it the role of the recognizer or the dialog? Or should we add middleware to translate the input into English? For this example, we will utilize the middleware approach because we are utilizing the translation service on both the incoming and outgoing content and want it to be as transparent to the rest of the bot as possible. If we had a set of culture-specific LUIS applications and localized output strings, we could use a mix of recognizers with dialog logic.

Before we begin, make sure you have created a Text Analytics API and Translator Text API resource in the Azure Portal, in the same way we created the Bing Spell Check v7 API resource. Both APIs have a free pricing tier, so make sure to select that. Note that the Text Analytics API requires that we select a region. All the cognitive services unrelated to Bing require this to be set. This obviously has availability and latency implications that are outside the scope of this book. Once created, we must save the keys into the .env file. Name the Text Analytics key as *TA_KEY* and the Translator key as *TRANSLATOR_KEY*. In addition, the *cognitive-services* package requires the endpoint to be specified. The endpoint maps to the region, so if we selected West US as the Text Analytics service region, the endpoint value is westus.api.cognitive.microsoft.com.[5] Set this to the TA_*ENDPOINT* key in the .env file.

---

[5]We can find all the other possible endpoint values in the Node.js package code; see `https://github.com/joshbalfour/node-cognitive-services/blob/master/src/language/textAnalytics.js`.

We will use the *cognitive-services* Node.js package to interact with the Text Analytics API; however, the Translator API is one of the services not supported by this package. We can install the *mstranslator* Node.js package.

```
npm install mstranslator --save
```

```
const translator = require('mstranslator');
```

Next, we can create a middleware module that contains the translation logic so that we can easily apply this functionality to any bot.

```
const TranslatorMiddleware = require('./translatorMiddleware').
TranslatorMiddleware;
bot.use(new TranslatorMiddleware());
```

The middleware code itself will depend on using the Text Analytics and Translator APIs.

```
const textAnalytics = new cognitiveServices.textAnalytics({
    apiKey: process.env.TA_KEY,
    endpoint: process.env.TA_ENDPOINT
});
const translatorApi = new translator({ api_key: process.env.
TRANSLATOR_KEY }, true); // the second parameter ensures that
the token is autogenerated
```

After that, we create a class TranslatorMiddleware with a map that tells us which users are using which language. This is needed to store a user's incoming language for the outgoing logic to be able to translate from English back into it.

```
const userLanguageMap = {};

class TranslatorMiddleware {
    ...
}
```

The receive logic skips anything that is not a message. If we have a message, the user's language is detected. If the language is English, we continue; otherwise, we translate the message into English, reset the message text to the English version (thereby losing the original language input), and continue. If there is an error while we translate the incoming message, we simply assume English.

```
receive(event, next) {
    if (event.type !== 'message') { next(); return; }

    if (event.text == null || event.text.length == 0) {
        // if there is not input and we already have a
        language, leave as is, otherwise set to English
        userLanguageMap[event.user.id] = userLanguageMap[event.
        user.id] || 'en';
        next();
        return;
    }

    textAnalytics.detectLanguage({
        body: {
            documents: [
                {
                    id: "1",
                    text: event.text
                }
            ]
        }
    }).then(result => {
        const languageOptions = _.find(result.documents, p =>
        p.id === "1").detectedLanguages;
        let lang = 'en';
```

```
if (languageOptions && languageOptions.length > 0) {
    lang = languageOptions[0].iso6391Name;
}
this.userLanguageMap[event.user.id] = lang;

if (lang === 'en') next();
else {
    translatorApi.translate({
        text: event.text,
        from: languageOptions[0].iso6391Name,
        to: 'en'
    }, function (err, result) {
        if (err) {
            console.error(err);
            lang = 'en';
            userLanguageMap[event.user.id] = lang;
            next();
        }
        else {
            event.text = result;
            next();
        }
    });
}
});
}
```

On the way out, we simply figure out the user's language and translate the outgoing message into that language. If the user's language is English, we skip the translation step.

```
send(event, next) {
    if (event.type === 'message') {
        const userLang = this.userLanguageMap[event.address.
        user.id] || 'en';

        if (userLang === 'en') { next(); }
        else {
            translatorApi.translate({
                text: event.text,
                from: 'en',
                to: userLang
            }, (err, result) => {
                if (err) {
                    console.error(err);
                    next();
                }
                else {
                    event.text = result;
                    next();
                }
            });
        }
    }
    else {
        next();
    }
}
```

Figure 10-7 displays the responses to a greeting in different languages.

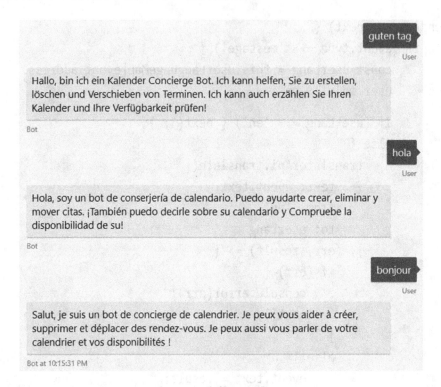

Figure 10-7. *Bot responding in different languages*

Congratulations, we now have a naïve multilanguage chat bot! Basic requests and responses seem OK, but there are some issues with collecting data. For example, the bot seems to switch languages midstream (Figure 10-8).

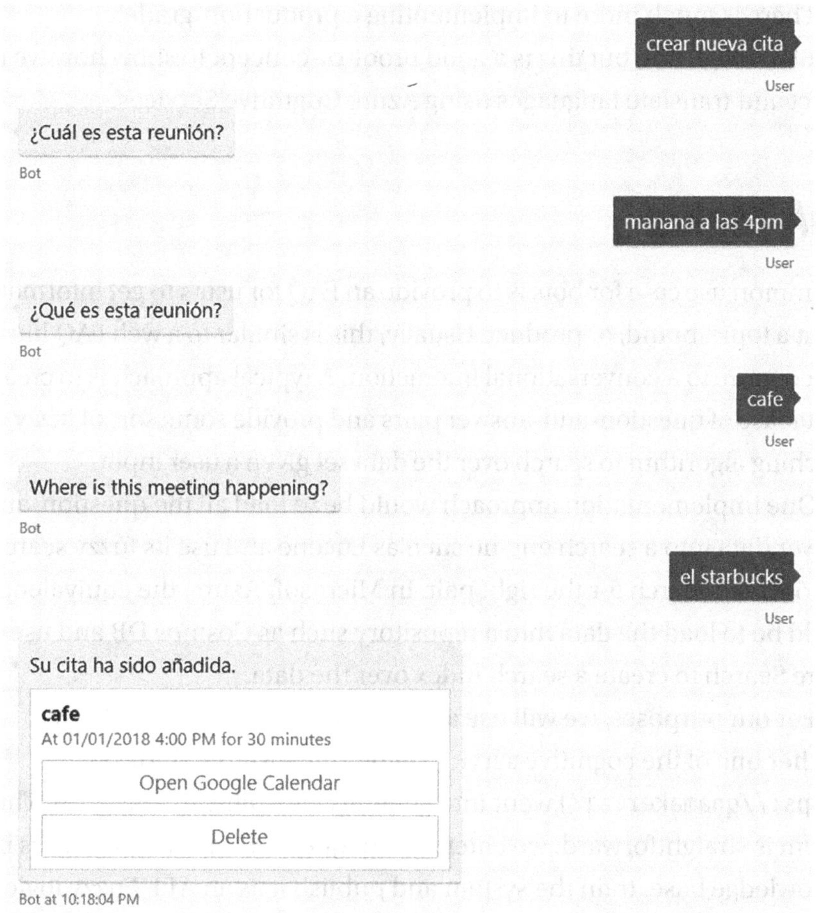

crear nueva cita

User

¿Cuál es esta reunión?

Bot

manana a las 4pm

User

¿Qué es esta reunión?

Bot

cafe

User

Where is this meeting happening?

Bot

el starbucks

User

Su cita ha sido añadida.

cafe
At 01/01/2018 4:00 PM for 30 minutes

| Open Google Calendar |
| Delete |

Bot at 10:18:04 PM

Figure 10-8. *Create appointment flow in Spanish, with a blip*

The problem is that the word *café* is valid in both English and Spanish. This perhaps calls for some sort of language lock-in during dialogs. The translation of "when is the meeting?" does not sound right either. The word *cuál* translates to *which*, not *when*. We could solve this by providing static localized output strings.

There is much more to implementing a production-grade multilanguage bot, but this is a good proof-of-concept to show how we can detect and translate languages using Azure Cognitive Services.

QnA Maker

A common use case for bots is to provide an FAQ for users to get information about a topic, brand, or product. Usually, this is similar to a web FAQ but geared more to a conversational interaction. A typical approach is to create a database of question-and-answer pairs and provide some sort of fuzzy matching algorithm to search over the data set given a user input.

One implementation approach would be to load all the question-and-answer data into a search engine such as Lucene and use its fuzzy search algorithm to search for the right pair. In Microsoft Azure, the equivalent would be to load the data into a repository such as Cosmos DB and use Azure Search to create a search index over the data.

For our purposes, we will use a simpler option called QnA Maker, another one of the cognitive services at our disposal. QnA Maker (`https://qnamaker.ai/`) went into general availability in May 2018. The system is straightforward: we enter a set of question-and-answer pairs into a knowledge base, train the system and publish it as an API. Fuzzy logic matching is then made available via an API that we host in an Azure App Service Plan, so we can tune its performance as necessary.

We must first log into the Azure Portal and create a new QnA Maker instance (Figure 10-9). The UI will collect a few pieces of data from us. We enter a name, the management service pricing tier (free pricing!), the resource group, the search service pricing tier (again, free!), search service location, service location, and whether we want to include Application Insights. The service will work just as well if you enable or disable Application Insights. Leaving it enabled allows you to view the logs of what users asked QnA Maker.

Figure 10-9. *Creating a new QnA Maker service*

After the Azure Portal does its thing, we end up with several resources. The search service hosts the search index, the app service hosts the API we will call, and Application Insights provides analytics around our service usage. Make sure to change the app service plan pricing tier to free!

At this point, we can go to the QnA Maker Portal. Log into `https://www.qnamaker.ai` using the same account you use for Azure. Click *Create a knowledge base*. You will see the screen in Figure 10-10. Select the QnA Service from your Azure subscription and name your knowledge base. There are several options to populate the content: you can supply a URL with an FAQ, upload a TSV file that contains the data, a PDF file, or enter the data manually. These are very interesting options we suggest you explore on your own.

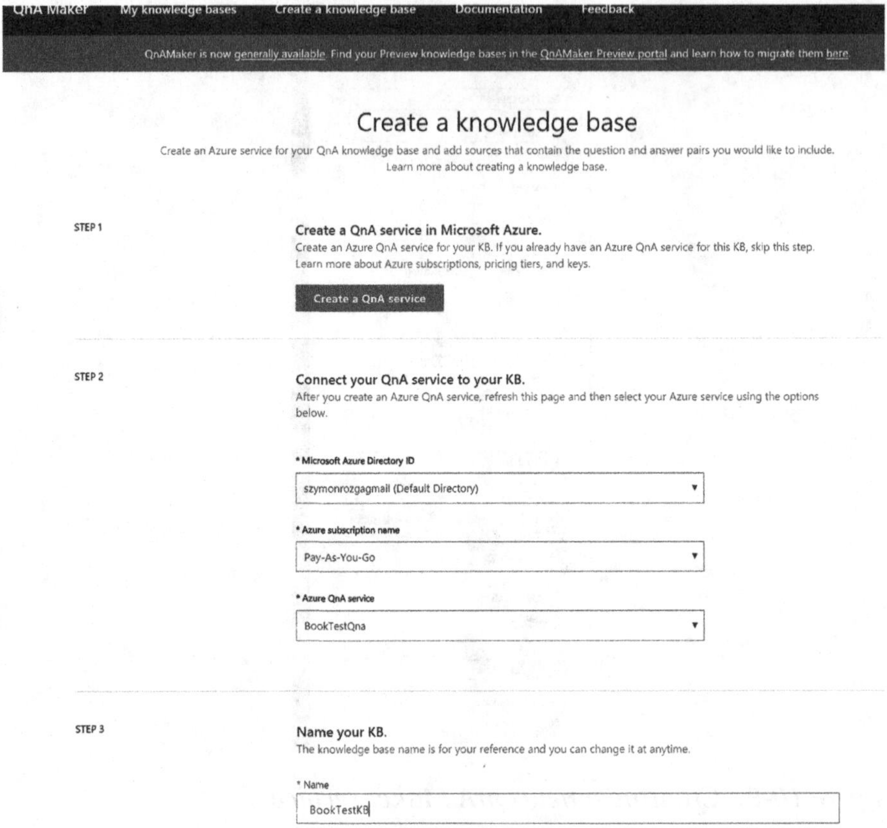

Figure 10-10. *Creating a new QnA knowledge base*

For our purposes, we will use the manual interface. After entering a service name, click *Create new KB*. We are met with a rich interface that allows us to edit content in our knowledge base and to save and retrain or publish it (Figure 10-11). We add a few pairs using the *+ Add new QnA pair* link in the top right.

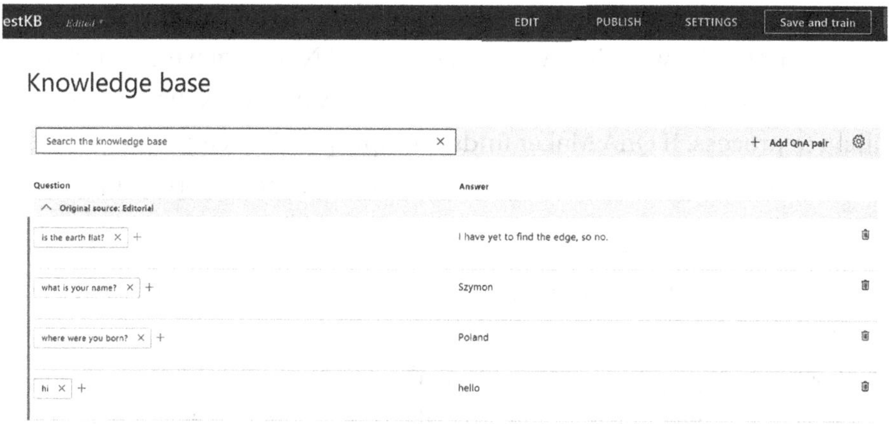

estKB   *Edited*   EDIT   PUBLISH   SETTINGS   Save and train

Knowledge base

| Search the knowledge base | ✕ | | + Add QnA pair | ⚙ |

Question	Answer	
∧ Original source: Editorial		
is the earth flat? ✕ +	I have yet to find the edge, so no.	🗑
what is your name? ✕ +	Szymon	🗑
where were you born? ✕ +	Poland	🗑
hi ✕ +	hello	🗑

Figure 10-11. *Adding more QnA pairs to our knowledge base*

We can now click *Save and train* and then click *Publish*. Clicking the *Publish* button will move the knowledge base into the Azure Search instance created in the Azure Portal. Once it's published, we will be presented with details on how to call the API (see Figure 10-12). Note that the URL corresponds to the app service we created in the Azure Portal.

Success! Your service has been deployed. What's next?

You can always find the deployment details in your service's settings.

Use the below HTTP request to build your bot. Learn how.

Sample HTTP request	POST /knowledgebases/ce45743a-62e5-42b1-a572-f912ea6836f9/generateAnswer Host: https://booktestqna.azurewebsites.net/qnamaker Authorization: EndpointKey f3c15268-40c1-4e66-8790-392c29f2f704 Content-Type: application/json {"question":"<Your question>"}

Need to fine-tune and refine? Go back and keep editing your service.

Edit Service

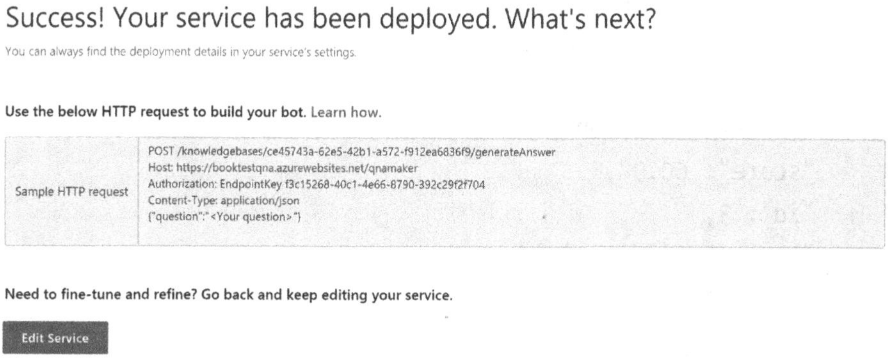

Figure 10-12. *We published a QnA Maker KB!*

Let's use curl to see the API in action. We'll try something we have not explicitly trained it with like "whats your name." Note that we can include the top parameter to indicate to QnA Maker how many results we are willing to process. If QnA Maker finds multiple possible candidate answers with a close enough score, it will return up to the value of top options.

```
curl -X POST
-H "Authorization: EndpointKey f3c15268-40c1-4e66-8790-
392c29f2f704"
-H "Content-Type: application/json"  "https://booktestqna.
azurewebsites.net/qnamaker/knowledgebases/ce45743a-62e5-42b1-
a572-f912ea6836f9/generateAnswer"
-d '{ "question": "whats your name?", "top": 5 }'
```

The response is as follows:

```
{
  "answers": [
    {
      "questions": [
        "what is your name?"
      ],
      "answer": "Szymon",
      "score": 60.98,
      "id": 3,
      "source": "Editorial",
      "metadata": []
    }
  ]
}
```

The response looks good. If we ask a question we have not trained, we get a "No good match found in the KB" response.

```
curl -X POST
-H "Authorization: EndpointKey f3c15268-40c1-4e66-8790-
392c29f2f704"
-H "Content-Type: application/json"  "https://booktestqna.
azurewebsites.net/qnamaker/knowledgebases/ce45743a-62e5-42b1-
a572-f912ea6836f9/generateAnswer"
-d '{ "question": "when are you going to give me your
bitcoin?", "top": 5 }'
{
  "answers": [
    {
      "questions": [],
      "answer": "No good match found in KB.",
      "score": 0.0,
      "id": -1,
      "metadata": []
    }
  ]
}
```

The result is what we would expect: no match. The user interface also provides a test capability that lets us ask the knowledge base questions in different phrasings to see what the model returns before we publish to a public API. If the algorithm picks up the wrong answer, we can point it to the right answer. You can also easily add alternative question phrasings (Figure 10-13).

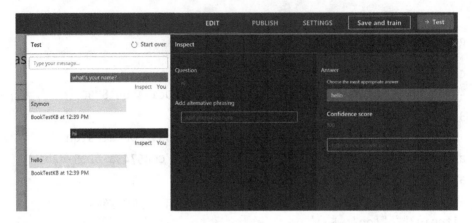

Figure 10-13. *QnA Maker test interface, a powerful way to add new question phrasings and add new pairs*

Microsoft provides a QnA Maker recognizer and dialog as part of its *BotBuilder-CognitiveServices*[6] Node.js package. If we would like our chat bot to utilize both QnA Maker and LUIS, we could use a custom recognizer that queries both services and picks the right course of action depending on the results from both services.

EXERCISE 10-1

Integrating with QnA Maker

The goal of this exercise is to add question-and-answer functionality to an existing chat bot.

1. Create a simple QnA Maker knowledge base that has answers to some questions about yourself. Name, date of birth, and number of siblings are some possibilities.

---

[6]The BotBuilder-CognitiveServices Node.js package provides helpers around accessing QnA Maker. The code can be found on GitHub at https://github.com/ Microsoft/BotBuilder-CognitiveServices/tree/master/Node.

2. Create a chat that utilizes the *BotBuilder-CognitiveServices* Node.js package to connect to your QnA Maker service.

3. Integrate your QnA Maker dialog and recognizer into a bot that also connects to LUIS. You can use Chapter 7's calendar bot as an example. Is the framework good at distinguishing between LUIS queries and QnA queries?

4. Try to train QnA Maker with utterances that are like those with which you trained your LUIS model. How does the bot behave? Does the behavior change if we change the order of recognizer registrations?

In this exercise you explored integrating QnA Maker into a chat bot. You also explored mixing the QnA Maker and LUIS recognizers, a good exercise in both Bot Builder mechanics and possible ordering pitfalls.

Computer Vision

Until now, all the cognitive services we have explored had some form of obvious application to chat bots. Spell-checking, sentiment analysis, translation and language detection, and fuzzy input matching are all clearly applicable to our everyday bot interactions. On the other hand, there are many machine learning tasks whose applicability to bots is not as clear. Computer Vision is one such example.

Microsoft's Azure Cognitive Services includes the Computer Vision family of services that provide several functions. For example, there is a service to detect and analyze faces and another one to analyze people's emotions. There is a content moderations service and a service that allows you to customize existing computer vision models to fit our use case (imagine trying to get an algorithm to become good at recognizing different types of trees). There is also a more general-purpose service called Computer Vision that returns a set of tags for the image with a confidence score. It can also create a text summary of the image and determine whether an image is racy or contains adult content, among other tasks.

Because of my unending amusement with mobile apps whose only task is to determine whether a photo is a hot dog or not, we will look at code for a bot that can tell whether the image sent by the user is a hot dog or not. The code can be found under the chapter10-hot-dog-or-not-hot-dog-bot folder of the book's GitHub repo.

Principally, we will exercise this bot using the emulator to ensure we can develop locally. When a user sends an image via any channel, the bot usually receives a URL for the image. We could send that URL to the service, but since the emulator sends a localhost address, this won't work. What our code will need to do is to download said image to a temporary directory and then upload it to the Computer Vision API. We will download the image using this code and using the *request* Node.js package.

```
const getImage = function (uri, filename) {
    return new Promise((resolve, reject) => {
        request.head(uri, function (err, res, body) {
            request(uri).pipe(fs.createWriteStream(filename))
                .on('error', () => { reject(); })
                .on('close', () => {
                    resolve();
                });
        });
    });
};
```

We then create a simple dialog that takes any input and runs it through the service to figure out whether a hot dog was identified.

```
bot.dialog('hot-dog-or-not-hot-dog', [
    (session, arg) => {
        if (session.message.attachments == null || session.
        message.attachments.length == 0 || session.message.
        attachments[0].contentType.indexOf('image') < 0) {
            session.send('Not supported. Require an image to be
            sent!');
            return;
        }

        // let them know we're thinking....
        session.sendTyping();

        const id = uuid();
        const dirName = 'images';

        if (!fs.existsSync(dirName)) {
            fs.mkdirSync(dirName);
        }
        const imagePath = dirName + '/' + id;
        const imageUrl = session.message.attachments[0].
        contentUrl;

        getImage(imageUrl, imagePath).then(() => {
            const cv = new cognitiveServices.computerVision({
            apiKey: process.env.CV_KEY, endpoint: process.env.
            CV_ENDPOINT });
            return cv.describeImage({
                headers: { 'Content-Type': 'application/octet-
                stream' },
```

```
              body: fs.readFileSync(imagePath)
        });
    }).then((analysis) => {
        // let's look at the raw object
        console.log(JSON.stringify(analysis));

        if (analysis.description.tags && ) {
            if (_.find(analysis.description.tags, p => p
            === 'hotdog')) {
                session.send('HOT DOG!');
            }
            else {
                session.send('not hot dog');
            }
        }
        else {
            session.send('not hot dog');
        }
        fs.unlinkSync(imagePath);
    });
    }
]);
```

If we upload this beautiful image of a hot dog (Figure 10-14), we get the following JSON result.

Figure 10-14. *A plain old hot dog*

```
{
    "description": {
        "tags": [
            "sitting", "food", "paper", "hot",
            "piece", "bun", "table", "orange",
            "top", "dog", "laying", "hotdog",
            "sandwich", "yellow", "close", "plate",
            "cake", "phone"
        ],
        "captions": [
            {
                "text": "a close up of a hot dog on a bun",
                "confidence": 0.5577123828705269
            }
        ]
    },
    "requestId": "4fa77b1a-1b27-491c-b895-8640d6a196fd",
    "metadata": {
        "width": 1200,
        "height": 586,
        "format": "Png"
    }
}
```

If we upload this Sonoran hot dog photo (Figure 10-15), whatever that is, we still get decent results.

Figure 10-15. *Another type of hot dog?*

```
{
    "description": {
        "tags": [
            "food", "sandwich", "dish", "box",
            "dog", "table", "hot", "sitting",
            "piece", "top", "square", "toppings",
            "paper", "slice", "close", "different",
            "hotdog", "holding", "pizza", "plate",
            "laying"
        ],
        "captions": [
```

```
        {
            "text": "a close up of a hot dog",
            "confidence": 0.9727350601423388
        }
    ]
},
"requestId": "11a12305-d36a-4db0-aca0-2a1870a8b9e7",
"metadata": {
    "width": 1280,
    "height": 960,
    "format": "Jpeg"
}
}
```

I don't know what a Sonoran hot dog is, but after reading about it, it sounds really tasty. I am slightly amused that the service could correctly determine it is a hotdog. I'm further amused that it also tagged the image with the tags *pizza* and *different*. It would be a fun exercise to see how crazy a hot dog one needs to completely trick this model.

There are a lot of fun things we can do with image detection and analysis, and although hot dog or not hot dog is a silly example, it should be clear how powerful this kind of general image description generation can be. Of course, more specific application requirements might mean that the general models provided by Microsoft or other providers are insufficient, and a custom model is more appropriate. The Custom Vision Service[7] has you covered for those use cases. In either case, the ability to quickly prototype these functions using an easy-to-use REST API cannot be understated.

---

[7]The Custom Vision Services allows us to augment the existing Computer Vision models with our application-specific imagery: https://azure.microsoft.com/en-us/services/cognitive-services/custom-vision-service/

EXERCISE 10-2

Exploring Computer Vision

Computer Vision allows us to do things other than just get tags. One of the more compelling actions we can do with the API is optical character recognition (OCR).

1. Get an access key for the Computer Vision API by using the Azure Portal. The process is the same as any other cognitive service.

2. Create a chat bot that accepts photos and extracts the text information from the photos. Handle image upload similarly as we did in the hot dog chat bot.

3. Try writing some text on a piece of paper and running it through your chat bot. Can it properly recognize your writing?

4. How bad can the contrast be in the image, or how bad can your writing get before the OCR struggles to recognize the text?

You have now exercised the Computer Vision API and tested its OCR algorithm's performance in an ad hoc manner.

Conclusion

The world is making much progress in the accuracy of machine learning algorithms, enough so that much of this functionality has been exposed to developers via REST APIs. The ability to access some of these algorithms through a simple REST endpoint, without the need to learn new environments and languages (like Anaconda, Python, and scikit-learn), has spurred a rush of developers to try new ideas and include AI functionality in their applications. Some services provided by big tech companies may not be as performant, cost effective, or accurate as custom-developed and curated models would be, but their ease of use and increasing accuracy and cost effectiveness over time is a catalyst for consideration in production scenarios.

As professionals in the chat bot space, we should have an idea of the type of cognitive offerings that can assist in our chat bot's development. Using all these great features can improve the conversational experience by leaps and bounds.

CHAPTER 11

Adaptive Cards and Custom Graphics

Throughout the book we have discussed the different ways in which bots can communicate to users. Bots can use text, voice, images, buttons, or carousels. These combined with the right tone and data become a powerful interface for users to quickly and efficiently accomplish their goals. We can easily build text with correct data, but text may not always be the most effective mechanism to communicate certain ideas. Let's take the example of a stock quote. What kind of data are users looking for when they ask for a quote for, say, Twitter?

Are they looking for the last price? Are they looking for volume? Are they looking for the bid/ask? Maybe they are looking to see what the 52-week high and low prices are. The truth is, each user may be looking for something slightly different. A text description of the stock may make sense to be read by a voice assistant. We would expect Alexa to say, "Twitter, symbol TWTR, is trading at $24.47 with a volume of 8.1 million. The 52-week range is $14.12 to $25.56. The current bid is $24.46, and the current ask is $24.47." Could you imagine receiving this data in a bot? Parsing through the text is, quite frankly, painful.

An appealing option is to lay out content inside a card, as in Figure 11-1. This sample comes from the TD Ameritrade Messenger bot. A lot of the same data that is included in the text message is communicated via the figure, yet this format is much easier for a human to consume.

© Szymon Rozga 2018

S. Rozga, *Practical Bot Development*, https://doi.org/10.1007/978-1-4842-3540-9_11

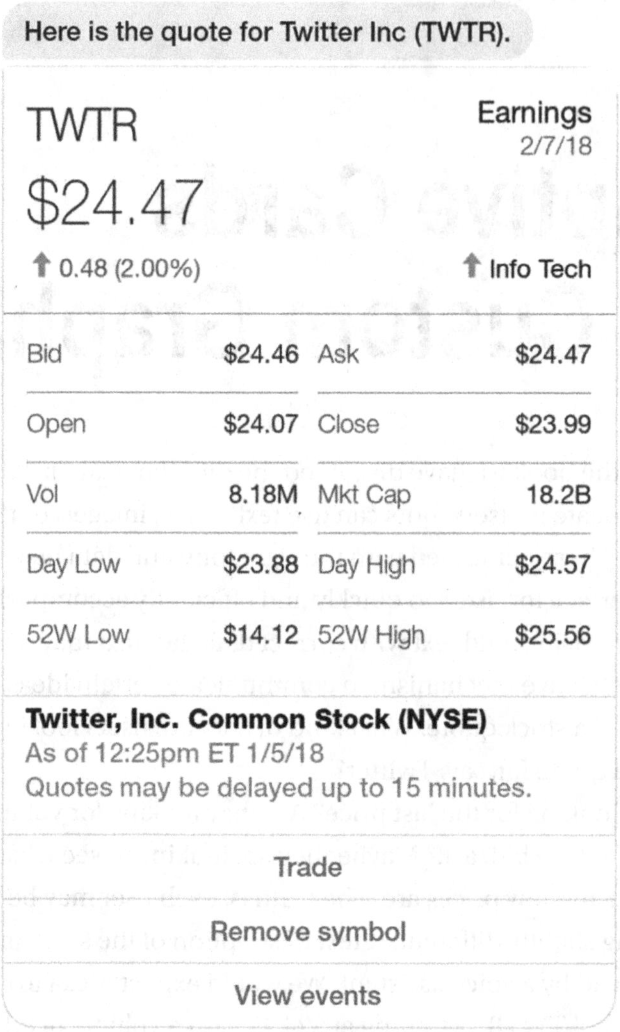

Here is the quote for Twitter Inc (TWTR).

TWTR		Earnings 2/7/18
$24.47		
↑ 0.48 (2.00%)		↑ Info Tech

Bid	$24.46	Ask	$24.47
Open	$24.07	Close	$23.99
Vol	8.18M	Mkt Cap	18.2B
Day Low	$23.88	Day High	$24.57
52W Low	$14.12	52W High	$25.56

Twitter, Inc. Common Stock (NYSE)
As of 12:25pm ET 1/5/18
Quotes may be delayed up to 15 minutes.

Trade
Remove symbol
View events

Figure 11-1. *A stock quote card*

A common hero card does not leave much room to create an interface like this. The title, subtitle, and buttons are easy, but the image is not. How do we include such visuals in our bot? In this chapter, we will explore two approaches: custom image rendering using headless browsers and Adaptive Cards, a format that Microsoft's connectors can render in a channel-specific manner. We will delve into Adaptive Cards first.

Adaptive Cards

When the Bot Framework was first released, Microsoft created hero cards. The hero card, as we explored in Chapters 4 and 5, is a great abstraction over the distinct ways in which different messaging platforms render images with text and buttons. However, it became evident that hero cards are a bit limiting since they are only composed of an image, title, subtitle, and optional buttons.

To provide more flexible user interfaces, Microsoft created Adaptive Cards. The Adaptive Card object model describes a much richer set of user interfaces within a messaging application. It is the channel connector's responsibility to render an Adaptive Card definition into whatever form is supported by the channel. Basically, it's a much richer version of the hero card.

Adaptive Cards were announced at the Build 2017 conference. As chat bot developers, we now have one format to describe a rich user interface. The format itself is a mix of a XAML-like layout engine with HTML-like concepts in a JSON format.

Here is an example of a restaurant card and its rendering in Figure 11-2:

```json
{
    "$schema": "http://adaptivecards.io/schemas/adaptive-card.
    json",
    "type": "AdaptiveCard",
    "version": "1.0",
    "body": [
        {
            "speak": "Tom's Pie is a Pizza restaurant which is
            rated 9.3 by customers.",
            "type": "ColumnSet",
            "columns": [
                {
                    "type": "Column",
                    "width": 2,
```

```
            "items": [
                {
                    "type": "TextBlock",
                    "text": "PIZZA"
                },
                {
                    "type": "TextBlock",
                    "text": "Tom's Pie",
                    "weight": "bolder",
                    "size": "extraLarge",
                    "spacing": "none"
                },
                {
                    "type": "TextBlock",
                    "text": "4.2 ★★★☆ (93) · $$",
                    "isSubtle": true,
                    "spacing": "none"
                },
                {
                    "type": "TextBlock",
                    "text": "**Matt H. said** \"I'm
                    compelled to give this place 5
                    stars due to the number of times
                    I've chosen to eat here this past
                    year!\"",
                    "size": "small",
                    "wrap": true
                }
            ]
        },
        {
            "type": "Column",
```

```
                    "width": 1,
                    "items": [
                        {
                            "type": "Image",
                            "url": "https://picsum.
                            photos/300?image=882",
                            "size": "auto"
                        }
                    ]
                }
            ]
        }
    ],
    "actions": [
        {
            "type": "Action.OpenUrl",
            "title": "More Info",
            "url": "https://www.youtube.com/watch?v=dQw4w9WgXcQ"
        }
    ]
}
```

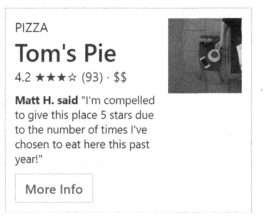

Figure 11-2. *A restaurant card rendering*

In an Adaptive Card, almost everything is a container that can include other containers or UI elements. The result is a UI object tree, just like any other standard UI platform. In this example we have a container with two columns. The first column is double the width of the second column and contains four *TextBlock* elements. The second column simply contains an image. Lastly, the card includes one action that opens a web URL. Here is another example and its rendering (Figure 11-3):

```
{
  "$schema": "http://adaptivecards.io/schemas/adaptive-card.json",
  "type": "AdaptiveCard",
  "version": "1.0",
  "body": [
    {
      "type": "ColumnSet",
      "columns": [
        {
          "type": "Column",
          "width": 2,
          "items": [
            {
              "type": "TextBlock",
              "text": "Tell us about yourself",
              "weight": "bolder",
              "size": "medium"
            },
            {
              "type": "TextBlock",
              "text": "We just need a few more details to get
              you booked for the trip of a lifetime!",
              "isSubtle": true,
              "wrap": true
            },
```

```
{
  "type": "TextBlock",
  "text": "Don't worry, we'll never share or sell
  your information.",
  "isSubtle": true,
  "wrap": true,
  "size": "small"
},
{
  "type": "TextBlock",
  "text": "Your name",
  "wrap": true
},
{
  "type": "Input.Text",
  "id": "myName",
  "placeholder": "Last, First"
},
{
  "type": "TextBlock",
  "text": "Your email",
  "wrap": true
},
{
  "type": "Input.Text",
  "id": "myEmail",
  "placeholder": "youremail@example.com",
  "style": "email"
},
{
  "type": "TextBlock",
  "text": "Phone Number"
},
```

```
          {
            "type": "Input.Text",
            "id": "myTel",
            "placeholder": "xxx.xxx.xxxx",
            "style": "tel"
          }
        ]
      },
      {
        "type": "Column",
        "width": 1,
        "items": [
          {
            "type": "Image",
            "url": "https://upload.wikimedia.org/wikipedia/
            commons/b/b2/Diver_Silhouette%2C_Great_Barrier_
            Reef.jpg",
            "size": "auto"
          }
        ]
      }
    ]
  }
],
"actions": [
  {
    "type": "Action.Submit",
    "title": "Submit"
  }
]
}
```

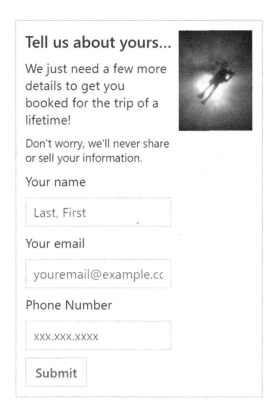

Figure 11-3. *A data-gathering template*

This has a similar overall layout with two columns that have a 2:1 width ratio. The first column contains text of varying sizes as well as three input fields. The second column contains an image.

We present one more example in Figure 11-4, recalling our stock ticker card discussion.

```
{
    "$schema": "http://adaptivecards.io/schemas/adaptive-card.
    json",
    "type": "AdaptiveCard",
    "version": "1.0",
    "speak": "Microsoft stock is trading at $62.30 a share,
    which is down .32%",
```

```
"body": [
    {
        "type": "Container",
        "items": [
            {
                "type": "TextBlock",
                "text": "Microsoft Corp (NASDAQ: MSFT)",
                "size": "medium",
                "isSubtle": true
            },
            {
                "type": "TextBlock",
                "text": "September 19, 4:00 PM EST",
                "isSubtle": true
            }
        ]
    },
    {
        "type": "Container",
        "spacing": "none",
        "items": [
            {
                "type": "ColumnSet",
                "columns": [
                    {
                        "type": "Column",
                        "width": "stretch",
                        "items": [
                            {
                                "type": "TextBlock",
                                "text": "75.30",
                                "size": "extraLarge"
```

```
                },
                {
                    "type": "TextBlock",
                    "text": "▼ 0.20 (0.32%)",
                    "size": "small",
                    "color": "attention",
                    "spacing": "none"
                }
            ]
        },
        {
            "type": "Column",
            "width": "auto",
            "items": [
                {
                    "type": "FactSet",
                    "facts": [
                        {
                            "title": "Open",
                            "value": "62.24"
                        },
                        {
                            "title": "High",
                            "value": "62.98"
                        },
                        {
                            "title": "Low",
                            "value": "62.20"
                        }
                    ]
                }
            ]
```

```
                    }
                ]
            }
        ]
    }
  ]
}
```

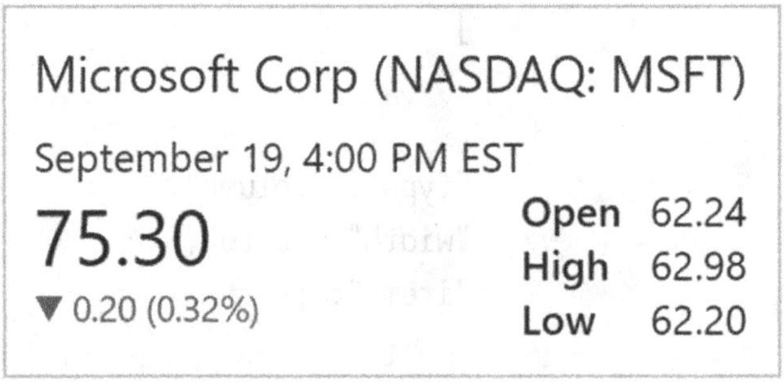

Microsoft Corp (NASDAQ: MSFT)

September 19, 4:00 PM EST

75.30

▼ 0.20 (0.32%)

Open	62.24
High	62.98
Low	62.20

Figure 11-4. *A stock quote rendering*

This template introduces a few more concepts. First, the card has two containers instead of columns. The first container simply displays the two TextBlocks with the data around the company name/ticker and the quote date. The second container contains two columns. One has the last price and change data, and the other has the Open/High/Low data. The latter data is stored in an object of type *FactSet*, a collection of name-value pairs that are rendered as a tightly spaced group.

The Adaptive Cards website provide a variety of rich samples.[1] On the same site, the Visualizer[2] makes it clear that Bot Framework chat bots are only a small part of Adaptive Cards. The individual Bot Framework channels are supported with varying degrees of fidelity. The emulator

---

[1]Adaptive cards samples: `http://adaptivecards.io/samples/`

[2]Adaptive cards Visualizer: `http://adaptivecards.io/visualizer/index.html`

renders the cards faithfully, but many other channels like Facebook Messenger result in images (Figure 11-5).

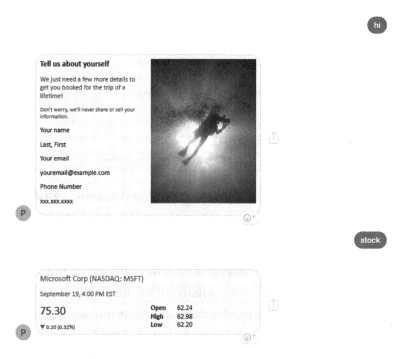

Figure 11-5. *Messenger renders the Adaptive Cards as images*

To be fair, Microsoft's Facebook connector returns a Bad Request (400) status code to any Adaptive Card with unsupported features. This truly captures the dilemma here. Having a common rich card format is a positive development, but only if it is widely supported. Lacking support in a platform like Facebook is detrimental. It is worth noting that the host app allowed in the Visualizer tells a broader adaptive cards story (Figure 11-6).

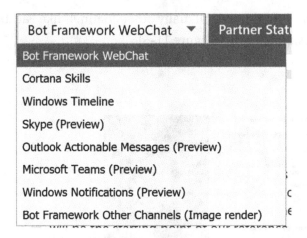

Figure 11-6. *Possible rendering options in the Adaptive Card Visualizer*

Note the first seven items (WebChat, Cortana Skills, Windows Timeline, Skype, Outlook Actionable Messages, Microsoft Team, and Windows Notifications) are all systems within Microsoft's control. Microsoft is building a common format to render cards across its numerous properties.

In short, if your application is targeting many of the Microsoft systems like Windows 10, Teams, and Skype, investing in reusable and consistent cross-platform Adaptive Cards is a good idea.

Microsoft also provides several SDKs to help your custom app render Adaptive Cards. For instance, there is an iOS SDK, a client-side JavaScript SDK, and a Windows SDK; each can take adaptive card JSON and render a native UI from it.

A Working Example

We will now look at a sample to get a better idea of how Adaptive Cards render and how they send input form messages back to the bot. We will use the Emulator as our channel since it implements all the important features. We will use a slightly modified card from a previous example to collect a user's name, phone number, and e-mail address.

```
{
    "$schema": "http://adaptivecards.io/schemas/adaptive-
    card.json",
    "type": "AdaptiveCard",
    "version": "1.0",
    "body": [
        {
            "type": "TextBlock",
            "text": "Tell us about yourself",
            "weight": "bolder",
            "size": "medium"
        },
        {
            "type": "TextBlock",
            "text": "Don't worry, we'll never share or sell
            your information.",
            "isSubtle": true,
            "wrap": true,
            "size": "small"
        },
        {
            "type": "TextBlock",
            "text": "Your name",
            "wrap": true
        },
        {
            "type": "Input.Text",
            "id": "name",
            "placeholder": "First Last"
        },
        {
            "type": "TextBlock",
```

```
            "text": "Your email",
            "wrap": true
        },
        {

            "type": "Input.Text",
            "id": "email",
            "placeholder": "youremail@example.com",
            "style": "email"
        },
        {

            "type": "TextBlock",
            "text": "Phone Number"
        },
        {

            "type": "Input.Text",
            "id": "tel",
            "placeholder": "xxx.xxx.xxxx",
            "style": "tel"
        }
    ],
    "actions": [
        {

            "type": "Action.Submit",
            "title": "Submit"
        },
        {

            "type": "Action.ShowCard",
            "title": "Terms and Conditions",
            "card": {
                "type": "AdaptiveCard",
                "body": [
                    {
```

```
                    "type": "TextBlock",
                    "text": "We will not share your
                    data with anyone. Ever.",
                    "size": "small",
                }
            ]
        }
    }
   ]
}
```

We will also allow the user to click any of two items: a *Submit* button
to send the data and a *Terms and Conditions* button that displays some
extra information when clicked. When a user clicks *Submit*, the data from
the fields is gathered and sent to the bot as an object exposed via the
message's *value* property. The object sent by the Adaptive Card defined
in the previous JSON will have three properties: name, email, and tel. The
property names correspond to the field *id*.

It follows that the code that gets the values is straightforward. It could
be as basic as simply checking whether the value exists and executing logic
based on it. If we send multiple cards, since they stay in the user's chat
history, it is again critical to ensure a consistent conversational experience.

```
const bot = new builder.UniversalBot(connector, [
    (session) => {

        let incoming = session.message;
        if (incoming.value) {
            // this means we are getting data from an adaptive
            card
            let o = incoming.value;
            session.send('Thanks ' + o.name.split(' ')[0] + ".
            We'll be in touch!");
        } else {
```

```
    let msg = new builder.Message(session);
    msg.addAttachment({
        contentType: 'application/vnd.microsoft.card.
        adaptive',
        content: adaptiveCardJson
    });
    session.send(msg);
    }
  }
]);
```

Figure 11-7 illustrates how this conversation can develop. Note that there is no actual logic within the cards themselves, save for some minor validation. There may be an ability to do so in the future, but for now all such logic must occur in the bot code.

Figure 11-7. *An input form Adaptive Card after expanding the Terms and Conditions and clicking Submit*

EXERCISE 11-1

Creating a Custom Adaptive Card

1. The goal of this exercise is to create a functioning weather update Adaptive Card. You will integrate with a Weather API to provide live weather to your chat bot's users. Create a bot that collects a user's location, perhaps simply a ZIP code, and returns a text message echoing the location.

2. Write the code necessary to integrate with the Yahoo Weather API. You can find information about using it at `https://developer.yahoo.com/weather/`.

3. Create an Adaptive Card that includes the various data points that the service provides. The Adaptive Cards website provides two weather samples; you can use one of these if you would prefer. Once done, switch some of the UI elements around in the adaptive card JSON. How easy is it to do so?

4. Add graphic image elements. For example, display a different graphic to represent sunny versus overcast weather. You may find some assets using an image search online or host some images locally. If you host them locally, make sure you are set up to serve static content.

Well done! You are now able to enrich your bot's conversational experience with Adaptive Cards.

Rendering Custom Graphics

Adaptive Cards simplify some types of layouts and allow us to declaratively define custom layouts that can be rendered into images. We do not, however, have control over how the image is utilized; as we saw on Messenger, the image is sent as a stand-alone image, devoid of any contextual buttons or text in card format. Among other minor limitations around sizing, margins, and layout control, we do not have a way to generate graphics. Say we wanted to generate a chart to represent a stock price over time. There is no way to do this using Adaptive Cards. What if we had an alternate way of doing this?

The best way to create custom graphics is to utilize technologies we are already familiar with, such as HTML, JavaScript, and CSS! If we could use HTML and CSS directly, we could create custom, branded, beautiful layouts to represent the various concepts in our conversational experience. Using SVG and JavaScript, we would enable us to create stunning data-driven graphics that bring our bot's content to life.

OK, we are sold. But how do we do this? We'll take a slight detour into a mechanism we can use to render these artifacts: headless browsers.

A standard run-of-the-mill browser like Firefox or Chrome has many components: the network layer; standards-compliant HTML engines such as Gecko, WebKit, or Chromium; and lastly the UI that allows you to view the actual content. A headless browser is a browser without the UI components. Typically, these browsers are controlled using either the command line or a scripting language. The original and most important use cases that headless browsers address are tasks such as functional tests in an environment where JavaScript and AJAX are enabled. Search engines, for example, can use headless browsers to index dynamic web page content. Phantom[3] is an example of a WebKit-based headless browser that

---

[3]PhantomJs: `http://phantomjs.org/`

was used heavily during the early AngularJS days. Firefox[4] and Chrome[5] have recently added support for headless modes in both of their browsers. One of the uses that is becoming more common in this space is image rendering. All headless browsers implement a screenshot functionality that we can leverage for image rendering needs.

We will continue with our stock quote example and build something that can return a quote as text. The full working code sample can be found under the `chapter11-image-rendering-bot` folder in the book's GitHub repo. To do so, we need access to a financial data provider. One easy-to-use provider is called Intrinio, which provides free accounts to start using their API. Go to `http://intrinio.com` and click the Start for Free button to create an account to use their APIs. Once we have completed the account creation process, we can access our access keys, which must be passed to the API via Basic HTTP authentication. Using a URL like `https://api.intrinio.com/data_point?ticker=AAPL&item=last_price,volume`, we receive the last price and volume for AAPL. The resulting data JSON is shown here:

```
{
    "data": [
        {
            "identifier": "AAPL",
            "item": "last_price",
            "value": 174.32
        },
        {
            "identifier": "AAPL",
            "item": "volume",
```

---

[4]Firefox Headless Mode: `https://developer.mozilla.org/en-US/Firefox/Headless_mode`

[5]Getting Started with Headless Chrome: `https://developers.google.com/web/updates/2017/04/headless-chrome`

```
            "value": 20179172
        }
    ],
    "result_count": 2,
    "api_call_credits": 2
}
```

Creating a bot to use this API can be done by using the following code, resulting in the conversation in Figure 11-8:

```javascript
require('dotenv-extended').load();

const builder = require('botbuilder');
const restify = require('restify');
const request = require('request');
const moment = require('moment');
const _ = require('underscore');
const puppeteer = require('puppeteer');
const vsprintf = require('sprintf').vsprintf;

// declare all of the data points we will be interested in
const datapoints = {
    last_price: 'last_price',
    last_year_low: '52_week_low',
    last_year_high: '52_week_high',
    ask_price: 'ask_price',
    ask_size: 'ask_size',
    bid_price: 'bid_price',
    bid_size: 'bid_size',
    volume: 'volume',
    name: 'name',
    change: 'change',
```

```
    percent_change: 'percent_change',
    last_timestamp: 'last_timestamp'
};

const url = "https://api.intrinio.com/data_
point?ticker=%s&item=" + _.map(Object.keys(datapoints), p =>
datapoints[p]).join(',');

// Setup Restify Server
const server = restify.createServer();
server.listen(process.env.port || process.env.PORT || 3978, ()
=> {
    console.log('%s listening to %s', server.name, server.url);
});

// Create chat bot and listen to messages
const connector = new builder.ChatConnector({
    appId: process.env.MICROSOFT_APP_ID,
    appPassword: process.env.MICROSOFT_APP_PASSWORD
});
server.post('/api/messages', connector.listen());

const bot = new builder.UniversalBot(connector, [
    session => {
        // get ticker and create request URL
        const ticker = session.message.text.toUpperCase();
        const tickerUrl = vsprintf(url, [ticker]);

        // make request to get the ticker data
        request.get(tickerUrl, {
            auth:
                {
                    user: process.env.INTRINIO_USER,
                    pass: process.env.INTRINIO_PASS
                }
```

```
    }, (err, response, body) => {
        if (err) {
            console.log('error while fetching data:\n' +
            err);
            session.endConversation('Error while fetching
            data. Please try again later.');
            return;
        }

        // parse JSON response and extract the last price
        const results = JSON.parse(body).data;
        const lastPrice = getval(results, ticker,
        datapoints.last_price).value;

        // send the last price as a response
        session.endConversation(vsprintf('The last price
        for %s is %.2f', [ ticker, lastPrice]));
    });
    }
]);

const getval = function(arr, ticker, data_point) {
    const r =  _.find(arr, p => p.identifier === ticker &&
    p.item === data_point);
    return r;
}

const inMemoryStorage = new builder.MemoryBotStorage();
bot.set('storage', inMemoryStorage);
```

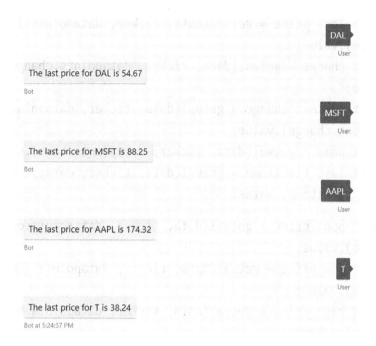

Figure 11-8. *Text stock quotes*

Great. We will now create an adaptive card and see how we can utilize what we just covered with headless browsers to render a richer graphic.

For the adaptive card, we will use a template modified from the previous stock update scenario. Instead of sending a string in the *endConversation* call, we send back a stock card. The *renderStockCard* function takes the data returned from the API and renders the adaptive card JSON.

```
const cardData = renderStockCard(results, ticker);
const msg = new builder.Message(session);
msg.addAttachment({
    contentType: 'application/vnd.microsoft.card.adaptive',
    content: cardData
});
session.endConversation(msg);

function renderStockCard(data, ticker) {
```

```
const last_price = getval(data, ticker, datapoints.last_
price).value;
const change = getval(data, ticker, datapoints.change).
value;
const percent_change = getval(data, ticker, datapoints.
percent_change).value;
const name = getval(data, ticker, datapoints.name).value;
const last_timestamp = getval(data, ticker, datapoints.
last_timestamp).value;

const open_price = getval(data, ticker, datapoints.open_
price).value;
const low_price = getval(data, ticker, datapoints.low_
price).value;
const high_price = getval(data, ticker, datapoints.high_
price).value;
const yearhigh = getval(data, ticker, datapoints.last_year_
high).value;
const yearlow = getval(data, ticker, datapoints.last_year_
low).value;

const bidsize = getval(data, ticker, datapoints.bid_size).
value;
const bidprice = getval(data, ticker, datapoints.bid_
price).value;
const asksize = getval(data, ticker, datapoints.ask_size).
value;
const askprice = getval(data, ticker, datapoints.ask_
price).value;

let color = 'default';
if (change > 0) color = 'good';
else if (change < 0) color = 'warning';
```

```
let facts = [
    { title: 'Bid', value: vsprintf('%d x %.2f', [bidsize,
    bidprice]) },
    { title: 'Ask', value: vsprintf('%d x %.2f', [asksize,
    askprice]) },
    { title: '52-Week High', value: vsprintf('%.2f',
    [yearhigh]) },
    { title: '52-Week Low', value: vsprintf('%.2f',
    [yearlow]) }
];

let card = {
    "$schema": "http://adaptivecards.io/schemas/adaptive-
    card.json",
    "type": "AdaptiveCard",
    "version": "1.0",
    "speak": vsprintf("%s stock is trading at $%.2f a
    share, which is down %.2f%%", [name, last_price,
    percent_change]),
    "body": [
        {
            "type": "Container",
            "items": [
                {
                    "type": "TextBlock",
                    "text": vsprintf("%s ( %s)", [name,
                    ticker]),
                    "size": "medium",
                    "isSubtle": false
                },
```

```
                {
                        "type": "TextBlock",
                        "text": moment(last_timestamp).
                        format('LLL'),
                        "isSubtle": true
                }
        ]
},
{
    "type": "Container",
    "spacing": "none",
    "items": [
            {
                "type": "ColumnSet",
                "columns": [
                        {
                            "type": "Column",
                            "width": "stretch",
                            "items": [
                                {
                                    "type": "TextBlock",
                                    "text":
                                    vsprintf("%.2f", [last_
                                    price]),
                                    "size": "extraLarge"
                                },
                                {

                                    "type": "TextBlock",
                                    "text": vsprintf("%.2f
                                    (%.2f%%)", [change,
                                    percent_change]),
                                    "size": "small",
```

```
                                    "color": color,
                                    "spacing": "none"
                                }
                            ]
                        },
                        {
                            "type": "Column",
                            "width": "auto",
                            "items": [
                                {
                                    "type": "FactSet",
                                    "facts": facts
                                }
                            ]
                        }
                    ]
                }
            ]
        }
    ]
}

    return card;
}
```

Now, if we send a ticker symbol to the bot, we will get a resulting adaptive card. The rendering on the emulator looks good (Figure 11-9). The Messenger rendering is a bit choppy and pixelated (Figure 11-10). We have also uncovered an inconsistency in how the two channels render the "warning" color. We can certainly do better.

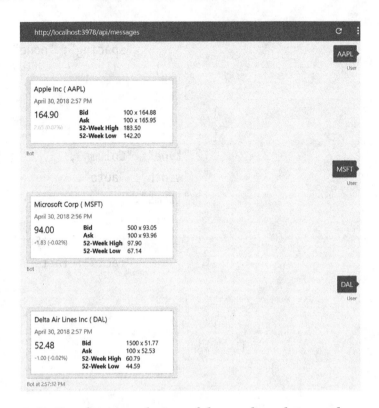

Figure 11-9. *Emulator rendering of the stock update card*

Figure 11-10. *Messenger rendering of the stock u-update card*

We will now create our own custom HTML template. Now, by trade, as an engineer, I do not do design, but Figure 11-11 is the card that I came up with. We display all the same pieces of data as earlier, but we also add a sparkline for the last 30 days of data.

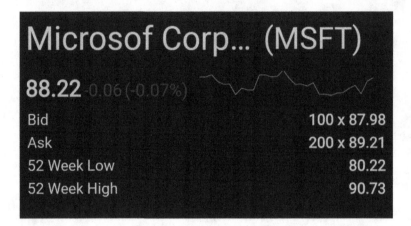

Figure 11-11. *The custom quote card we would like to support*

The HTML and CSS for the earlier template is presented here:

```
<html>
<head>
    <style>
        body {
            background-color: white;
            font-family: 'Roboto', sans-serif;
            margin: 0;
            padding: 0;
        }

        .card {
            color: #dddddd;
            background-color: black;
            width: 564px;
            height: 284px;
            padding: 10px;
        }
```

```css
.card .symbol {
    font-size: 48px;
    vertical-align: middle;
}

.card .companyname {
    font-size: 52px;
    display: inline-block;
    vertical-align: middle;
    overflow-x: hidden;
    white-space: nowrap;
    text-overflow: ellipsis;
    max-width: 380px;
}

.card .symbol::before {
    content: '(';
}

.card .symbol::after {
    content: ')';
}

.card .priceline {
    margin-top: 20px;
}

.card .price {
    font-size: 36px;
    font-weight: bold;
}

.card .change {
    font-size: 28px;
}
```

```css
.card .changePct {
    font-size: 28px;
}

.card .positive {
    color: darkgreen;
}

.card .negative {
    color: darkred;
}

.card .changePct::before {
    content: '(';
}

.card .changePct::after {
    content: ')';
}

.card .factTable {
    margin-top: 10px;
    color: #dddddd;
    width: 100%;
}

.card .factTable .factTitle {
    width: 50%;
    font-size: 24px;
    padding-bottom: 5px;
}

.card .factTable .factValue {
    width: 50%;
    text-align: right;
    font-size: 24px;
    font-weight: bold;
```

```
            padding-bottom: 5px;
        }
        .sparkline {
            padding-left: 10px;
        }
        .sparkline embed {
            width: 300px;
            height: 40px;
        }
    </style>
    <link href="https://fonts.googleapis.com/css?family=Roboto"
    rel="stylesheet">
</head>

<body>
    <div class="card">
        <div class="header">
                <span class="companyname">Microsoft</span>
                <span class="symbol">MSFT</span>
        </div>
        <div class="priceline">
            <span class="price">88.22</span>
            <span class="change negative">-0.06</span>
            <span class="changePct negative">-0.07%</span>
            <span class="sparkline">
                <embed src="http://sparksvg.me/line.svg?174.33,
                174.35,175,173.03,172.23,172.26,169.23,171.08,
                170.6,170.57,175.01,175.01,174.35,174.54,176.42,
                173.97,172.22,172.27,171.7,172.67,169.37,169.32,
                169.01,169.64,169.8,171.05,171.85,169.48,173.07,
                174.09&rgba:255,255,255,0.7"
                    type="image/svg+xml">
            </span>
```

```
        </div>
        <table class="factTable">
            <tr>
                <td class="factTitle">Bid</td>
                <td class="factValue">100 x 87.98</td>
            </tr>
            <tr>
                <td class="factTitle">Ask</td>
                <td class="factValue">200 x 89.21</td>
            </tr>
            <tr>
                <td class="factTitle">52 Week Low</td>
                <td class="factValue">80.22</td>
            </tr>
            <tr>
                <td class="factTitle">52 Week High</td>
                <td class="factValue">90.73</td>
            </tr>
        </table>
    </div>

</body>

</html>
```

Note that we are doing three things that are not obviously possible with adaptive cards: the fine granular control over styling that CSS allows, custom web fonts (in this case, Google's Roboto font), and an SVG object to draw the sparkline. At this point, all we really must do is modify the appropriate data in the HTML template and render it. How do we do this?

From the different options we mentioned earlier, one of the better options today is Chrome. The easiest way to integrate with headless

Chrome is to use the Node.js package called Puppeteer.[6] This library can be used for many tasks such as automating Chrome, taking screenshots, gathering timeline data for websites, and running automated test suites. We'll use the basic API to take a screenshot of a page.

Puppeteer samples use the async/await[7] features introduced in Node version 7.6. The syntax waits for a Promise value to return in one line, instead of writing chains of *then* method calls. The code for rendering an HTML snippet will look as follows:

```
async function renderHtml(html, width, height) {
    var browser = await puppeteer.launch();
    const page = await browser.newPage();

    await page.setViewport({ width: width, height: height });
    await page.goto(`data:text/html,${html}`, { waitUntil:
    'load' });
    const pageResultBuffer = await page.screenshot({
    omitBackground: true });
    await page.close();
    browser.disconnect();
    return pageResultBuffer;
}
```

We launch a new instance of headless chrome, open a new page, set the size of the viewport, load the HTML, and then take a screenshot. The *omitBackground* option allows us to have transparent backgrounds in the HTML, which result in transparent screenshot backgrounds.

The resulting object is a Node.js buffer. A buffer is simply a collection of binary data, and Node.js provides numerous functions to consume this

---

[6]Puppeteer, the headless Chrome Node.js API: https://github.com/GoogleChrome/puppeteer

[7]Mozilla Developers Networks await Documentation: https://developer.mozilla.org/en-US/docs/Web/JavaScript/Reference/Operators/await

data. We can call our *renderHtml* method and convert the buffer into a base64 string. Once we have this, we can simply send the base64 image as part of a Bot Builder attachment.

```
renderHtml(html, 600, 312).then(cardData => {
    const base64image = cardData.toString('base64');
    const contentType = 'image/png';
    const attachment = {
        contentUrl: util.format('data:%s;base64,%s',
        contentType, base64image),
        contentType: contentType,
        name: ticker + '.png'
    }

    const msg = new builder.Message(session);
    msg.addAttachment(attachment);
    session.endConversation(msg);
});
```

Constructing the HTML is string manipulation to ensure that the proper values are populated. We add some placeholders into the HTML to make it easy to do string replace calls to place the data into the appropriate locations. A snippet of this is shown here:

```
<div class="priceline">
    <span class="price">${last_price}</span>
    <span class="change ${changeClass}">${change}</span>
    <span class="changePct ${changeClass}">${percent_change}
    </span>
    <span class="sparkline">
        <embed src="http://sparksvg.me/line.svg?${sparklinedata
        }&rgba:255,255,255,0.7" type="image/svg+xml">
    </span>
</div>
```

The following is the full code to fetch the data from the Intrinio endpoints, read the card template HTML, substitute the right values, render the HTML, and send it as an attachment. Some sample results are illustrated in Figure 11-12.

```
request.get(tickerUrl, opts, (quote_error, quote_
response, quote_body) => {
    request.get(pricesTickerUrl, opts, (prices_error,
    prices_response, prices_body) => {
        if (quote_error) {
            console.log('error while fetching data:\n'
            + quote_error);
            session.endConversation('Error while
            fetching data. Please try again later.');
            return;
        } else if (prices_error) {
            console.log('error while fetching data:\n'
            + prices_error);
            session.endConversation('Error while
            fetching data. Please try again later.');
            return;
        }

        const quoteResults = JSON.parse(quote_body).data;
        const priceResults = JSON.parse(prices_body).data;

        const prices = _.map(priceResults, p => p.close);
        const sparklinedata = prices.join(',');

        fs.readFile("cardTemplate.html", "utf8",
        function (err, data) {
            const last_price = getval(quoteResults,
            ticker, datapoints.last_price).value;
            const change = getval(quoteResults, ticker,
            datapoints.change).value;
```

```
const percent_change = getval(quoteResults,
ticker, datapoints.percent_change).value;
const name = getval(quoteResults, ticker,
datapoints.name).value;
const last_timestamp = getval(quoteResults,
ticker, datapoints.last_timestamp).value;
const yearhigh = getval(quoteResults,
ticker, datapoints.last_year_high).value;
const yearlow = getval(quoteResults,
ticker, datapoints.last_year_low).value;

const bidsize = getval(quoteResults,
ticker, datapoints.bid_size).value;
const bidprice = getval(quoteResults,
ticker, datapoints.bid_price).value;
const asksize = getval(quoteResults,
ticker, datapoints.ask_size).value;
const askprice = getval(quoteResults,
ticker, datapoints.ask_price).value;

data = data.replace('${bid}', vsprintf('%d
x %.2f', [bidsize, bidprice]));
data = data.replace('${ask}', vsprintf('%d
x %.2f', [asksize, askprice]));
data = data.replace('${52weekhigh}',
vsprintf('%.2f', [yearhigh]));
data = data.replace('${52weeklow}',
vsprintf('%.2f', [yearlow]));
data = data.replace('${ticker}', ticker);
data = data.replace('${companyName}', name);
data = data.replace('${last_price}',
last_price);

let changeClass = '';
```

```
if(change > 0) changeClass = 'positive';
else if(change < 0) changeClass = 'negative';

data = data.replace('${changeClass}',
changeClass);
data = data.replace('${change}',
vsprintf('%.2f%%', [change]));
data = data.replace('${percent_change}',
vsprintf('%.2f%%', [percent_change]));
data = data.replace('${last_timestamp}',
moment(last_timestamp).format('LLL'));
data = data.replace('${sparklinedata}',
sparklinedata);

renderHtml(data, 584, 304).then(cardData => {
    const base64image = cardData.
    toString('base64');
    const contentType = 'image/png';
    const attachment = {
        contentUrl: util.
        format('data:%s;base64,%s',
        contentType, base64image),
        contentType: contentType,
        name: ticker + '.png'
    }

    const msg = new builder.Message(session);
    msg.addAttachment(attachment);
    session.endConversation(msg);
});
        });
    });
});
```

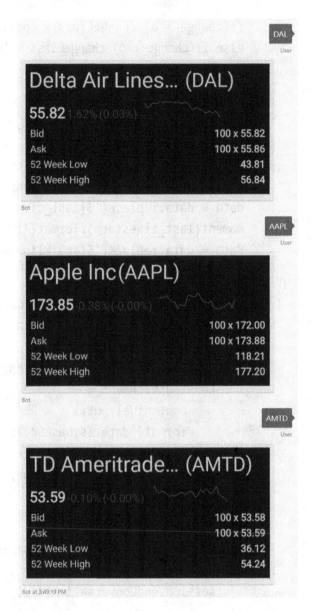

Figure 11-12. Different renderings of the custom HTML images

These are really good results considering the short amount of time we spent on this! The image renders great on Messenger as well (Figure 11-13).

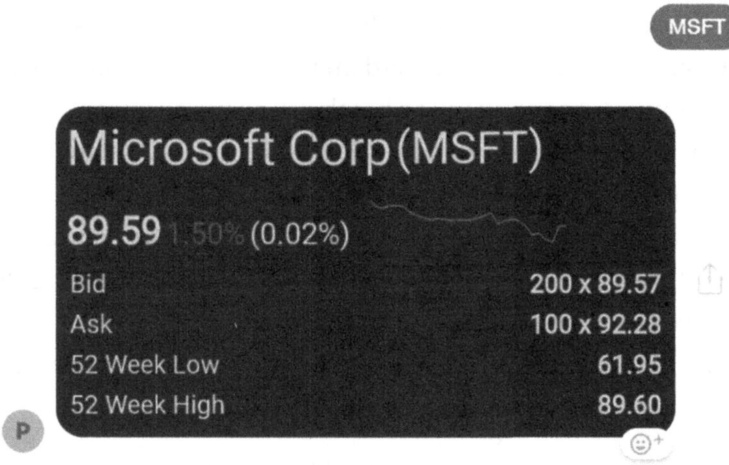

Figure 11-13. *Image rendering in Messenger*

However, we had set a goal of creating custom cards. OK, so we change the code to the following:

```
const card = new builder.HeroCard(session)
    .buttons([
        builder.CardAction.postBack(session, ticker, 'Quote
        Again')])
    .images([
        builder.CardImage.create(session, imageUri)
    ])
    .title(ticker + ' Quote')
    .subtitle('Last Updated: ' + moment(last_timestamp).
    format('LLL'));

const msg = new builder.Message(session);msg.
addAttachment(card.toAttachment());
session.send(msg);
```

This renders perfectly fine in the emulator, but we get no result in Messenger. If we look at the Node output, we will quickly notice that Facebook returns an HTTP 400 (*BadRequest*) response. What's happening? Although Facebook supports data URIs with an embedded Base64 image, it does not support this format for card images. We can go through the effort of creating an endpoint in our bot that returns the image, but Facebook has yet another limitation: a webhook and the URI for the card image cannot have the same hostname.

The solution is for our bot to host the resulting images elsewhere. A great place to start is a cloud-based Blob store like Amazon's S3 or Microsoft's Azure Storage. Since we are focusing on Microsoft's stack, we'll go ahead and use Azure's Blob Storage. We will use the relevant Node.js package.

```
npm install azure-storage --save
const blob = azureStorage.createBlobService(process.env.IMAGE_
STORAGE_CONNECTION_STRING);
```

IMAGE_STORAGE_CONNECTION_STRING is an environment variable that stores the Azure Storage connection string, which can be found in the Azure Portal after creating a storage account resource. After we generate the image into a local file, our code must ensure a blob container exists and create the blob from our image. We then use the new blob's URL as the source of our image.

```
renderHtml(data, 584, 304).then(cardData => {
    const uniqueId = uuid();

    const name = uniqueId + '.png';
    const pathToFile = 'images/' + name;
    fs.writeFileSync(pathToFile, cardData);

    const containerName = 'image-rendering-bot';
    blob.createContainerIfNotExists(containerName, {
        publicAccessLevel: 'blob'
    }, function (error, result, response) {
```

```
if (!error) {
    blob.createBlockBlobFromLocalFile(containerNa
    me, name, pathToFile, function (error, result,
    response) {
        if (!error) {
            fs.unlinkSync(pathToFile);
            const imageUri = blob.getUrl(containerName,
            name);

            const card = new builder.HeroCard(session)
                .buttons([
                    builder.CardAction.postBack(session,
                    ticker, 'Quote Again')])
                .images([
                    builder.CardImage.create(session,
                    base64Uri)
                ])
                .title(ticker + ' Quote')
                .subtitle('Last Updated: ' +
                moment(last_timestamp).format('LLL'));

            const msg = new builder.Message(session);
            msg.addAttachment(card.toAttachment());
            session.send(msg);
        } else {
            console.error(error);
        }
    });
} else {
    console.error(error);
}
});
});
```

The card is now rendering as expected, as per Figure 11-14.

Figure 11-14. *The card now renders!*

EXERCISE 11-2

<u>Rendering Your Graphic Using Headless Chrome</u>

In this exercise, you will take the code from your weather bot from Exercise 11-1 and add custom HTML rendering.

1. In your adaptive card, add a placeholder that can contain an image to represent the temperature forecast in a chart.

2. Render an image using headless chrome that shows the forecast using a line chart. You can utilize the same sparkline approach as earlier.

3. Store the resulting image in blob storage.

4. Ensure the adaptive card includes the custom rendered image in the designated spot and that it can render in the emulator and Facebook Messenger.

You have now mixed a custom HTML rendering with an adaptive card. No one said we couldn't do that, right?

Conclusion

In this chapter, we explored two approaches to communicating complex ideas and our chat bot's brand via rich graphics. Adaptive Cards are a quick way to get started and allow for deeper integration with platforms that support the format natively. Custom HTML-based image rendering allows for much more customization and control over the resulting graphic and is especially valuable where there is no native Adaptive Card support. Both are great choices for highly engaging chat bot experiences.

CHAPTER 12

Human Handoff

Chat bots almost never live in isolation. Companies and brands have invested significant time, energy, and money interacting with their customers via social media, such as Twitter, Facebook, Instagram, Snapchat, and others. There is an ongoing competition among social media companies to provide the best platform for businesses to interact with their customers. Each of these platforms wants to connect its users in the interest of driving platform usage and selling products. In addition, customer service systems from Zendesk, LiveChat, FreshDesk, and ServiceNow, as well as tech behemoths like Oracle Service Cloud, Remedy, and Salesforce Service Cloud, are building up systems that connect consumers to a brand's customer service representatives (CSRs) over all types of channels from SMS to Messenger to live chat.

Today, chat bots are taking on workloads that have much to gain by being automated. As discussed throughout this book, however, there are many limitations to what a chat bot can do. In its current state, the technology is not able to handle some requests that a human customer service representative could easily solve. Despite the amount of investment put into the different customer service systems, team training, and reporting, it would be shortsighted to exclude humans from the conversations with a product's users. In this chapter, we will address what a customer service system does and, most important, what are our options when it comes to integrating with them and providing a seamless chat bot to CSR handoff.

© Szymon Rozga 2018
S. Rozga, *Practical Bot Development*, https://doi.org/10.1007/978-1-4842-3540-9_12

We Still Need Humans

Chat bots are starting to handle some of the queries being asked of businesses. Even though some of these questions might be easily answered via a simple Google search or by looking at the company's FAQ page, a segment of customers will still reach out via a live chat or the company's Facebook page. There is a significant opportunity to automate some of the work to answer these customers' questions.

That said, bots currently cannot always handle questions gracefully. As a relatively new technology, chat bots may be insufficiently tested and yield confusing or inconsistent experiences. A bug in the chat bot itself may create a situation where the bot becomes unresponsive, and a CSR must step in and manually take over a conversation to ensure client satisfaction. As such, a company that automates a workload using chat bot technology typically will not see an immediate reduction in workload. In fact, it is not uncommon that a new set of skills focused on working with the bot itself becomes necessary. As the technology and our understanding of its uses improve, we may get to a point where humans are replaced, but do not expect that to happen immediately. Human CSRs must remain in the loop to intercede as needed.

Chat Bots from a Customer Service Perspective

There are three main classes of chat bots popular in the customer service industry. The type of bot a company builds is directly correlated to the number of cases it thinks a chat bot can handle correctly and to its users' willingness and savvy to talk to a computer via natural language.

Always-On Chat Bot

An always-on chat bot is directly connected to the user's channel and awaits questions or instructions. It assumes that it can handle every input, even if it is by saying the dreaded "I don't know" response. The key here is balance; a bot can try to handle every query, but it must be clear in its limitations and in its ability to point users to possible sources of help. Of course, if the bot is not able to handle the request, providing an alternate way of contacting a human is suggested. If seamless human escalation integration is unavailable, even providing a reference number for continuity is better than not.

Sometimes-On Chat Bot

A sometimes-on chat bot can handle a smaller closed set of questions and user inputs, but if it is not sure or does not know an answer, it immediately forwards the question to a human agent. This is an effective way of mitigating the risk of a user being stuck in a loop with a chat bot and not being able to get any help. On the other hand, if a forward-thinking customer is trying to explore bot functionality and is being redirected to a human on pretty much any input, it can become a frustrating experience. A nice compromise is to suggest to the user that they can speak to a human agent when, at any point, the bot does not understand the user's intent. Again, if no seamless human escalation functionality exists, any way of contacting the business is better than none.

CSR-Facing Chat Bot

A CSR-facing bot acts as an extension of the CSR system and provides suggestions to the human agent about what the response to a user's query should be. This one is an interesting approach if only because it slightly inverts the concept of a chat bot. It is also a great way to gather data to train a chat bot based on user queries and the agent's responses. This approach is an effective technique to build up use cases and content for a chat bot. We have also observed this type of chat bot to perform well in cases where a business's customers are not tech savvy or much rather prefer to speak to a human.

Typical Customer Service System Concepts

A customer service system can be many things. It can be a knowledge base. It can be a ticketing system. It can be a call center system. It can be a messaging system. Among the big players in the space mentioned in the chapter introduction, all include some combination of these functionalities in their products. In fact, because of the rich set of data that these systems obtain from their customers, such as detailed knowledge bases and rich conversation histories, many of these players are developing their own virtual assistant solutions. For instance, an obvious start is to create a virtual assistant that queries a knowledge base for answers to known problems. A ticketing system could very well provide a chat bot that can check on ticket status and perform basic edits on existing tickets.

Customer service systems will generally organize every interaction between a user and the business into an item known as a *case*. A customer asking the business for help with a password issue, for example, opens a new case in the system. The new item might come into an inbox that all active agents see on their desktops. The case gets assigned to whoever selects the item, or maybe the system automatically assigns the case to a CSR who is available and not handling many cases at the moment. Once the agent is done helping the customer with the issue, the case is closed. The agent may have created a new ticket for the customer, linking the case with the ticket. The CSR system is aware of multiple pieces of data. It knows when an agent is available. It knows how quickly agents typically handle cases. It knows the call center's operating hours, thus perhaps not allowing any live chats during off-hours.

All this data makes for very rich reporting. These systems will typically provide detailed reports for everything such as total chats, chat engagement, queue waiting times, time to close cases, first response time, and many other interesting data points. Naturally, the CSR team will be evaluated and compensated on these kinds of measures.

As bot developers, we should not expect the CSR team to change its workflow or data reporting structure. In fact, many of these systems provide bot integration points that treat the chat bot as an agent. Every system is slightly different, but they generally follow this paradigm. One of the benefits of this approach is that the system's reporting capabilities are not broken by introducing a chat bot as a virtual CSR.

Integrating with a customer service system means that we need to write code to initiate and close out cases. Case initiation may happen automatically when a new message arrives from a customer. Case close-out occurs when the chat bot is finished helping the user with their query. The definition of a case will vary. A case may be defined as from the moment that a user asks a question until an answer is presented by the chat bot. Alternatively, a case may be defined as any interactions between the chat bot and user until there is 15 minutes of activity in the conversation.

Integration Approaches

There are multiple approaches to seamlessly integrate chat bots with customer service systems. We will take a look at three options. The level of integration we select is dictated by the support team's maturity and available tools. We will address this as we explore each type of integration.

Custom-Built Interface

A custom-built interface might be the best for teams with a highly specialized workflow or teams that do not have any existing customer service staff or systems. Furthermore, if we are deploying the bot to a channel without existing affordable tools, we may not have an option other than building your own. Although a custom-built interface is not recommended, there are developers who have created the interfaces themselves. Here is an example: `https://ankitbko.github.io/2017/03/human-handover-bot`. The general approach is to build a customer service–like system on top of existing bot functionality. Obviously, the issue is now that our development team owns the customer service interface and has the added responsibility of keeping that system live.

On Platform

If you do not have an existing customer service system but are aiming to deploy to a channel that has its own support tools, you are in luck. Facebook pages, for example, allow customers to interact with businesses via Messenger. Pages include many features for page owners, one of them being a sleek inbox (Figure 12-1). As messages from customers arrive, they will appear on the left-side panel. The page body contains the chat history and allows the business to interact with the user.

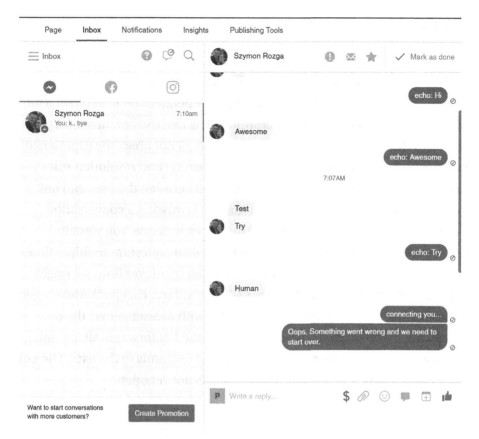

Figure 12-1. *Facebook page inbox user interface*

Suffice it to say that the user interface is a powerful way for page owners to respond to many types of user queries. The challenge, of course, is that if the bot is deployed to channels other than Facebook, an on-platform interface will not support those live chat scenarios.

Product

If a team already has a customer service system with live chat support in place, we will most likely want to develop an integration into the existing system. The process for doing this is highly dependent on the system. One of the most important tasks in this approach is that the bot must be a good citizen to the customer Service system and must not break the experience for the other agents. This means that case opening and resolution rules must be obeyed, and all messages exchanged between the user and bot must be logged. If an agent opens a case that is missing a conversation history, it would prove to be a bad customer experience. You want to witness a frustrated customer? Ask them the same question multiple times.

If we naively begin implementing a human handover flow, we might end up with what's shown in Figure 12-2. We will use Facebook Messenger as an example. The chat bot communicates with Messenger via the bot connector. In the normal conversation flow, the bot forwards all incoming messages to the customer service system and responds to the user. The bot is also responsible for opening a case if one is not yet open.

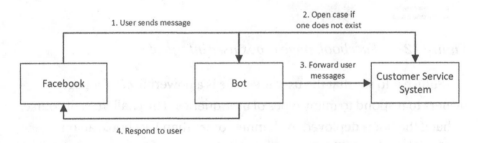

Figure 12-2. *A normal conversation flow without a human agent*

When the flow of the conversation necessitates human handover, the chat bot acts as a proxy, sending the user's messages into the agent chat and forwarding the agent's responses back to the user. This is illustrated in Figure 12-3. If the case has been solved by the agent, the case must be closed.

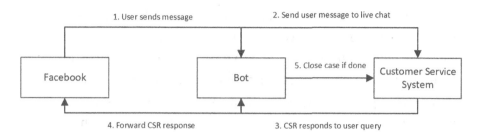

Figure 12-3. *Customer interacting with human agent*

This model is not popular. The main reason is that the customer service system is typically connected to an existing social channel, such as Facebook. The connections between the chat bot, Facebook, and the customer service system look more like Figure 12-4.

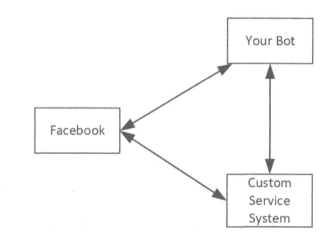

Figure 12-4. *Connections between the chat bot, Facebook, and customer service system in practice*

Social platforms typically do not support having multiple applications listen to a conversation simultaneously. As such, a choice needs to be made around which system owns the connection. Since customer service systems can provide integration above and beyond chat integration and are usually in place before a decision to build a chat bot is made, they end up owning the connection.

In the case of Facebook, we can use something called the Handover Protocol, which allows us to work around the limitation of only one application owning the connection at a time. Using this protocol, we can designate one app as the primary, and any others are secondary. The primary app will always be contacted when a user first starts a conversation with a page. The primary app can then transfer the conversation thread to a secondary app. When an app is not active in a user's conversation, it is in standby mode. There is a way to ensure that the apps receive the user's messages when in standby mode by implementing the standby channel. You can find more documentation at `https://developers.facebook.com/docs/messenger-platform/handover-protocol`. Figure 12-5 shows the setup described.

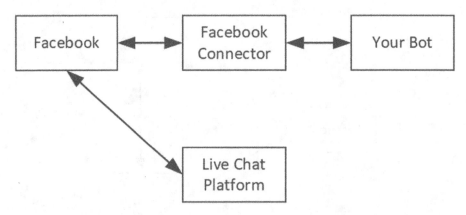

Figure 12-5. *A Handover Protocol implementation on Facebook Messenger. Out bot app is designated as primary, and the live chat platform of our choice is secondary.*

Unfortunately for us, not every channel supports the multi-application paradigm, and not every customer service system implements the handover protocol. Not to mention, we are assuming a Facebook-only bot. Adding more channels would create further challenges within this approach.

Figure 12-6 illustrates another approach to integrating human handover. Using this approach, the customer service system acts as a proxy for messages intended for the bot until the conversation is transferred to a human. At that point, the chat bot does not see any pieces of the conversation. This setup also means that the Facebook channel connector is out of the loop, so we need to implement a custom translator that receives Messenger format messages, converts them to the Bot Builder SDK format, and forwards the messages into the chat bot using Direct Line, like we did in Chapter 9.

This approach is a lot more common since it is easier to integrate the back end into the customer service system's ecosystem than share the Facebook page between two systems. This approach is also effective at supporting human handoff on any system that the customer service system supports.

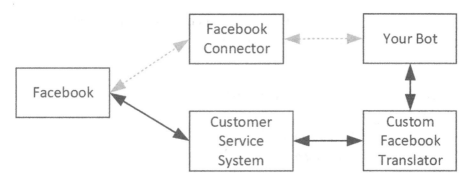

Figure 12-6. *A more common architectural approach to chat bot integration with customer service systems*

Facebook Messenger Handover Sample

It would be difficult to demonstrate a fully integrated product-based human handover scenario, but if we pretend that Facebook pages are the customer service system in the previous figures, it becomes easier to do so. In this section, we will add human handover integration to the calendar bot that we have been building throughout the book.

The approach that we use will be the following. First, we will create a new intent to handle a customer's explicit request to speak to a human agent. Next, we will create a dialog to handle the logic to transfer the user. We will designate our bot as the primary app and the inbox as the secondary app. We will demonstrate how to transfer thread control over from our app to the inbox. Lastly, we will show how we can support a customer via the Facebook page inbox and then send control back to the chat bot.

Let's create a new version of our calendar bot model. In this version, we will create an intent called *HumanHandover* and provide it with sample utterances like the following:

- "Talk to agent"

- "Give me a human"

- "I want to speak with a human"

We train and publish the LUIS app. Our chat bot will not be able to receive the intent and do something with it.

```
{
  "query": "take me to your leader",
  "topScoringIntent": {
    "intent": "HumanHandover",
    "score": 0.883278668
  },
  "intents": [
    {
      "intent": "HumanHandover",
      "score": 0.883278668
    },
    {
      "intent": "None",
      "score": 0.3982243
    },
```

```
  {
    "intent": "EditCalendarEntry",
    "score": 0.00692663854
  },
  {
    "intent": "Login",
    "score": 0.00396537
  },
  {
    "intent": "CheckAvailability",
    "score": 0.00346317887
  },
  {
    "intent": "AddCalendarEntry",
    "score": 0.00215073861
  },
  {
    "intent": "ShowCalendarSummary",
    "score": 0.0006825995
  },
  {
    "intent": "PrimaryCalendar",
    "score": 2.43631575E-07
  },
  {
    "intent": "DeleteCalendarEntry",
    "score": 4.69401E-08
  },
  {
    "intent": "Help",
    "score": 2.26313137E-08
  }
```

```
  ],
  "entities": []
}
```

The Facebook Handoff Protocol is composed of two main actions: passing thread control and taking thread control. Any time a new conversation begins, the primary app receives the user's message. The primary app determines when to pass control to a secondary app. The primary app will either know the hard-coded identifier of the secondary app, or it can query the page for a list of secondary apps and select one at runtime. If our page has multiple secondary apps depending on the functional area, the chat bot can figure out the destination of the transfer based on the user's input. After the secondary app is done, it can pass control back to the primary app.

In the context of Facebook pages, the page's inbox can be considered a secondary application. From a functional perspective, this means that anyone managing the page inbox should not see a message unless the chat bot has handed it to the inbox. We can set this up in the page's Messenger Platform settings (Figure 12-7).

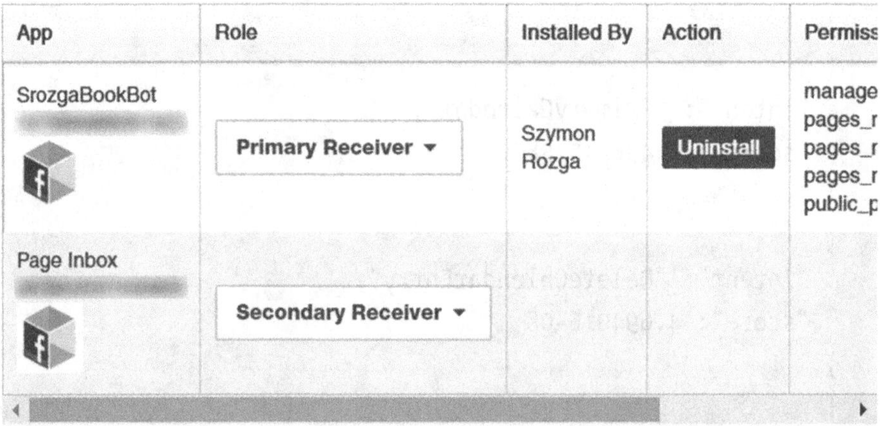

App	Role	Installed By	Action	Permiss
SrozgaBookBot	Primary Receiver ▾	Szymon Rozga	Uninstall	manage pages_r pages_r pages_r public_p
Page Inbox	Secondary Receiver ▾			

Figure 12-7. Setting up the primary and secondary receivers for a Facebook page

Next, we create the dialog responsible for invoking the handover logic. The requests to the Facebook APIs will be to either of these two endpoints, although our demo will only need to contact the *pass_thread_control* endpoint.

```
const pass_thread_control = 'https://graph.facebook.com/v2.6/
me/pass_thread_control?access_token=' + pageAccessToken;
const take_thread_control = 'https://graph.facebook.com/v2.6/
me/take_thread_control?access_token=' + pageAccessToken;
```

No matter which endpoint we call, we must include the user's ID and may include some metadata. The *pass_thread_control* method also requires a *target_app_id* to be passed to indicate which application the thread is being transferred to. The Facebook documentation states that handing over to the page inbox requires the *target_app_id* to be the value 263902037430900. The code then to call Facebook endpoints is shown next. We use the request Node.js package to make new HTTP requests.

```
function makeFacebookGraphRequest(d, psid, metadata, procedure,
pageAccessToken) {
    const data = Object.assign({}, d);
    data.recipient = { 'id': psid };
    data.metadata = metadata;

    const options = {
        uri: "https://graph.facebook.com/v2.6/me/" + procedure +
        "?access_token=" + pageAccessToken,
        json: data,
        method: 'POST'
    };
    return new Promise((resolve, reject) => {
        request(options, function (error, response, body) {
            if (error) {
                console.log(error);
```

```
                reject(error);
                return;
            }
            console.log(body);
            resolve();
        });
    });
}

const secondaryApp = 263902037430900; // Inbox App ID

function handover(psid, pageAccessToken) {
    return makeFacebookGraphRequest({ 'target_app_id':
    secondaryApp }, psid, 'test', 'pass_thread_control',
    pageAccessToken);
}

function takeControl(psid, pageAccessToken) {
    return makeFacebookGraphRequest({}, psid, 'test',
    'take_thread_control', pageAccessToken);
}
```

The code for the dialog quite simply calls the handover method.

```
const builder = require('botbuilder');
const constants = require('../constants');
const request = require('request');

const libName = 'humanEscalation';
const escalateDialogName = 'escalate';
```

```
const lib = new builder.Library(libName);

let pageAccessToken = null;
exports.pageAccessToken = (val) => {
    if(val) pageAccessToken = val;
    return pageAccessToken;
};

exports.escalateToHuman = (session, pageAccessTokenArg, userId)
=> {
    session.beginDialog(libName + ':' + escalateDialogName, {
    pageAccessToken: pageAccessTokenArg || pageAccessToken });
};

lib.dialog(escalateDialogName, (session, args, next) => {
    handover(session.message.address.user.id, args.
    pageAccessToken || pageAccessToken);
    session.endDialog('Just hold tight... getting someone for
    you...');
}).triggerAction({
    matches: constants.intentNames.HumanHandover
});

exports.create = () => { return lib.clone(); }
```

Let's see what this interaction looks like on the Facebook inbox. Before we run the bot, we note that the inbox in the Facebook page is empty (Figure 12-8).

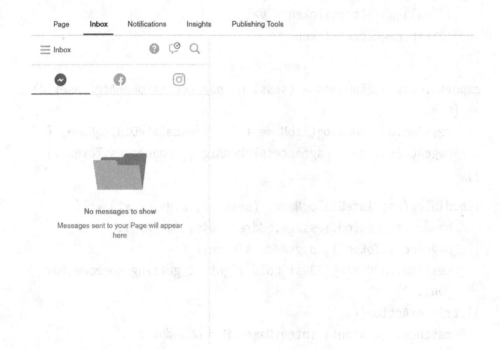

***Figure 12-8.** Empty inbox*

We can exchange a few messages with the calendar bot. Figure 12-9 shows a sample interaction.

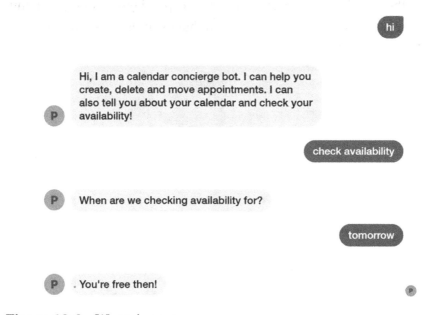

Figure 12-9. *Warming up*

Note that the Facebook page inbox remains empty; that is by design. Since the primary app is taking care of the user's messages, there is no need for the page inbox to get involved. If we expand the hamburger menu on the top left of the interface, we will find that the inbox has multiple folders (Figure 12-10).

Figure 12-10. *We have located the inbox folders*

Lo and behold, if we click the Done folder, we will find the conversation we just had with the chat bot (Figure 12-11). We could very well type our reply into the response textbox, but that will just confuse the user as both the bot and a human would be responding to the customer since the bot is still in the loop.

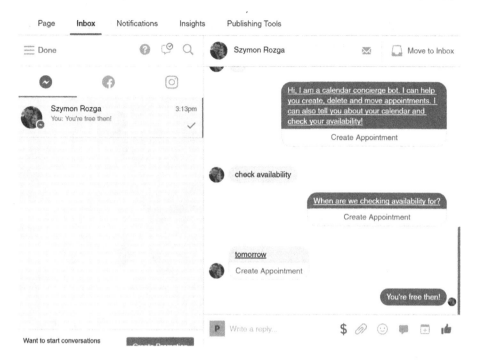

Figure 12-11. *We found our conversation!*

Let's back up into the Inbox folder. We also go back into Messenger as the customer and ask to speak to a human (Figure 12-12).

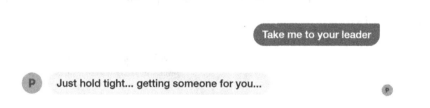

Figure 12-12. *I demand to speak to her!*

If you refresh the page inbox, you'll note that the conversation appears in the inbox (Figure 12-13).

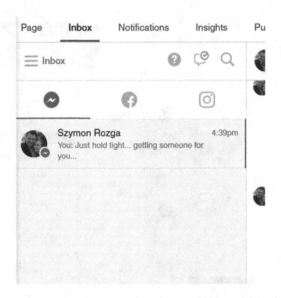

Figure 12-13. *OK, it's time to talk to our customer!*

At this point the chat bot does not see any customer messages, and any message sent from the Facebook page inbox appear in the customer's chat (Figure 12-14).

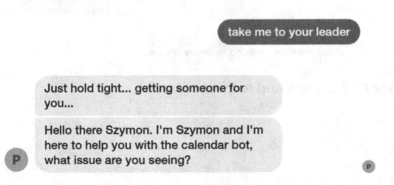

Figure 12-14. *Oh wow, seamless human escalation integration!*

Now, the next step is to disconnect from the secondary app. If we had two Facebook apps, we would have to either take control back or pass control back to the primary app using the code we wrote. In this instance, the page inbox has the functionality built right in. In the top-right corner of any conversation, we will find a button with green text labeled "Mark as done" (Figure 12-15).

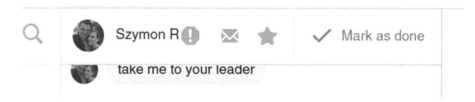

Figure 12-15. *Transferring the user back to the chat bot by clicking the "Mark as done" button*

Once the conversation is over, the agent clicks that button, and the conversation is transferred back to the bot. From the Facebook page inbox perspective, the conversation is moved back into the Done folder, and the bot is once again active (Figure 12-16)! From a customer's perspective, it is completely seamless.

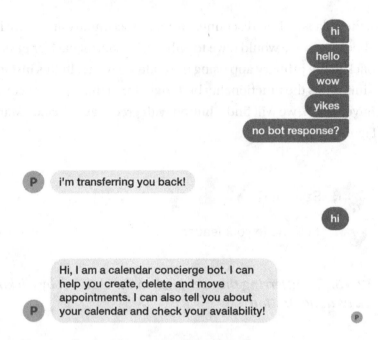

Figure 12-16. *The bot is once again active*

If the user gets into trouble again, he can once again ask for a human agent and resolve an issue.

Conclusion

The focus of our work in this chapter has been seamless human handover. That is a key experience requirement for our customers and agents. The experience provided for both parties should be as frictionless as possible. The chat bot should be a helpful assistant, which will increase the likelihood that the chat bot gains support from both internal and external parties.

Although the sample we demonstrated in this chapter was limited in scope to Facebook, it illustrates the general approach that most chat bot integrations with live chat systems will follow. There are, of course, many details to figure out, and there is no single approach to the problem, but the work we did in this chapter should be sufficient to get our chat bot's human handoff functionality going in the right direction.

CHAPTER 13

Chat Bot Analytics

Now that we are equipped with the necessary skills to develop great conversational experiences for our customers, it is clear you will create the next killer bot. It will integrate with a bunch of APIs and accomplish things unheard of in the industry to date. I'm not a great sales guy, but you get it. You are excited about your idea, and you are even more excited to bring it to market. The bot is deployed, and, to everyone's disappointment, it is not gaining traction. Users do not engage with it. Suddenly, you realize you do not have a good understanding of what users are doing and when they abandon the conversation with your chat bot. What we need is analytics!

All chat bots constantly generate data. Every interaction between a user and a bot, every time the NLU platform resolves a user's intent, every time the user curses at the bot, and every time the bot has no idea what users are asking it to do are critical points in the conversation that lend insight into users' behaviors and, more importantly, into how to improve the conversational experience.

What are the ways in which we can capture all this data? What kinds of questions are we trying to answer? How do we get to this data? This chapter aims to answer some of these questions and provide an introduction to integrating a Bot Framework chat bot with an analytics platform.

© Szymon Rozga 2018
S. Rozga, *Practical Bot Development*, https://doi.org/10.1007/978-1-4842-3540-9_13

Common Data Questions

It is worth examining what insights we should be looking to gain from user interactions with our chat bot. We are certainly interested in how long our users converse with the bot. We are also interested in what topics users are messaging about. Surely, we are interested in the raw input, but we can probably get better insights if we knew the exact intent that was resolved. We also want to know what percentage of user input our bot knew how to handle versus, perhaps, what it should know how to handle.

In general, chat bot analytics platforms all gather and report similar data. On top of generic analytics functions, many can perform channel-specific analytics on the bot. For example, Dashbot, one of the platforms we will look at in the next section, can gather specific analytics data from Slack and Facebook Messenger among others. On Slack, we can see statistics such as how many Slack channels have installed our bot. Not surprisingly, analytics tools should allow us to ask for channel-specific data. In the general case, the questions we will be asking are not novel: web analytics platforms answer a lot of similar questions. For chat bots we look at several categories of analytics next.

Generic Data

Generic data is raw, numerical data such as number of messages, number of user sessions, number of messages exchanged per session, session duration, number of sessions per user, and so on. This data should be displayed in a chart plotted against time and, ideally, aggregated by any time bucket. This data allows us to see some simple trends such as when users typically interact with the bot, how many times, and for how long. If you have a million users, congratulations! But if they interact with your bot for only two messages ever, that is not success. Figure 13-1 illustrates a simple active users chart provided by Google's Chatbase. Figure 13-2 is an example of a user engagement chart by Dashbot.

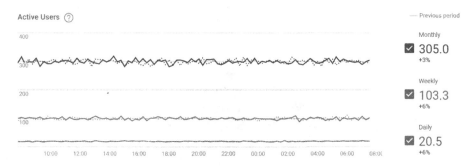

Figure 13-1. *Chatbase's active users chart*

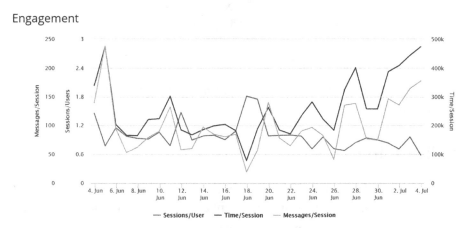

Figure 13-2. *Dashbot's engagement chart*

Demographics

This category comprises data such as location, gender, age, and language. This data is not available for all channels. Figure 13-3 is an example of user language distribution from Dashbot.

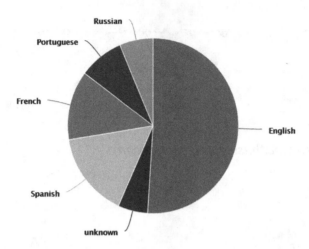

Figure 13-3. *This chat bot should definitely support multiple languages*

Sentiment

Now we are getting into some interesting territory. Ideally, we would like to examine average conversation sentiment correlated with other measures such as session duration and intent. For example, does one piece of functionality really frustrate users? Does the user get more frustrated with the bot over time? This might indicate a need for aggressive transfer to a human live chat, if supported. Does sentiment correlate with something beyond our control like time of day? Figure 13-4 is an example of Dashbot's overall sentiment visualization.

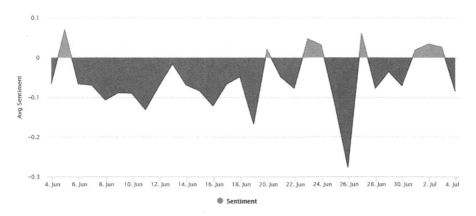

Figure 13-4. *Overall sentiment tracking. June 26 was not a good day.*

User Retention

As a chat bot developer or product owner, one of the most interesting bits of data is how often users come back to the experience. We want our conversational experience to be "sticky." The analytics platforms will typically include some visualization showing how many users return to the chat bot week after week. Of course, a good analytics tool will also let us explore the retention metrics based on the manner in which the users initially interacted with the chat bot. Google's Chatbase is a platform that does just that (Figure 13-5). By default, we see what percentage of users come back to the bot a week after interacting with it in any way whatsoever. We can break this down to consider intent as part of the equation, leading us to correlate intents with retention. This can be a good metric to understand which pieces of functionality may be driving user retention and which areas need work.

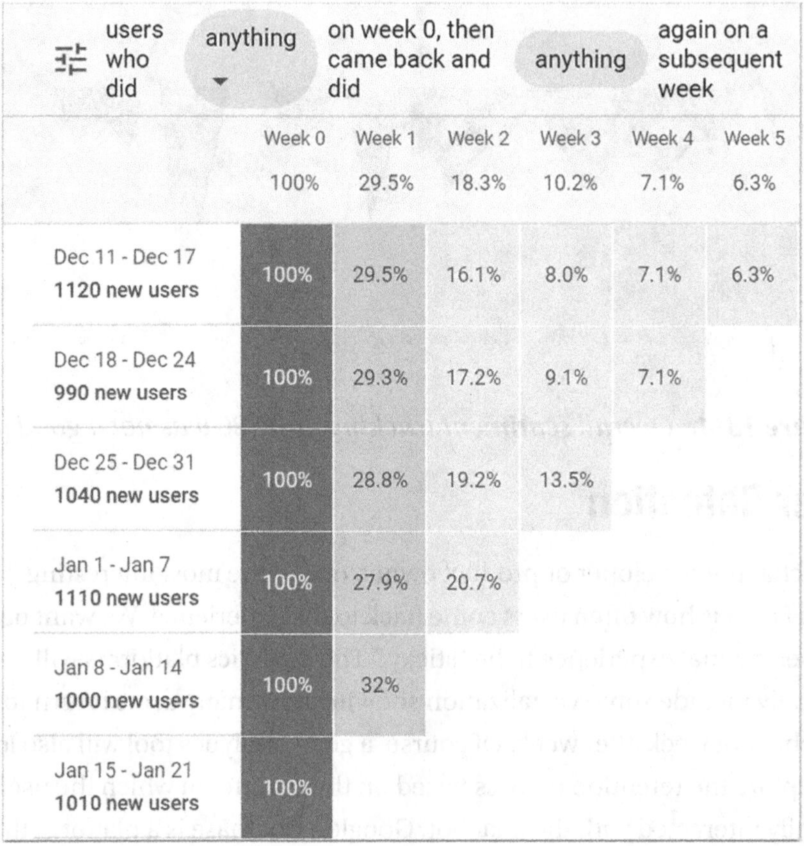

⊟↕ users who did	anything ▾	on week 0, then came back and did		anything	again on a subsequent week	
	Week 0	Week 1	Week 2	Week 3	Week 4	Week 5
	100%	29.5%	18.3%	10.2%	7.1%	6.3%
Dec 11 - Dec 17 1120 new users	100%	29.5%	16.1%	8.0%	7.1%	6.3%
Dec 18 - Dec 24 990 new users	100%	29.3%	17.2%	9.1%	7.1%	
Dec 25 - Dec 31 1040 new users	100%	28.8%	19.2%	13.5%		
Jan 1 - Jan 7 1110 new users	100%	27.9%	20.7%			
Jan 8 - Jan 14 1000 new users	100%	32%				
Jan 15 - Jan 21 1010 new users	100%					

Figure 13-5. User retention table

User Session Flows

There are many ways of visualizing user behavior, but user flows are among
the most common approaches. Typically, the analytics platform will show
the most common actions that users took upon session start and what
percentage of users took this action. Next, for every action, it will show
every subsequent action that users took, including the percentage of users
who did so and the drop-off rate. That is, we gain an understanding of how
many users kept interacting with the bot and through which actions versus
how many users simply stopped talking to the bot altogether. Again, this

kind of visualization is common in the web analytics space, and it is natural to use it with chat bots. Figure 13-6 shows an example from Chatbase. One of the insights we may gain from this visualization is that the team might consider supporting rental car customers that specify they want the car *today* as opposed to requiring them to enter the date. Note that the path to Rent-Car Today indicates the Today intent is not supported.

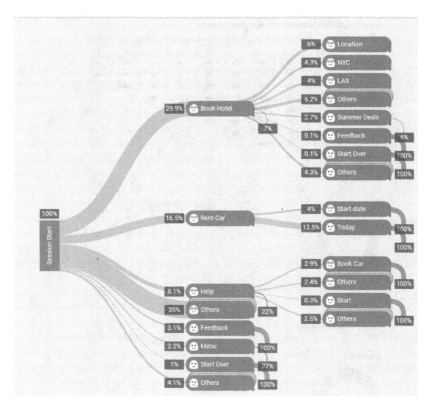

Figure 13-6. *A sample Chatbase session flow diagram*

Analytics Platforms

There are several chat bot analytics platforms. First, most chat bot development platforms and some channels have some sort of analytics dashboards. For example, Microsoft's Bot Framework includes an analytics dashboard (Figure 13-7) that provides the total number of messages and users, a basic retention table, number of users per channel over time, and number of messages per channel over time.

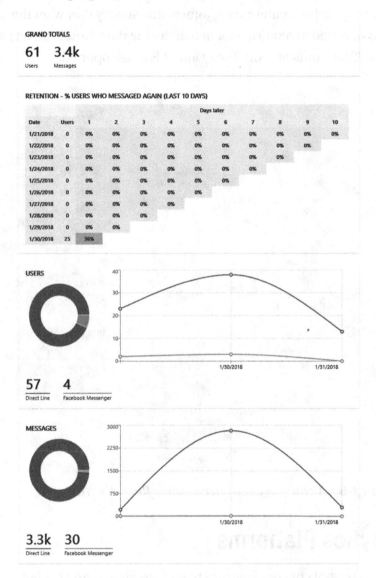

Figure 13-7. *Azure Bot Service analytics dashboard*

Facebook provides Facebook Analytics (Figure 13-8), a platform-wide analytics dashboard that includes detailed Facebook bot data. Amazon provides an Alexa Skill dashboard. The problem is that the Bot Service analytics are somewhat lacking in their depth and usability, and the Facebook and Alexa dashboards each support only one channel.

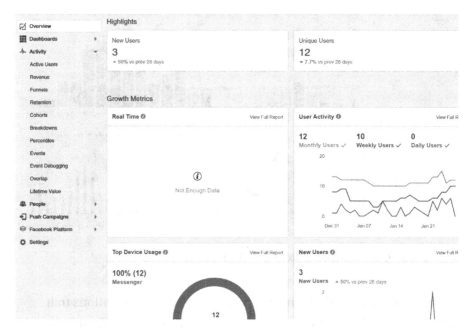

Figure 13-8. *Facebook Analytics for bots*

Many customers have existing investments in analytics platforms spanning multiple product lines. For example, one analytics system may own all the data gathered from web properties, mobile apps, and multiple chat bot. In such an environment, the data and user behavior can be correlated across the different platforms. If there is a way to identify a user on a mobile device and correlate that to a user on the chat bot (perhaps via an account linking process), then we can gain a much broader understanding of that user's behavior across the platforms and cater to their needs accordingly. Typically, this would involve an enterprise data storage solution, either on premises or in the cloud, with custom visualizations built using something like Microsoft's Power BI (Figure 13-9) or Tableau.

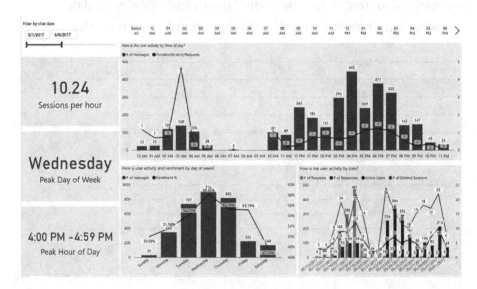

Figure 13-9. *A sample Power BI dashboard*

There are also flexible third-party chat bot analytics solutions that provide APIs and SDKs that we can integrate with our bot. We mentioned two that we will work with in the rest of the chapter: Dashbot (https:// dashbot.io) and Google's Chatbase (https://chatbase.com). There are other options such as Botanalytics (https://botanalytics.co/) and BotMetrics (https://www.getbotmetrics.com/). Many of these vendors also support analytics for voice interfaces such as Alexa, Cortana, and Google Home. We encourage you to do your own research to understand the options and make the best choice based on their requirements.

Integrating with Dashbot and Chatbase

We have chosen these two platforms to show two styles of analytics integration and the kinds of reports they provide. We will look at Dashbot's out-of-the-box Node Bot Builder support, which leverages Bot middleware to install incoming and outgoing message handlers to send analytics data to Dashbot. (Recall that we used the concept of bot middleware before in the context of multilanguage support in Chapter 10.) That is a great start. Google's Chatbase, in contrast, is a bit more focused on ensuring a richer story around the analytics data. Specifically, when reporting data to an analytics system, it may be useful not only to send the user's input but also to determine whether the input resolved to an intent, whether the input was handled, and whether the input was a command or simply feedback to a bot question. This additional metadata, something that simple integration via middleware will be pressed to capture, can yield incredibly rich analytics. Getting it done right requires effort to make each dialog analytics-aware. Let's look at a couple of samples that illustrate the two approaches.

Let's start with Dashbot. First, we sign up for a free account by going to `https://dashbot.io/`. Once logged in, we will be taken to an empty bots list. Click the Add a Bot, Skill, or Action button (Dashbot supports Alexa skills and Google actions, could you tell?). The interface will ask us for the platform or channel we are targeting (Figure 13-10). This is Dashbot's way of providing analytics optimizations and opportunities for further data integration based on the channel.

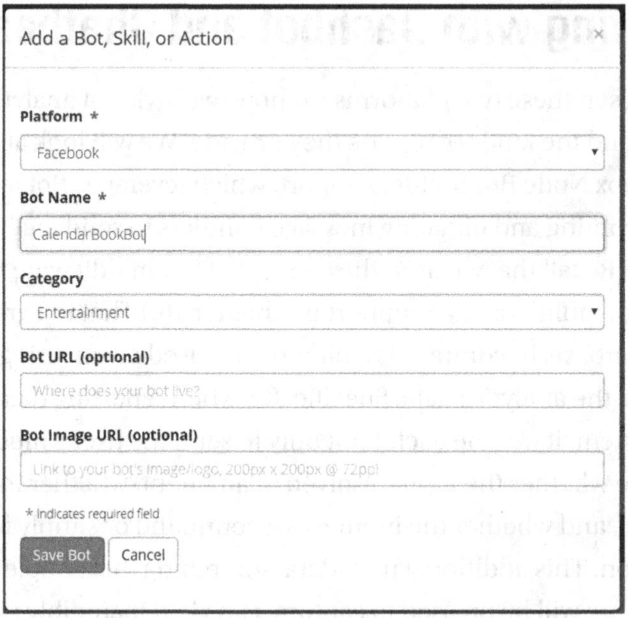

Figure 13-10. *Creating a new Dashbot entry*

Once created, Dashbot will show us the bot's analytics API key. Let's connect our chat bot to this Dashbot entry. First, install the *Node.js* package.

```
npm install dashbot --save
```

Lastly, we add the following code to our app.js file after we create a bot:

```
// setup dashbot
const dashbotApiMap = {
    facebook: process.env.DASHBOT_FB_KEY
};
const dashbot = require('dashbot')(dashbotApiMap).microsoft;
// optional and recommended for Facebook Bots
dashbot.setFacebookToken(process.env.PAGE_ACCESS_TOKEN);
bot.use(dashbot);
```

There are several things happening here. First, we are specifying the Dashbot API keys. In Dashbot, each platform can get its own distinct dashboard, or you can create multiplatform dashboards. If the bot supported additional channels and we had additional API keys for those channels, we would set them in the *dashbotApiMap*. Next, we import the Dashbot middleware for the Bot Framework and add it to the bot by using *bot.use*. As we do so, we are also providing the Facebook page access token. This isn't required, but it provides Dashbot with the ability to fetch additional data from Facebook and integrate it into the dashboards.

And, that's it! The code for Dashbot's Bot Framework middleware is very concise. We present it here for reference:

```
that.receive = function (session, next) {
    logDashbot(session, true, next);
};
that.send = function (session, next) {
    logDashbot(session, false, next);
};
function logDashbot(session, isIncoming, next) {
    if (that.debug) {
        //console.log('\n*** MSFTBK Debug: ', (isIncoming ?
        'incoming' : 'outgoing'), JSON.stringify(session,
        null, 2))
    }

    var data = {
        is_microsoft: true,
        dashbot_timestamp: new Date().getTime(),
        json: session
    };
    var platform = session.source ? session.source :
    _.get(session, 'address.channelId');
```

```
// hack for facebook token
if (platform === 'facebook' && that.facebookToken != null)
{

    data.token = that.facebookToken;
}

var apiKey = apiKeyMap[platform]
if (!apiKey) {
    console.warn('**** Warning: No Dashbot apiKey for
    platform:(' + platform + ') Data not saved. ')
    next();
    return;
}

// if the platform is not supported by us, use generic
if (_.indexOf(['facebook', 'kik', 'slack'], platform) ===
-1) {
    platform = 'generic';
}

var url = that.urlRoot + '?apiKey=' +
    apiKey + '&type=' + (isIncoming ? 'incoming' :
    'outgoing') +
    '&platform=' + platform + '&v=' + VERSION + '-npm';
if (that.debug) {
    console.log('\n*** Dashbot MSFT Bot Framework Debug **');
    console.log(' *** platform is ' + platform);
    console.log(' *** Dashbot Url: ' + url);
    console.log(JSON.stringify(data, null, 2));
}
makeRequest({
    uri: url,
    method: 'POST',
```

```
    json: data
}, that.printErrors, that.config.redact);

next();
}
```

After speaking to our bot for a couple of minutes, we produced the data in Figure 13-11.

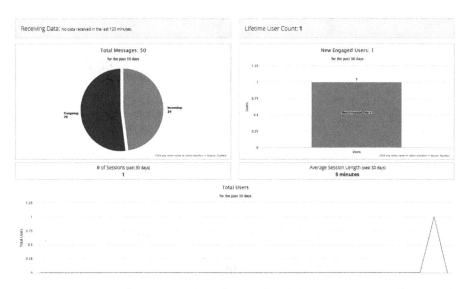

Figure 13-11. *One conversation's worth of data*

That was easy. There are many other data points we can look at on Dashbot. Figure 13-12 shows a listing of the possibilities and includes details about users, retention, demographics, top messages and intents, and even raw conversation transcriptions. Naturally, things like intent data are not populated. Per our earlier point, if we wanted to support that, our dialogs would have to incorporate analytics reporting functions.

Behavior	ⓘ		Top Users	
Goal Funnels	🔒		Demographics	
Behavior Flow	NEW		Conversations	ⓘ
Market Metrics	ⓘ		Word Clouds	NEW
Message Percentile	🔒		Message Count	
User Percentile	🔒		Top Messages In	
Live	ⓘ		Top Messages Out	
Firehose			Top Intents In	
Live Transcripts			Top Intents Out	
Message Rate			Top Exit Message	NEW
Audience	ⓘ		Sentiment	
Users			Transcripts	
Lifetime Users	NEW		Referrals	
Sessions				
Engagement				
Retention				

Figure 13-12. *Different analytics provided by Dashbot*

Google's Chatbase API does not contain prebuilt Bot Framework middleware integration; however, building this out ourselves is not too challenging. We could take Dashbot's code as a starting point. In fact, we do so but only for outgoing messages. The incoming message data will be sent from within the individual dialogs.

To begin, we create a new bot on https://chatbase.com, via the Add Your Bot button. We will need to enter a name, country, industry, and business case. As a result, we will get an API key from Chatbase. We first install the Node.js package.

```
npm install @google/chatbase --save
```

We then write a few helper methods to build Chatbase messages and the middleware send handler. We can place this in its own Node.js module. In the following build method, we ask the caller for the message text, user ID, dialog arguments (from which we can try extracting the intent), and handled flag. Chatbase allows us to report whether a certain input was handled or not. For example, if there is unrecognized input from users, we would want to report it as such.

```
require('dotenv-extended').load();

const chatbase = require('@google/chatbase')
    .setApiKey(process.env.CHATBASE_KEY) // Your Chatbase API Key
    .setAsTypeUser()
    .setVersion('1.0')
    .setPlatform('SAMPLE'); // The platform you are interacting
    with the user over

exports.chatbase = chatbase;
chatbase.build = function (text, user_id, args, handled) {
    let intent = args;
    if (typeof (intent) !== 'string') {
        intent = args && args.intent && args.intent.intent;
    }

    var msg = chatbase.newMessage();
    msg.setIntent(intent).setUserId(user_id).setMessage(text);

    if (handled === undefined && !intent) {
        msg.setAsNotHandled();
    } else if (handled === true) {
        msg.setAsHandled();
    } else if (handled === false) {
        msg.setAsNotHandled();
    }
```

```
        return msg;
}

exports.middleware = {
    send: function (event, next) {
        if (event.type === 'message') {
            const msg = chatbase.newMessage()
                .setAsTypeAgent()
                .setUserId(event.address.user.id)
                .setMessage(event.text);
            if (!event.text && event.attachments) {
                msg.setMessage(event.attachmentLayout);
            }
            msg.send()
                .then(() => {
                    next();
                })
                .catch(err => {
                    console.error(err);
                    next();
                });
        } else {
            next();
        }
    }
};
```

All that is left to do in our app.js is to install the Bot Builder middleware.

```
const chatbase = require('./chatbase');
bot.use(chatbase.middleware); // install the sender middleware
```

Next, we need to add the analytics call wherever in our dialogs it is needed. For example, in the summarize dialog, we can use this call to report a successful entry into the dialog.

```
chatbase.build(session.message.text, session.message.address.
user.id, args, true).send();
```

This code has been integrated into the calendar bot we have been working on throughout the book. The branch chapter-13 in the repo has been integrated with the previous code.

Figure 13-13 is a sample dashboard of data gathered using this approach. We are particularly interested in the messages that were not handled by the chat bot. We did ask the calendar bot for the meaning of life, something we would not expect to get a satisfactory answer to. The unhandled utterance data certainly is important information for us to consider. Figure 13-14 displays the handled inputs.

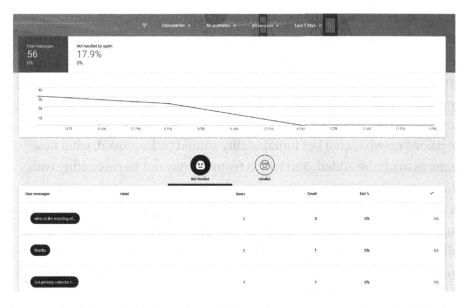

Figure 13-13. *A dashboard consisting of one conversation with the bot*

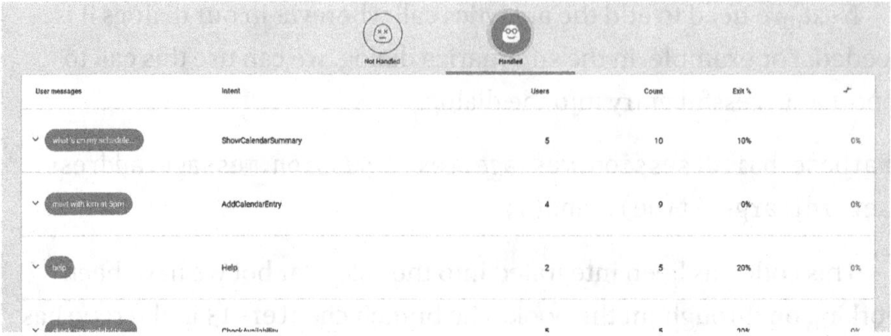

User messages	Intent	Users	Count	Exit %	
what's on my schedule...	ShowCalendarSummary	5	10	10%	0%
meet with kim at 3pm	AddCalendarEntry	4	9	0%	0%
help	Help	2	5	20%	0%
	Check Availability				

Figure 13-14. *The handled messages for the same conversation*

Again, the previous data is scarce, but as your chat bot gains usage, the picture will become clearer and much more valuable.

Conclusion

This chapter only scratched the surface of how to properly instrument a chat bot for analytics collection. The different analytics platforms are not yet as rich as the mature web analytics platforms, but they are making good progress. Our focus as a chat bot developer is to become familiar with the systems and be able to integrate them in our code so that the right data is flowing into the analytics dashboards. Then, our team can make informed decisions on what chat bot functionality should be improved, what new features might be added, and which features may not be resonating with your users. Chat bots are still a new space; customers are going to react in all kinds of ways to a conversational interface, especially if deployed to customers who are not tech savvy or who are not enamored in messaging with a computer. Understanding those challenges and improving the conversational experience based on analytics is essential to ensuring successful adoption over the years to come. Analytics will play a lead role in that evolution.

CHAPTER 14

Applying Our Learnings: Alexa Skills Kit

One of book's goals is to emphasize that the ideas, techniques, and skills introduced throughout apply to many types of applications. In this chapter, by creating a simple Alexa skill, we demonstrate how we can apply our knowledge of intent classification, entity extraction, and dialog construction to create a natural language voice experience. We begin by creating an Alexa skill in the simplest way possible, by using the Alexa Skills Kit SDK for Node.js. Since we already have a bot service back end, you may inevitably ask whether we can integrate Alexa with this back end. The answer is a resounding yes. Once we have our Alexa skill basics down, we will show how to power an Alexa skill via Direct Line and a Bot Framework bot.

Introduction

Alexa is Amazon's intelligent personal assistant. The first Alexa-enabled devices were the Echo and Echo Dot followed by the screen-enabled Echo Show and Spot. Amazon is also exploring a chat bot platform called Lex. Alexa skills are developed by declaring a set of intents and slots (another name for entities) and writing a webhook to handle incoming Alexa messages. A message from Alexa will include the resolved intent

© Szymon Rozga 2018
S. Rozga, *Practical Bot Development*, https://doi.org/10.1007/978-1-4842-3540-9_14

and slot data. Our webhook responds with data that includes speech and user interface elements. In the first iteration of the Echo and Echo Dot, there was no physical screen, so the only user interface was the Alexa app on the user's phone. The main user interface element on the app is a card, not much different from the hero cards we encountered in the Bot Builder SDK. For instance, a message from Alexa to our webhook will look as follows. Note that the message formats presented in this section are pseudocode because the actual messages are significantly more verbose.

```
{
    "id": "0000001",
    "session": "session00001",
    "type": "IntentRequest",
    "intent": {
        "intent": "QuoteIntent",
        "slots": [
            {
                "type": "SymbolSlot",
                "value": "apple"
            }
        ]
    }
}
```

The response would look like this:

```
{
    "speech": "The latest price for AAPL is 140.61",
    "card": {
        "title": "AAPL",
        "text": "The latest price for Apple (AAPL) is $140.61.",
        "img": "https://fakebot.ngrok.io/img/d5fa618b"
    }
}
```

We may want to allow additional functionality such as playing audio files. In keeping with the financial scenario, maybe we have audio briefing content that we would like to play for our users. A message to accomplish this task would look something like this:

```
{
    "speech": "",
    "directives": [
        {
            "type": "playAudio",
            "parameters": {
                "href": "https://fakebot.ngrok.io/audio/
                audiocontent1",
                "type": "audio/mpeg"
            }
        }
    ]
}
```

In addition, the system may want to provide an indication of whether the user cancelled audio playback or listened to the entire clip. More generically, the system may need a way to send events to our webhook. In those cases, an incoming message may look like this:

```
{
    "id": "0000003",
    "session": "session00001",
    "type": " AudioFinished"
}
```

If we gain use of a screen like the Echo Show device provides, the potential for more actions and behaviors grows. For example, we can now play videos. Or we can present a user interface with images and buttons to our users. If we display a list of items, perhaps we want the device to send an event when an item is tapped. We will then create a user interface render directive, so perhaps our earlier response for a quote will now include a user interface element as follows:

```
{
    "speech": "The latest price for AAPL is 140.61",
    "card": {
        "title": "AAPL",
        "text": "The latest price for Apple (AAPL) is $140.61.",
        "img": "https://fakebot.ngrok.io/img/d5fa618b"
    },
    "directives": [
        {
            "type": "render",
            "template": "single_image_template",
            "param": {
                "title": "AAPL",
                "subtitle": "Apple Corp.",
                "img": "https://fakebot.ngrok.io/img/
                largequoteaapl"
            }
        }
    ]
}
```

The great thing about directives is that they are declarative; it is up to the device to determine what to do with them. The Echo Show and Echo Spot devices, for example, may render templates in a slightly different but consistent manner. The Echo and Echo Dot might ignore or raise an error in the case that they receive an unsupported directive, such as playing a video.

Creating a New Skill

Creating a new Alexa skill requires having access to an Amazon developer account for skill registration and an Amazon Web Services (AWS) account to host the skill code. To get started, navigate to `https://developer.amazon.com` and click the *Developer Console* link. If you have an account, sign into it. Otherwise, click *Create your Amazon Developer Account.* We will be asked for an e-mail and a password, our contact information, and a developer or company name; we will also need to accept the app distribution agreement and to answer a couple of questions about whether our skill will accept payments or display ads. We can leave both answers selected as *No* to those last two questions. At this point, we will be taken to the dashboard (Figure 14-1).

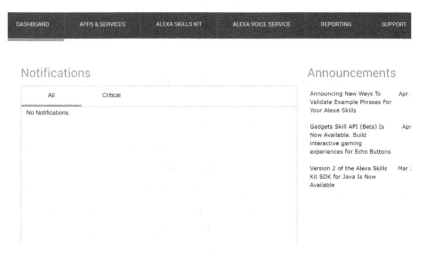

Figure 14-1. *Not much on this dashboard*

Click the Alexa Skills Kit header item. We will now be placed in the Alexa Skills Kit Developer Console, with an empty list of skills. After clicking Create Skill, we must enter a skill name. After that, we must select a model to add to the skill. There are a few types of skills with prebuilt natural

595

language models to choose from, but for this case we choose to build our own models, so we select the Custom skill.[1] After selecting the Custom type, click the Create Skill button. We are now met with the skill dashboard (Figure 14-2). The dashboard includes the ability to create the skill's language models, as well as configure, test, and even publish the skill.

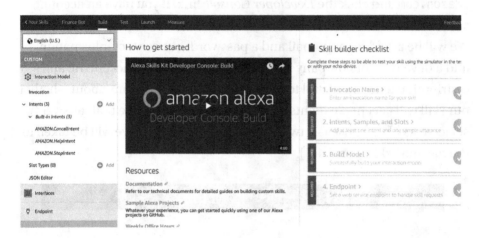

Figure 14-2. *New custom skill dashboard*

There is a convenient *Skill builder checklist* area on the right side of the page that we will follow. We will begin by setting our skill's invocation name. This is the phrase used to identify the skill when users want to invoke it on their Alexa device. For example, in the "Alexa, ask Finance Bot to quote Apple" utterance, *Finance Bot* is the invocation name. Clicking the *Invocation Name* checklist item loads the screen to set this up (Figure 14-3). After entering the name, click *Save Model*.

---

[1]Understanding the Different Types of Alexa Skills: `https://developer.amazon.com/docs/ask-overviews/understanding-the-different-types-of-skills.html`

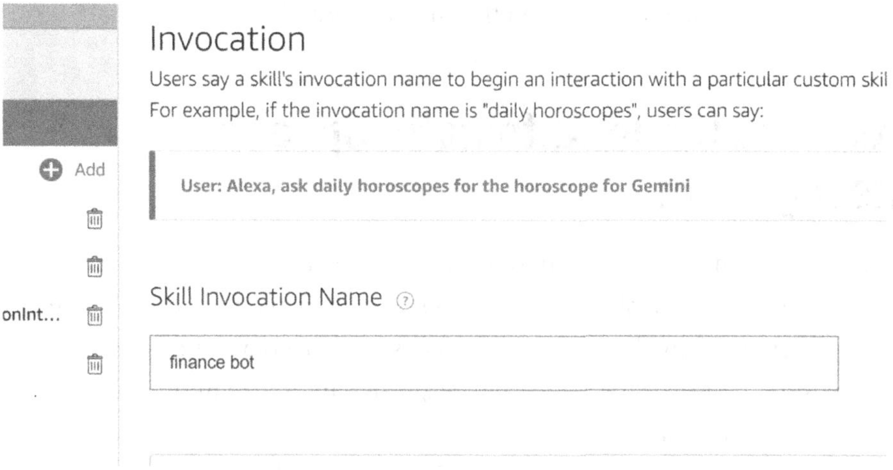

Invocation

Users say a skill's invocation name to begin an interaction with a particular custom skil
For example, if the invocation name is "daily horoscopes", users can say:

⊕ Add

🗑

🗑

onInt...   🗑

🗑

> User: Alexa, ask daily horoscopes for the horoscope for Gemini

Skill Invocation Name ⑦

finance bot

Figure 14-3. *Setting up a skill invocation name*

Before we jump into setting up our natural language model, or
interaction model, we need to enable the right interfaces. Recall that
we spoke about the ability to send directives to the device such as to
play audio files or render a user interface element. We have to explicitly
enable those features in our skill. Click the *Interfaces* link on the left-side
navigation pane. Within this UI, enable *Audio Player, Display Interface*,
and *Video App* (Figure 14-4). We will experiment with all of these in our
chapter exercises.

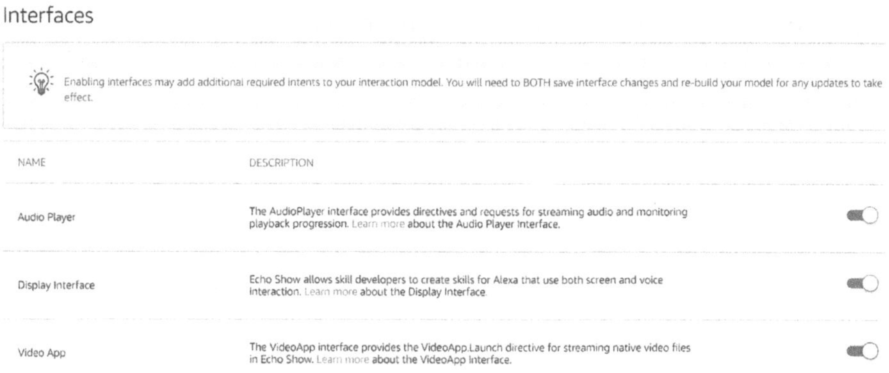

Interfaces

🔅 Enabling interfaces may add additional required intents to your interaction model. You will need to BOTH save interface changes and re-build your model for any updates to take
effect.

NAME	DESCRIPTION	
Audio Player	The AudioPlayer interface provides directives and requests for streaming audio and monitoring playback progression. Learn more about the Audio Player Interface.	◉○
Display Interface	Echo Show allows skill developers to create skills for Alexa that use both screen and voice interaction. Learn more about the Display Interface.	◉○
Video App	The VideoApp interface provides the VideoApp.Launch directive for streaming native video files in Echo Show. Learn more about the VideoApp Interface.	◉○

Figure 14-4. *Enabling Alexa interfaces*

We are now ready to work on the Alexa interaction model.

Alexa NLU and Automatic Speech Recognition

You may have noticed that when we first created the skill, we had three built-in intents in our skill's model. These are displayed on the left-side pane. After enabling the various interfaces, we now have about 16 intents. As the Alexa system adds more features, more and more intents will be added to all the skills.

This highlights the first difference between the Alexa interaction model and Language Understanding Intelligent Service (LUIS), explored in depth in Chapter 3. LUIS is a general-purpose natural language understanding (NLU) platform that can be utilized in just about any natural language application. Alexa is a specific ecosystem around digital assistant devices. To create a consistent experience across all Alexa skills, Amazon provides a set of common built-in intents for all skills prefixed by *AMAZON*. (Figure 14-5). For the best user experience, our skill should implement as many of these as possible or fail gracefully if they do not apply. Amazon will review all of these during the skill review process. As an aside, we do not cover skill review and certification in this book; Amazon provides ample detailed documentation around this process.

Figure 14-5. *Built-in Alexa intents*

As if the set of 16 listed is not enough, Amazon provides a total of 133 built-in intents for our skills to take advantage of. It is useful for us to become familiar with the set provided by Amazon, as the list continues evolving independent of our skills. Of course, writing a custom skill implies adding custom intents. As we create a finance bot skill, we will create a quote intent that will allow us to get a quote either for a company or for a symbol. To add a new custom intent, click the Add button next to the Intents header on the left. Select the *Create custom intent* checkbox, enter the name, and click the *Create custom intent* button (Figure 14-6).

Figure 14-6. *Adding the QuoteIntent custom intent*

We are taken to the Intents screen where we can enter sample utterances (Figure 14-7). Note that the intent is added on the left-side pane and there is a trash button next to it should we choose to remove the intent from our model.

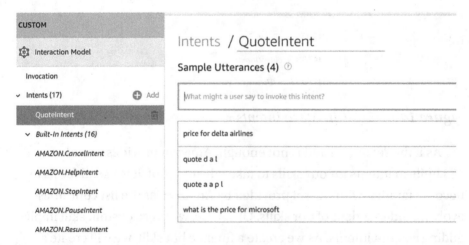

Figure 14-7. *Populating sample utterance for QuoteIntent*

Next, we need to be able to extract the name of the company or symbol that we want to get a quote for. In LUIS we would create a new entity for this purpose; in the Alexa world, this is known as a *slot*. We will create a custom slot type called *QuoteItem* and give it a few examples of company names or symbols. We first add a new slot type by clicking the Add button next to the Slot Types header in the left pane (Figure 14-8). Note that there are 96 built-in slot types! Those include everything from dates and numbers to actors, sports, and even video games. There is a Corporation slot type that could fit our purpose, but we choose to proceed with a custom slot type as an exercise. Select the *Create custom slot type* radio button, enter a name, and click the *Create custom slot type* button.

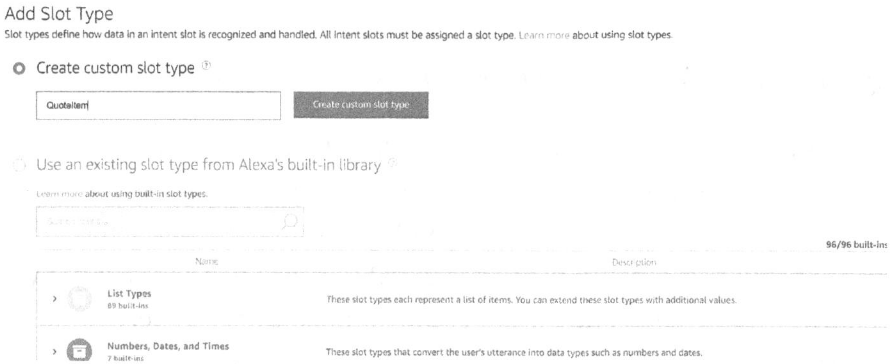

Add Slot Type

Slot types define how data in an intent slot is recognized and handled. All intent slots must be assigned a slot type. Learn more about using slot types.

○ Create custom slot type ⑦

| QuoteItem | | Create custom slot type |

⦿ Use an existing slot type from Alexa's built-in library ⑦

Learn more about using built-in slot types.

96/96 built-ins

Name		Description
> ○	List Types 89 built-ins	These slot types each represent a list of items. You can extend these slot types with additional values.
> 🗊	Numbers, Dates, and Times 7 built-ins	These slot types that convert the user's utterance into data types such as numbers and dates.

Figure 14-8. *Adding a new slot type*

Next, we enter the various values for the *QuoteItem* slot type (Figure 14-9).

Slot Types / QuoteItem

Slot Values (9) ⑦   Search

Enter a new value for this slot type

VALUE ⑦	ID (OPTIONAL) ⑦	SYNONYMS (OPTIONAL) ⑦	
royal caribbean	Enter ID	Add synonym	+
united airlines	Enter ID	Add synonym	+
d a l	Enter ID	Add synonym	+
t w t r	Enter ID	Add synonym	+
a a p l	Enter ID	Add synonym	+
delta airlines	Enter ID	Add synonym	+
apple	Enter ID	Add synonym	+

Figure 14-9. *Adding new values to a custom slot type*

This is a limited set, of course, but it will do for now. The universe
of company names and ticker symbols is quite large, and we are not
expecting to enter all of them in the sample slot values. However, the
more examples we provide, the better the NLU engine will be at correctly
identifying *QuoteItems,* and the better the Automatic Speech Recognition
(ASR) engine will be. The reason for this latter point is that speech
recognition systems such as Alexa, Google Home, and Microsoft's Cortana
can all be primed with different utterances. Priming is an important step
in the ASR process as it gives clear hints to the engine about the skill's
vocabulary. This allows the ASR system to understand context and better
transcribe users' utterances.

Let's go back into the QuoteIntent. In Alexa's NLU, we must explicitly
add slot types to intents. Below the sample utterances, the intent user
interface lets us add slots. Give the slot a name and click the + button.
Now, we are able to assign a slot type (Figure 14-10).

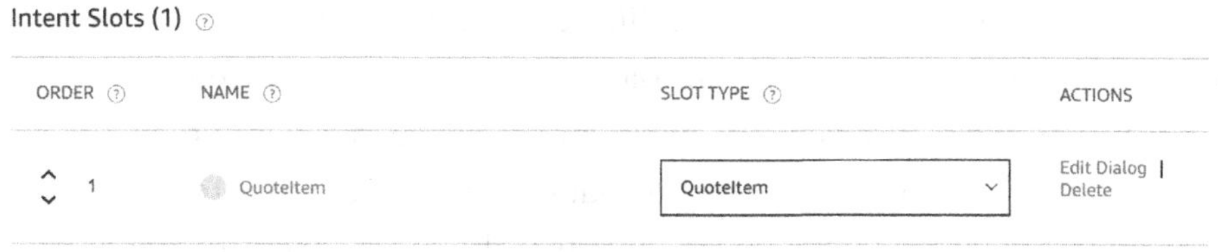

Intent Slots (1) ⑦

ORDER ⑦	NAME ⑦	SLOT TYPE ⑦	ACTIONS
⌃ 1 ⌄	🔲 QuoteItem	QuoteItem ⌄	Edit Dialog | Delete

Figure 14-10. *Adding the QuoteItem slot type to QuoteIntent*

Finally, we must correctly label the slot in each utterance. We can do this by selecting a word or set of consecutive words in the sample utterance interface. We will see a pop-up with the intent slots you can assign to the selected substring. After choosing QuoteItem for each one, our QuoteIntent will look like Figure 14-11.

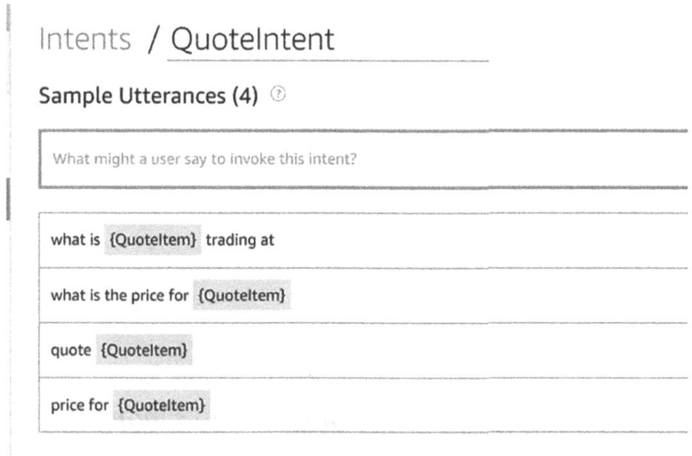

Intents / QuoteIntent
_____

Sample Utterances (4) ⑦

> What might a user say to invoke this intent?

what is {QuoteItem} trading at

what is the price for {QuoteItem}

quote {QuoteItem}

price for {QuoteItem}

Figure 14-11. *The QuoteIntent is now ready*

We will add one more intent. We want the ability to ask for information about specific account types using utterances like "get information for 401k account" or "what is a roth ira?" Let's call this intent *GetAccountTypeInfoIntent*. Before we create the intent, let's create the supporting slot type. In the same way that we added the QuoteItem slot type, let's add an AccountType custom slot type.

Once it's created, enter a set of different account types and different ways of expressing them. For example, 401k can also be referred to as 401(k). Note, we also specify the word spelling of each account type (Figure 14-12). The reason for this is that the ASR system may transcribe user input as words, not numbers. Note that the set of account types will most likely be a closed set for our application, so this presents a different use case from the open concept of a QuoteItem in our QuoteIntent.

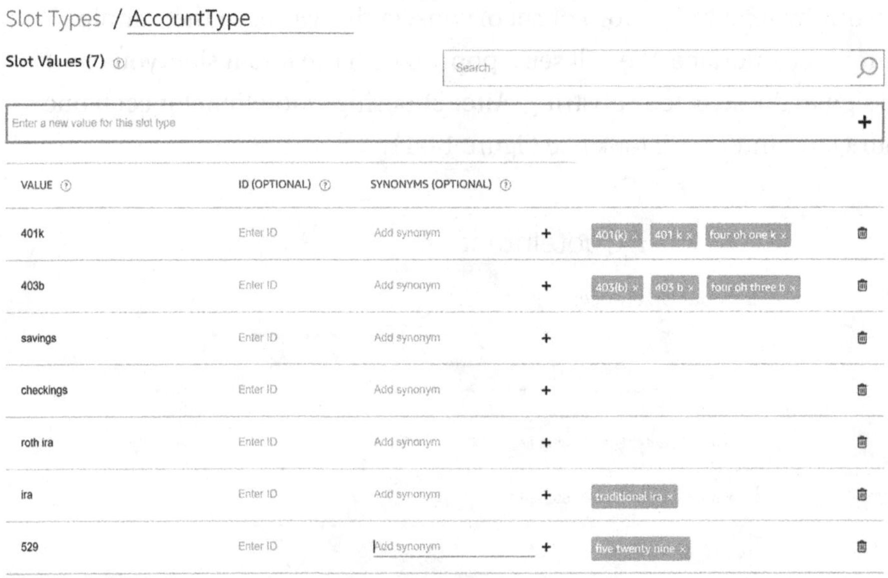

Slot Types / AccountType

Slot Values (7) ⑦

VALUE ⑦	ID (OPTIONAL) ⑦	SYNONYMS (OPTIONAL) ⑦		
401k	Enter ID	Add synonym	+	401(k) ×	401 k ×	four oh one k ×
403b	Enter ID	Add synonym	+	403(b) ×	403 b ×	four oh three b ×
savings	Enter ID	Add synonym	+	
checkings	Enter ID	Add synonym	+	
roth ira	Enter ID	Add synonym	+	
ira	Enter ID	Add synonym	+	traditional ira ×
529	Enter ID	Add synonym	+	five twenty nine ×

Figure 14-12. Creating a custom slot type with synonyms

Now we can create a new custom intent called
GetAccountTypeInformationIntent. Add the AccountType as an intent
slot. Then we can enter some sample utterances. The result is found in
Figure 14-13.

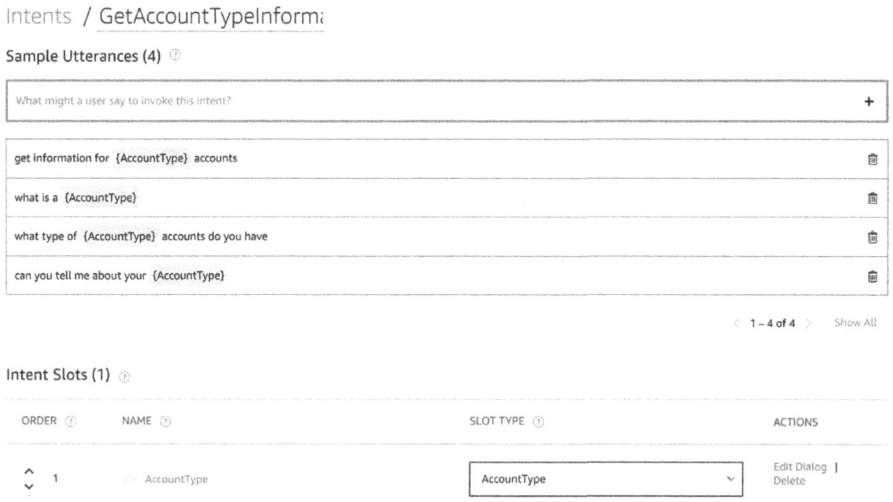

Intents / GetAccountTypeInform;

Sample Utterances (4) ⓘ

What might a user say to invoke this intent?	+

get information for {AccountType} accounts	🗑
what is a {AccountType}	🗑
what type of {AccountType} accounts do you have	🗑
can you tell me about your {AccountType}	🗑

< 1 – 4 of 4 >   Show All

Intent Slots (1) ⓘ

ORDER ⓘ	NAME ⓘ	SLOT TYPE ⓘ	ACTIONS
⌃⌄ 1	AccountType	AccountType ⌄	Edit Dialog | Delete

Figure 14-13. *Finalized GetAccountTypeInformationIntent*

At this point, we have finished the first draft of our interaction model.
Click the Save Model button, followed by the Build Model button. Building
the model will utilize all the data we have provided to train the system.
Note that at any point we can see the model JSON format using the JSON
Editor link in the left pane. The JSON encapsulates everything that was
added to the model. Figure 14-14 shows an excerpt of it. The easiest way
to share a model is to share this JSON content. Of course, there are also
command-line tools to further automate this process.

```
 67            "name": "AMAZON.ScrollUpIntent",
 68            "samples": []
 69        },
 70        {
 71            "name": "QuoteIntent",
 72            "slots": [
 73                {
 74                    "name": "QuoteItem",
 75                    "type": "QuoteItem"
 76                }
 77            ],
 78            "samples": [
 79                "what is {QuoteItem} trading at",
 80                "what is the price for {QuoteItem}",
 81                "quote {QuoteItem}",
 82                "price for {QuoteItem}"
 83            ]
 84        },
 85        {
 86            "name": "GetAccountTypeInformationIntent",
 87            "slots": [
 88                {
 89                    "name": "AccountType",
 90                    "type": "AccountType"
 91                }
 92            ],
 93            "samples": [
 94                "get information for {AccountType} accounts",
 95                "what is a {AccountType}",
 96                "what type of {AccountType} accounts do you have",
 97                "can you tell me about your {AccountType}"
 98            ]
 99        }
100    ],
101    "types": [
102        {
103            "name": "QuoteItem",
104            "values": [
105                {
106                    "name": {
107                        "value": "royal caribbean"
108                    }
109                },
110                {
111                    "name": {
112                        "value": "united"
```

Figure 14-14. *An excerpt of the Alexa interaction model we just created*

For the purposes of this chapter, this is all we will cover about Alexa's NLU. To be clear, we did not do it justice. The system is rich and worth learning about.

Diving Into Alexa Skills Kit for Node

Back in the dashboard, the last step in the *Skill builder checklist* is to set up the endpoint. The endpoint is the code that will receive the incoming messages from Amazon and respond with speech, cards, and directives.

There are two approaches we can take here. First, we can host an endpoint ourselves, give Amazon the URL, parse each request, and respond accordingly. Using this approach, we gain control but must implement the verification and parsing logic ourselves. We would also own the deployment tasks.

The second alternative, which is quite common these days, is to use serverless computing.[2] This gives us the ability to create bits of code in the cloud that run and scale according to demand. On AWS, this is Lambda. In Azure, the equivalent would be Functions. Amazon provides the Amazon Alexa Skills Kit SDK for Node.js for this very purpose (`https://github.com/alexa/alexa-skills-kit-sdk-for-nodejs`). In this section, we dive into running Alexa Skills on AWS Lambda.

The structure of a skill built using the Alexa Skills Kit SDK is shown next. We register all the intents we want to handle in the code. The emit function sends responses to Alexa. There are many different overloads of emit documented on the SDK's GitHub site.[3]

```
const handlers = {
    'LaunchRequest': function () {
        this.emit('HelloWorldIntent');
    },
```

---

[2]What Serverless Computing Really Means:`https://www.infoworld.com/article/3093508/cloud-computing/what-serverless-computing-really-means.html`

[3]Alexa Skill Kit for Node.js: Response vs. ResponseBuilder: `https://github.com/alexa/alexa-skills-kit-sdk-for-nodejs#response-vs-responsebuilder`

```
    'HelloWorldIntent': function () {
        this.emit(':tell', 'Hello World!');
    }
};
```

Finally, we register the skill and handlers with the Alexa SDK.

```
const Alexa = require('alexa-sdk');

exports.handler = function(event, context, callback) {
    const alexa = Alexa.handler(event, context, callback);
    alexa.registerHandlers(handlers);
    alexa.execute();
};
```

This code is sufficient to run a basic skill that responds with "hello world" when launched or when the *HelloWorldIntent* intent is matched. Conceptually, we will follow the same approach when creating the code for our financial skill. Before we continue, though, how do we connect our skill to an AWS Lambda?

First, we will need to have an AWS account. We can create an AWS free tier account here: `https://aws.amazon.com/free/`. The free tier is a perfect way to get started and become familiar with AWS. Click Create Free Account. We will be asked for an e-mail address, a password, and an AWS account name (Figure 14-15).

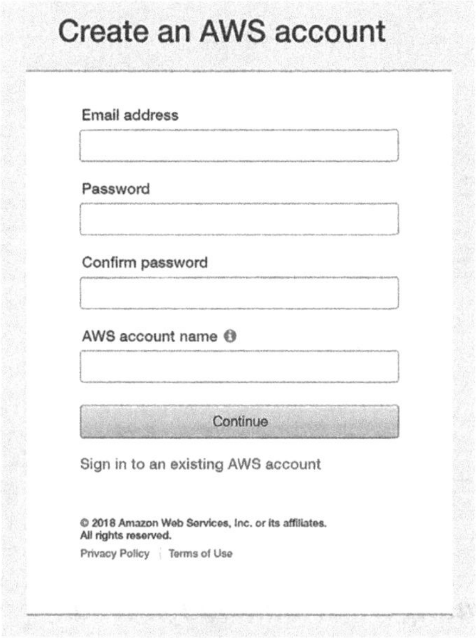

Figure 14-15. *Creating a new AWS account*

Next, we will enter our personal contact information. We will need to enter our payment information for *identity verification purposes* (you will not be charged while in the free tier) and verify our phone number. Once completed, we will be taken to the AWS Management Console. At this point, we can find Lambda in the "All services" list and navigate to it.

Now we can start creating a Lambda function. Click "Create a function," select Blueprints, find and select the alexa-skill-kit-sdk-factskill, and click the Configure button. We give the function a name unique to our account's function list, set Role to *Create new role from template(s)*, give the role a name, and select the *Simple Microservice permissions* template (Figure 14-16).

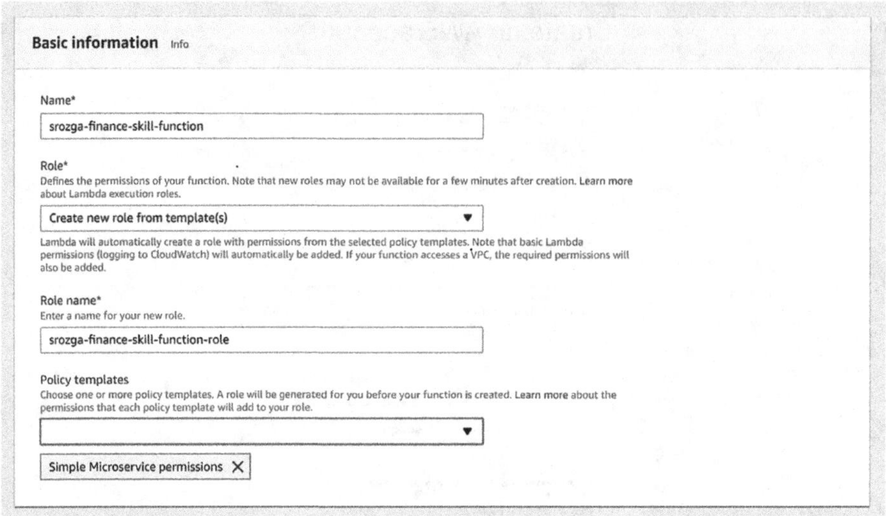

Figure 14-16. *Creating a new Lambda function*

Below the data entry fields, we will see our Lambda code. The runtime should be set to Node.js 6.10, though it is safe to assume Amazon may update this any time. We leave the code as is for now. After clicking the *Create Function* button, you will be taken to the function configuration screen (Figure 14-17).

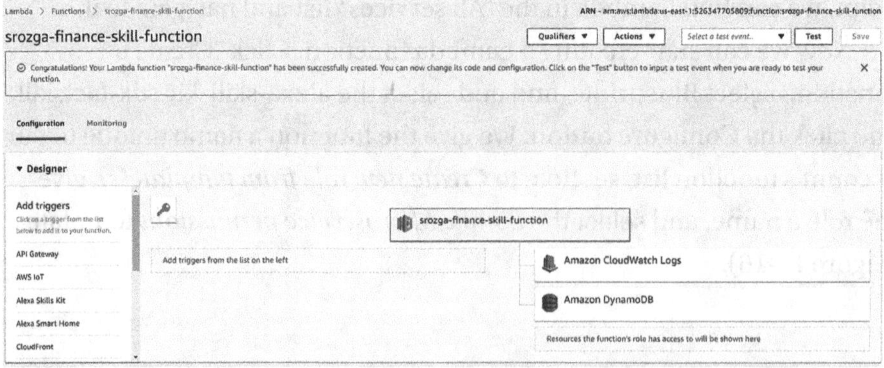

Figure 14-17. *Function configuration screen*

There are many actions we can perform on this screen. First, the top right shows the Lambda identifier. We will need to present this to the Alexa skill momentarily. We also see that the function has access to CloudWatch logs (all Lambda logs are sent to CloudWatch) and DynamoDB, Amazon's managed cloud NoSQL database. Alexa skills can use DynamoDB to store skill state.

In the Designer section, we need to set a trigger that can invoke our new function. For our purposes, find and click the Alexa Skills Kit trigger. Once you do so, a Configure Triggers section will appear below. Enter the skill ID from the Alexa Skill dashboard. It should look like *amzn1.ask. skill.5d364108-7906-4612-a465-9f560b0bc16f*. Once you have entered the ID, click *Add* for the trigger and then save the function configuration. At this point, the Lambda function is ready to be called from our skill.

Before we do so, we select the function in the Designer (in this case, srozga-finance-skill-function as per Figure 14-17); we will be greeted with the code editor. We have a few different options of how code is loaded into Lambda. One option is to write the code manually in the editor; another option is to upload a zip with all the code. Doing this manual labor in a real application gets tiring very quickly; you can utilize the AWS[4] and ASK CLI[5] to deploy a skill from the command line. For now, we will simply use the editor. Replace the code in the editor with the following:

```
'use strict';

const Alexa = require('alexa-sdk');
const handlers = {
    'LaunchRequest': function () {
        this.emit(':tell', 'Welcome!');
    },
```

---

[4]AWS CLI: https://aws.amazon.com/cli/

[5]Alexa Skills Kit (ASK) CLI: https://developer.amazon.com/docs/smapi/quick-start-alexa-skills-kit-command-line-interface.html

```
    'QuoteIntent': function () {
        this.emit(':tell', 'Quote by company.');
    },
    'GetAccountTypeInformationIntent': function () {
        this.emit(':tell', 'Getting account type.');
    }
};

exports.handler = function (event, context, callback) {
    const alexa = Alexa.handler(event, context, callback);
    alexa.registerHandlers(handlers);
    alexa.execute();
};
```

Before we leave, copy the Lambda function's Amazon Resource Name (ARN) from the top-right area of the screen. The identifier looks like this: *arn:aws:lambda:us-east-1:526347705809:function:srozga-finance-skill-function.*

Let's switch back into the Alexa Skill configuration screen for our skill. Select the Endpoint link in the right-side pane. Select the *AWS Lambda ARN* checkbox and enter the Lambda ARN in the Default Region text box (Figure 14-18).

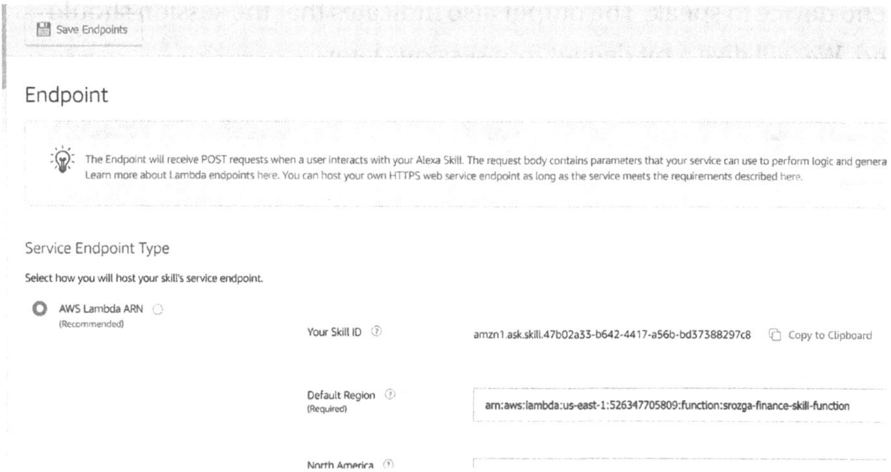

Figure 14-18. *Alexa skill Lambda ARN endpoint configuration*

Click the Save Endpoints button. If there are issues here, you may not have correctly added the Alexa Skills Kit trigger for the Lambda function.

At this point we can navigate into the Test section, using the top navigation panel. By default, the skill is not enabled for test. Toggle the checkbox. Now, we can test the skill from the Alexa test interface, any Echo device connected to the developer account, or third-party tools such as EchoSim.[6] You may be prompted to allow microphone access if you want to speak to the test application.

We can send input utterances by either speaking or typing, and we will receive our lambda function's response, as shown in Figure 14-19. Make sure to preface your utterances with "Ask {Invocation Name}." Note that this interface presents the raw input and output JSON content. Take some time to examine it; it contains a lot of information we covered earlier in the chapter. For example, the incoming request includes the resolved intent and slots from our interaction model. The output contains SSML for the

---

[6]EchoSim is a browser-based interface to Alexa. It helps in testing development skills. As the Alexa test tool has improved substantially in recent months, it remains to be seen how effective of a tool EchoSim will be; see `https://echosim.io`.

Echo device to speak. The output also indicates that the session should end. We will dive a bit deeper into sessions later.

Figure 14-19. *Success!*

Now that we see the incoming JSON and the slot format, we can extend the code to extract the slot values. In the context of an intent handler, the *this.event.request* object contains the resolved intent and slot values. From there, it's simply a matter of extracting the values and doing something with them. The following code extracts the slot values and includes them in the Alexa voice response:

```
'use strict';

const Alexa = require('alexa-sdk');
const handlers = {
    'LaunchRequest': function () {
        this.emit(':tell', 'Welcome!');
    },
    'QuoteIntent': function () {
        console.log(JSON.stringify(this.event));
        let intent = this.event.request.intent;
        let quoteitem = intent.slots['QuoteItem'].value;
```

```
        this.emit(':tell', 'Quote for ' + quoteitem);
    },
    'GetAccountTypeInformationIntent': function () {
        console.log(JSON.stringify(this.event));
        let intent = this.event.request.intent;
        let accountType = intent.slots['AccountType'].value;
        this.emit(':tell', 'Getting information for account
        type ' + accountType);
    }
};

exports.handler = function (event, context, callback) {
    const alexa = Alexa.handler(event, context, callback);
    alexa.registerHandlers(handlers);
    alexa.execute();
};
```

A sample interaction with input "ask finance bot what is an ira" is presented in Figure 14-20. If you speak the utterance, it will come through as "ask finance bot what is an I R A." Make sure "I R A" is one of the synonyms for the IRA account type slot type.

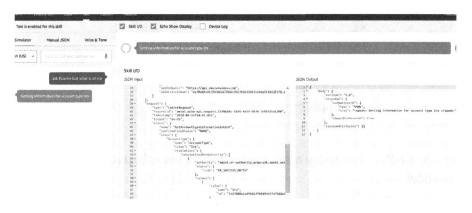

Figure 14-20. *Successfully extracting AccountType slot values from Alexa request*

Note that if we send the skill something that the built-in Amazon intents should handle, as perhaps "cancel," the skill might return an error. The reason for this is that we do not yet handle some of those built-in intents. In addition, we do not include unhandled intent logic. We can easily handle both cases by adding the following handlers:

```
'AMAZON.CancelIntent': function() {
    this.emit(':tell', 'Ok. Bye.');
},
'Unhandled': function() {
    this.emit(':tell', "I'm not sure what you are talking
    about.");
}
```

Now, telling the skill "cancel" results in a good-bye message (Figure 14-21).

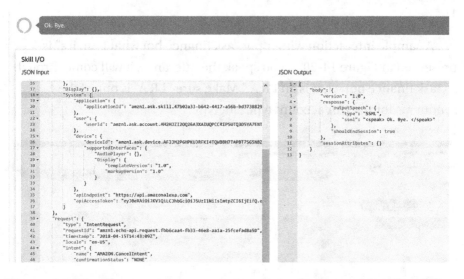

Figure 14-21. *The sassy message we promised when asking the skill to cancel*

Great. This works well, but how do we model a dialog into an Alexa Skill? The SDK for Node.js includes the concept of state. Think of it as the user's current dialog. For each state, we provide a set of handlers for each intent supported by that state. Essentially, we are encoding a dialog graph by using a set of state names and handlers. The code for this skill follows:

```
'use strict';

const Alexa = require('alexa-sdk');
const defaultHandlers = {
    'LaunchRequest': function () {
        this.emit(':ask', 'Welcome to finance skill!  I can get
        your information about quotes or account types.', 'What
        can I help you with?');
    },
    'GetAccountTypeInformationIntent': function () {
        this.handler.state = 'AccountInfo';
        this.emitWithState(this.event.request.intent.name);
    },
    'QuoteIntent': function () {
        this.handler.state = 'Quote';
        this.emitWithState(this.event.request.intent.name);
    },
    'AMAZON.CancelIntent': function () {
        this.emit(':tell', 'Ok. Bye.');
    },
    'Unhandled': function () {
        console.log(JSON.stringify(this.event));
        this.emit(':ask', "I'm not sure what you are talking
        about.", 'What can I help you with?');
    }
};
```

```
const quoteStateHandlers = Alexa.CreateStateHandler('Quote', {
    'LaunchRequest': function () {
        this.handler.state = '';
        this.emitWithState('LaunchRequest');
    },
    'AMAZON.MoreIntent': function () {
        this.emit(':ask', 'More information for quote item ' +
        this.attributes.quoteitem, 'What else can I help you
        with?');
    },
    'AMAZON.CancelIntent': function () {
        this.handler.state = '';
        this.emitWithState(this.event.request.intent.name);
    },
    'QuoteIntent': function () {
        console.log(JSON.stringify(this.event));
        let intent = this.event.request.intent;
        let quoteitem = null;
        if (intent && intent.slots.QuoteItem) {
            quoteitem = intent.slots.QuoteItem.value;
        } else {
            quoteitem = this.attributes.quoteitem;
        }
        this.attributes.quoteitem = quoteitem;
        this.emit(':ask', 'Quote for ' + quoteitem, 'What else
        can I help you with?');
    },
    'GetAccountTypeInformationIntent': function () {
        this.handler.state = '';
        this.emitWithState(this.event.request.intent.name);
    },
```

```
    'Unhandled': function () {
        console.log(JSON.stringify(this.event));
        this.emit(':ask', "I'm not sure what you are talking
        about.", 'What can I help you with?');
    }
});

const accountInfoStateHandlers =
Alexa.CreateStateHandler('AccountInfo', {
    'LaunchRequest': function () {
        this.handler.state = '';
        this.emitWithState('LaunchRequest');
    },
    'AMAZON.MoreIntent': function () {
        this.emit(':ask', 'More information for account ' +
        this.attributes.accounttype, 'What else can I help you
        with?');
    },
    'AMAZON.CancelIntent': function () {
        this.handler.state = '';
        this.emitWithState(this.event.request.intent.name);
    },
    'GetAccountTypeInformationIntent': function () {
        console.log(JSON.stringify(this.event));
        let intent = this.event.request.intent;
        let accounttype = null;
        if (intent && intent.slots.AccountType) {
            accounttype = intent.slots.AccountType.value;
        } else {
            accounttype = this.attributes.accounttype;
        }
```

```
        this.attributes.accounttype = accounttype;
        this.emit(':ask', 'Information for ' + accounttype,
        'What else can I help you with?');
    },
    'QuoteIntent': function () {
        this.handler.state = '';
        this.emitWithState(this.event.request.intent.name);
    },
    'Unhandled': function () {
        console.log(JSON.stringify(this.event));
        this.emit(':ask', "I'm not sure what you are talking
        about.", 'What can I help you with?');
    }
});

exports.handler = function (event, context, callback) {
    const alexa = Alexa.handler(event, context, callback);
    alexa.registerHandlers(defaultHandlers, quoteStateHandlers,
    accountInfoStateHandlers);
    alexa.execute();
};
```

Note that this skill has two states: Quote and AccountInfo. Within the context of these states, each intent may produce different behavior. If a user asks about an account in the Quote state, the skill redirects to the default state to decide what to do with the request. Likewise, if a user asks about a quote in the AccountInfo state, similar logic happens. An illustration of the dialogs is presented in Figure 14-22. Note that in the code, we use *this.emit(':ask')* if we want to keep the session open and *this.emit(':tell')* if we simply want to speak and answer and close the session. If the session stays open, we do not have to preface each utterance to Alexa with ask finance bot." It is implicit since the session between the user and our skill stays open.[7] There is another way to build responses by utilizing the ResponseBuilder. We can read about it in SDK documentation, and we will use it in Exercise 14-1 to build responses with render template directives.

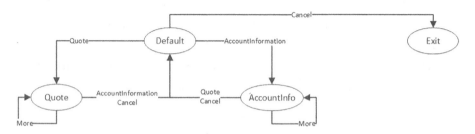

Figure 14-22. *An illustration of the dialogs and transitions in our skill*

Go ahead and run this sample to gain familiarity with the ideas behind the flow. Of importance is that we take advantage of two fields for state storage: *this.handler.state* for the name of the current state and *this.attributes*, which acts as a user conversation data store. Think of *this. attributes* as the *privateConversationData* dictionary in Bot Builder. These values are not persisted when a session ends by default, but the Alexa Skills Kit for Node.js supports DynamoDB integration for state storage. This would enable our skill to continue an interaction with a user whenever they invoke the skill again.

Other Options

We conveniently ignored a few other options along the way. The skill developer console for our skill contains the Account Linking and Permissions links. Account linking is the process of redirecting the user to

---

[7]Alexa sessions are an interesting topic that deserves more examination. More information can be found online at `https:// developer.amazon.com/alexa-skills-kit/big-nerd-ranch/ alexa-voice-user-interfaces-and-sessions`.

an authorization experience via an OAuth flow managed by Alexa. Alexa stores the tokens and sends them to our endpoint as part of each request. Part of the reason this is managed in this manner is that the original Echo did not have a screen. As an affordance, authorization is conducted through the Alexa mobile app, so the Alexa servers need to own the entire OAuth flow.

The Permissions screen lets us request access to certain data on the user's device such as the device address or Alexa shopping lists (Figure 14-23).

Request users to access resources and capabilities. ☉   **Device Address**

○ Full Address ☉

○ Country & Postal Code Only ☉

Lists Read ☉

Lists Write ☉

Figure 14-23. *The Alexa Permissions screen*

You can find more information on both topics in the Alexa documentation.[8]

EXERCISE 14-1

Connecting to Real Data and Rendering Imagery

In Chapter 11 we integrated with a service called Intrinio to fetch financial data and render it in an image. The goal of this exercise is to connect your Alexa Skill code to the same service and render the image on screen-enabled Echo devices.

---

[8]Account Linking Documentation: https://developer.amazon.com/docs/ custom-skills/link-an-alexa-user-with-a-user-in-your-system.html. Using the Device Address API: https://developer.amazon.com/docs/custom-skills/device-address-api.html. Working with Alexa's To Do and Shopping Lists: https://developer.amazon.com/docs/custom-skills/access-the-alexa-shopping-and-to-do-lists.html.

1. Use the code in the previous section as a starting point. Revisit
    the code from Chapter 11 and ensure that your quote state
    QuoteIntent handler retrieves quote data from Intrinio and
    responds with the latest price in voice.

2. Integrate Chapter 11's HTML-to-image generation code into
    your Alexa skill. Remember to add the necessary packages into
    the `package.json` file in the Lambda function.

3. Visit `https://developer.amazon.com/docs/custom-`
    `skills/display-interface-reference.html` to get
    familiar with how to render display templates. Specifically, you
    will be using BodyTemplate[7] to render the image generated in
    the previous step.

4. To render the template using the Node.js SDK for Alexa Skills
    Kit you will need to utilize the response builder (`https://`
    `github.com/alexa/alexa-skills-kit-sdk-for-`
    `nodejs#response-vs-responsebuilder`). The SDK
    has helpers to generate the template JSON (`https://`
    `github.com/alexa/alexa-skills-kit-sdk-for-`
    `nodejs#display-interface`).

5. Test the functionality in the Alexa Test utility, EchoSim, and, if
    available, real Echo devices. What is the behavior of the code in
    a device without a display?

Your skill should now be rendering your financial quote image on display-
enabled Echo devices, and you should have gained hands-on experience
testing an Alexa skill using several methods.

Connecting to Bot Framework

The features we have presented thus far are just a fraction of the Alexa Skills Kit capabilities but are sufficient to gain an appreciation for applying this book's concepts to emerging voice platforms. The process of connecting an Alexa skill to a Bot Framework bot follows a recipe similar to our voice bot implementation for Twilio in Chapter 8. We will show code on how to accomplish this connection given our existing Alexa Skills Kit interaction model. Before we dive into the code, we will discuss several implementation decisions for our solution.

Implementation Decisions Around Bot Framework and Alexa Skills Kit Integration

Typically, we do not suggest that a stand-alone Alexa skill be implemented by using the Bot Framework. If the requirements truly suggest a single platform, staying within the confines of an Alexa interaction model and the Alexa Skills Kit SDK for Node.js running on an AWS Lambda function is sufficient. In the case that our product should support multiple natural language text and voice interfaces, we may want to consider one platform to run our business logic, and the Bot Framework lends itself well to this approach. Once we start down the path of connecting an Alexa skill to the Bot Framework, several important implementation decisions follow. These apply to all types of systems, not just Alexa.

Natural Language Understanding

In the context of our current effort, which NLU platform should we utilize: LUIS or Alexa's interaction model? If we were to use Alexa's interaction model, we would have to pass the Alexa intent and slot objects through Direct Line calls into our bot implementation. We could then build a custom recognizer that detects this object's existence and translates it to the correct intent and entity response object in the Bot Builder SDK. To make it very clear, this is where the utility of recognizers shines: the bot doesn't care where the intent data comes from.

On the other hand, if we choose to utilize LUIS, we must find a way to pass raw input from Alexa into the bot. The way to achieve this is to mark the entire user input as an AMAZON.LITERAL slot type.[9] This allows developers to pass the raw user input into the skill code. This does not mean our skill interaction model becomes nonexistent. Remember, Alexa uses the interaction model for its ASR, so we want to give as many examples of utterances and input types that we expect in our skill's vocabulary. We would need to include all our LUIS utterances in the Alexa interaction model.

In general, since the bot may support more channels than Alexa, maintaining one NLU system, such as LUIS, is be a more maintainable approach. There is no way to break away completely. We still need to ensure our bot correctly handles the built-in intents, such as Stop and Cancel. In the following code sample, in the interest of expediency, we will assume the entire NLU model lives in Alexa and demonstrate a custom recognizer approach.

Channel-Agnostic vs. Channel-Specific Dialogs

When we develop one bot that handles multiple channels, we must decide whether the one dialog implementation can handle all channels or whether each channel should have its own dialog implementation. There are arguments to be made for each, although if you think in terms of the Model

---

[9]There has been much debate around the LITERAL slot type and its use. Amazon has tried to deprecate the slot type for some time now. It is easy to understand why. The natural language models and Alexa's ability to prime the Automatic Speech Recognition engine by using the models are only as good as the models' content. If some of the NLU is offloaded to a separate system, the Alexa NLU and Speech Recongition suffer. That being said, even though Amazon has espoused alternatives, the slot type has not yet been removed. See `https://developer.amazon.com/post/Tx3IHSFQSUF3RQP/ Why-a-Custom-Slot-is-the-Literal-Solution`.

View Controller (MVC) pattern,[10] we can come up with an elegant solution. If we consider a dialog to be the controller and the APIs we talk to the model, then we are left with the question of what takes on the role of the view.

We want to create separate pieces of code that can render messages based on the channel. Although the bot service attempts to abstract the channel, we will run into channel-specific behavior at one point or another. For example, we will treat Alexa differently from a text channel. One approach is to create a default view renderer that is used in the dialog with the addition of channel-specific view renderers to support behavior or imagery that diverges from the default. A more generic approach is to simply have different view renderers for voice versus text channels. Figure 14-24 shows a sample flow of this approach in the case of a message from a voice channel.

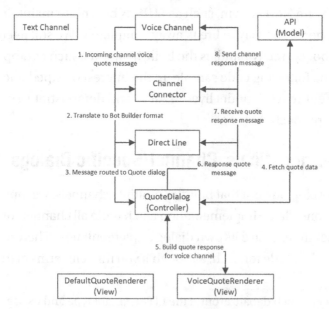

Figure 14-24. *A sample flow of a message incoming from a voice channel such as Alexa and its flow through our system all the way to the view renderers*

---

[10]Model View Controller: https://en.wikipedia.org/wiki/Model%E2%80%93view%E2%80%93controller

Alexa Constructs

The Bot Builder SDK abstracts the concept of a text conversation well, but mapping the concepts directly to Alexa is nontrivial. A couple of examples come to mind.

First, when a speech utterance is sent to the Alexa service, it may include an initial speech string plus a re-prompt speech string. The re-prompt is spoken to the user if Alexa poses a question, and the user does not respond in time. Bot Builder activities contain a property for speech but not for re-prompt. In our sample code, we leverage the custom Channel Data field to send this information.

A second example is the Alexa render templates. Although we are not covering them here, Alexa supports a number (seven by the latest count) of templates to display content on display-enabled Echo devices. Each template is a different JSON structure representing a user interface. Although we could try to come up with a way to utilize the hero card objects to communicate these templates to a connector, it is simpler to generate the JSON in a renderer and send in the channel data. Instructing the Echo device to play a video presents a similar dilemma.

A solution to all these problems is to try to render as much as possible using the Bot Builder SDK objects and drop to channel data only when necessary. As illustrated in Figure 14-24, we could even utilize the Bot Builder SDK objects and translate them to channel-specific constructs on the connector layer. In general, though, is it easier to generate the Alexa channel data for each response in an Alexa renderer.

Callback Support

Most channels can send events that have nothing to do with user messages. For example, Facebook sends events about referrals, app handover, checkouts, and payments among others. These are channel-specific messages that need to be handled in the bot, sometimes outside the structure of a dialog. Alexa is no stranger to such events. When a video or audio file is playing on an Echo device, various events about progress, interruptions, and errors are sent to the skill. It is up to our bot code to interpret those events correctly.

A good approach to this interaction is to create custom recognizers that can identify the different types of messages and then direct these messages to the right dialogs. For events that require a JSON response, the dialogs should send a payload using the channel data.

Sample Integration

Let's dig into what a sample integration would look like. We split the implementation into three components: the connector, the recognizer, and the bot. The full sample code can be found under the chapter14-alexa-skill-connector-bot folder in the book's GitHub repo.

The connector consists of an HTTP handler that Alexa will send messages to. The goal of the handler is to resolve the conversation, call the bot, wait for a response from the bot, and send the message back to Alexa. There is a bit of code here, so let's walk through it step-by-step.

The message comes into the handler. We extract the request body and the user ID. We then create an MD5 hash of the user ID. The reason for doing this is that Alexa user IDs are longer than the Bot Framework supports. A hash helps us keep the length manageable.

```
const cachedConversations = {};

exports.handler = function (req, res, next) {
    const reqContents = req.body;
    console.log('Incoming message', reqContents);

    const userId = reqContents.session.user.userId;
    const userIdHash = md5(userId);

    ...
};
```

We next either retrieve a cached conversation for that user or create a new one. Note, we store the conversations in memory, so every server restart will create new Direct Line conversations. In production, we would use a persistent store using a service such as Cosmos DB or Azure Table Storage. Alexa also includes a flag that informs us whether a session has just started. In the case that we do not have a cached conversation or the session is new, we create a new Direct Line conversation and cache it.

```
const cachedConv = cachedConversations[userId];
let p = Promise.resolve(cachedConv);
if (reqContents.session.new || !cachedConv) {
    p = startConversation(process.env.DL_KEY).then(conv => {
        cachedConversations[userId] = { id: conv.
        conversationId, watermark: null, lastAccessed:
        moment().format() };
        console.log('created conversation [%s] for user [%s]
        hash [%s]', conv.conversationId, userId, userIdHash);
        return cachedConversations[userId];
    });
}

p.then(conv => {
    ...
});
```

After we retrieve the conversation, we post an activity to the bot. Note that since we decided to pass the resolved Alexa interaction model intents and slots, we simply pass the Alexa message through the channel data in the sourceEvent property.

```
postActivity(process.env.DL_KEY, conv.id, {
    from: { id: userIdHash, name: userIdHash }, // required
    (from.name is optional)
    type: 'message',
```

```
        text: '',
        sourceEvent: {
            'directline': {
                alexaMessage: reqContents
            }
        }
    }).then(() => {
        ...
    });
```

If Alexa sent a SessionEndedRequst, we automatically respond with an HTTP 200 status code.

```
if (reqContents.request.type === 'SessionEndedRequest') {
    buildAndSendSessionEnd(req, res, next);
    return;
}
function buildAndSendSessionEnd(req, res, next) {
    let responseJson =
        {
            "version": "1.0"
        };
    res.send(200, responseJson);
    next();
}
```

Otherwise, we use the Direct Line polling mechanism to try to get the activity response from the bot. We time out after six seconds. Once a response activity has been identified, we extract some Alexa-specific information from the activity and build a response to Alexa. If the message had timed out, we send back an HTTP 504 status code.

```
let timeoutAttempts = 0;
const intervalSleep = 500;
```

```
const timeoutInMs = 10000;
const maxTimeouts = timeoutInMs / intervalSleep;
const interval = setInterval(() => {

    getActivities(process.env.DL_KEY, conv.id, conv.watermark).
    then(activitiesResponse => {
        const temp = _.filter(activitiesResponse.activities,
        (m) => m.from.id !== userIdHash);
        if (temp.length > 0) {
            clearInterval(interval);
            const responseActivity = temp[0];
            console.log('Bot response:', responseActivity);

            conv.watermark = activitiesResponse.watermark;
            conv.lastAccessed = moment().format();
            const keepSessionOpen = responseActivity.
            channelData && responseActivity.channelData.
            keepSessionOpen;
            const reprompt = responseActivity.channelData &&
            responseActivity.channelData.reprompt;
            buildAndSendSpeech(responseActivity.speak,
            keepSessionOpen, reprompt, req, res, next);
        } else {
            // no-op
        }
        timeoutAttempts++;

        if (timeoutAttempts >= maxTimeouts) {
            clearInterval(interval);
            buildTimeoutResponse(req, res, next);
        }
    });
}, intervalSleep);
```

That's it! The code to build the response messages follows.

```
function buildTimeoutResponse(req, res, next) {
    res.send(504);
    next();
}

function buildAndSendSpeech(speak, keepSessionOpen, reprompt,
req, res, next) {
    let responseJson =
        {
            "version": "1.0",
            "response": {
                "outputSpeech": {
                    "type": "PlainText",
                    "text": speak
                },
                // TODO REPROMPT
                "shouldEndSession": !keepSessionOpen
            }
        };
    if (reprompt) {
        responseJson.reprompt = {
            outputSpeech: {
                type: 'PlainText',
                text: reprompt
            }
        };
    }
    console.log('Final response to Alexa:', responseJson);
    res.send(200, responseJson);
    next();
}
```

```
function buildAndSendSessionEnd(req, res, next) {
    let responseJson =
        {
            "version": "1.0"
        };
    res.send(200, responseJson);
    next();
}
```

The Direct Line functions are the same as those we showed in Chapter 9.

What happens with the message on the bot side of things? First it will hit our custom recognizer. The recognizer first ensures we are getting an Alexa message and that it is either an IntentRequest, LaunchRequest, or SessionEndedRequest request. If it is an IntentRequest, we resolve the Alexa intent and slots as the intent and entities for LUIS. As the comments note, the format of the slots object is different from the LUIS entities object. If we were to mix both NLU systems in one bot to use the same dialogs, we would have to ensure that the format is normalized. If the request is LaunchRequest or SessionEndedRequest, we simply pass through those strings as bot intents.

```
exports.recognizer = {
    recognize: function (context, done) {
        const msg = context.message;

        // we only look at directline messages that include
        additional data
        if (msg.address.channelId === 'directline' && msg.
        sourceEvent) {

            const alexaMessage = msg.sourceEvent.directline.
            alexaMessage;
```

```
// skip if no alexaMessage
if (alexaMessage) {
    if (alexaMessage.request.type ===
    'IntentRequest') {
        // Pass IntentRequest into the dialogs.
        // The odd thing is that the slots and
        entities structure is different. If we mix
        LUIS/Alexa
        // it would make sense to normalize the
        format.
        const alexaIntent = alexaMessage.request.
        intent;
        const response = {
            intent: alexaIntent.name,
            entities: alexaIntent.slots,
            score: 1.0
        };
        done(null, response);
        return;
    } else if (alexaMessage.request.type ===
    'LaunchRequest' || alexaMessage.request.type
    === 'SessionEndedRequest') {
        // LaunchRequest and SessionEndedRequest
        are simply passed through as intents
        const response = {
            intent: alexaMessage.request.type,
            score: 1.0
        };
        done(null, response);
        return;
    }
}
```

```
    }
    done(null, { score: 0 });
  }
};
```

Let's come back to the bot code. We first register our custom Alexa HTTP handler, custom recognizer, and the default response. Note our use of the custom Direct Line data. If we ask the skill something it doesn't support, the session is terminated.

```
server.post('/api/alexa', (req, res, next) => {
    alexaConnector.handler(req, res, next);
});

const bot = new builder.UniversalBot(connector, [
    session => {
        let response = 'Sorry, I am not sure how to help you on
        this one. Please try again.';
        let msg = new builder.Message(session).text(response).
        speak(response).sourceEvent({
            directline: {
                keepSessionOpen: false
            }
        });
        session.send(msg);
    }
]);

bot.recognizer(alexaRecognizer);
```

Next, we create the QuoteDialog dialog. Note the following:

- It reads the quote item from the entities as our Alexa skill code did.

- It sends a response via the speak property but also includes a reprompt in the custom Direct Line channel data.

- Within the context of this dialog, if the bot detects the AMAZON.MoreIntent, the MoreQuoteDialog dialog is invoked.

- After the MoreQuoteDialog dialog executes, it yields control back to QuoteDialog.

```javascript
bot.dialog('QuoteDialog', [
    (session, args) => {
        let quoteitem = args.intent.entities.QuoteItem.value;
        session.privateConversationData.quoteitem = quoteitem;

        let response = 'Looking up quote for ' + quoteitem;
        let reprompt = 'What else can I help you with?';
        let msg = new builder.Message(session).text(response).
        speak(response).sourceEvent({
            directline: {
                reprompt: reprompt,
                keepSessionOpen: true
            }
        });
        session.send(msg);
    }
])
    .triggerAction({ matches: 'QuoteIntent' })
    .beginDialogAction('moreQuoteAction', 'MoreQuoteDialog', {
    matches: 'AMAZON.MoreIntent' });

bot.dialog('MoreQuoteDialog', session => {
    let quoteitem = session.privateConversationData.quoteitem;
    let response = 'Getting more quote information for ' +
    quoteitem;
    let reprompt = 'What else can I help you with?';
```

```
    let msg = new builder.Message(session).text(response).
    speak(response).sourceEvent({
        directline: {
            reprompt: reprompt,
            keepSessionOpen: true
        }
    });
    session.send(msg);
    session.endDialog();
});
```

The same pattern is repeated for the
GetAccountTypeInformationIntent intent. Lastly, we add some handlers to
support things such as canceling the skill and handling the LaunchRequest
and SessionEndedRequest events.

```
bot.dialog('CloseSession', session => {
    let response = 'Ok. Good bye.';
    let msg = new builder.Message(session).text(response).
    speak(response).sourceEvent({
        directline: {
            keepSessionOpen: false
        }
    });
    session.send(msg);
    session.endDialog();
}).triggerAction({ matches: 'AMAZON.CancelIntent' });

bot.dialog('EndSession', session => {
    session.endConversation();
}).triggerAction({ matches: 'SessionEndedRequest' });
```

```
bot.dialog('LaunchBot', session => {
    let response = 'Welcome to finance skill!  I can get your
    information about quotes or account types.';
    let msg = new builder.Message(session).text(response).
    speak(response).sourceEvent({
        directline: {
            keepSessionOpen: true
        }
    });
    session.send(msg);
    session.endDialog();
}).triggerAction({ matches: 'LaunchRequest' });
```

That completes our integration with Alexa. If we run the code, we will
see similar behavior to the Lambda skill we had developed earlier. There
are many unhandled intents and contingencies in both the bot code and
the connector code, but we are well on our way to integrating the Alexa
Skills Kit with Microsoft's Bot Framework.

EXERCISE 14-2

Integrate Data and Quote Imagery into Bot Builder Code

In Exercise 14-1, we connected the Lambda function code to data and
generated an image to render the quote on screen-enabled Echo devices. In
this exercise, we will migrate both components into our Bot Builder code.

1. Utilize the previous section's code as a starting point.

2. Extract the appropriate image generation code from the
   Lambda function and add it to your bot. Make sure you install
   the necessary Node.js packages.

3. Generate the display template within the dialog and add it into your custom channel data. You can include the Alexa Skills Kit SDK for Node.js as a dependency to use the template builder types.

4. Ensure the connector is translating the channel data template correctly into a final response back to Alexa.

5. Run your integrated Alexa skill and Bot Framework bot and test it using the same methods you used in Exercise 14-2.

6. What does it take to modify the bot code so that you can utilize your bot through the Bot Framework emulator? After all the knowledge you have gained in this book, you should be able to create a LUIS application to complete the experience.

What a great feeling getting this one working! It can be quite fun and interesting to develop voice chat bots, especially on a rich ecosystem like Alexa.

Conclusion

This chapter has enabled us to coalesce the learnings of this book to leverage Amazon's Alexa platform and, additionally, integrate it with the Bot Builder SDK. A modern conversational interface can be reduced to NLU intents and entities plus a dialog engine to drive the conversation. Whether it is Alexa or other channels like Google Assistant, all these systems share common core concepts. There are those who will draw a strong enough distinction between voice and text communications to argue for a need for distinct ways of handling both interactions. Although it is true that the voice and text communications are distinct enough to warrant different front-end experiences, the ability to handle the generic idea of a conversation is well developed in the Bot Builder SDK. The idea that we can connect different NLU systems to pass their own intents into our Bot Framework bot is powerful. It means that a message into our bot can be much more than just text. It can be any kind of complex object only limited by our imagination. Granted, there is always some level of overhead to run a generic system connected to many specific interfaces, but, as we hope to have demonstrated in this chapter, the extra effort required to build the connecting layer is well within our grasp.

Index

A

Action parameters, 24
Active learning, 115–116
Adaptive cards, 155, 166, 218, 501
  creating custom, 517
  data-gathering template, 507
  example, 507–509
  Facebook Messenger, 511
  rendering, 504–506
  rendering custom graphics, 518
    AAPL, 519–520, 522
    Azure's Blob Storage, 542–543
    custom quote card, 530
    emulator rendering, 528
    fetching data, 537, 539
    headless browsers, 518
    headless Chrome, 544–545
    HTML and CSS, 530–534
    Intrinio, 519
    Messenger rendering, 529
    Puppeteer, 535
    rendering HTML, 535–536, 540
    rendering in Messenger, 541
    renderStockCard function,
      523–525, 527
    string manipulation, 536
    text stock quotes, 523
  restaurant card, 501–504
  SDKs, 512
  stock quote rendering, 510
  Visualizer, 512
  working example, 512, 514–516
Alexa Skills Kit
  connecting to Bot
    Framework, 624
    Alexa constructs, 627
    callback support, 627
    channel-agnostic *vs.*
      channel-specific
      dialogs, 625–626
    implementations, 624
    NLU, 624–625
    sample integration, 628–630,
      632–636, 638
  creating new skill, 595
  interfaces, 597
  invocation name, 597
  NLU and ASR, 598
    AccountType, 605
    Amazon, 598–599
    Build Model button, 605–606
    Intents, 600
    LUIS, 598
    QuoteIntent, 602–604
    QuoteItem, 601–602

D